The Illustrated Golden Bough

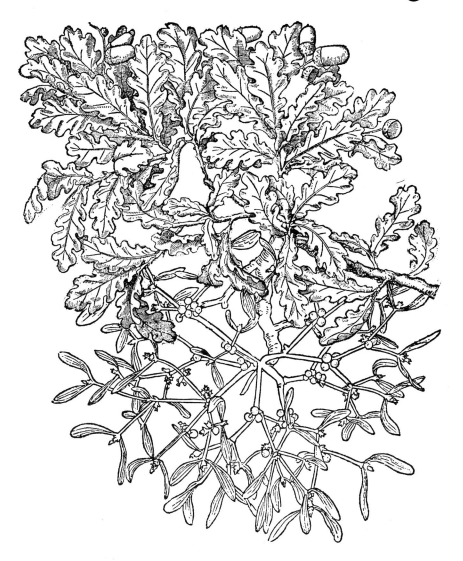

Sir James George Frazer

General Editor
Mary Douglas

Abridged and Illustrated by
Sabine MacCormack

Book Club Associates
London

The Illustrated Golden Bough

The publishers are indebted to the Curators of the
Bodleian Library, Oxford; the Trustees of the British Museum, London;
the Trustees of the National Gallery, London;
and the Trustees of the Wallace Collection, London,
for permission to reproduce their photographs.

This edition published 1978 by
Book Club Associates
By arrangement with Macmillan London Limited

Designed and produced by
George Rainbird Limited
36 Park Street
London W1Y 4DE

House Editor: Felicity Luard
Pictures and captions: Sabine MacCormack
Designer: Alan Bartram
Indexer: Christopher Wallis

Colour originated by Gilchrist Bros. Limited, Leeds
Printed and bound by Jarrold and Sons Limited, Norwich

The golden bough

TITLE PAGE. The sibyl of Cumae, prophetess and protector
of Aeneas on his venture to found Rome, holds up the
golden branch that would give Aeneas access to the
world of souls, where he was to behold Rome's future
greatness. In the background is the Lake of Nemi, home
of Diana. *The Golden Bough*, engraving by Turner,
British Museum, London. (Turner's painting, on page 250,
is reproduced by courtesy of the Tate Gallery, London.)

Contents

Colour Plates

Introduction by Mary Douglas

Ghosts and human sacrifice hardly present a serious problem in modern culture, and the same goes for demon worship and cannibalism. If blood-smeared idols have any place in our scheme of ideas, they appear in science fiction and horror films. The endings of these ghoulish stories never explain the cruelty of priests and their fanatical devotees except by either introducing the touch of fantasy, hinting at satanic powers loose in the world or – more tamely – by getting the villains labelled as dangerous lunatics. But these very themes, now a source of entertainment, filled an important intellectual slot and provoked serious reflection among scholars a hundred years ago.

The dawn of human thought was a central problem for the thinkers of the nineteenth century. At some point our ancestors must have separated themselves out from wild beasts. Their self-awareness must have gradually shed its animal beginnings. Their earliest efforts to understand the world would surely have been marked by bestial cruelties and gross mistakes. The customs of primitive peoples gave some clues to archaic thinking, and new information about crazy-seeming beliefs came pouring in from explorers' and traders' and missionaries' reports. To make sense of what seemed senseless and absurd was the great challenge of the day. Popular attention was focused upon the anthropologists who were in an international race to crack a code that seemed then as exciting as anything that physicists could tell a modern audience about life on other planets.

James Frazer may well be said to have won the race, so thoroughly that with the last volume of *The Golden Bough* the race could be declared ended. The esteem he gained in his lifetime shows that he beat his rivals. For the first time in the world a university chair in Social Anthropology was created in 1907, for him. He was knighted in 1914, he became a Fellow of the Royal Society in 1920, he received the Order of Merit in 1925. Many universities in Britain and abroad gave him honorary degrees. Some scholars earn high prestige in their lifetime and are afterwards forgotten. But this has not been Frazer's fate. Though most anthropologists disagree with him on one point or another, there is hardly anyone so great that he thinks it beneath him or a waste of his time to criticize Frazer. He has not been left alone; often attacked while the names of his contemporary critics are ignored: this is the evidence that his work must still be significant. Thirteen volumes of *The Golden Bough* is a massive monument. How did it develop? What is it worth now? How relevant is it to our present preoccupations?

Before seeing how the thirteen volumes of *The Golden Bough* developed, or considering its strengths and weaknesses, we must look at Frazer against his background. He should be read and known for a representative nineteenth-century thinker, and also for his elegant style.

Frazer was born in 1856. His father read a passage from the Bible out aloud every day to the family, but always closed the book without comment. The reading was an act of pious ritual. I surmise that from this childhood experience Frazer took his lifelong sense of reverence for religious feeling but was left with a notable lack of religious intuition. Evidently the strange stories impressed his youthful imagination. Abraham was prepared to plunge the sacrificial knife into his own child, there were miraculous interventions, punishing floods over the entire world, boys unharmed in the fiery furnace, the Red Sea divided. God was always present to his people, mysterious and often cruel, requiring them to behave in risky or immoral ways. In 1878 Frazer graduated in classics at Cambridge. Here he had occasion to read more about exotic religions. The profound moral teaching and ecstatic vision of the Graeco-Roman tradition inspired a reverence for what he called the poetry of religion, but he was also intrigued by tales of Greek gods, unscrupulous and lustful, chasing after each other or after human boys or girls, jealous and vengeful. They might have seemed almost human, but surely not quite: an inconsequentiality and disconnectedness marks their intentions and lives. How to explain the cruelties and irrationalities enshrined in mythology was one of the great puzzles of scholarship in the 1870–1910 period.

The Golden Bough opens on a note of mystery: a sacred grove in Italy, a priest prowling round a tree, sword on the draw, a myth that he was the attendant of Diana's shrine and that his fate was to be killed by his successor, the conjecture that the tree was an oak, that the priest was protecting a bunch of mistletoe, and that he was the human spouse of the goddess Diana – it scarcely seems possible that thirteen volumes were needed to unravel the origins of such a story, contrived from such flimsy evidence. Why did Frazer give it so much prominence? It has even been said that *The Golden Bough* is merely one long, rambling footnote to a line in Ovid about the shrine of Diana near the lake at Nemi (*Fasti*, vi, 756). If so, why did Frazer pick on that line rather than on any other, and why did he keep reverting to the story?

In my opinion the priest at Nemi, and even the bunch of golden mistletoe, are not the origin or main purpose of the book, but contrivances in the skilful narrator's box of tricks. The priest of Diana, and the Norse god Balder, starting and ending the book, are what Henry James called a 'ficelle', a necessary string, holding the narrative firmly together and helping the reader to feel the structure before it is all revealed.

One of the regular complaints about *The Golden Bough* is that Frazer piled fact upon fact, with only the weakest connection between them, and that the whole edifice became so top-heavy that the initial idea was lost from sight. Frazer tends to be dismissed as an incoherent, doddering old collector of curious facts, as

indeed he may have seemed in his old age. Even his good friend, Professor E. O. James, said, 'As the book grew in his hands, the slender thread of connection with his original subject threatened to snap under the weight of each successive edition of the work.' (*Dictionary of National Biography*.) But this is really off the mark. If ever a scholar had a one-track mind, it was Frazer. He never wanders from his theme of the slain god. Our new edition disengages the central argument from the massive detail. Dr MacCormack, who skilfully reduced the thirteen volumes to this modest size, insists that Frazer never wandered from his argument. I believe she has produced an abridgment that keeps the meaning clear and the interest strong, without clipping the famous style. In her note on page 251 she describes how the book grew and the editorial decisions she had to take in order to present the text in this straightforward way.

Frazer's theory was sketched out in three stages. The first stage was in 1888, when he wrote the articles on Totemism and Taboo for the *Encyclopædia Britannica*. He tells us that at that time and always he was deeply influenced by his friend William Robertson Smith, author of the justly famed *Religion of the Semites* to be published in 1889. It is likely that as a scholar Frazer's first intention was to do for the Graeco-Latin tradition what his friend had done for the Judaic.

Robertson Smith remained all his life a devout and committed Christian. His scholarly task was to submit the Bible to strict historical scrutiny and by doing so to protect it from the destructive criticisms of scientists. His way of defending the Bible from the intellectual assault it was staggering under was to pick out what was noble and rational in it and to throw overboard what seemed primitive and irrational. He and Frazer were originally writing in the twenty to fifty years after Darwin's *The Origin of Species* so disturbed the old fundamentalist interpretation of the Bible: was man created by a single divine act, as the Bible said, or did he evolve from apes? Robertson Smith's ingenious way of playing back the ball of biblical criticism was to show that the history of the Jewish religion had also evolved. The strains of justice and mercy had always been there, viable and full of energy to survive, while the barbaric strains had been gradually selected against. Magic, he taught, was connected with the worship of free-floating evil demons, not connected with the community god. Magic eventually gave way, in Judaism, to the worship of one God. Bloody sacrifice gave way to the repentance of a humble heart, the slain animal representing the community god gave way to a spiritual conception of sacrificial worship.

The core of Frazer's lifelong theme of the slain god appears in this first article on Totemism in which he describes a mimed death and revival in initiation ceremonies, and suggests that the totemic rites are really sacrifices in which the god dies for his people.

The second stage was when Frazer brought out the first edition of *The Golden Bough* in 1890 (dedicated to 'My friend W. R. Smith'). He says in his preface that the central idea of the book is the conception of the slain god, derived from Robertson Smith. This is where the doomed priest at Nemi and the dying Norse god, Balder, make their first appearance. The aim of the book is to uncover the original unity of religious thought from the primitive worship of the Aryans, through the oakwoods of Gaul and Prussia and Scandinavia, and maintained nearly in its original form in the sacred grove at Nemi: 'The King of the wood lived and died as an incarnation of the supreme Aryan god whose life was in the mistletoe or Golden Bough.' The religions were all based on a close communion between worshippers and their priest god.

When he said that the slain god is the central idea of *The Golden Bough*, he must be supposed to have meant it. With Robertson Smith, Frazer believed in a process of social evolution that had by now passed an irreversible judgment against all ritual slaying, whether the victim be animal or a human being, or the god himself slain to be offered to himself on behalf of his people. The full ambition of *The Golden Bough* is to place the sacrificial doctrines of Christianity, together with the doctrines of the Incarnation and of the Virgin Birth and of the Resurrection into the same perspective as totemic worship, together with the lusty antics of the Greek pantheon and with the burnt or bleeding carcasses on ancient altars of the Israelites. Whatever the stories were, they would be regarded as partial, imperfect versions. A fuller, more profound and powerful insight now appeared. This modern insight identifies the smooth evolution of religion from carnal to fine spiritual meanings. It could not have seemed a wildly risky idea to promote in the rationalist mood of the 1890s. Those still committed to fundamentalist religious dogma would object. But for enlightened scholarship the task ahead for the successive volumes of *The Golden Bough* would be the adducing of more and more evidence for that worldwide evolution towards a purer spirituality.

But between 1890 and 1910, in the third stage of his thought, Frazer had developed new ideas about how magical thinking worked and how it fitted into modern psychology. Basically, he argued that the earliest stage of philosophical evolution was magical, the second religious, and the third scientific. Frazer agreed that the primitives could reason well enough when it came to building a house, catching deer, or delivering babies, but without the advantages of modern science they strengthened their efforts by appeals to sympathetic magic. It was generally acknowledged that all magic worked by a sympathetic principle. But Frazer distinguished two sorts of sympathy: sympathy of organic parts, and sympathy of observed similarity. The first supposed that things that had once been together and now were separated had a permanent power over each other: as when two friends drank each other's blood so that each would thereafter be in direct physical communication with the other, one would know when dangers threatened the other and even wilt or die when the other was attacked. This is quite different from the second. If for example gold is a good yellow and jaundice is a bad yellow, then gold will be used in the curing of jaundice, to overwhelm the wrong kind of yellow colour. These two principles of contagion and similarity had to be reckoned with as a powerful influence in primitive thought.

All through the literature of primitive thinking these sympathies recur. By organizing them as similarity and contagion (or contiguity) Frazer linked them with the current psychology of mental association and so updated his whole subject.

Even today the principles of association occupy a curious place in psychology and philosophy. They tend to be treated as a spontaneous, uncontrolled energy in the individual mind, an energy gradually tamed and taught by analytic reasoning. That it takes a lot of analytic power to recognize likeness at all is only just beginning to be admitted. We are all subject to mistaken association of ideas. We break out of our subjection by the route that has led to science. But for Frazer the primitive mind was not haphazardly at the mercy of mistaken associations. He was intent on revealing a particular bias, a concern that preoccupied our ancestors, this concern was age-long meditation on humanity as part of nature. It infused all nature with animate spirits, and called for a sense of wonder, harnessing guilt and impossible hopes. It produced the prototype of all religion, the belief in God incarnate, dying to redeem his people and being resurrected in due course.

I should here mention some criticisms levelled nowadays against *The Golden Bough*. The main modern one is, first, that Frazer was insufferably arrogant about primitive mentality, and second, that he dealt superficially with deep matters. It is true that he does make the so-called savages out to be perfect idiots. If anyone were to write of primitive mentality in that way nowadays he would be accused of racialism. But Frazer was not a racialist in any ordinary way. He never visited any of the peoples or places he described, and his examples are as often drawn from his own race, from London, Scotland, Ireland, France, or Germany, as from more distant lands. It is also true that he trivializes grave reflections on death and divinity. He did tend to churn gods and goblins impartially through the same analytical machine. But the mistake is to treat him as a writer of the twentieth century just because he lived until 1941. He was not dealing with a modern problem. His thought was formed by 1910 and his chosen audience remained the scholars of his youth. Frazer regarded his work on religion as to do with prehistory, something past and done: 'The long tragedy of human folly and suffering which has unrolled itself before the readers of these volumes and on which the curtain is now about to fall.' Professor E. O. James, who knew him well, said that 'Frazer was mainly impressed by what seemed to him to be the utter futility of the world he surveyed.' To consider whether he deserved these criticisms of superficiality and arrogance we should place him correctly in his period.

Frazer's colleagues certainly thought that the age of dogmatic religion and superstition was coming to a close. Criticisms of superficiality and arrogance only get their bite by taking Frazer out of context. His view of primitive mentality was positively elevated by comparison with some of his very learned and respected contemporaries. One of them considered seriously whether humanity had passed through a phase of temporary madness – and concluded that it must have done so. Max Müller, the great philologist, tried to imagine our first emergent ancestors struggling with speech, using only a few tenses and unable to develop abstract ideas. Naturally they would get horribly muddled about transfers of meaning between individuals named after events and events which had given names to individuals. Supposing every word implied an individual and gave it grammatical gender, then with a masculine gender word for sun, such as 'the shining one', and a feminine gender word for dawn, 'the burning one', it would be impossible to say the sun follows the dawn without implying a male chasing after a female. Like all the other scholars of the time, Müller thought it was easy to understand stories about noble and reasonable gods, but some theory about primitive mental confusion had to be invoked to understand 'the silly, senseless and savage element'. Explaining myths by mistakes between words for things in nature suggests that all myths arose originally as nature myths. The trouble here is that anything you like can be seen as a nature myth. Even the Little Red Riding Hood story can sound like a nature myth, if we take the red cloak and her youthfulness to be the dawn, the aged grandmother the dying daylight, and the big wolf who swallows the grandmother whole in his black jaws the night; luckily the mythical woodman rescues dawn and so the sun rises, again and again.

From the very first Frazer was scornful of all these theories based on verbal misunderstandings. A hundred years on we have all learned better than to speculate too wildly upon the first moment of human speech, although we recognize it as a fascinating theme.

Frazer's own theories were certainly much less superficial than those the mythologists put forth. Instead of finding early humanity locked in puzzlement caused by its first clumsy efforts to speak, he finds it contemplating the same themes as Christians of his own day. This is why he is ready to speak of the virgin goddess Diana in the same breath as the Virgin Mary, and to evoke slain gods and incarnate deities in the perspective of Christian theology. Given his early upbringing and reverence for other people's religion, he is careful not to give offence. He does not try to score off Christians, nor to embarrass them. But nor does he try to save their doctrine from scientific attack. For him the key to future understanding lay in science, not in religion or magic. Many would agree with him: there is progress in science, proof of cumulative change, but in religion the real truths seem to be the old truths, and there is a continual effort to recapture and protect a threatened ancient vision.

Yet for all this, Frazer cannot escape the charge of superficiality. He chose to deal with reflections on life and death, humanity and animality, divinity and immortality. 'What narrowness of spiritual life we find in Frazer,' exclaimed Ludwig Wittgenstein, 'and as a result how impossible for him to understand a different way of life from the English one of his time!' ('Remarks on Frazer's Golden Bough', *The Human World*, May 1971). It is partly a matter of style. When he writes wittily, the idea is well turned and comes across well, but when Frazer puts on his solemn tone, there is something portentous and even false about it. It is as if he knows that it is easy to snigger at other people's religion, and is trying to avoid the solecism by an unctuous tone of voice.

Superficiality is not the difference that separates modern anthropology from Frazer's viewpoint. No modern anthropologist, however sensitive, can apply the tools of his trade to a foreign religious system and entirely escape that same criticism. The most modern tools of analysis are necessarily clumsy, what they reveal is partial, the final view is crude and often cynical. The essential difference is that the modern anthropologist intends to study a symbolic system, whereas Frazer put less emphasis on conscious symbolizing and more on unconscious mistakes about physical reality. To quote Wittgenstein on Frazer again: 'I read among many similar examples, of a rain king in Africa to whom the people appeal for rain *when the rainy season comes*. But surely this means that they do not actually think he can make rain, otherwise they would do it in the dry period in which the land is "a parched and arid desert". For if we do assume that it was stupidity that once led the people to institute this office of Rain King, still they obviously knew from experience that the rains begin in March, and it would have been the Rain King's duty to perform in other periods of the year. Or again: towards morning, when the sun is about to rise, people celebrate the rites of the coming of the day, but not at night, for then they simply burn lamps.' Even though Frazer recognized the ritual was not automatically effective as a magic rite, the whole pressure of his argument is to discover the characteristic primitive way of thinking.

The modern approach to Frazer's chosen problem is to emphasize the symbolic side of human behaviour, the rites of celebration, without trying too much to distinguish what is symbolic and what is practical, a task that is much more difficult than it appears. The anthropologist homes in on the local culture as if it was a complete system with all its explanations contained within itself. No hopping from one culture in Borneo to another in Peru or ancient Rome is expected to give good answers. The first job is to understand a cultural system as a rational way of behaving for people who know each other and who make the same assumptions. Beliefs in fiends and gods, witches and mysterious powers of blessing and cursing make sense if we know the full context in which they are used. The biggest change from Frazer's way of putting the problem is to suppose that all the beliefs are actively employed. He seemed to think

that they are framed off in a kind of Sunday-school mood of contemplation. Today it is more in fashion to treat them as being put to practical use in the here-and-now bustle of social life. So if a king is thought to be able to make rain, and if rain-making is his main responsibility to his people, then the political interest does focus on the moment when the rain is late in falling – was he angry? Was someone committing an offence against the kingdom which he and the ancestors could see? If so, the crime should be forthwith brought to the light of day, confessed and expiated, so that the king will be pacified enough to unloose the rain clouds. Special political interest focuses on dynastic rivalry. Suppose the drought persists because the wrong king got the crown and has banished the right one who has the real power to make rain? Then the pretender should be unmasked and the rightful heir installed. So we see how ideas about rain magic can be put to great political use, providing a kind of meteorological test of political legitimacy. This is how we tend nowadays to interpret magic. The example shows the scope for cynicism and for diminishing the rich fabric of beliefs that a foreign culture presents for analysis. The task of understanding has become much more difficult than before. Instead of trying to understand the whole thing, anthropologists now tend to chip off a bit and to develop refined tools for interpreting that bit. There is a concentration on tools, on methods, and with it a humility amounting to doubt as to whether we can ever understand another culture. For the moment, the major problem that interested Frazer's contemporaries so passionately is laid aside.

They really thought that the great cruelties of man to man were in the past. They could feel appalled at the practice of human sacrifice or ritual cannibalism, and feel amazed that anyone should believe in blood-sucking ghosts or in a heaven inhabited by orgiastic, atrocity-condoning deities. There were plenty of cruelties being committed by man to man in the 1890s but our scholars in those days lived very sheltered lives. They could be hopeful about human evolution. It is hard for us to realize how blinkered and protected the intellectual elite could be. Even university teachers could be spared the face-to-face confrontation with students. Frazer himself, after being appointed to the Liverpool Chair of Social Anthropology, soon found it more convenient to spend all his time working twelve hours a day on his researches in Trinity College, Cambridge, though he did not think it necessary to resign from the Chair at Liverpool.

A change has taken place in our consciousness. Two world wars have helped to shake our confidence in human kindness; a greater depth colours our perception of our own potential for cruel action and our own blindness to cruelty around us. Living with urban guerrilla warfare, bomb explosions, and open terrorism, we cannot believe that the book of human folly has been closed. This makes a difference. Anyone who criticizes Frazer now is criticizing not so much a writer, as a whole period that he represented, a period of about a hundred years ago. This is in itself a reason for reading *The Golden Bough*. It is not so certain that the pinnacle from which we look back to that time is so clearly elevated above it. We have our own self-esteem and arrogance which mark us as members of our own civilization. For example, some of us are shocked at Frazer writing that ignorant and dull-witted people tend to magic beliefs. But to balk at that seems to be rather mealy-mouthed for anyone convinced of the invincible superiority of our modern science. Less than a hundred years from now our own attitudes will seem as patronizing as Frazer's. By then we may have met people ignorant of science yet perfectly versed in the meaning of dreams, or able to speak with animals, or able to master their own thoughts and bodies in ways that our science cannot comprehend.

MARY DOUGLAS

Preface to the 1911 edition

When I originally conceived the idea of the work, of which the first part is now laid before the public in a third and enlarged edition, my intention merely was to explain the strange rule of the priesthood or sacred kingship of Nemi and with it the legend of the Golden Bough, immortalised by Virgil, which the voice of antiquity associated with the priesthood. The explanation was suggested to me by some similar rules formerly imposed on kings in Southern India, and at first I thought that it might be adequately set forth within the compass of a small volume. But I soon found that in attempting to settle one question I had raised many more: wider and wider prospects opened out before me; and thus step by step I was lured on into far-spreading fields of primitive thought which had been but little explored by my predecessors. Thus the book grew on my hands, and soon the projected essay became in fact a ponderous treatise, or rather a series of separate dissertations loosely linked together by a slender thread of connexion with my original subject. With each successive edition these dissertations have grown in number and swollen in bulk by the accretion of fresh materials, till the thread on which they are strung at last threatened to snap under their weight. Accordingly, following the hint of a friendly critic, I decided to resolve my over-grown book into its elements, and to publish separately the various disquisitions of which it is composed. The present volumes, forming the first part of the whole, contain a preliminary enquiry into the principles of Magic and the evolution of the Sacred Kingship in general. They will be followed shortly by a volume which discusses the principles of Taboo in their special application to sacred or priestly kings. The remainder of the work will be mainly devoted to the myth and ritual of the Dying God, and as the subject is large and fruitful, my discussion of it will, for the sake of convenience, be divided into several parts, of which one, dealing with some dying gods of antiquity in Egypt and Western Asia, has already been published under the title of *Adonis, Attis, Osiris.*

But while I have thus sought to dispose my book in its proper form as a collection of essays on a variety of distinct, though related, topics, I have at the same time preserved its unity, as far as possible, by retaining the original title for the whole series of volumes, and by pointing out from time to time the bearing of my general conclusions on the particular problem which furnished the starting-point of the enquiry. It seemed to me that this mode of presenting the subject offered some advantages which out-weighed certain obvious drawbacks. By discarding the austere form, without, I hope, sacrificing the solid substance, of a scientific treatise, I thought to cast my materials into a more artistic mould and so perhaps to attract readers, who might have been repelled by a more strictly logical and systematic arrangement of the facts. Thus I put the mysterious priest of Nemi, so to say, in the forefront of the picture, grouping the other sombre figures of the same sort behind him in the background, not certainly because I deemed them of less moment, but because the picturesque natural surroundings of the priest of Nemi among the wooded hills of Italy, the very mystery which enshrouds him, and not least the haunting magic of Virgil's verse, all combine to shed a glamour on the tragic figure with the Golden Bough, which fits him to stand as the centre of a gloomy canvas. But I trust that the high relief into which he has thus been thrown in my pages will not lead my readers either to overrate his historical importance by comparison with that of some other figures which stand behind him in the shadow, or to attribute to my theory of the part he played a greater degree of probability than it deserves. Even if it should appear that this ancient Italian priest must after all be struck out from the long roll of men who have masqueraded as gods, the single omission would not sensibly invalidate the demonstration, which I believe I have given, that human pretenders to divinity have been far commoner and their credulous worshippers far more numerous than had been hitherto suspected. Similarly, should my whole theory of this particular priesthood collapse – and I fully acknowledge the slenderness of the foundations on which it rests – its fall would hardly shake my general conclusions as to the evolution of primitive religion and society, which are founded on large collections of entirely independent and well-authenticated facts.

Friends versed in German philosophy have pointed out to me that my views of magic and religion and their relations to each other in history agree to some extent with those of Hegel. The agreement is quite independent and to me unexpected, for I have never studied the philosopher's writings nor attended to his speculations. As, however, we have arrived at similar results by very different roads, the partial coincidence of our conclusions may perhaps be taken to furnish a certain presumption in favour of their truth.

With regard to the history of the sacred kingship which I have outlined in these volumes, I desire to repeat a warning which I have given in the text. While I have shewn reason to think that in many communities sacred kings have been developed out of magicians, I am far from supposing that this has been universally true. The causes which have determined the establishment of monarchy have no doubt varied greatly in different countries and at different times: I make no pretence to discuss or even enumerate them all: I have merely selected one particular cause because it· bore directly on my special enquiry; and I have laid emphasis on it because it seems to have been overlooked by writers on the origin of political institutions, who, themselves sober and rational according to modern standards, have not laid their account sufficiently with the enormous influence which superstition has exerted in shaping the human past. But I have no wish to exaggerate the importance of this particular cause at the expense of others which may have been equally or even more influential. No one can be more sensible than I am of the risk of stretching an hypothesis too far, of crowding a multitude of incongruous particulars under one narrow formula, of reducing the vast, nay inconceivable complexity of nature and history to a delusive appearance of theoretical simplicity. It may well be that I have erred in this direction again and again; but at least I have been well aware of the danger of error and have striven to guard myself and my readers against it. How far I have succeeded in that and the other objects I have set before me in writing this work, I must leave to the candour of the public to determine.

J. G. FRAZER

At Nemi, near Rome, there was a shrine where, down to imperial times, Diana, goddess of woodlands and animals and giver of offspring, was worshipped with a male consort, Virbius. The rule of the shrine was that any man could be its priest, and take the title King of the Wood, provided he first plucked a branch – the Golden Bough – from a certain sacred tree in the temple grove and then killed the priest. This was the regular mode of succession to the priesthood. The aim of The Golden Bough is to answer two questions: why did the priest have to kill his predecessor, and why did he first have to pick the branch?

Because there is no simple answer to either question, Frazer collects and compares analogies to the custom of Nemi. For by showing that similar rules existed all over the world and throughout history, he hopes to reach an understanding of how the primitive mind works, and then to use his understanding to shed light on the rule of Nemi. In collecting analogies, Frazer does not look for total parallels, but breaks up the custom of Nemi into its component parts and examines each in turn. Indeed, one piece of evidence may be used for more than one aspect of the question.

Throughout The Golden Bough Frazer is interested in how primitive thought seeks to control and regulate the world. According to him the problem of causation – how one thing affects another – is tackled by two sorts of association. The first is association by similarity, that is, a cause resembles its effect. For instance, a person wishing to harm an enemy will damage an effigy in the hope that this will rebound on the enemy. The second is association by contiguity, that is, things that once were joined together and afterwards parted continue to have an effect on each other. In this case, a personal belonging of the enemy will be damaged rather than an effigy.

These two modes of association also apply to the very structure of The Golden Bough itself. For in his selection of evidence, Frazer relates to the priesthood of Nemi what is similar in other cultures and other periods, i.e. sacred personages who were ritually or otherwise killed, and what is contiguous, for example the nature of the goddess at Nemi, the myths of the cult site and its religious observances. There is, therefore, a crucial link between Frazer's evidence and his method of interpreting it, between practice and theory.

Part 1. The Magic Art and the Evolution of Kings

Frazer begins by setting out the rule of the priesthood of Nemi. He then launches on a discussion of magic. Magic is relevant to answering the question, why did the king have to die (The Dying God)? But it also helps to illuminate the role of the King of the Wood in his lifetime, for magic is a means of controlling nature and therefore an essential function of kingship. Frazer distinguishes two types of magic: imitative (or similarity) magic – rain will fall after a ceremony that in some way imitates the falling of rain; and contagious (or contiguity) magic – a lover may win the affections of a lady by casting a spell on clippings of her hair.

Next, Frazer explores the significance of the wood at Nemi and more particularly of the tree from which the claimant to the priesthood had to break a branch. He finds that in many societies fertilizing powers are attributed to trees and that in ancient Europe the oak was the most important tree in this respect. It is therefore appropriate that Diana, goddess of fertility, should have a woodland shrine, and we deduce her sacred tree to have been an oak. Virbius, Diana's partner in the shrine, emerges as a local manifestation of Jupiter, god of the oak and the sky, and the King of the Wood as this god's human incarnation.

Magicians and shamans have extraordinary powers to aid and protect their fellow humans, because they are able to converse with and contend against invisible spirits of all kinds. Such powers are communicated in both actions and attributes. Thus, this Florida shaman of the 16th century is depicted with a bird, and in the attitude of taking off to fly. De Bry, *America*, 1590, Bodleian Library, Oxford

1. The King of the Wood

The still glassy lake that sleeps
  Beneath Aricia's trees –
Those trees in whose dim shadow
  The ghastly priest doth reign,
The priest who slew the slayer,
  And shall himself be slain.
                                    MACAULAY

Diana and Virbius

Who does not know Turner's picture of the Golden Bough? The scene, suffused with the golden glow of imagination in which the divine mind of Turner steeped and transfigured even the fairest natural landscape, is a dream-like vision of the little woodland lake of Nemi – 'Diana's Mirror', as it was called by the ancients. No one who has seen that calm water, lapped in a green hollow of the Alban hills, can ever forget it. The two characteristic Italian villages which slumber on its banks, and the equally Italian palace whose terraced gardens descend steeply to the lake, hardly break the stillness and even the solitariness of the scene. Diana herself might still linger by this lonely shore, still haunt these woodlands.

Here, in the very heart of the wooded hills, under the abrupt declivity now crested by the village of Nemi, the sylvan goddess Diana had an old and famous sanctuary, the resort of pilgrims from all parts of Latium. It was known as the sacred grove of Diana Nemorensis, that is, Diana of the Wood. Sometimes the lake and grove were called, after the nearest town, the lake and grove of Aricia. But the town, the modern Ariccia, lay three miles away at the foot of the mountains, and separated from the lake by a long and steep descent. A spacious terrace or platform contained the sanctuary. On the north and east it was bounded by great retaining walls which cut into the hillsides and served to support them. Semicircular niches sunk in the walls and faced with columns formed a series of chapels, which in modern times have yielded a rich harvest of votive offerings. On the side of the lake the terrace rested on a mighty wall, over seven hundred feet long by thirty feet high, built in triangular buttresses, like those which we see in front of the piers of bridges to break floating ice. At present this terrace-wall stands back some hundred yards from the lake; in other days its buttresses may have been lapped by the water. Compared with the extent of the sacred precinct, the temple itself was not large; but its remains prove it to have been neatly and solidly built of massive blocks of peperino, and adorned with Doric columns of the same material. Elaborate cornices of marble and friezes of terra-cotta contributed to the outward splendour of the edifice, which appears to have been further enhanced by tiles of gilt bronze.

Multitudes of statuettes of Diana, appropriately clad in the short tunic and high buskins of a huntress, with the quiver slung over her shoulder, have been found on the spot. Some of them represent her with her bow in her hand or her hound at her side. Bronze and iron spears, and images of stags and hinds, discovered within the precinct, may have been offerings of huntsmen to the huntress goddess for success in the chase. Similarly the bronze tridents, which have also come to light at Nemi, were perhaps presented by fishermen who had speared fish in the lake, or maybe by hunters who had stabbed boars in the forest. The wild boar was still hunted in Italy down to the end of the first century of our era; for the younger Pliny tells us

The mistress of the animals

The cult of the winged goddess holding lions was brought to Italy from the Near East in early historic times. In Greece and Rome, this ancient deity of the wilds came to be worshipped as Diana the patroness of hunters. BELOW. Diana with her lions on a gold necklace from Rhodes, 8th century BC, British Museum, London

BOTTOM LEFT. Terracotta frieze from the temple of Diana at Nemi, Castle Museum, Nottingham. Photo from G. H. Wallis, *Classical Antiquities from Nemi*, 1893
BOTTOM RIGHT. The Emperor Trajan sacrifices to Diana after the hunt. Tondo from the Arch of Constantine, Rome. Photo: Anderson

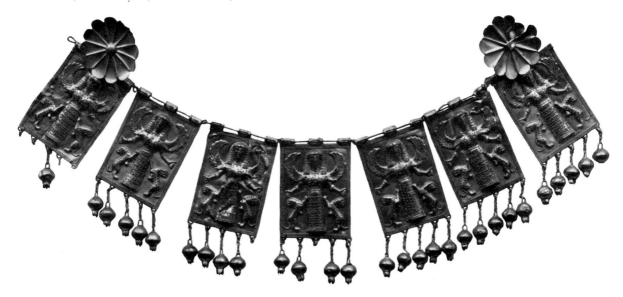

how, with his usual charming affectation, he sat meditating and reading by the nets, while three fine boars fell into them. Indeed, some fourteen-hundred years later boar-hunting was a favourite pastime of Pope Leo the Tenth. A frieze of painted reliefs in terra-cotta, which was found in the sanctuary at Nemi, and may have adorned Diana's temple, portrays the goddess in the character of what is called the Asiatic Artemis, with wings sprouting from her waist and a lion resting its paws on each of her shoulders. A few rude images of cows, oxen, horses, and pigs dug up on the site may perhaps indicate that Diana was here worshipped as the patroness of domestic animals as well as of the wild creatures of the wood.

Down to the decline of Rome a custom was observed at Nemi which seems to transport us at once from civilisation to savagery. In the sacred grove there grew a certain tree round which at any time of the day, and probably far into the night, a grim figure might be seen to prowl. In his hand he carried a drawn sword, and he kept peering warily about him as if at every instant he expected to be set upon by an enemy. He was a priest and a murderer; and the man for whom he looked was sooner or later to murder him and hold the priesthood in his stead. Such was the rule of the sanctuary. A candidate for the priesthood could only succeed to office by slaying the priest, and having slain him, he retained office till he was himself slain by a stronger or a craftier. The post which he held by this precarious tenure carried with it the title of king; but surely no crowned head ever lay uneasier, or was visited by more evil dreams, than his. For year in year out, in summer and winter, in fair weather and in foul, he had to keep his lonely watch, and whenever he snatched a troubled slumber it was at the peril of his life.

The strange rule of this priesthood has no parallel in classical antiquity, and cannot be explained from it. To find an explanation we must go farther afield. No one will probably deny that such a custom savours of a barbarous age, and, surviving into imperial times, stands out in striking isolation from the polished Italian society of the day, like a primaeval rock rising from a smooth-shaven lawn. It is the very rudeness and barbarity of the custom which allow us a hope of explaining it. For recent researches into the early history of man have revealed the essential similarity with which, under many superficial differences, the human mind has elaborated its first crude philosophy of life. Accordingly, if we can shew that a barbarous custom, like that of the priesthood of Nemi, has existed elsewhere; if we can detect the motives which led to its institution; if we can prove that these motives have operated widely, perhaps universally, in human society, producing in varied circumstances a variety of institutions specifically different but generically alike; if we can shew, lastly, that these very motives, with some of their derivative institutions, were actually at work in classical antiquity; then we may fairly infer that at a remoter age the same motives gave birth to the priesthood of Nemi. Such an inference, in default of direct evidence as to how the priesthood did actually arise, can never amount to demonstration. But it will be more or less probable according to the degree of completeness with which it fulfils the conditions I have indicated. The object of this book is, by meeting these conditions, to offer a probable explanation of the priesthood of Nemi.

I begin by setting forth the few facts and legends which have come down to us on the subject. According to one story the worship of Diana at Nemi was instituted by Orestes, who, after killing Thoas, King of the Tauric Chersonese (the Crimea), fled with his sister to Italy, bringing with him the image of the Tauric Diana hidden in a faggot of sticks. After his death his bones were transported from Aricia to Rome and buried in front of the temple of

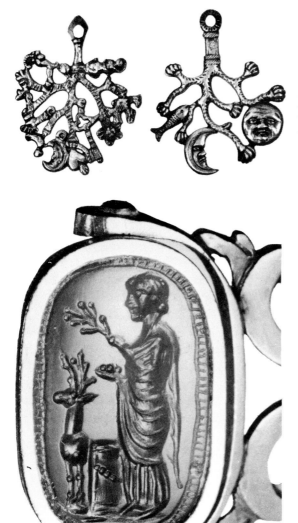

Diana, goddess of nature
Cimurata, silver sprigs of rue with magical symbols on them, have been regarded as a survival of the cult of Diana. In 19th-century Italy, they were still used as talismans for good fortune and prosperity. Two thousand years ago, similar objects could have been offered to Diana. On the Roman gem stone Diana holds a branch and a bowl of fruit. At her side is her sacred stag.
TOP. Cimurata, 19th century, Pitt Rivers Museum, University of Oxford
ABOVE. Gem stone, Antikenmuseum, Bildarchiv, Preussischer Kulturbesitz, Berlin (West). Photo: Isolde Luckert

Saturn, on the Capitoline slope, beside the temple of Concord. The bloody ritual which legend ascribed to the Tauric Diana is familiar to classical readers; it is said that every stranger who landed on the shore was sacrificed on her altar. But transported to Italy, the rite assumed a milder form. Within the sanctuary at Nemi grew a certain tree of which no branch might be broken. Only a runaway slave was allowed to break off, if he could, one of its boughs. Success in the attempt entitled him to fight the priest in single combat, and if he slew him he reigned in his stead with the title of King of the Wood (*Rex Nemorensis*). According to the public opinion of the ancients the fateful branch was that Golden Bough which, at the Sibyl's bidding, Aeneas plucked before he essayed the perilous journey to the world of the dead. The flight of the slave represented, it was said, the flight of Orestes; his combat with the priest was a reminiscence of the human sacrifices once offered to the Tauric Diana. This rule of succession by the sword was observed down to imperial times; for amongst his other freaks Caligula, thinking that the priest of Nemi had held office too long, hired a more stalwart ruffian to slay him; and a Greek traveller, who visited Italy in the age of the Antonines, remarks that down to his time the priesthood was still the prize of victory in a single combat.

Of the worship of Diana at Nemi some leading features can still be made out. From the votive offerings which have been found on the site, it appears that she was conceived of especially as a huntress, and further as blessing men and women with offspring, and granting expectant mothers an easy delivery. Again, fire seems to have played a foremost part in her ritual. For during her annual festival, held on the thirteenth of August, at the hottest time of the year, her grove shone with a multitude of torches, whose ruddy glare was reflected by the lake; and throughout the length and breadth of

Italy the day was kept with holy rites at every domestic hearth. Bronze statuettes found in her precinct represent the goddess herself holding a torch in her raised right hand; and women whose prayers had been heard by her came crowned with wreaths and bearing lighted torches to the sanctuary in fulfilment of their vows. Some one unknown dedicated a perpetually burning lamp in a little shrine at Nemi for the safety of the Emperor Claudius and his family. The terra-cotta lamps which have been discovered in the grove may perhaps have served a like purpose for humbler persons. If so, the analogy of the custom to the Catholic practice of dedicating holy candles in churches would be obvious. Further, the title of Vesta borne by Diana at Nemi points clearly to the maintenance of a perpetual holy fire in her sanctuary.

At her annual festival, which was celebrated all over Italy on the thirteenth of August, hunting dogs were crowned and wild beasts were not molested; young people went through a purificatory ceremony in her honour; wine was brought forth, and the feast consisted of a kid, cakes served piping hot on plates of leaves, and apples still hanging in clusters on the boughs. The Christian Church appears to have sanctified this great festival of the virgin goddess by adroitly converting it into the festival of the Assumption of the Blessed Virgin on the fifteenth of August. The discrepancy of two days between the dates of the festivals is not a fatal argument against their identity; for a similar displacement of two days occurs in the case of St George's festival on the twenty-third of April, which is probably identical with the ancient Roman festival of the Parilia on the twenty-first of April. On the reasons which prompted this conversion of the festival of the Virgin Diana into the festival of the Virgin Mary, some light is thrown by a passage in the Syriac text of *The Departure of My Lady Mary from This World*, which runs thus: 'And the apostles also ordered

Diana is honoured at the vintage
ABOVE. Head crowned with leaves and grapes, a Roman votive offering from Nemi, Castle Museum, Nottingham. Photo from G.H. Wallis, *Classical Antiquities from Nemi*, 1893
OPPOSITE. Children with torches and offerings of grapes before an image of Diana. Wall painting from Ostia, 1st century, Vatican, Rome. Photo: Anderson

that there should be a commemoration of the blessed one on the thirteenth of Ab [that is, August], on account of the vines bearing bunches [of grapes], and on account of the trees bearing fruit, that clouds of hail, bearing stones of wrath, might not come, and the trees be broken, and their fruits, and the vines with their clusters.' Here the festival of the Assumption of the Virgin is definitely said to have been fixed on the thirteenth or fifteenth of August for the sake of protecting the ripening grapes and other fruits. To this day in Greece the ripening grapes and other fruits are brought to the churches to be blest by the priests on the fifteenth of August. Now we hear of vineyards and plantations dedicated to Artemis, fruits offered to her, and her temple standing in an orchard. Hence we may conjecture that her Italian sister Diana was also revered as a patroness of vines and fruit-trees, and that on the thirteenth of August the owners of vineyards and orchards paid their

respects to her at Nemi along with other classes of the community.

Diana did not reign alone in her grove at Nemi. Two lesser divinities shared her forest sanctuary. One was Egeria, the nymph of the clear water which, bubbling from the basaltic rocks, used to fall in graceful cascades into the lake at the place called Le Mole, because here were established the mills of the modern village of Nemi. Women with child used to sacrifice to Egeria, because she was believed, like Diana, to be able to grant them an easy delivery. Tradition ran that the nymph had been the wife or mistress of the wise king Numa, that he had consorted with her in the secrecy of the sacred grove, and that the laws which he gave the Romans had been inspired by communion with her divinity. Plutarch compares the legend with other tales of the loves of goddesses for mortal men, such as the love of Cybele and the Moon for the fair youths Attis and Endymion. We may suppose that the spring which fell into the lake of Nemi was the true original Egeria, and that when the first settlers moved down from the Alban hills to the banks of the Tiber they brought the nymph with them and found a new home for her in a grove outside the gates. The remains of baths which have been discovered within the sacred precinct, together with many terra-cotta models of various parts of the human body, suggest that the waters of Egeria were used to heal the sick, who may have signified their hopes or testified their gratitude by dedicating likenesses of the diseased members to the goddess, in accordance with a custom which is still observed in many parts of Europe. To this day it would seem that the spring retains medicinal virtues.

The other of the minor deities at Nemi was Virbius. Legend had it that Virbius was the young Greek hero Hippolytus, chaste and fair, who learned the art of venery from the centaur Chiron, and spent all his days in the greenwood chasing wild beasts with the virgin huntress Artemis (the Greek counterpart of Diana) for his only comrade. Proud of her divine society, he spurned the love of women, and this proved his bane. For Aphrodite, stung by his scorn, inspired his stepmother Phaedra with love of him; and when he disdained her wicked advances she falsely accused him to his father Theseus. The slander was believed, and Theseus prayed to his sire Poseidon to avenge the imagined wrong. So while Hippolytus drove in a chariot by the shore of the Saronic Gulf, the sea-god sent a fierce bull forth from the waves. The terrified horses bolted, threw Hippolytus from the chariot, and dragged him at their hoofs to death. But Diana, for the love she bore Hippolytus, persuaded the leech Aesculapius to bring her fair young hunter back to life and then bore him far away to the dells of Nemi, where she entrusted him to the nymph Egeria, to live there, unknown and solitary, under the name of Virbius, in the depth of the Italian forest. There he reigned a king, and there he dedicated a precinct to Diana. Virbius was worshipped as a god not only at Nemi but elsewhere; for in Campania we hear of a special priest devoted to his service. Horses were excluded from the Arician grove and sanctuary because horses had killed Hippolytus. It was unlawful to touch his image. Some thought that he was the sun. 'But the truth is', says Servius, 'that he is a deity associated with Diana, as Attis is associated with the Mother of the Gods, and Erichthonius with Minerva, and Adonis with Venus.'

It needs no elaborate demonstration to convince us that the stories told to account for Diana's worship at Nemi are unhistorical. The incongruity of these Nemi myths is transparent, since the foundation of the worship is traced now to Orestes and now to Hippolytus, according as this or that feature of the ritual has to be accounted for. The real value of such tales is that they serve to illustrate the nature of the

worship by providing a standard with which to compare it; and further, that they bear witness indirectly to its venerable age by shewing that the true origin was lost in the mists of a fabulous antiquity.

Artemis and Hippolytus

The Arician legends of Orestes and Hippolytus, though worthless as history, have a certain value in so far as they may help us to understand the worship at Nemi better by comparing it with the ritual and myths of other sanctuaries. We must ask ourselves, Why did the author of these legends pitch upon Orestes and Hippolytus in order to explain Virbius and the King of the Wood? In regard to Orestes, the answer is obvious. He and the image of the Tauric Diana, which could only be appeased with human blood, were dragged in to render intelligible the murderous rule of succession to the Arician priesthood. In regard to Hippolytus the case is not so plain. The manner of his death suggests readily enough a reason for the exclusion of horses from the grove; but this by itself seems hardly enough to account for the identification. We must try to probe deeper by examining the worship as well as the legend or myth of Hippolytus.

He had a famous sanctuary at his ancestral home of Troezen, situated on a beautiful, almost landlocked bay. Across the blue water of the tranquil bay, which it shelters from the open sea, rises Poseidon's sacred island, its peaks veiled in the sombre green of the pines. Within the sanctuary stood a temple with an ancient image. The service was performed by a priest who held office for life: every year a sacrificial festival was held in his honour; and his untimely fate was yearly mourned, with weeping and doleful chants, by unwedded maids, who also dedicated locks of their hair in his temple before marriage. His grave existed at Troezen, though the people would not shew it. It has been suggested, with great plausibility, that in the handsome Hippolytus, beloved of Artemis, cut off in his youthful prime, and yearly mourned by damsels, we have one of those mortal lovers of a goddess who appear so often in ancient religion, and of whom Adonis is the most familiar type. The rivalry of Artemis and Phaedra for the affection of Hippolytus reproduces, it is said, under different names, the rivalry of Aphrodite and Proserpine for the love of Adonis, for Phaedra is merely a double of Aphrodite. Certainly in the *Hippolytus* of Euripides the tragedy of the hero's death is traced directly to the anger of Aphrodite at his contempt for her power, and Phaedra is nothing but a tool of the goddess. Moreover, within the precinct of Hippolytus at Troezen there stood a temple of Peeping Aphrodite, which was so named, we are told, because from this spot the amorous Phaedra used to watch Hippolytus at his manly sports. Clearly the name would be still more appropriate if it was Aphrodite herself who peeped. And beside this temple of Aphrodite grew a myrtle-tree with pierced leaves, which the hapless Phaedra, in the pangs of love, had pricked with her bodkin. Now the myrtle, with its glossy evergreen leaves, its red and white blossom, and its fragrant perfume, was Aphrodite's own tree, and legend associated it with the birth of Adonis. At Athens also Hippolytus was intimately associated with Aphrodite, for on the south side of the Acropolis, looking towards Troezen, a barrow or sepulchral mound in his memory was shewn, and beside it stood a temple of Aphrodite, said to have been founded by Phaedra, which bore the name of the temple of Aphrodite and Hippolytus. The conjunction, both in Troezen and in Athens, of his grave with a temple of the goddess of love is significant.

If this view of the relation of Hippolytus to Artemis and Aphrodite is right, it is somewhat remarkable that both his divine mistresses appear to have been associated at Troezen with oaks.

For Aphrodite was here worshipped under the title of Askraia, that is, She of the Fruitless Oak; and Hippolytus was said to have met his death not far from a sanctuary of Saronian Artemis, that is, Artemis of the Hollow Oak, for here the wild olive-tree was shewn in which the reins of his chariot became entangled, and so brought him to the ground.

Another point in the myth of Hippolytus which deserves attention is the frequent recurrence of horses in it. His name signifies either 'horse-loosed' or 'horse-looser'; he consecrated twenty horses to Aesculapius at Epidaurus; he was killed by horses; the Horse's Fount probably flowed not far from the temple which he built for Wolfish Artemis; and horses were sacred to his grandsire Poseidon, who had an ancient sanctuary in the wooded island across the bay, where the ruins of it may still be seen in the pine-forest. Lastly, Hippolytus's sanctuary at Troezen was said to have been founded by Diomede, whose mythical connexion both with horses and wolves is attested. Thus Hippolytus was associated with the horse in many ways, and this association may have been used to explain more features of the Arician ritual than the mere exclusion of the animal from the sacred grove.

The custom observed by Troezenian girls of offering tresses of their hair to Hippolytus before their wedding brings him into a relation with marriage, which at first sight seems out of keeping with his reputation as a confirmed bachelor. According to Lucian, youths as well as maidens at Troezen were forbidden to wed till they had shorn their hair in honour of Hippolytus, and we gather from the context that it was their first beard which the young men thus polled. However we may explain it, a custom of this sort appears to have prevailed widely both in Greece and the East. Plutarch tells us that formerly it was the wont of boys at puberty to go to Delphi and offer of their hair to Apollo; Theseus, the father of Hippolytus, complied with the custom, which lasted down into historical times. Argive maidens, grown to womanhood, dedicated their tresses to Athena before marriage. At the entrance to the temple of Artemis in Delos the grave of two maidens was shewn under an olive-tree. It was said that long ago they had come as pilgrims from a far northern land with offerings to Apollo, and dying in the sacred isle were buried there. The Delian virgins before marriage used to cut off a lock of their hair, wind it on a spindle, and lay it on the maidens' grave. The young men did the same, except that they twisted the down of their first beard round a wisp of grass or a green shoot.

In the sanctuary of the great Phoenician goddess Astarte at Byblus at the annual mourning for the dead Adonis, the women had to shave their heads, and such of them as refused to do so were bound to prostitute themselves to strangers and to sacrifice to the goddess with the wages of their shame. Though Lucian, who mentions the custom, does not say so, there are some grounds for thinking that the women in question were generally maidens, of whom this act of devotion was required as a preliminary to marriage. In any case, it is clear the goddess accepted the sacrifice of chastity as a substitute for the sacrifice of hair. The meaning of this sacrifice was that the women gave of their fecundity to the goddess, whether they offered their hair or their chastity. But why, it may be asked, should they make such an offering to Astarte, who was herself the great goddess of love and fertility? What need had she to receive fecundity from her worshippers? Was it not rather for her to bestow it on them? Thus put, the question overlooks an important side of polytheism, perhaps we may say of ancient religion in general. The gods stood as much in need of their worshippers as the worshippers in need of them. The benefits conferred were mutual. If the gods made the earth to bring forth abundantly, the flocks and herds to teem, and the

human race to multiply, they expected that a portion of their bounty should be returned to them in the shape of tithe or tribute. On this tithe, indeed, they subsisted, and without it they would starve. Their divine bellies had to be filled, and their divine reproductive energies to be recruited; hence men had to give of their meat and drink to them, and to sacrifice for their benefit what is most manly in man and womanly in woman. Sacrifices of the latter kind have too often been overlooked or misunderstood by the historians of religion. Other examples of them will meet us in the course of our enquiry. At the same time it may well be that the women who offered their hair to Astarte hoped to benefit through the sympathetic connexion which they thus established between themselves and the goddess; they may in fact have expected to fecundate themselves by contact with the divine source of fecundity. And it is probable that a similar motive underlay the sacrifice of chastity as well as the sacrifice of hair.

If the sacrifice of hair, especially of hair at puberty, is sometimes intended to strengthen the divine beings to whom it is offered by feeding or fertilising them, we can the better understand, not only the common practice of offering hair to the shadowy dead, but also the Greek usage of shearing it for rivers, as the Arcadian boys of Phigalia did for the stream that runs in the depths of the tremendous woody glen below the city. For next perhaps to rain and sunshine, nothing in nature so obviously contributes to fertilise a country as its rivers. Again, this view may set in a clearer light the custom of the Delian youths and maidens, who offered their hair on the maidens' tomb under the olive-tree. For at Delos, as at Delphi, one of Apollo's many functions was to make the crops grow and to fill the husbandman's barns; hence at the time of harvest tithe-offerings poured in to him from every side in the form of ripe sheaves, or, what was perhaps still more acceptable, golden models of them, which went by the name of the 'golden summer'. The festival at which these first-fruits were dedicated may have been the sixth and seventh of the harvest-month Thargelion, corresponding to the twenty-fourth and twenty-fifth of May, for these were the birthdays of Artemis and Apollo respectively. In Hesiod's day the corn-reaping began at the morning rising of the Pleiades, which then answered to our 9th of May, and in Greece the wheat is still ripe about that time. In return for these offerings the god sent out a sacred new fire from both his great sanctuaries at Delos and Delphi, thus radiating from them, as from central suns, the divine blessings of heat and light. A ship brought the new fire every year from Delos to Lemnos, the sacred island of the fire-god Hephaestus, where all fires were put out before its arrival, to be afterwards rekindled at the pure flame. The fetching of the new fire from Delphi to Athens appears to have been a ceremony of great solemnity and pomp.

Now the maidens on whose grave the Delian youths and damsels laid their shorn locks before marriage, were said to have died in the island after bringing the harvest offering, wrapt in wheaten straw, from the land of the Hyperboreans in the far north. Thus they were in popular opinion the mythical representatives of those bands of worshippers who bore, year by year, the yellow sheaves with dance and song to Delos. But in fact they had once been much more than this. For an examination of their names, which are commonly given as Hekaerge and Opis, has led modern scholars to conclude, with every appearance of probability, that these maidens were originally mere duplicates of Artemis herself. Perhaps indeed we may go a step farther. For sometimes one of this pair of Hyperboreans appears as a male, not a female, under the name of the Far-shooter (Hekaergos), which was a common epithet of Apollo. This suggests that the two were originally the heavenly twins themselves, Apollo and Artemis,

and that the two graves which were shewn at Delos, one before and the other behind the sanctuary of Artemis, may have been at first the tombs of these great deities, who were thus laid to their rest on the spot where they had been born. As the one grave received offerings of hair, so the other received the ashes of the victims which were burned on the altar. Both sacrifices, if I am right, were designed to strengthen and fertilise the divine powers who made the earth to wave with the golden harvest, and whose mortal remains, like the miracle-working bones of saints in the Middle Ages, brought wealth to their fortunate possessors. Ancient piety was not shocked by the sight of the tomb of a dead god.

But how, it may be asked, does all this apply to Hippolytus? Why attempt to fertilise the grave of a bachelor who paid all his devotions to a barren virgin? What seed could take root and spring up in so stony a soil? The question implies the popular modern notion of Diana or Artemis as the pattern of a strait-laced maiden lady with a taste for hunting. No notion could well be further from the truth. To the ancients, on the contrary, she was the ideal and embodiment of the wild life of nature – the life of plants, of animals, and of men – in all its exuberant fertility and profusion. The word *parthenos* applied to Artemis, which we commonly translate virgin, means no more than an unmarried woman, and in early days the two things were by no means the same. With the growth of a purer morality among men a stricter code of ethics is imposed by them upon their gods; the stories of the cruelty, deceit, and lust of these divine beings are glossed lightly over or flatly rejected as blasphemies, and the old ruffians are set to guard the laws which before they broke. In regard to Artemis, even the ambiguous *parthenos* seems to have been merely a popular epithet, not an official title. There was no public worship of Artemis the chaste; so far as her sacred titles bear on the relation of the sexes, they shew that, on the contrary, she was, like Diana in Italy, specially concerned with the loss of virginity and with child-bearing, and that she not only assisted but encouraged women to be fruitful and multiply; indeed, if we may take Euripides's word for it, in her capacity of midwife she would not even speak to childless women. Further, it is highly significant that while her titles and the allusions to her functions mark her out clearly as the patroness of childbirth, we find none that recognise her distinctly as a deity of marriage. Nothing, however, sets the true character of Artemis as a goddess of fecundity, though not of wedlock, in a clearer light than her constant identification with the unmarried, but not chaste, Asiatic goddesses of love and fertility, who were worshipped with rites of notorious profligacy at their popular sanctuaries. At Ephesus, the most celebrated of all the seats of her worship, her universal motherhood was set forth unmistakably in her sacred image.

To return now to Troezen, we shall probably be doing no injustice either to Hippolytus or to Artemis if we suppose that the relation between them was once of a tenderer nature than appears in classical literature. We may conjecture that if he spurned the love of women, it was because he enjoyed the love of a goddess. On the principles of early religion, she who fertilises nature must herself be fertile, and to be that she must necessarily have a male consort. If I am right, Hippolytus was the consort of Artemis at Troezen, and the shorn tresses offered to him by the Troezenian youths and maidens before marriage were designed to strengthen his union with the goddess, and so to promote the fruitfulness of the earth, of cattle, and of

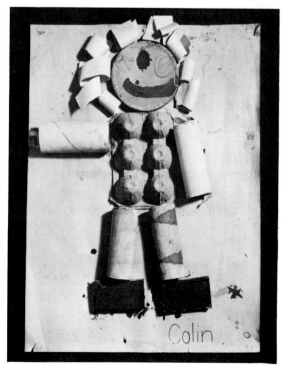

Diana, goddess of human fertility – and counterpart
TOP. Cult statue of Diana of Ephesus, 2nd century, Capitoline Museum, Rome. Photo: DAI, Rome
RIGHT. Colin, aged five, portrays his mother. Photo: Hamlyn Group Picture Library

mankind. Man and goddess did not stand side by side as lovers in Troezen only and the legends which traced the spilt blood of the human partner in the purple bloom of the violet, the scarlet stain of the anemone, or the crimson flush of the rose were no idle poetic emblems of youth and beauty fleeting as the summer flowers. Such fables contain a deeper philosophy of the relation of the life of man to the life of nature – a sad philosophy which gave birth to a tragic practice. What that philosophy and that practice were we shall learn later on.

Recapitulation

We can now perhaps understand why the ancients identified Hippolytus, the consort of Artemis, with Virbius, who, according to Servius, stood to Diana as Adonis to Venus, or Attis to the Mother of the Gods. For Diana, like Artemis, was a goddess of fertility in general, and of childbirth in particular. As such she, like her Greek counterpart, needed a male partner. That partner, if Servius is right, was Virbius. In his character of the founder of the sacred grove and first king of Nemi, Virbius is clearly the mythical predecessor or archetype of the line of priests who served Diana under the title of Kings of the Wood, and who came, like him, one after the other, to a violent end. It is natural, therefore, to conjecture that they stood to the goddess of the grove in the same relation in which Virbius stood to her; in short, that the mortal King of the Wood had for his queen the woodland Diana herself. If the sacred tree which he guarded with his life was supposed, as seems probable, to be her special embodiment, her priest may not only have worshipped it as his goddess but embraced it as his wife. There is at least nothing absurd in the supposition, since even in the time of Pliny a noble Roman used thus to treat a beautiful beech-tree in another sacred grove of Diana on the Alban hills. He embraced it, he kissed it, he lay under its shadow, he poured wine on its trunk. Apparently he took the tree for the goddess. The custom of physically marrying men and women to trees is still practised in India and other parts of the East. Why should it not have obtained in ancient Latium?

Reviewing the evidence as a whole, we may conclude that the worship of Diana in her sacred grove at Nemi was of great importance and immemorial antiquity; that she was revered as the goddess of woodlands and of wild creatures, probably also of domestic cattle and of the fruits of the earth; that she was believed to bless men and women with offspring and to aid mothers in childbed; that her holy fire, tended by chaste virgins, burned perpetually in a round temple within the precinct; that associated with her was a water-nymph Egeria who discharged one of Diana's own functions by succouring women in travail, and who was popularly supposed to have mated with an old Roman king in the sacred grove; further, that Diana of the Wood herself had a male companion, Virbius by name, who was to her what Adonis was to Venus, or Attis to Cybele; and, lastly, that this mythical Virbius was represented in historical times by a line of priests known as Kings of the Wood, who regularly perished by the swords of their successors, and whose lives were bound up with a certain tree in the grove, because so long as that tree was uninjured they were safe from attack.

Clearly these conclusions do not of themselves suffice to explain the peculiar rule of succession to the priesthood. But perhaps the survey of a wider field may lead us to think that they contain in germ the solution of the problem.

2. Priestly Kings

The questions which we have set ourselves to answer are mainly two: first, why had Diana's priest at Nemi, the King of the Wood, to slay his predecessor? second, why before doing so had he to pluck the branch of a certain tree which the public opinion of the ancients identified with Virgil's Golden Bough? The two questions are to some extent distinct, and it will be convenient to consider them separately. We begin with the first. In the last part of the book I shall suggest an answer to the second question.

The first point on which we fasten is the priest's title. Why was he called the King of the Wood? Why was his office spoken of as a kingdom?

The union of a royal title with priestly duties was common in ancient Italy and Greece. At Rome and in other cities of Latium there was a priest called the Sacrificial King or King of the Sacred Rites, and his wife bore the title of Queen of the Sacred Rites. In republican Athens the second annual magistrate of the state was called the King, and his wife the Queen; the functions of both were religious. Many other Greek democracies had titular kings, whose duties, so far as they are known, seem to have been priestly, and to have centred round the Common Hearth of the state.

This combination of priestly functions with royal authority is familiar to every one. Asia Minor, for example, was the seat of various great religious capitals peopled by thousands of sacred slaves, and ruled by pontiffs who wielded at once temporal and spiritual authority, like the popes of mediaeval Rome. Such priest-ridden cities were Zela and Pessinus. Teutonic kings, again, in the old heathen days seem to have stood in the position, and to have exercised the powers, of high priests. The Emperors of China offer public sacrifices, the details of which are regulated by the ritual books. The King of Madagascar was high-priest of the realm. At the great festival of the new year, when a bullock was sacrificed for the good of the kingdom, the king stood over the sacrifice to offer prayer and thanksgiving, while his attendants slaughtered the animal. In the monarchical states which still maintain their independence among the Gallas of Eastern Africa, the king sacrifices on the mountain tops and regulates the immolation of human victims; and the dim light of tradition reveals a similar union of temporal and spiritual power, of royal and priestly duties, in the kings of that delightful region of Central America whose ancient capital, now buried under the rank growth of the tropical forest, is marked by the stately and mysterious ruins of Palenque.

But when we have said that the ancient kings were commonly priests also, we are far from having exhausted the religious aspect of their office. In those days the divinity that hedges a king was no empty form of speech, but the expression of a sober belief. Kings were revered, in many cases not merely as priests, that is, as intercessors between man and god, but as

God revealed in human form
When the Dalai Lama of Tibet, the reincarnate divine Buddha, dies, the monks of the country look for a young successor who will prove by his more than human knowledge that he is the bearer of the same divine spirit that inspired his predecessor.
OPPOSITE. The young Dalai Lama presides at a sacred fire ceremony, Tibet. Granada Television Limited, *Disappearing World*

themselves gods, able to bestow upon their subjects and worshippers those blessings which are commonly supposed to be beyond the reach of mortals, and are sought, if at all, only by prayer and sacrifice offered to superhuman and invisible beings. Thus kings are often expected to give rain and sunshine in due season, to make the crops grow, and so on. Strange as this expectation appears to us, it is quite of a piece with early modes of thought. A savage hardly conceives the distinction commonly drawn by more advanced peoples between the natural and the supernatural. To him the world is to a great extent worked by supernatural agents, that is, by personal beings acting on impulses and motives like his own, liable like him to be moved by appeals to their pity, their hopes, and their fears. In a world so conceived he sees no limit to his power of influencing the course of nature to his own advantage. Prayers, promises, or threats may secure him fine weather and an abundant crop from the gods; and if a god should happen, as he sometimes believes, to become incarnate in his own person, then he need appeal to no higher being; he, the savage, possesses in himself all the powers necessary to further his own well-being and that of his fellow-men.

This is one way in which the idea of a man-god is reached. But there is another. Along with the view of the world as pervaded by spiritual forces, savage man has a different, and probably still older, conception in which we may detect a germ of the modern notion of natural law or the view of nature as a series of events occurring in an invariable order without the intervention of personal agency. The germ of which I speak is involved in that sympathetic magic, as it may be called, which plays a large part in most systems of superstition. In early society the king is frequently a magician as well as a priest; indeed he appears to have often attained to power by virtue of his supposed proficiency in the black or white art. Hence in order to understand the evolution of the kingship and the sacred character with which the office has commonly been invested in the eyes of savage or barbarous peoples, it is essential to have some acquaintance with the principles of magic and to form some conception of the extraordinary hold which that ancient system of superstition has had on the human mind in all ages and all countries. Accordingly I propose to consider the subject in some detail.

Contagious magic
Contact is communication, so that the essence of a person can be passed on through any one of his parts. Minatarres, like other North American Indians, believed that they acquired the strength of their enemies through their scalps.
OPPOSITE. Scalp dance of the Minatarres. Painting by Bodmer, from Maximilian Prince of Wied, *Travels in North America, c.*1840, British Museum, London

3. Sympathetic Magic

The Principles of Magic

If we analyse the principles of thought on which magic is based, they will probably be found to resolve themselves into two: first, that like produces like, or that an effect resembles its cause; and, second, that things which have once been in contact with each other continue to act on each other at a distance after the physical contact has been severed. The former principle may be called the Law of Similarity, the latter the Law of Contact or Contagion. From the first of these principles, namely the Law of Similarity, the magician infers that he can produce any effect he desires merely by imitating it: from the second he infers that whatever he does to a material object will affect equally the person with whom the object was once in contact, whether it formed part of his body or not. Charms based on the Law of Similarity may be called Homoeopathic or Imitative Magic. Charms based on the Law of Contact or Contagion may be called Contagious Magic. To denote the first of these branches of magic the term Homoeopathic is perhaps preferable, for the alternative term Imitative or Mimetic suggests, if it does not imply, a conscious agent who imitates, thereby limiting the scope of magic too narrowly. For the same principles which the magician applies in the practice of his art are implicitly believed by him to regulate the operations of inanimate nature; in other words, he tacitly assumes that the Laws of Similarity and Contact are of universal application and are not limited to human actions. In short, magic is a spurious system of natural law as well as a fallacious guide of conduct; it is a false science as well as an abortive art. Regarded as a system of natural law, that is, as a statement of the rules which determine the sequence of events throughout the world, it may be called Theoretical Magic: regarded as a set of precepts which human beings observe in order to compass their ends, it may be called Practical Magic. At the same time it is to be borne in mind that the primitive magician knows magic only on its practical side; he never analyses the mental processes on which his practice is based, never reflects on the abstract principles involved in his actions. With him, as with the vast majority of men, logic is implicit, not explicit: he reasons just as he digests his food in complete ignorance of the intellectual and physiological processes which are essential to the one operation and to the other. In short, to him magic is always an art, never a science; the very idea of science is lacking in his undeveloped mind. It is for the philosophic student to trace the train of thought which underlies the magician's practice; to draw out the few simple threads of which the tangled skein is composed; to disengage the abstract principles from their concrete applications; in short, to discern the spurious science behind the bastard art.

If my analysis of the magician's logic is correct, its two great principles turn out to be merely two different misapplications of the association of ideas. Homoeopathic magic is founded on the association of ideas by similarity: contagious magic is founded on the association of ideas by contiguity. Homoeopathic magic commits the mistake of assuming that things which resemble each other are the same: contagious magic commits the mistake of assuming that things which have once been in contact with each other are always in contact. But in practice the two branches are often combined; or, to be more exact, while homoeopathic or imitative magic may be practised by itself, contagious magic will generally be found to involve an application of the homoeopathic or imitative principle. Thus generally stated the two things may be a little difficult to grasp, but they will readily become intelligible when they are illustrated by particular examples. Both trains of thought are in fact extremely simple and elementary. It could hardly be otherwise, since they are familiar in the concrete, though certainly not in the abstract, to the crude intelligence not only of the savage, but of ignorant and dull-witted people everywhere. Both branches of magic, the homoeopathic and the contagious, may conventionally be comprehended under the general name of Sympathetic Magic, since both assume that things act on each other at a distance through a secret sympathy, the impulse being transmitted from one to the other by means of what we may conceive as a kind of invisible ether, not unlike that which is postulated by modern science for a precisely similar purpose, namely, to explain how things can physically affect each other through a space which appears to be empty.

It may be convenient to tabulate as follows the branches of magic according to the laws of thought which underlie them:

SYMPATHETIC MAGIC
Law of Sympathy

| HOMOEOPATHIC MAGIC | CONTAGIOUS MAGIC |
| *Law of Similarity* | *Law of Contact* |

I will now illustrate these two great branches of sympathetic magic by examples, beginning with homoeopathic magic.

Belief in magic dies hard
A mandrake being pulled up by a wolfhound, 'the only way to capture and tear it from the ground'. Medieval bestiary, MS Ashmole 1431, fol. 31R, Bodleian Library, Oxford

Black bryony root brought to the Pitt Rivers Museum, University of Oxford, by a workman in 1906. He believed it to be a mandrake plant with magical potency.

Homoeopathic or Imitative Magic

Perhaps the most familiar application of the principle that like produces like is the attempt which has been made by many peoples in many ages to injure or destroy an enemy by injuring or destroying an image of him, in the belief that, just as the image suffers, so does the man, and that when it perishes he must die. This form of magic has been practised through the ages and all over the world. For thousands of years ago it was known to the sorcerers of ancient India, Babylon, and Egypt, as well as of Greece and Rome, and at this day it is still resorted to by cunning and malignant savages in Australia, Africa, and Scotland. Thus the North American Indians, we are told, believe that by drawing the figure of a person in sand, ashes, or clay, or by considering any object as his body, and then pricking it with a sharp stick or doing it any other injury, they inflict a corresponding injury on the person represented. For example, when an Ojebway Indian desires to work evil on any one, he makes a little wooden image of his enemy and runs a needle into its head or heart, or he shoots an arrow into it, believing that wherever the needle pierces or the arrow strikes the image, his foe will the same instant be seized with a sharp pain in the corresponding part of his body; but if he intends to kill the person outright, he burns or buries the puppet, uttering certain magic words as he does so. So when a Cora Indian of Mexico wishes to kill a man, he makes a figure of him out of burnt clay, strips of cloth, and so forth, and then, muttering incantations, runs thorns through the head or stomach of the figure to make his victim suffer correspondingly. Sometimes the Cora Indian makes a more beneficent use of this sort of homoeopathic magic. When he wishes to multiply his flocks or herds, he models a figure of the animal he wants in wax or clay, or carves it from tuff, and deposits it in a cave of the mountains; for these Indians believe that the mountains are masters of all riches, including

cattle and sheep. For every cow, deer, dog, or hen he wants, the Indian has to sacrifice a corresponding image of the creature. This may help us to understand the meaning of the figures of cattle, deer, horses, and pigs which were dedicated to Diana at Nemi. They may have been the offerings of farmers or huntsmen who hoped thereby to multiply the cattle or the game.

The Chinese also are perfectly aware that you can harm a man by maltreating or cursing an image of him, especially if you have taken care to write on it his name and horoscope. This mode of venting spite on an enemy is said to be commonly practised in China. In Amoy such images, roughly made of bamboo splinters and paper, are called 'substitutes of persons' and may be bought very cheap for a small sum apiece at any shop which sells paper articles for the use of the dead or the gods; for the frugal Chinese are in the habit of palming off paper imitations of all kinds of valuables on the simple-minded ghosts and gods, who take them in all good faith for the genuine articles. As usual, the victim suffers a hurt corresponding to that done to his image.

In ancient Babylonia also it was a common practice to make an image of clay, pitch, honey, fat, or other soft material in the likeness of an enemy, and to injure or kill him by burning, burying, or otherwise ill-treating it. Thus in a hymn to the fire-god Nusku we read:

Those who have made images of me, reproducing my features,
Who have taken away my breath, torn my hairs,
Who have rent my clothes, have hindered my feet from treading the dust,
May the fire-god, the strong one, break their charm.

But both in Babylon and in Egypt this ancient tool of superstition, so baneful in the hands of the mischievous and malignant, was also pressed into the service of religion and turned to glorious account for the confusion and overthrow of demons. In a Babylonian incantation we meet with a long list of evil spirits whose effigies were

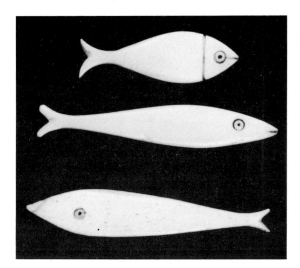

Imitative magic: like produces like
Models of fish will ensure a good catch, and disease will
be healed by means of votive offerings depicting the
afflicted part of the body in a healthy state.
TOP. Fisherman's bone models of fish, 19th century, from
Great Yarmouth, England. Pitt Rivers Museum,
University of Oxford
ABOVE. Silver votive offerings for cures, 19th century,
from the Mediterranean. Pitt Rivers Museum, University
of Oxford

burnt by the magician in the hope that, as their
images melted in the fire, so the fiends themselves might melt away and disappear.

If homoeopathic or imitative magic, working
by means of images, has commonly been practised for the spiteful purpose of putting obnoxious people out of the world, it has also, though
far more rarely, been employed with the benevo-
lent intention of helping others into it. In other
words, it has been used to facilitate childbirth
and to procure offspring for barren women.
Thus among the Esquimaux of Bering Strait a
barren woman desirous of having a son will con-
sult a shaman, who commonly makes, or causes
her husband to make, a small doll-like image
over which he performs certain secret rites, and
the woman is directed to sleep with it under her
pillow. In Japan, when a marriage is unfruitful,
the old women of the neighbourhood come to
the house and go through a pretence of delivering the wife of a child. The infant is represented
by a doll. The Maoris had a household god
whose image was in the form of an infant. The
image was very carefully made, generally life-
size, and adorned with the family jewels. Barren
women nursed it and addressed it in the most en-
dearing terms in order to become mothers.

The ancient Hindoos performed an elaborate
ceremony, based on homoeopathic magic, for
the cure of jaundice. Its main drift was to banish
the yellow colour to yellow creatures and yellow
things, such as the sun, to which it properly belongs, and to procure for the patient a healthy
red colour from a living, vigorous source, namely
a red bull. With this intention, a priest recited
the following spell: 'Up to the sun shall go thy
heart-ache and thy jaundice: in the colour of the
red bull do we envelop thee! We envelop thee in
red tints, unto long life. May this person go un-
scathed and be free of yellow colour! The cows
whose divinity is Rohini, they who, moreover,
are themselves red [*rohinih*] – in their every form
and every strength we do envelop thee. Into the

parrots, into the thrush, do we put thy jaundice, and, furthermore, into the yellow wagtail do we put thy jaundice.' While he uttered these words, the priest, in order to infuse the rosy hue of health into the sallow patient, gave him water to sip which was mixed with the hair of a red bull; he poured water over the animal's back and made the sick man drink it; he seated him on the skin of a red bull and tied a piece of the skin to him. Then in order to improve his colour by thoroughly eradicating the yellow taint, he proceeded thus. He first daubed him from head to foot with a yellow porridge made of turmeric or curcuma (a yellow plant), set him on a bed, tied three yellow birds, to wit a parrot, a thrush, and a yellow wagtail, by means of a yellow string to the foot of the bed; then pouring water over the patient, he washed off the yellow porridge, and with it no doubt the jaundice, from him to the birds. After that, by way of giving a final bloom to his complexion, he took some hairs of a red bull, wrapt them in gold leaf, and glued them to the patient's skin.

One of the great merits of homoeopathic magic is that it enables the cure to be performed on the person of the doctor instead of on that of his victim, who is thus relieved of all trouble and inconvenience, while he sees his medical man writhe in anguish before him. For example, the peasants of Perche, in France, labour under the impression that a prolonged fit of vomiting is brought about by the patient's stomach becoming unhooked, as they call it, and so falling down. Accordingly, a practitioner is called in to restore the organ to its proper place. After hearing the symptoms he at once throws himself into the most horrible contortions, for the purpose of unhooking his own stomach. Having succeeded in the effort, he next hooks it up again in another series of contortions and grimaces, while the patient experiences a corresponding relief. Fee five francs.

Further, homoeopathic and in general sympathetic magic plays a great part in the measures taken by the rude hunter or fisherman to secure an abundant supply of food. On the principle that like produces like, many things are done by him and his friends in deliberate imitation of the result which he seeks to attain; and, on the other hand, many things are scrupulously avoided because they bear some more or less fanciful resemblance to others which would really be disastrous.

The Indians of British Columbia live largely upon the fish which abound in their seas and rivers. If the fish do not come in due season, and the Indians are hungry, a Nootka wizard will make an image of a swimming fish and put it into the water in the direction from which the fish generally appear. This ceremony, accompanied by a prayer to the fish to come, will cause them to arrive at once. The islanders of Torres Straits use models of dugong and turtles to charm dugong and turtle to their destruction. A Malay who has baited a trap for crocodiles, and is awaiting results, is careful in eating his curry always to begin by swallowing three lumps of rice successively; for this helps the bait to slide more easily down the crocodile's throat. He is equally scrupulous not to take any bones out of his curry; for, if he did, it seems clear that the sharp-pointed stick on which the bait is skewered would similarly work itself loose, and the crocodile would get off with the bait. Hence in these circumstances it is prudent for the hunter, before he begins his meal, to get somebody else to take the bones out of his curry, otherwise he may at any moment have to choose between swallowing a bone and losing the crocodile.

This last rule is an instance of the things which the hunter abstains from doing lest, on the principle that like produces like, they should spoil his luck. For it is to be observed that the system of sympathetic magic is not merely composed of positive precepts; it comprises a very large number of negative precepts, that is, prohibitions. It tells you not merely what to do, but also what to leave undone. The positive precepts are charms: the negative precepts are taboos. In fact the whole doctrine of taboo, or at all events a large part of it, would seem to be only a special application of sympathetic magic, with its two great laws of similarity and contact. Though these laws are certainly not formulated in so many words nor even conceived in the abstract by the savage, they are nevertheless implicitly believed by him to regulate the course of nature quite independently of human will. He thinks that if he acts in a certain way, certain consequences will inevitably follow in virtue of one or other of these laws; and if the consequences of a particular act appear to him likely to prove disagreeable or dangerous, he is naturally careful not to act in that way lest he should incur them. In other words, he abstains from doing that which, in accordance with his mistaken notions of cause and effect, he falsely believes would injure him; in short, he subjects himself to a taboo. Thus taboo is so far a negative application of practical magic. Positive magic or sorcery says, 'Do this in order that so and so may happen.' Negative magic or taboo says, 'Do not do this, lest so and so should happen.' The aim of positive magic or sorcery is to produce a desired event, the aim of negative magic or taboo is to avoid an undesirable one. But both consequences, the desirable and the undesirable, are supposed to be brought about in accordance with the laws of similarity and contact. And just as the desired consequence is not really effected by the observance of a magical ceremony, so the dreaded consequence does not really result from the violation of a taboo. If the supposed evil necessarily followed a breach of taboo, the taboo would not be a taboo but a precept of morality or common sense. It is not a taboo to say, 'Do not put your hand in the fire'; it is a rule of common sense, because the forbidden action entails a real, not an imaginary evil. In short,

those negative precepts which we call taboo are just as vain and futile as those positive precepts which we call sorcery. The two things are merely opposite sides or poles of one great disastrous fallacy, a mistaken conception of the association of ideas. Of that fallacy, sorcery is the positive, and taboo the negative pole. If we give the general name of magic to the whole erroneous system, both theoretical and practical, then taboo may be defined as the negative side of practical magic. To put this in tabular form:

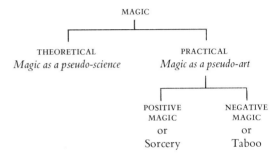

I have made these remarks on taboo and its relations to magic because I am about to give some instances of taboos observed by hunters, fishermen, and others, and I wished to shew that they fall under the head of Sympathetic Magic, being only particular applications of that general theory. Thus, it is a rule with the Galeareese that when you have caught fish and strung them on a line, you may not cut the line through, or next time you go a-fishing your fishing-line will be sure to break. Among the Esquimaux of Baffin Land boys are forbidden to play cat's cradle, because if they did so their fingers might in later life become entangled in the harpoon-line. Here the taboo is obviously an application of the law of similarity, which is the basis of homoeopathic magic: as the child's fingers are entangled by the string in playing cat's cradle, so they will be entangled by the harpoon-line when he is a man and hunts whales. Again, among the Huzuls, who inhabit the wooded north-eastern slopes of the Carpathian Mountains, the wife of a hunter

Imitative actions: like produces like
TOP. The buffalo dance of the Mandan Indians never
failed because they would continue dancing until a herd
of buffalo appeared. G. Catlin, *North American Indian
Portfolio*, 1845, Bodleian Library, Oxford
ABOVE. In this bushman rock painting from South Africa,
women dance disguised as the animals their menfolk are
to hunt. Copy by G. Stow, 1868, Bodleian Library,
Oxford

may not spin while her husband is hunting, or the
game will turn and wind like the spindle, and the
hunter will be unable to hit it. Here again the
taboo is clearly derived from the law of similarity. So, too, in most parts of ancient Italy

women were forbidden by law to spin on the
highroads as they walked, or even to carry their
spindles openly, because any such action was
believed to injure the crops. Probably the notion
was that the twirling of the spindle would twirl
the corn-stalks and prevent them from growing
straight. So, too, among the Ainos of Saghalien
a pregnant woman may not spin nor twist ropes
for two months before her delivery, because they
think that if she did so the child's guts might be
entangled like the thread.

Among the many beneficent uses to which a
mistaken ingenuity has applied the principle of
homoeopathic or imitative magic, is that of causing trees and plants to bear fruit in due season.
The eminent novelist, Mr Thomas Hardy, was
once told that the reason why certain trees in
front of his house, near Weymouth, did not
thrive, was that he looked at them before break-
fast on an empty stomach. In many parts of
Europe dancing or leaping high in the air are
approved homoeopathic modes of making the
crops grow high. Thus in Franche-Comté they
say that you should dance at the Carnival in
order to make the hemp grow tall. When a
Catholic priest remonstrated with the Indians of
the Orinoco on allowing their women to sow
the fields in the blazing sun, with infants at their
breasts, the men answered, 'Father, you don't
understand these things, and that is why they vex
you. You know that women are accustomed to
bear children, and that we men are not. When
the women sow, the stalk of the maize bears two
or three ears, the root of the yucca yields
two or three basketfuls, and everything multi-
plies in proportion. Now why is that? Simply
because the women know how to bring forth,
and know how to make the seed which they sow
bring forth also. Let them sow, then; we men
don't know as much about it as they do.' For the
same reason, probably, the Tupinambas of Brazil
thought that if a certain earth-almond were
planted by the men, it would not grow.

Thus on the theory of homoeopathic magic a person can influence vegetation either for good or for evil according to the good or the bad character of his acts or states: for example, a fruitful woman makes plants fruitful, a barren woman makes them barren. Hence this belief in the noxious and infectious nature of certain personal qualities or accidents has given rise to a number of prohibitions or rules of avoidance: people abstain from doing certain things lest they should homoeopathically infect the fruits of the earth with their own undesirable state or condition. All such customs of abstention or rules of avoidance are examples of negative magic or taboo.

In the foregoing cases a person is supposed to influence vegetation homoeopathically. He infects trees or plants with qualities or accidents, good or bad, resembling and derived from his own. But on the principle of homoeopathic magic the influence is mutual: the plant can infect the man just as much as the man can infect the plant. In magic, as I believe in physics, action and reaction are equal and opposite. The Cherokee Indians are adepts in practical botany of the homoeopathic sort. Before Cherokee braves went forth to war the medicine-man used to give each man a small charmed root which made him absolutely invulnerable. On the eve of battle the warrior bathed in a running stream, chewed a portion of the root and spat the juice on his body in order that the bullets might slide from his skin like the drops of water. Some of my readers perhaps doubt whether this really made the men bomb-proof. There is a barren and paralysing spirit of scepticism abroad at the present day which is most deplorable. However, the efficacy of this particular charm was proved in the Civil War, for three hundred Cherokees served in the army of the South; and they were never, or hardly ever, wounded in action.

Again, animals are often conceived to possess qualities or properties which might be useful to man, and homoeopathic or imitative magic seeks to communicate these properties to human beings in various ways. Thus some Bechuanas wear a ferret as a charm, because, being very tenacious of life, it will make them difficult to kill. Others wear a certain insect, mutilated, but living, for a similar purpose. The Wajaggas of Eastern Africa think that if they wear a piece of the wing-bone of a vulture tied round their leg they will be able to run and not grow weary, just as the vulture flies unwearied through the sky. The Esquimaux of Baffin Land fancy that if part of the intestines of a fox is placed under the feet of a baby boy, he will become active and skilful in walking over thin ice, like a fox. One of the ancient books of India prescribes that when a sacrifice is offered for victory, the earth out of which the altar is to be made should be taken from a place where a boar has been wallowing, since the strength of the boar will be in that earth.

On the principle of homoeopathic magic, inanimate things, as well as plants and animals, may diffuse blessing or bane around them, according to their own intrinsic nature and the skill of the wizard to tap or dam, as the case may be, the stream of weal or woe. In Samaracand women give a baby sugar candy to suck and put glue in the palm of its hand, in order that, when the child grows up, his words may be sweet and precious things may stick to his hands as if they were glued. The Greeks thought that a garment made from the fleece of a sheep that had been torn by a wolf would hurt the wearer, setting up an itch or irritation in his skin. They were also of opinion that if a stone which had been bitten by a dog were dropped in wine, it would make all who drank of that wine to fall out among themselves.

Amongst the things which homoeopathic magic seeks to turn to account are the great powers of nature, such as the waxing and the waning moon, the rising and the setting sun, the stars, and the sea. The ancient books of the Hindoos lay down a rule that after sunset on his marriage night a man should sit silent with his wife till the stars begin to twinkle in the sky. When the pole-star appears, he should point it out to her, and, addressing the star, say, 'Firm art thou; I see thee, the firm one. Firm be thou with me, O thriving one!' Then, turning to his wife, he should say, 'To me Brihaspati has given thee; obtaining offspring through me, thy husband, live with me a hundred autumns.' The intention of the ceremony is plainly to guard against the fickleness of fortune and the instability of earthly bliss by the steadfast influence of the constant star. It is the wish expressed in Keats's last sonnet:

Bright star! would I were steadfast as thou art –
  Not in lone splendour hung aloft the night.

A like fancy still lingers in some parts of Europe. On the Cantabrian coast of Spain they think that persons who die of chronic or acute diseases expire at the moment when the tide of the sea begins to recede.

Contagious magic: for good or ill the part stands for the whole
Contact with a saint's relic, part of his body or clothing, will cure or aid the devotee as the saint himself would have done. Silver box containing bone relic of a Buddhist saint, from Tibet, E. M. Scratton Collection, Gulbenkian Museum of Oriental Art, Durham

Contagious Magic

Thus far we have been considering chiefly that branch of sympathetic magic which may be called homoeopathic or imitative. Its leading principle, as we have seen, is that like produces like, or, in other words, that an effect resembles its cause. The other great branch of sympathetic magic, which I have called Contagious Magic, proceeds upon the notion that things which have once been conjoined must remain ever afterwards, even when quite dissevered from each other, in such a sympathetic relation that whatever is done to the one must similarly affect the other. Thus the logical basis of Contagious Magic, like that of Homoeopathic Magic, is a mistaken association of ideas: its physical basis, if we may speak of such a thing, like the physical basis of Homoeopathic Magic, is a material medium of some sort which, like the ether of modern physics, is assumed to unite distant objects and to convey impressions from one to the other. The most familiar example of Contagious Magic is the magical sympathy

which is supposed to exist between a man and any severed portion of his person, as his hair or nails; so that whoever gets possession of human hair or nails may work his will, at any distance, upon the person from whom they were cut. This superstition is worldwide; instances of it in regard to hair and nails will be noticed later on in this work. While like other superstitions it has had its absurd and mischievous consequences, it has nevertheless indirectly done much good by furnishing savages with strong, though irrational, motives for observing rules of cleanliness which they might never have adopted on rational grounds. How the superstition has produced this salutary effect will appear from a single instance, which I will give in the words of an experienced observer. Amongst the natives of the Gazelle Peninsula in New Britain 'it is as a rule necessary for the efficiency of a charm that it should contain a part of the person who is to be enchanted (for example, his hair), or a piece of his clothing, or something that stands in some relation to him,

such as his excrements, the refuse of his food, his spittle, his footprints, etc. All such objects can be employed as *panait*, that is, as a medium for a *papait* or charm, consisting of an incantation or murmuring of a certain formula, together with the blowing into the air of some burnt lime which is held in the hand. It need hardly, therefore, be said that the native removes all such objects as well as he can. Thus the cleanliness which is usual in the houses and consists in sweeping the floor carefully every day, is by no means based on a desire for cleanliness and neatness in themselves, but purely on the effort to put out of the way anything that might serve an ill-wisher as a charm.' I will now illustrate the principles of Contagious Magic by examples, beginning with its application to various parts of the human body.

Among the parts which are commonly believed to remain in a sympathetic union with the body, after the physical connexion has been severed, are the navel-string and the afterbirth, including the placenta. So intimate, indeed, is

BELOW. But evil will befall a person if a spell is wrought on something that was once a part of him. Thus, a Santal baby's first hair is ceremonially shaved to be then carefully disposed of. Photo: W. G. Archer
BELOW RIGHT. If it is dangerous for a person to lose control of part of his body in this life, the same may

apply in the next. Therefore, in China, those who in their lives had suffered punitive amputation were buried with jade replicas of their missing limbs. Jade replica of a hand from China, 3rd to 4th century, Sir Charles Hardinge Collection, Gulbenkian Museum of Oriental Art, Durham

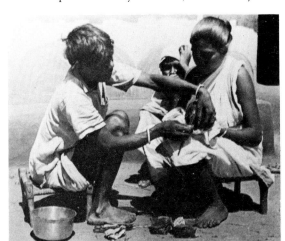

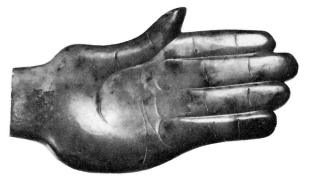

the union conceived to be, that the fortunes of the individual for good or evil throughout life are often supposed to be bound up with one or other of these portions of his person, so that if his navel-string or afterbirth is preserved and properly treated, he will be prosperous; whereas if it be injured or lost, he will suffer accordingly. Thus among the Maoris, when the navel-string dropped off, the child was carried to a priest to be solemnly named by him. But before the ceremony of naming began, the navel-string was buried in a sacred place and a young sapling was planted over it. Ever afterwards that tree, as it grew, was a *tohu oranga* or sign of life for the child.

A Chinese medical work prescribes that 'the placenta should be stored away in a felicitous spot under the salutary influences of the sky or the moon, deep in the ground, and with earth piled up over it carefully, in order that the child may be ensured a long life. If it is devoured by a swine or dog, the child loses its intellect; if insects or ants eat it, the child becomes scrofulous; if crows or magpies swallow it, the child will have an abrupt or violent death; if it is cast into the fire, the child incurs running sores.' The Japanese preserve the navel-string most carefully and bury it with the dead in the grave.

A curious application of the doctrine of contagious magic is the relation commonly believed to exist between a wounded man and the agent of the wound, so that whatever is subsequently done by or to the agent must correspondingly affect the patient either for good or evil. Thus Pliny tells us that if you have wounded a man and are sorry for it, you have only to spit on the hand that gave the wound, and the pain of the sufferer will be instantly alleviated.

In Suffolk if a man cuts himself with a billhook or a scythe he always takes care to keep the weapon bright, and oils it to prevent the wound from festering. If he runs a thorn or, as he calls it, a bush into his hand, he oils or greases the ex-

tracted thorn. A man came to a doctor with an inflamed hand, having run a thorn into it while hedging. On being told that the hand was festering, he remarked, 'That didn't ought to, for I greased the bush well arter I pulled it out.'

Sometimes the magical sympathy is supposed to exist between the man and his clothes, so that the garment by itself is enough to give the sorcerer a hold upon his victim. The witch in Theocritus, while she melted an image or lump of wax in order that her faithless lover might melt with love of her, did not forget to throw into the fire a shred of his cloak which he had dropped in her house. Again, magic may be wrought on a man sympathetically, not only through his clothes and severed parts of himself, but also through the impressions left by his body in sand or earth. In particular, it is a world-wide superstition that by injuring footprints you injure the feet that made them. Thus the natives of south-eastern Australia think that they can lame a man by placing sharp pieces of quartz, glass, bone, or charcoal in his footprints. Rheumatic pains are often attributed by them to this cause. It was a maxim with the Pythagoreans that in rising from bed you should smooth away the impression left by your body on the bed-clothes. The rule was simply an old precaution against magic, forming part of a whole code of superstitious maxims which antiquity fathered on Pythagoras, though doubtless they were familiar to the barbarous forefathers of the Greeks long before the time of that philosopher.

The Magician's Progress

We have now concluded our examination of the general principles of sympathetic magic. The examples by which I have illustrated them have been drawn for the most part from what may be called private magic, that is from magical rites and incantations practised for the benefit or the injury of individuals. But in savage society there is commonly to be found in addition what we

The diviner
Among the Basuto of South Africa and in Edwardian
England.
ABOVE. Early 20th-century photograph from the
Duggan-Cronin Gallery, Alexander McGregor
Memorial Museum, Kimberley

Broadsheet from John Johnson Collection, Bodleian
Library, Oxford

may call public magic, that is, sorcery practised
for the benefit of the whole community. Wherever ceremonies of this sort are observed for the
common good, it is obvious that the magician
ceases to be merely a private practitioner and becomes to some extent a public functionary. The
development of such a class of functionaries is of
great importance for the political as well as the
religious evolution of society. For when the welfare of the tribe is supposed to depend on the
performance of these magical rites, the magician
rises into a position of much influence and repute, and may readily acquire the rank and
authority of a chief or king.

Thus, so far as the public profession of magic
affected the constitution of savage society, it
tended to place the control of affairs in the hands
of the ablest man: it shifted the balance of power
from the many to the one: it substituted a monarchy for a democracy, or rather for an oligarchy
of old men; for in general the savage community
is ruled, not by the whole body of adult males,
but by a council of elders. The change, by whatever causes produced, and whatever the character of the early rulers, was on the whole very
beneficial. For the rise of monarchy appears to
be an essential condition of the emergence of
mankind from savagery. No human being is so

hidebound by custom and tradition as your democratic savage; in no state of society consequently is progress so slow and difficult.

Hence, it is no accident that all the first great strides towards civilisation have been made under despotic and theocratic governments, like those of Egypt, Babylon, and Peru, where the supreme ruler claimed and received the servile allegiance of his subjects in the double character of a king and a god. It is hardly too much to say that at this early epoch despotism is the best friend of humanity and, paradoxical as it may sound, of liberty. For after all there is more liberty in the best sense – liberty to think our own thoughts and to fashion our own destinies – under the most absolute despotism, the most grinding tyranny, than under the apparent freedom of savage life, where the individual's lot is cast from the cradle to the grave in the iron mould of hereditary custom.

So far, therefore, as the public profession of magic has been one of the roads by which the ablest men have passed to supreme power, it has contributed to emancipate mankind from the thraldom of tradition and to elevate them into a larger, freer life, with a broader outlook on the world. This is no small service rendered to humanity. And when we remember further that in another direction magic has paved the way for science, we are forced to admit that if the black art has done much evil, it has also been the source of much good; that if it is the child of error, it has yet been the mother of freedom and truth.

From magic to religion
Christian priests and bishops, like magicians in primitive societies, have powers to protect their fellow humans that are expressed in their insignia. The Bishop's mitre represents the fire of the Holy Spirit, while the cross stands for victory over evil. Dr Michael Ramsey, former Archbishop of Canterbury. Portrait study by Karsh of Ottawa, Camera Press, London

4. The Magical Control of the Weather

The patient reader may remember that we were led to plunge into the labyrinth of magic by a consideration of two different types of man-god. The two types of human gods may conveniently be distinguished as the religious and the magical man-god respectively. In the former, a being of an order different from and superior to man is supposed to become incarnate, for a longer or a shorter time, in a human body, manifesting his superhuman power and knowledge by miracles wrought and prophecies uttered through the medium of the fleshly tabernacle in which he has deigned to take up his abode. This may also appropriately be called the inspired or incarnate type of man-god. In it the human body is merely a frail earthly vessel filled with a divine and immortal spirit. On the other hand, a man-god of the magical sort is nothing but a man who possesses in an unusually high degree powers which most of his fellows arrogate to themselves on a smaller scale; for in rude society there is hardly a person who does not dabble in magic. Thus, whereas a man-god of the former or inspired type derives his divinity from a deity who has stooped to hide his heavenly radiance behind a dull mask of earthly mould, a man-god of the latter type draws his extraordinary power from a certain physical sympathy with nature. He is not merely the receptacle of a divine spirit. His whole being, body and soul, is so delicately attuned to the harmony of the world that a touch of his hand or a turn of his head may send a thrill vibrating through the universal framework of things; and conversely his divine organism is acutely sensitive to such slight changes of environment as would leave ordinary mortals wholly un-affected. But the line between these two types of man-god, however sharply we may draw it in theory, is seldom to be traced with precision in practice, and in what follows I shall not insist on it.

We have seen that in practice the magic art may be employed for the benefit either of individuals or of the whole community, and that according as it is directed to one or other of these two objects it may be called private or public magic. Further, I pointed out that the public magician occupies a position of great influence, from which, if he is a prudent and able man, he may advance step by step to the rank of a chief or king. Thus an examination of public magic conduces to an understanding of the early kingship, since in savage and barbarous society many chiefs and kings appear to owe their authority in great measure to their reputation as magicians.

Among the objects of public utility which magic may be employed to secure, the most essential is an adequate supply of food. The purveyors of food – the hunter, the fisher, the farmer – all resort to magical practices in the pursuit of their callings, as private individuals, for the benefit of themselves. But a great step in advance has been taken when a special class of magicians has been instituted; when, in other words, a number of men have been set apart for the express purpose of benefiting the whole community by their skill, whether that skill be directed to the healing of diseases, the forecasting of the future, the regulation of the weather, or any other object of general utility.

The Magical Control of Rain

Of the things which the public magician sets

himself to do for the good of the tribe, one of the chief is to control the weather and especially to ensure an adequate fall of rain. Water is the first essential of life, and in most countries the supply of it depends upon showers. Without rain vegetation withers, animals and men languish and die. Hence in savage communities the rain-maker is a very important personage; and often a special class of magicians exists for the purpose of regulating the heavenly water-supply. The methods by which they attempt to discharge the duties of their office are commonly, though not always, based on the principle of homoeopathic or imitative magic. If they wish to make rain they simulate it by sprinkling water or mimicking clouds: if their object is to stop rain and cause drought, they avoid water and resort to warmth and fire for the sake of drying up the too abundant moisture. Such attempts are by no means confined, as the cultivated reader might imagine, to the naked inhabitants of those sultry lands like Central Australia and some parts of Eastern and Southern Africa, where often for months together the pitiless sun beats down out of a blue and cloudless sky on the parched and gaping earth. They are, or used to be, common enough among outwardly civilised folk in the moister climate of Europe.

When the rains do not come in due season the people of Central Angoniland repair to what is called the rain-temple. Here they clear away the grass, and the leader pours beer into a pot which is buried in the ground, while he says, 'Master *Chauta*, you have hardened your heart towards us, what would you have us do? We must perish indeed. Give your children the rains, there is the beer we have given you.' Then they all partake of the beer that is left over, even the children being made to sip it. Next they take branches of trees and dance and sing for rain. When they return to the village they find a vessel of water set at the doorway by an old woman; so they dip their branches in it and wave them aloft,

so as to scatter the drops. After that the rain is sure to come driving up in heavy clouds. In these practices we see a combination of religion with magic; for while the scattering of the water-drops by means of branches is a purely magical ceremony, the prayer for rain and the offering of beer are purely religious rites. In Laos the festival of the New Year takes place about the middle of April and lasts three days. The people assemble in the pagodas, which are decorated with flowers and illuminated. The Buddhist monks perform the ceremonies, and when they come to the prayers for the fertility of the earth the worshippers pour water into little holes in the floor of the pagoda as a symbol of the rain which they hope Buddha will send down on the rice-fields in due time.

It is interesting to observe that where an opposite result is desired, primitive logic enjoins the weather-doctor to observe precisely opposite rules of conduct. In the tropical island of Java, where the rich vegetation attests the abundance of the rainfall, ceremonies for the making of rain are rare, but ceremonies for the prevention of it are not uncommon. When a man is about to give a great feast in the rainy season and has invited many people, he goes to a weather-doctor and asks him to 'prop up the clouds that may be lowering'. If the doctor consents to exert his professional powers, he begins to regulate his behaviour by certain rules as soon as his customer has departed. He must observe a fast, and may neither drink nor bathe; what little he eats must be eaten dry, and in no case may he touch water. The host, on his side, and his servants,

Reality behind the myth
The Greek myth of Andromeda, who was to be sacrificed to a sea monster, reflects an earlier practice of sacrificing women to water spirits for the benefit of vegetation. The myth marks the point in human thought when this practice was being discarded, for Andromeda was saved by her human lover Perseus.
OPPOSITE. *Perseus and Andromeda* by Titian, Wallace Collection, London. Photo: John Freeman

Krishna

Kuchita wife of
Ayana Ghosha
(maternal uncle of Krishna)

Krishna fell in love with her.

both male and female, must neither wash clothes nor bathe so long as the feast lasts, and they have all during its continuance to observe strict chastity. The doctor seats himself on a new mat in his bedroom, and before a small oil-lamp he murmurs, shortly before the feast takes place, the following prayer or incantation: 'Grandfather and Grandmother Sroekoel' (the name seems to be taken at random; others are sometimes used), 'return to your country. Akkemat is your country. Put down your water-cask, close it properly, that not a drop may fall out.' While he utters this prayer the sorcerer looks upwards, burning incense the while.

In south-eastern Europe at the present day ceremonies are observed for the purpose of making rain which rest on the same general train of thought as the preceding. Among the Greeks of Thessaly and Macedonia, for instance, when a drought has lasted a long time, it is customary to send a procession of children round to all the wells and springs of the neighbourhood. At the head of the procession walks a girl adorned with flowers, whom her companions drench with water at every halting-place while they sing an invocation. Similarly, at Poona in India, when rain is needed, the boys dress up one of their number in nothing but leaves and call him King of Rain (*Mrüj raja*). Then they go round to every house in the village where the householder or his wife sprinkles the Rain King with water, and gives the party food of various

The marriage between gods and mortal women
OPPOSITE. The god Krishna with his human beloved, the shepherd girl Radha. This relationship can signify on the one hand the ideal relationship between the sexes, on which depends the reproduction of life, and on the other spiritual union with god. 'No one knows the purpose of thy action, O Lord, in the guise of a human being. Thou hast neither any favourite nor any foe, although men wrongly think of thee as having such.' (Prayer to Sri Krishna.) Kalighat market painting, 19th century, India, Victoria and Albert Museum, London. Crown Copyright

kinds. When they have thus visited all the houses, they strip the Rain King of his leafy robes and feast upon what they have gathered.

There exists an entirely different mode of procuring rain, to which people sometimes have recourse in extreme cases, when the drought is long and their temper short. At such times they will drop the usual hocus-pocus of imitative magic altogether, and being far too angry to waste their breath in prayer they seek by threats and curses or even downright physical force to extort the waters of heaven from the supernatural being who has, so to say, cut them off at the main.

The Chinese are adepts in the art of taking the kingdom of heaven by storm. Thus, when rain is wanted they make a huge dragon of paper or wood to represent the rain-god, and carry it about in procession; but if no rain follows, the mock-dragon is execrated and torn to pieces. At other times they threaten and beat the god if he does not give rain; sometimes they publicly depose him from the rank of deity. On the other hand, if the wished-for rain falls, the god is promoted to a higher rank by an imperial decree. About the year 1710 the island of Tsong-ming, which belongs to the province of Nanking, was afflicted with a drought. The viceroy of the province, after the usual attempts to soften the heart of the local deity by burning incense-sticks had been made in vain, sent word to the idol that if rain did not fall by such and such a day, he would have him turned out of the city and his temple razed to the ground. The threat had no effect on the obdurate divinity; the day of grace came and went, and yet no rain fell. Then the indignant viceroy forbade the people to make any more offerings at the shrine of this unfeeling deity, and commanded that the temple should be shut up and seals placed on the doors. This soon produced the desired effect. Cut off from his base of supplies, the idol had no choice but to surrender at discretion. Rain fell in a few

days, and thus the god was restored to the affections of the faithful.

·Like other peoples, the Greeks and Romans sought to obtain rain by magic, when prayers and processions had proved ineffectual. The Athenians sacrificed boiled, not roast meat to the Seasons, begging them to avert drought and dry heat and to send due warmth and timely rain. This is an interesting example of the admixture of religion with sorcery, of sacrifice with magic. The Athenians dimly conceived that in some way the water in the pot would be transmitted through the boiled meat to the deities, and then sent down again by them in the form of rain. In a similar spirit the prudent Greeks made it a rule always to pour honey, but never wine, on the altars of the sun-god, pointing out, with great show of reason, how expedient it was that a god on whom so much depended should keep strictly sober.

The rule of total abstinence which Greek prudence and piety imposed on the sun-god introduces us to a second class of natural phenomena which primitive man commonly supposes to be in some degree under his control and dependent on his exertions. As the magician thinks he can make rain, so he fancies he can cause the sun to shine, and can hasten or stay its going down. At an eclipse the Ojebways used to imagine that the sun was being extinguished. So they shot fire-tipped arrows in the air, hoping thus to rekindle his expiring light. The Sencis of eastern Peru also shot burning arrows at the sun during an eclipse, but apparently they did this not so much to relight his lamp as to drive away a savage beast with which they supposed him to be struggling. Sometimes the mode of making sunshine is the converse of that of making rain. Thus in the Timorese sacrifice a white or red victim is sacrificed for sunshine, while a black one is sacrificed for rain. Some of the New Caledonians drench a skeleton to make rain, but burn it to make sunshine.

Magical control of the weather
Throughout the world, meteorological phenomena have been divinized, for sun, moon, thunder and lightning can be more readily approached by man as anthropomorphic gods than as pure natural phenomena.
TOP. Some Greek myths, such as the one of Aeolus, king of wind and clouds, reflect the practices of an earlier period. Aeolus chases the clouds into their cave to make fair weather. Athenian vessel, 5th century BC, British Museum, London
ABOVE. Inti Huatana, Machu Picchu, Peru, where the Incas 'tied' the sun, their god and father, on the shortest day of the year to ensure his return. Photo: C. N. Wallis

When the mists lay thick on the Sierras of Peru, the Indian women used to rattle the silver and copper ornaments which they wore on their breasts, and they blew against the fog, hoping thus to disperse it and make the sun shine through. Another way of producing the same effect was to burn salt or scatter ashes in the air.

Jerome of Prague, travelling among the heathen Lithuanians early in the fifteenth century, found a tribe who worshipped the sun and venerated a large iron hammer. The priests told him that once the sun had been invisible for several months, because a powerful king had shut it up in a strong tower; but the signs of the zodiac had broken open the tower with this very hammer and released the sun. Therefore they adored the hammer.

Magicians as Kings

The foregoing evidence may satisfy us that in many lands and many races magic has claimed to control the great forces of nature for the good of man. If that has been so, the practitioners of the art must necessarily be personages of importance and influence in any society which puts faith in their extravagant pretensions, and it would be no matter for surprise if, by virtue of the reputation which they enjoy and of the awe which they inspire, some of them should attain to the highest position of authority over their credulous fellows. In point of fact magicians appear to have often developed into chiefs and kings.

In Africa, the evidence for the evolution of the chief out of the magician, and especially out of the rainmaker, is comparatively plentiful. Thus among the Wambugwe, a Bantu people of East Africa, the original form of government was a family republic, but the enormous power of the sorcerers, transmitted by inheritance, soon raised them to the rank of petty lords or chiefs. Of the three chiefs living in the country in 1894 two were much dreaded as magicians, and the wealth of cattle they possessed came to them almost wholly in the shape of presents bestowed for their services in that capacity. Their principal art was that of rain-making. The chiefs of the Wataturu, another people of East Africa, are said to be nothing but sorcerers destitute of any direct political influence. Again, among the Wagogo of German East Africa the main power of the

chiefs, we are told, is derived from their art of rain-making. If a chief cannot make rain himself, he must procure it from some one who can. Again, in the powerful Masai nation of the same region the medicine-men are not uncommonly the chiefs, and the supreme chief of the race is almost invariably a powerful medicine-man. These *Laibon*, as they are called, are priests as well as doctors, skilled in interpreting omens and dreams, in averting ill-luck, and in making rain. The head chief or medicine-man, who has been called the Masai pope, is expected not only to make rain, but to repel and destroy the enemies of the Masai in war by his magic art.

In many other parts of the world kings have been expected to regulate the course of nature for the good of their people and have been punished if they failed to do so. It appears that the Scythians, when food was scarce, used to put their king in bonds. In ancient Egypt the sacred kings were blamed for the failure of the crops, but the sacred beasts were also held responsible for the course of nature. When pestilence and other calamities had fallen on the land, in consequence of a long and severe drought, the priests took the animals by night and threatened them, but if the evil did not abate they slew the beasts. On the coral island of Niuē or Savage Island, in the South Pacific, there formerly reigned a line of kings. But as the kings were also high priests, and were supposed to make the food grow, the people became angry with them in times of scarcity and killed them; till at last, as one after another was killed, no one would be king, and the monarchy came to an end. Ancient Chinese writers inform us that in Corea the blame was laid on the king whenever too much or too little rain fell and the crops did not ripen. Some said that he must be deposed, others that he must be slain. The Chinese emperor himself is deemed responsible if the drought is at all severe, and many are the self-condemnatory edicts on this subject published in the pages of the venerable

Peking Gazette. In extreme cases the emperor, clad in humble vestments, sacrifices to heaven and implores its protection. The Toorateyas of southern Celebes hold that the prosperity of the rice depends on the behaviour of their princes, and that bad government, by which they mean a government which does not conform to ancient custom, will result in a failure of the crops. In the time of the Swedish king Domalde a mighty famine broke out, which lasted several years, and could be stayed by the blood neither of beasts nor of men. Therefore, in a great popular assembly held at Upsala, the chiefs decided that King Domalde himself was the cause of the scarcity and must be sacrificed for good seasons. So they slew him and smeared with his blood the altars of the gods. Again, we are told that the Swedes always attributed good or bad crops to their kings as the cause. Now, in the reign of King Olaf, there came dear times and famine, and the people thought that the fault was the king's, because he was sparing in his sacrifices. So, mustering an army, they marched against him, surrounded his dwelling, and burned him in it, 'giving him to Odin as a sacrifice for good crops'.

Perhaps the last relic of such superstitions which lingered about our English kings was the notion that they could heal scrofula by their touch. The disease was accordingly known as the King's Evil. Queen Elizabeth often exercised this miraculous gift of healing. On Midsummer Day 1633, Charles the First cured a hundred patients at one swoop in the chapel royal at Holyrood. But it was under his son Charles the Second that the practice seems to have attained its highest vogue. It was the twenty-ninth of May 1660 when he was brought home in triumph from exile and on the sixth of July that he began to touch for the King's Evil. The ceremony is thus described by Evelyn, who may have witnessed it. 'His Majestie began first to *touch for ye evil*, according to costome, thus: His Matie sitting under his state in the Banqueting House, the chirurgeons cause the sick to be brought or led up to the throne, where they kneeling, ye King strokes their faces or cheekes with both his hands at once, at which instant a chaplaine in his formalities says, "He put his hands upon them and he healed them." This is sayd to every one in particular. When they have been all touch'd they come up again in the same order, and the other chaplaine kneeling, and having angel gold strung on white ribbon on his arme, delivers them one by one to his Matie, who puts them about the necks of the touched as they pass, whilst the first chaplaine repeats, "That is ye true light who came into ye world." Then follows an Epistle (as at first a Gospell) with the liturgy, prayers for the sick, with some alteration, lastly ye blessing; and then the Lo. Chamberlaine and the Comptroller of the Household bring a basin, ewer and towell, for his Majesty to wash.'

On the whole, then, we seem to be justified in inferring that in many parts of the world the king is the lineal successor of the old magician or medicine-man. When once a special class of sorcerers has been segregated from the community and entrusted by it with the discharge of duties on which the public safety and welfare are believed to depend, these men gradually rise to wealth and power, till their leaders blossom out into sacred kings. And while the distinction between the human and the divine is still imperfectly drawn, it is often imagined that men may themselves attain to godhead, not merely after their death, but in their lifetime, through the temporary or permanent possession of their whole nature by a great and powerful spirit. No class of the community has benefited so much as kings by this belief in the possible incarnation of a god in human form. The doctrine of that incarnation, and with it the theory of the divinity of kings in the strict sense of the word, will form the subject of the following chapter.

5. Divine Kings

Incarnate Human Gods

The instances which in the preceding chapters I have drawn from the beliefs and practices of rude peoples all over the world, may suffice to prove that the savage fails to recognise those limitations to his power over nature which seem so obvious to us. In a society where every man is supposed to be endowed more or less with powers which we should call supernatural, it is plain that the distinction between gods and men is somewhat blurred, or rather has scarcely emerged.

The notion of a man-god, or of a human being endowed with divine or supernatural powers, belongs essentially to that earlier period of religious history in which gods and men are still viewed as beings of much the same order, and before they are divided by the impassable gulf which, to later thought, opens out between them. Strange, therefore, as may seem to us the idea of a god incarnate in human form, it has nothing very startling for early man, who sees in a man-god or a god-man only a higher degree of the same supernatural powers which he arrogates in perfect good faith to himself. Nor does he draw any very sharp distinction between a god and a powerful sorcerer. His gods are often merely invisible magicians who behind the veil of nature work the same sort of charms and incantations which the human magician works in a visible and bodily form among his fellows. And as the gods are commonly believed to exhibit themselves in the likeness of men to their worshippers, it is easy for the magician, with his supposed miraculous powers, to acquire the reputation of being an incarnate deity. Thus beginning as little more than a simple conjurer, the medicine-man or magician tends to blossom out into a full-blown god and king in one. Only in speaking of him as a god we must beware of importing into the savage conception of deity those very abstract and complex ideas which we attach to the term. When the savage uses his word for god, he has in his mind a being of a certain sort: when the civilised man uses his word for god, he has in his mind a being of a very different sort; and if, as commonly happens, the two men are equally unable to place themselves at the other's point of view, nothing but confusion and mistakes can result from their discussions.

An early Portuguese historian informs us that the Quiteve or king of Sofala, in south-eastern Africa, is a woolly-haired Kaffir, a heathen who adores nothing whatever, and has no knowledge of God; on the contrary he esteems himself the god of all his lands, and is so looked upon and reverenced by his subjects. When they suffer necessity or scarcity they have recourse to the king, firmly believing that he can give them all that they desire or have need of, and can obtain anything from his dead predecessors, with whom they believe that he holds converse. For this reason they ask the king to give them rain when it is required, and other favourable weather for their harvest, and in coming to ask for any of these things they bring him valuable presents, which the king accepts, bidding them return to their homes and he will be careful to grant their petitions. They are such barbarians that though they see how often the king does not give them what they ask for, they are not undeceived, but make him still greater offerings, and many days are spent in these comings and

54

goings, until the weather turns to rain, and the Kaffirs are satisfied, believing that the king did not grant their request until he had been well bribed and importuned, as he himself affirms, in order to maintain them in their error.

But the persons in whom a deity is thought to reveal himself are by no means always kings or descendants of kings; the supposed incarnation may take place even in men of the humblest rank. Thus, the Buddhist Tartars believe in a great number of living Buddhas, who officiate as Grand Lamas at the head of the most important monasteries. When one of these Grand Lamas dies his disciples do not sorrow, for they know that he will soon reappear, being born in the form of an infant. Their only anxiety is to discover the place of his birth. If at this time they see a rainbow they take it as a sign sent them by the departed Lama to guide them to his cradle. Sometimes the divine infant himself reveals his identity. 'I am the Grand Lama,' he says, 'the living Buddha of such and such a temple. Take me to my old monastery. I am its immortal head.' In whatever way the birthplace of the Buddha is revealed, whether by the Buddha's own avowal or by the sign in the sky, tents are struck, and the joyful pilgrims, often headed by the king or one of the most illustrious of the royal family, set forth to find and bring home the infant god. Generally he is born in Tibet, the holy land, and to reach him the caravan has often to traverse the most frightful deserts. When at last they find the child they fall down and worship him. Before, however, he is acknowledged as the Grand Lama whom they seek he must satisfy them of his identity. He is asked the name of the monastery of which he claims to be the head, how far off it is, and how many monks live in it; he must also describe the habits of the deceased Grand Lama and the manner of his death. Then various articles, as prayer-books, tea-pots, and cups, are placed before him, and he has to point out those used by

The association between kings and gods
TOP. Manco Inca, son of the divine sun and moon, one of the last Inca kings, enthroned and surrounded by nobles. Facsimile of Guaman Poma de Ayala, *Nueva Corónica* (*c.* 1615), Institut d'Ethnologie, Paris
ABOVE. Augustus, 'son of the deified' Caesar, wearing the laurel wreath, an attribute of the gods. Roman coin, British Museum, London

himself in his previous life. If he does so without a mistake his claims are admitted, and he is conducted in triumph to the monastery. At the head of all the Lamas is the Dalai Lama of Lhasa, the Rome of Tibet. He is regarded as a living god, and at death his divine and immortal spirit is born again in a child. According to some accounts the mode of discovering the Dalai Lama is similar to the method, already described, of discovering an ordinary Grand Lama.

We may now conclude that the claim to divine and supernatural powers put forward by the monarchs of great historical empires like those of Egypt, China, Mexico, and Peru, was not the simple outcome of inflated vanity or the empty expression of a grovelling adulation; it was merely a survival and extension of the old savage apotheosis of living kings. Thus, for example, as children of the Sun the Incas of Peru were revered like gods; they could do no wrong, and no one dreamed of offending against the person, honour, or property of the monarch or of any of the royal family.

The kings of Egypt, like those of other countries in the ancient Mediterranean, were deified in their lifetime, sacrifices were offered to them, and their worship was celebrated in special temples and by special priests. Indeed the worship of the kings sometimes cast that of the gods into the shade. Thus in the reign of Merenra a high official declared that he had built many holy places in order that the spirits of the king, the ever-living Merenra, might be invoked 'more than all the gods'. Historically, the institution of sacred kingship appears to have originated in the order of public magicians or medicine-men; logically it rests on a mistaken deduction from the association of ideas. Men mistook the order of their ideas for the order of nature, and hence imagined that the control which they have, or seem to have, over their thoughts, permitted them to exercise a corresponding control over things.

Departmental Kings of Nature

In the case of Diana's priest at Nemi, this control over nature was exercised specifically in his abode, the forest of Aricia, which gave him his title, King of the Wood. Unlike the titular and priestly kings in the republics of ancient Greece and Italy, Diana's priest ruled, not in the city, but in the greenwood. He was thus a king of nature, and of a special side of nature, namely, the woods from which he took his title. If we could find instances of what we may call departmental kings of nature, that is of persons supposed to rule over particular elements or aspects of nature, they would probably present a closer analogy to the King of the Wood than the divine kings we have been hitherto considering, whose control of nature is general rather than special.

The most appropriate example for our present purpose comes from Cambodia. There, in the backwoods, live two mysterious sovereigns known as the King of the Fire and the King of the Water. Their fame is spread all over the south of the great Indo-Chinese peninsula; but only a faint echo of it has reached the West. Down to a few years ago no European, so far as is known, had ever seen either of them; and their very existence might have passed for a fable, were it not that till lately communications were regularly maintained between them and the King of Cambodia, who year by year exchanged presents with them. The Cambodian gifts were passed from tribe to tribe till they reached their destination; for no Cambodian would essay the long and perilous journey. The tribe amongst whom the Kings of Fire and Water reside is the Chréais or Jaray, a race with European features but a sallow complexion, inhabiting the forest-clad mountains and high tablelands which separate Cambodia from Annam. Their royal functions are of a purely mystic or spiritual order; they have no political authority; they are simple peasants, living by the sweat of their brow and the offerings of the faithful. According to one account they live in absolute solitude, never meeting each other and never seeing a human face. They inhabit successively seven towers perched upon seven mountains, and every year they pass from one tower to another. People come furtively and cast within their reach what is needful for their subsistence. The kingship lasts seven years, the time necessary to inhabit all the towers successively; but many die before their time is out. The offices are hereditary in one or (according to others) two royal families, who enjoy high consideration, have revenues assigned to them, and are exempt from the necessity of tilling the ground. But naturally the dignity is not coveted and when a vacancy occurs, all eligible men (they must be strong and have children) flee and hide themselves. The kings enjoy extraordinary privileges and immunities, but their authority does not extend beyond the few villages of their neighbourhood. Like many other sacred kings, of whom we shall read in the sequel, the Kings of Fire and Water are not allowed to die a natural death, for that would lower their reputation. Accordingly when one of them is seriously ill, the elders hold a consultation and if they think he cannot recover they stab him to death. His body is burned and the ashes are piously collected and publicly honoured for five years. Part of them is given to the widow, and she keeps them in an urn, which she must carry on her back when she goes to weep on her husband's grave.

We are told that the Fire King, the more important of the two, whose supernatural powers have never been questioned, officiates at marriages, festivals, and sacrifices in honour of the *Yan* or spirit. On these occasions a special place is set apart for him; and the path by which he approaches is spread with white cotton cloths. A reason for confining the royal dignity to the same family is that this family is in possession of certain famous talismans which would lose their virtue or disappear if they passed out of the family. These talismans are three: the fruit of a creeper called *Cui*, gathered ages ago at the time of the last deluge, but still fresh and green; a rattan, also very old but bearing flowers that never fade; and lastly, a sword containing a *Yan* or

spirit, who guards it constantly and works miracles with it. The spirit is said to be that of a slave, whose blood chanced to fall upon the blade while it was being forged, and who died a voluntary death to expiate his involuntary offence. By means of the two former talismans the Water King can raise a flood that would drown the whole earth. If the Fire King draws the magic sword a few inches from its sheath, the sun is hidden and men and beasts fall into a profound sleep; were he to draw it quite out of the scabbard, the world would come to an end. To this wondrous brand sacrifices of buffaloes, pigs, fowls, and ducks are offered for rain. It is kept swathed in cotton and silk; and amongst the annual presents sent by the King of Cambodia were rich stuffs to wrap the sacred sword.

In return the Kings of Fire and Water sent him a huge wax candle and two calabashes, one full of rice and the other of sesame. The candle bore the impress of the Fire King's middle finger, and was probably thought to contain the seed of fire, which the Cambodian monarch thus received once a year fresh from the Fire King himself. This holy candle was kept for sacred uses. On reaching the capital of Cambodia it was entrusted to the Brahmans, who laid it up beside the regalia, and with the wax made tapers which were burned on the altars on solemn days. As the candle was the special gift of the Fire King, we may conjecture that the rice and sesame were the special gift of the Water King. The latter was doubtless king of rain as well as of water, and the fruits of the earth were boons conferred by him on men. In times of calamity, as during plague, floods, and war, a little of this sacred rice and sesame was scattered on the ground 'to appease the wrath of the maleficent spirits'. Contrary to the common usage of the country, which is to bury the dead, the bodies of both these mystic monarchs are burnt, but their nails and some of their teeth and bones are religiously preserved as amulets.

Departmental kings of nature
Oba Ohe, King of Benin, is shown with mud-fish feet to indicate his possession by the sea god Olokun and swings leopards as symbols of his power and royalty. Benin bronze plaque, late 16th century, British Museum, London

But it is a far cry to Italy from the forests of Cambodia. And though Kings of Water and Fire have been found we have still to discover a King of the Wood to match the Arician priest who bore that title. Perhaps we shall find him nearer home.

6. The Worship of Trees

Tree-Spirits

In the religious history of the Aryan race in Europe the worship of trees has played an important part. Nothing could be more natural. For at the dawn of history Europe was covered with immense primaeval forests, in which the scattered clearings must have appeared like islets in an ocean of green. Germans whom

The worship of trees

King Ashurnasirpal of Assyria, 'the king of the world . . . who has subjugated all mankind', with his divinities the winged sun disk and the tree of life. The relief, from Ashurnasirpal's palace at Nimrud, 9th century BC, shows the king twice, on either side of the sacred emblems. British Museum, London

Caesar questioned had travelled through the Hercynian forest without reaching the end. In the reign of Henry II, the citizens of London still hunted the wild boar in the woods of Hampstead. Classical writers make many references to Italian forests which have now disappeared. In Greece, beautiful woods of pine, oak and other trees still linger in some areas, but they are mere fragments of the forests which clothed great tracts in antiquity, and which at a more remote epoch may have spanned the Greek peninsula from sea to sea.

Amongst the Celts the oak-worship of the Druids is familiar to every one, and their old word for a sanctuary seems to be identical in origin and meaning with the Latin *nemus*, a grove or woodland glade, which still survives in the name of Nemi. At Upsala, the old religious capital of Sweden, there was a sacred grove in which every tree was regarded as divine. The heathen Slavs worshipped trees and groves. The Lithuanians were not converted to Christianity till towards the close of the fourteenth century, and amongst them at the date of their conversion the worship of trees was prominent. Some of them revered remarkable oaks and other great shady trees, from which they received oracular responses. Some maintained holy groves about their villages or houses, where even to break a twig would have been a sin. Proofs of the prevalence of tree-worship in ancient Greece and Italy are abundant. In the sanctuary of Aesculapius at Cos, for example, it was forbidden to cut down the cypress-trees under a penalty of a thousand drachms. But nowhere, perhaps, in the ancient world was this antique form of religion better preserved than in the heart of the great

metropolis itself. In the Forum, the busy centre of Roman life, the sacred fig-tree of Romulus was worshipped down to the days of the empire, and the withering of its trunk was enough to spread consternation through the city.

But it is necessary to examine in some detail the notions on which the worship of trees and plants is based. To the savage the world in general is animate, and trees and plants are no exception to the rule. He thinks that they have souls like his own, and he treats them accordingly. 'They say', writes the ancient vegetarian Porphyry, 'that primitive men led an unhappy life, for their superstition did not stop at animals but extended even to plants. For why should the slaughter of an ox or a sheep be a greater wrong than the felling of a fir or an oak, seeing that a soul is implanted in these trees also?' Similarly, the Hidatsa Indians of North America believe that every natural object has its spirit, or to speak more properly, its shade. To these shades some consideration or respect is due, but not equally to all. For example, the shade of the cottonwood, the greatest tree in the valley of the Upper Missouri, is supposed to possess an intelligence which, if properly approached, may help the Indians in certain undertakings; but the shades of shrubs and grasses are of little account.

If trees are animate, they are necessarily sensitive and the cutting of them down becomes a delicate surgical operation, which must be performed with as tender a regard as possible for the feelings of the sufferers, who otherwise may turn and rend the careless or bungling operator.

Trees in holy places
TOP. The temple of Vesta in Rome, with Vesta's sacred oak tree. Marble relief, Uffizi, Florence. Photo: Alinari
CENTRE. An oak tree at the shrine of a Muslim saint, Iran. Photo: David Brooks
LEFT. Church of St Mary, Painswick, England, famed for its ninety-nine clipped yews. Photo: Gloucestershire Record Office

When an oak is being felled 'it gives a kind of shriekes or groanes, that may be heard a mile off, as if it were the genius of the oake lamenting. E. Wyld, Esq., hath heard it several times.' Similar observations have been recorded in many other parts of the world.

The conception of trees and plants as animated beings naturally results in treating them as male and female, who can be married to each other in a real, and not merely a figurative or poetical sense of the word. The ancients knew the difference between the male and the female date-palm, and fertilised them artificially by shaking the pollen of the male tree over the flowers of the female. The fertilisation took place in spring. Among the heathen of Harran the month during which the palms were fertilised bore the name of the Date Month, and at this time they celebrated the marriage festival of all the gods and goddesses. In the Moluccas, when the clove-trees are in blossom, they are treated like pregnant women. No noise may be made near them; no light or fire may be carried past them at night; no one may approach them with his hat on, all must uncover in their presence. These precautions are observed lest the tree should be alarmed and bear no fruit, or should drop its fruit too soon, like the untimely delivery of a woman who has been frightened in her pregnancy.

In Corea the souls of people who die of the plague or by the roadside, and of women who expire in childbed, invariably take up their abode in trees. To such spirits offerings of cake, wine, and pork are made on heaps of stones piled under the trees. In China it has been customary from time immemorial to plant trees on graves in order thereby to strengthen the soul of the deceased and thus to save his body from corruption; and as the evergreen cypress and pine are deemed to be fuller of vitality than other trees, they have been chosen by preference for this purpose. Hence the trees that grow on graves are sometimes identified with the souls of the departed.

In most, if not all, of these cases the spirit is viewed as incorporate in the tree; it animates the tree and must suffer and die with it. But, according to another and probably later opinion, the tree is not the body, but merely the abode of the tree-spirit, which can quit it and return to it at pleasure.

Not a few ceremonies observed at cutting down haunted trees are based on the belief that the spirits have it in their power to quit the trees at pleasure or in case of need. A French officer engaged in surveying the country inhabited by the primitive Moïs of Indo-China witnessed one such ceremony of propitiation performed by the natives before felling a tree. He says, 'It sometimes happened in the course of our geodetical survey that we were compelled to cut down a tree which interrupted the field of view of our instruments. A most interesting scene preceded the act of destruction. The "foreman" of our Moï coolies approached the condemned tree and addressed it much as follows: "Spirit who hast made thy home in this tree, we worship thee and are come to claim thy mercy. The white mandarin, our relentless master, whose commands we cannot but obey, has bidden us to cut down thy habitation, a task which fills us with sadness, and which we only carry out with regret. I adjure thee to depart at once from this place and seek a new dwelling-place elsewhere, and I pray thee to forget the wrong we do thee, for we are not our own masters."'

Thus the tree is regarded, sometimes as the body, sometimes as merely the house of the tree-spirit; and when we read of sacred trees which may not be cut down because they are the seat of spirits, it is not always possible to say with certainty in which way the presence of the spirit in the tree is conceived.

Beneficent Powers of Tree-Spirits

When a tree comes to be viewed, no longer as the body of the tree-spirit, but simply as its abode which it can quit at pleasure, an important advance has been made in religious thought. Animism is passing into polytheism. In other words, instead of regarding each tree as a living and conscious being, man now sees in it merely a lifeless, inert mass, tenanted for a longer or shorter time by a supernatural being who, as he can pass freely from tree to tree, thereby enjoys a certain right of possession or lordship over the trees, and, ceasing to be a tree-soul, becomes a forest god. As soon as the tree-spirit is thus in a measure disengaged from each particular tree, he begins to change his shape and assume the body of a man, in virtue of a general tendency of early thought to clothe all abstract spiritual beings in concrete human form. Hence in classical art the sylvan deities are depicted in human shape, their woodland character being denoted by a branch or some equally obvious symbol. But this change of shape does not affect the essential character of the tree-spirit. The powers which he exercised as a tree-soul incorporate in a tree, he still continues to wield as a god of trees.

Trees or tree-spirits are believed to give rain and sunshine. When the missionary Jerome of Prague was persuading the heathen Lithuanians to fell their sacred groves, a multitude of women besought the Prince of Lithuania to stop him, saying that with the woods he was destroying the house of god from which they had been wont to get rain and sunshine. The Mundaris in Assam think that if a tree in the sacred grove is felled the sylvan gods evince their displeasure by withholding rain.

Similarly, tree-spirits make the crops to grow. Amongst the Mundaris every village has its sacred grove, and 'the grove deities are held responsible for the crops, and are especially honoured at all the great agricultural festivals'. The negroes of the Gold Coast are in the habit

Rituals to ensure good crops
The Thulung of Nepal dance round a pole that represents the cosmic tree and squirt fermented liquid from gourds imitating male reproductive powers, and encouraging the fertility of the land. Photo: Nick Allen

of sacrificing at the foot of certain tall trees, and they think that if one of these were felled all the fruits of the earth would perish. In Northern India the *Emblica officinalis* is a sacred tree. On the eleventh of the month Phalgun (February) libations are poured at the foot of the tree, a red or yellow string is bound about the trunk, and prayers are offered to it for the fruitfulness of women, animals, and crops. In the town of Qua, near Old Calabar, there used to grow a palm-tree which ensured conception to any barren woman who ate a nut from its branches. In Europe the May-tree or May-pole is apparently supposed to possess similar powers over both women and cattle. But in Europe it seems that the influence of the tree, bush, or bough is really protective rather than generative; it does not so much fill the udders of the cows as prevent them from being drained dry by witches, who ride on broomsticks or pitchforks through the air on the Eve of May Day (the famous Walpurgis Night) and steal the milk from the cattle.

Relics of Tree-Worship in Modern Europe

From the foregoing review of the beneficent qualities commonly ascribed to tree-spirits, it is easy to understand why customs like the May-tree or May-pole have prevailed so widely and figured so prominently in the popular festivals of European peasants. In spring or early summer or even on Midsummer Day, it was and still is in many parts of Europe the custom to go out to the woods, cut down a tree and bring it into the village, where it is set up amid general rejoicings; or the people cut branches in the woods, and fasten them on every house. The intention of these customs is to bring home to the village, and to each house, the blessings which the tree-spirit has in its power to bestow. Hence the custom in some places of planting a May-tree before every house, or of carrying the village May-tree from door to door, that every household may receive its share of the blessing. It appears that a hoop wreathed with rowan and marsh marigold, and bearing suspended within it two balls, is still carried on May Day by villagers in some parts of Ireland. The balls, which are sometimes covered with gold and silver paper, are said to have originally represented the sun and moon. In Corfu the children go about singing May songs on the first of May. The boys carry small cypresses adorned with ribbons, flowers, and the fruits of the season. They receive a glass of wine at each house. The girls carry nosegays. One of them is dressed up like an angel, with gilt wings, and scatters flowers. Down to the present day May-trees decked with flowers and ribbons are set up on May Day in every village and hamlet of gay Provence. Under them the young folk make merry and the old folk rest.

The object of such customs, which used to be very widely spread in Europe, was to bring in the fructifying spirit of vegetation, newly awakened in spring. Amongst the Slavs of Carinthia, on St George's Day (the twenty-third of April), the young people deck with flowers and garlands a tree which has been felled on the eve of the festival. The tree is then carried in procession, accompanied with music and joyful acclamations, the chief figure in the procession being the Green George, a young fellow clad from head to foot in green birch branches. At the close of the ceremonies the Green George, that is an effigy of him, is thrown into the water. It is the aim of the lad who acts Green George to step out of his leafy envelope and substitute the effigy so adroitly that no one shall perceive the change. In many places, however, the lad himself who plays the part of Green George is ducked in a river or pond, with the express intention of thus ensuring rain to make the fields and meadows green in summer. In some places the cattle are crowned and driven from their stalls to the accompaniment of a song:

Relics of tree-worship
May King and Queen in the 19th century. Victorian engraving, John Johnson Collection, Bodleian Library, Oxford

Green George we bring,
Green George we accompany,
May he feed our herds well.
If not, to the water with him.

Here we see that the same powers of making rain and fostering the cattle, which are ascribed to the tree-spirit regarded as incorporate in the tree, are also attributed to the tree-spirit represented by a living man.

In spring processions of this kind the spirit of vegetation is often represented both by the May-tree and in addition by a man dressed in green leaves or flowers or by a girl similarly adorned. The mummer was regarded not as an image but as an actual representative of the spirit of vegetation; hence the wish expressed by the attendants of the May-rose and the May-tree that those who refuse them gifts of eggs, bacon, and so forth, may have no share in the blessings which it is in the power of the itinerant

spirit to bestow. We may conclude that these begging processions with May-trees or May-boughs from door to door ('bringing the May or the summer') had everywhere originally a serious and, so to speak, sacramental significance; people really believed that the god of growth was present unseen in the bough; by the procession he was brought to each house to bestow his blessing.

Often the leaf-clad person who represents the spirit of vegetation is known as the king or the queen; thus, for example, he or she is called the May King, Whitsuntide King, Queen of May, and so on. These titles imply that the spirit incorporate in vegetation is a ruler, whose creative power extends far and wide. Again the spirit of vegetation is sometimes represented by a bridegroom and bride. Here again the parallelism holds between the anthropomorphic and the vegetable representation of the tree-spirit,

Dancing round the Maypole in the 20th century. Photo: John Topham Picture Library

for we have seen above that trees are sometimes married to each other. In the neighbourhood of Briançon (Dauphiné) on May Day the lads wrap up in green leaves a young fellow whose sweetheart has deserted him or married another. He lies down on the ground and feigns to be asleep. Then a girl who likes him, and would marry him, comes and wakes him, and raising him up offers him her arm and a flag. So they go to the alehouse, where the pair lead off the dancing. But they must marry within the year, or they are treated as old bachelor and old maid, and are debarred the company of the young folk. The lad is called the bridegroom of the month of May (*le fiancé du mois de Mai*). In the alehouse he puts off his garment of leaves, out of which, mixed with flowers, his partner in the dance makes a nosegay, and wears it at her breast next day, when he leads her again to the alehouse.

Often the marriage of the spirit of vegetation in spring, though not directly represented, is implied by naming the human representative of the spirit, 'the Bride', and dressing her in wedding attire. Thus in some villages of Altmark at Whitsuntide, while the boys go about carrying a May-tree or leading a boy enveloped in leaves and flowers, the girls lead about the May Bride, a girl dressed as a bride with a great nosegay in her hair. They go from house to house, the May Bride singing a song in which she asks for a present, and tells the inmates of each house that if they give her something they will themselves have something the whole year through; but if they give her nothing they will themselves have nothing.

Tree-worship and Christianity
This 19th-century Queen of May from the Mediterranean carries a picture of the Virgin Mary and a rosary on her Maypole. The old pagan festival has acquired a Christian element. John Johnson Collection, Bodleian Library, Oxford

7. The Influence of the Sexes on Vegetation

From the preceding examination of the spring and summer festivals of Europe we may infer that our rude forefathers personified the powers of vegetation as male and female, and attempted, on the principle of homoeopathic or imitative magic, to quicken the growth of trees and plants by representing the marriage of the sylvan deities in the persons of a King and Queen of May, a Whitsun Bridegroom and Bride, and so forth. Such representations were accordingly no mere symbolic or allegorical dramas, pastoral plays designed to amuse or instruct a rustic audience. They were charms intended to make the woods to grow green, the fresh grass to sprout, the corn to shoot, and the flowers to blow.

In the Ukraine on St George's Day (the twenty-third of April) the priest in his robes, attended by his acolytes, goes out to the fields of the village, where the crops are beginning to shew green above the ground, and blesses them. After that the young married people lie down in couples on the sown fields and roll several times over on them, in the belief that this will promote the growth of the crops. Similarly, for four days before they committed the seed to the earth the Pipiles of Central America kept apart from their wives 'in order that on the night before planting they might indulge their passions to the fullest extent; certain persons are even said to have been appointed to perform the sexual act at the very moment when the first seeds were deposited in the ground'. The use of their wives at that time was indeed enjoined upon the people by the priests as a religious duty, in default of which it was not lawful to sow the seed. The only possible explanation of this custom seems to be that the Indians confused the process by which human beings reproduce their kind with the process by which plants discharge the same function, and fancied that by resorting to the former they were simultaneously forwarding the latter.

To the student who cares to track the devious course of the human mind in its gropings after truth, it is of some interest to observe that the same theoretical belief in the sympathetic influence of the sexes on vegetation, which has led some peoples to indulge their passions as a means of fertilising the earth, has led others to seek the same end by directly opposite means. From the moment that they sowed the maize till the time that they reaped it, the Indians of Nicaragua lived chastely, keeping apart from their wives and sleeping in a separate place. They ate no salt, and drank neither cocoa nor *chicha*, the fermented liquor made from maize; in short the season was for them, as the Spanish historians observe, a time of abstinence.

Again, the sympathetic relation supposed to exist between the commerce of the sexes and the fertility of the earth manifests itself in the belief that illicit love tends, directly or indirectly, to mar that fertility and to blight the crops. Such a belief prevails, for example, among the Karens of Burma. They imagine that adultery or fornication has a powerful influence to injure the harvest. Hence if the crops have been bad for a year or two, and no rain falls, the villagers set down the dearth to secret sins of this kind, and say that the God of heaven and earth is angry with them on that account; and they all unite in making an offering to appease him. Further, whenever adultery or fornication is detected, the elders decide that the sinners must buy a hog

Nature is brought to participate in the union of marriage
TOP. At Malay weddings, the relatives of the bride present a sacred tree to the relatives of the groom.
ABOVE. A native priest sprinkles rice over the groom and his following. Photos: William D. Wilder

and kill it. Then the woman takes one foot of the hog, and the man takes another, and they scrape out furrows in the ground with each foot, and fill the furrows with the blood of the hog. Next they scratch the ground with their hands and pray: 'God of heaven and earth, God of the mountains and hills, I have destroyed the productiveness of the country. Do not be angry with me, do not hate me; but have mercy on me,

and compassionate me. Now I repair the mountains, now I heal the hills, and the streams and the lands. May there be no failure of crops, may there be no unsuccessful labours, or unfortunate efforts in my country. Let them be dissipated to the foot of the horizon. Make thy paddy fruitful, thy rice abundant. Make the vegetables to flourish. If we cultivate but little, still grant that we may obtain a little.' After each has prayed thus, they return to the house and say they have repaired the earth.

It would seem that the ancient Greeks and Romans entertained similar notions as to the wasting effect of incest. Under the Emperor Claudius, a Roman noble was accused of incest with his sister. He committed suicide, his sister was banished, and the emperor ordered that certain ancient ceremonies traditionally derived from the laws of King Servius Tullius should be performed, and that expiation should be made by the pontiffs at the sacred grove of Diana, probably the famous Arician grove, which has furnished the starting-point of our enquiry. As Diana appears to have been a goddess of fertility in general and of the fruitfulness of women in particular, the atonement made at her sanctuary for incest may perhaps be accepted as evidence that the Romans, like other peoples, attributed to sexual immorality a tendency to blast the fruits both of the earth and of the womb. This inference is strengthened by a precept laid down by grave Roman writers that bakers, cooks, and butlers ought to be strictly chaste and continent, because it was most important that food and cups should be handled either by persons under the age of puberty, or at all events by persons who indulged very sparingly in sexual intercourse; for which reason if a baker, a cook, or a butler broke this rule of continence it was his bounden duty to wash in a river or other running water before he applied himself again to his professional duties. But for all such duties the services of a boy or of a virgin were preferred.

8. The Sacred Marriage

The Marriage of the Gods

In the last chapter we saw that according to a widespread belief, which is not without a foundation in fact, plants reproduce their kinds through the sexual union of male and female elements, and that on the principle of homoeopathic or imitative magic this reproduction can be stimulated by the real or mock marriage of men and women, who masquerade for the time being as spirits of vegetation. Such magical dramas have played a great part in the popular festivals of Europe, and based as they are on a very crude conception of natural law, it is clear that they must have been handed down from a remote antiquity. I would therefore suggest that in certain festivals of the ancients we may be able to detect the equivalents of our May Day, Whitsuntide, and Midsummer celebrations, with this difference, that in those days the ceremonies had not yet dwindled into mere shows and pageants, but were still religious or magical rites, in which the actors consciously supported the high parts of gods and goddesses. Now in the first chapter of this book we found reason to believe that the priest who bore the title of King of the Wood at Nemi had for his mate the goddess of the grove, Diana herself. May not he and she, as King and Queen of the Wood, have been serious counterparts of the merry mummers who play the King and Queen of May, the Whitsuntide Bridegroom and Bride in modern Europe? and may not their union have been yearly celebrated in a *theogamy* or divine marriage? Such dramatic weddings of gods and goddesses were carried out as solemn religious rites in many parts of the ancient world; hence there is no intrinsic improbability in the supposition that the sacred grove at Nemi may have been the scene of an annual ceremony of this sort. The aim of such a union would be to promote the fruitfulness of the earth, of animals, and of mankind; and it might naturally be thought that this object would be more surely attained if the sacred nuptials were celebrated every year, the parts of the divine bride and bridegroom being played either by their images or by living persons. In the absence of direct evidence, this theory must be based on the analogy of similar customs elsewhere and at other times in history.

At Babylon the imposing sanctuary of Bel rose like a pyramid above the city in a series of eight towers or stories, planted one on the top of the other. On the highest tower, reached by an ascent which wound about all the rest, there stood a spacious temple, and in the temple a great bed, magnificently draped and cushioned, with a golden table beside it. In the temple no image was to be seen, and no human being passed the night there, save a single woman, whom, according to the Chaldean priests, the god chose from among all the women of Babylon. They said that the deity himself came into the temple at night and slept in the great bed; and the woman, as a consort of the god, might have no intercourse with mortal man. As Bel at Babylon was identified with Marduk, the chief god of the city, the woman who thus shared his bed was doubtless one of the 'wives of Marduk' mentioned in the code of Hammurabi.

At Thebes in Egypt a woman slept in the temple of Ammon as the consort of the god, and, like the human wife of Bel at Babylon, she was said to have no commerce with a man. In Egyptian texts she is often mentioned as 'the

Marriage of the gods
The first meeting of the Greek divinities Zeus and Hera.
Metope from Greek temple at Selinus, Sicily, 5th century
BC, Museo Nazionale, Palermo. Photo: Anderson

divine consort', and usually she was no less a personage than the Queen of Egypt herself. For, according to the Egyptians, their monarchs were actually begotten by the god Ammon, who assumed for the time being the form of the reigning king, and in that disguise had intercourse with the queen. The divine procreation is carved and painted in great detail on the walls of the oldest temples in Egypt, those of Deir el Bahari and Luxor; and the inscriptions attached to the paintings leave no doubt as to the meaning of the scenes.

The custom of marrying gods to images was, and still is, widely spread. The Indians of a village in Peru have been known to marry a beautiful girl, about fourteen years of age, to a stone shaped like a human being, which they regarded as a god (*huaca*). All the villagers took part in the marriage ceremony, which lasted three days, and was attended with much revelry. The girl thereafter remained a virgin and sacrificed to the idol for the people. They shewed her the utmost reverence and deemed her divine.

A Berber ceremony furnishes another type of example of what we may call a sacred marriage, that is, a marriage of two divinities; here both are represented by living human beings. This ceremony is still observed in spring by some of the Berbers of Morocco. It takes place at the little village of Douzrou in the Anti-Atlas Mountains, and the time of it is the return of spring. In the morning, at daybreak, the young girls of the village go out into the forest to pluck grass and gather dead wood. Their return is signalled by the shot of a musket. Immediately the women remaining in the village advance to meet them, escorting a young girl called the Bride of the Good (*Fiancée du Bien*). The bride, apparelled as for a wedding, dressed entirely in white, is mounted upon a white she-ass, and holds in her hands a white hen. When the two processions meet the young girls put down their bundles of grass, and begin to dance, singing some such words as these:

We shall accompany the bride of the good to the
    mosque of the village,
That God may bring, for the Musulmans,
    health and abundance.

For their part, the boys go into the gardens to gather wood, which they take to the mosque. Then, like their sisters, they go into the forest to gather dry grass. They have chosen from among them a young man who is the Bridegroom of the Good (*Fiancé du Bien*). Dressed in white like the bride, he is also mounted upon a white male ass, and holds in his hands a cock of white plumage. He goes at the head of the small procession which makes its way into the fields; but when they have got halfway his companions leave him, committing him to the care of one of their number who stays by him, armed with a musket to protect him against

The union of gods and mortal women
Zeus comes to Danaë in a shower of gold. From the
union was born the great hero of Greek myth, Perseus.
Painting by Titian, Museo del Prado, Madrid

the evil spirits, or jinn. Then the boys, bringing armfuls of grass, return and take their places round the bridegroom. Then one of them hobbles the feet of the ass, and with the same rope ties the neck of the bridegroom, who is stooping over the shoulders of his mount. At this moment the guardian fires a shot with his musket. This signal, heard in the village, excites there a lively agitation. The men, seizing their arms, rush towards the bride, seated upon her ass in the centre of the group of women, and lead her, in wild career, towards the hobbled bridegroom. They call out, 'Hold on. Do not fall, that the new year may be favourable to us. Do not fall.' The procession stops near the bridegroom. Then, without losing a moment, the young girl cuts with a knife the rope that binds the bridegroom, after which she calls out: 'We have cut the neck of Hunger: May God resusci-

tate the neck of the Good.' Accompanied by the young man who guards the bridegroom, the bride then returns alone to the village, and when she has taken her place among the women, her guardian discharges his musket. This is another signal, for at once the men and boys lead, with the same precipitation, the now delivered bridegroom. They shout to him from all sides, 'Hold on. Do not fall, that the new year may be favourable to us.' Songs, dances, cries, and musket-shots announce the happy return of the bridegroom. That ends the first part of the ceremony. Doubtless the bridegroom, freed from his bonds and returning triumphant, personifies the renewal of Nature, and the bride the spirit of vegetation. Their union is expected to influence the renewal of the life of spring and render it fertile. The bride and bridegroom side by side now march at the head of the procession, in which the boys follow behind the bridegroom and the girls behind the bride, all singing, but without mingling with each other. The happy crowd repeats incessantly, 'We are bringing back the Good.'

In this curious and picturesque array the emblematic couple are conducted to the mosque. Bride and bridegroom alone enter the sanctuary, in accordance with prescribed custom. The two doors close upon them. Upon the threshold of one the crowd remains, keeping silence: on the other a severe guardian, his musket loaded, mounts guard, and keeps at a distance the curious and indiscreet who might wish to pierce the mystery that is taking place in the temple, become, for an hour, the scene of sacred prostitution. What takes place there is little known; but it is said that the bride and bridegroom go to the place called 'The Tomb of the Archangel Gabriel', and that there the bridegroom cuts the throat of the white cock which he has not abandoned in the course of the preceding ceremonies, and then does the same to the white hen of his bride. After having cooked and eaten the flesh of the two victims, he claims the rights which his bride does not contest, for on the consummation of their transitory union depends the prosperity of the clan. When night falls the bride and bridegroom separate to follow different paths. Then follows the third and last act of the ceremony, a tragic act, in the course of which the bride is to die. The bride and bridegroom separate and each go towards a door of the sanctuary. 'Fire!' cries the bridegroom to his guardian. At this signal the men rush towards the bridegroom's door, and kindle large heaps of dry grass which are placed there. and when the bridegroom comes forth he is confronted by high flames which he leaps over at a single bound, while the bride, languid and exhausted, lets herself fall into the small fire that her sisters have kindled for her at her door. It is further said that the young people of the village

imitate the example set by the bride and bridegroom of the Good, to facilitate, in the same manner, the return of the life of the spring. They meet in couples in a public place, and pass together, the girls and boys, that which they call 'the night of happiness'.

In Kengtung, one of the principal Shan states of Upper Burma, the spirit of the Nawng Tung lake is regarded as very powerful, and is propitiated with offerings in the eighth month (about July) of each year. A remarkable feature of the worship of this spirit consists in the dedication to him of four virgins in marriage. Custom requires that this should be done once in every three years. It was actually done by the late king or chief (Sawbwa) in 1893, but down to 1901 the rite had not been performed by his successor. The four girls are selected from among the unmarried women of suitable age and must be as beautiful as can be. After a public festival, they are formally presented to the spirit, along with the various sacrifices and offerings. They are next taken to the chief's residence, where strings are tied round their wrists by the ministers and elders to guard them against ill-luck. Usually they sleep a night or two at the palace, after which they may return to their homes. There seems to be no objection to their marrying afterwards. If nothing happens to any of the four, it is believed that the spirit of the lake loves them but little; but if one of them dies soon after the ceremony, it shews that she has been accepted by him. The spirit is propitiated with the sacrifice of pigs, fowls, and sometimes a buffalo.

In this last custom the death of the woman is regarded as a sign that the god has taken her to himself. Sometimes, apparently, it has not been left to the discretion of the divine bridegroom to take or leave his human bride; she was made over to him once for all in death. When the Arabs conquered Egypt they learned that at the annual rise of the Nile the Egyptians were wont

Gods and queens
The union of Queen Mutemwia and the god Ammon,
who hands to her the sign of life. Relief from the temple
of Luxor, Egypt, *c*.1400 BC. Drawing after H. Brunner,
Die Geburt des Gottkönigs, 1964, Otto Harrassowitz Verlag

to deck a young virgin in gay apparel and throw
her into the river as a sacrifice, in order to
obtain a plentiful inundation. The Arab general
abolished the barbarous custom.

The Kings of Rome

From the foregoing survey of custom and legend
we may infer that the sacred marriage of the
powers both of vegetation and of water has been
celebrated by many peoples for the sake of promoting the fertility of the earth, on which the
life of animals and men ultimately depends, and

that in such rites the part of the divine bridegroom or bride is often sustained by a man or
woman. The evidence may, therefore, lend
some countenance to the conjecture that in the
sacred grove at Nemi, where the powers of
vegetation and of water manifested themselves
in the fair forms of shady woods, tumbling cascades, and glassy lake, a marriage like that of our
King and Queen of May was annually celebrated
between the mortal King of the Wood and the
immortal Queen of the Wood, Diana. In this
connexion an important figure in the grove was
the water-nymph Egeria, who was worshipped
by pregnant women because she, like Diana,
could grant them an easy delivery. From this it
seems fairly safe to conclude that, like many
other springs, the water of Egeria was credited
with a power of facilitating conception as well
as delivery. The votive offerings found on the
spot, which clearly refer to the begetting of
children, may possibly have been dedicated to
Egeria rather than to Diana, or perhaps we
should rather say that the water-nymph Egeria
is a local representative of Diana.

Roman legend has it that Egeria was wedded
to the Roman king and lawgiver Numa, whom
she inspired with his more than mortal wisdom.
When we remember how very often in early
society the king is held responsible for the fall of
rain and the fruitfulness of the earth, it seems
hardly rash to conjecture that in the legend of
the nuptials of Numa and Egeria we have a
reminiscence of a sacred marriage which the old
Roman kings regularly contracted with a goddess of vegetation and water for the purpose of
enabling him to discharge his divine or magical
functions. In such a rite the part of the goddess
might be played either by an image or a woman,
and if by a woman, probably by the Queen. The
legend of Numa and Egeria points to a sacred
grove rather than to a house as the scene of the
nuptial union, which, like the marriage of the
King and Queen of May, or of the vine-god

and the Queen of Athens, may have been annually celebrated as a charm to ensure the fertility not only of the earth but of man and beast. Now, according to some accounts, the scene of the marriage was no other than the sacred grove of Nemi, and on quite independent grounds we have been led to suppose that in that same grove the King of the Wood was wedded to Diana. The convergence of the two distinct lines of enquiry suggests that the legendary union of the Roman king with Egeria may have been a reflection or duplicate of the union of the King of the Wood with Egeria or her double Diana. This does not imply that the Roman kings ever served as Kings of the Wood in the Arician grove, but only that they may originally have been invested with a sacred character of the same general kind, and may have held office on similar terms. To be more explicit, it is possible that they reigned, not by right of birth, but in virtue of their supposed divinity as representatives or embodiments of a god, and that as such they mated with a goddess, and had to prove their fitness from time to time to discharge their divine functions by engaging in a severe bodily struggle, which may often have proved fatal to them, leaving the crown to their victorious adversary. Our knowledge of the Roman kingship is far too scanty to allow us to affirm any one of these propositions with confidence; but at least there are some scattered hints or indications of a similarity in all these respects between the priests of Nemi and the kings of Rome, or perhaps rather between their remote predecessors in the dark ages which preceded the dawn of legend.

It would seem that the Roman king personated no less a deity than Jupiter himself. For down to imperial times victorious generals celebrating a triumph, and magistrates presiding at the games in the Circus, wore the costume of Jupiter, which was borrowed for the occasion from his great temple on the Capitol; and it has been held with a high degree of probability both by ancients and moderns that in so doing they copied the traditionary attire and insignia of the Roman kings. They rode a chariot drawn by four laurel-crowned horses through the city, where every one else went on foot; they wore purple robes embroidered or spangled with gold; in the right hand they bore a branch of laurel and in the left hand an ivory sceptre topped with an eagle; a wreath of laurel crowned their brows; their face was reddened with vermilion; and over their head a slave held a heavy crown of massy gold fashioned in the likeness of oak leaves. The eagle was the bird of Jove, the oak was his sacred tree, and the face of his image standing in his four-horse chariot on the Capitol was in like manner regularly dyed red on festivals; indeed, so important was it deemed to keep the divine features properly rouged that one of the first duties of the censors was to contract for having this done.

The legend of Numa and Egeria appears to embody a reminiscence of a time when the priestly king himself played the part of the divine bridegroom; and as we have seen reason to suppose that the Roman kings personated the oak-god, while Egeria is said by Plutarch to have been an oak-nymph, the story of their union in the sacred grove raises a presumption that at Rome in the regal period a marriage was periodically performed between the king of Rome and the oak-goddess, which must have been intended to quicken the growth of vegetation by homoeopathic magic. We may take it that the antecedents of this rite go back to the time when the forefathers of the Romans married the tree-god to the tree-goddess in the vast oak forests of Central and Northern Europe. In the England of our day the forests have mostly disappeared, yet still on many a village green and in many a country lane a faded image of the sacred marriage lingers in the rustic pageantry of May Day.

9. The Worship of the Oak

Some reasons have been given for thinking that the early Latin kings posed as living representatives of Jupiter, the god of the oak, the sky, the rain, and the thunder, and that in this capacity they attempted to exercise the fertilising functions which were ascribed to the god. The probability of this view will be strengthened if it can be proved that the same god was worshipped under other names by other branches of the Aryan stock in Europe, and that the Latin kings were not alone in arrogating to themselves his powers and attributes. In this chapter I propose briefly to put together a few of the principal facts which point to this conclusion.

Long before the dawn of history Europe was covered with vast primaeval woods, which must have exercised a profound influence on the thought as well as on the life of our rude ancestors who dwelt dispersed under the gloomy shadow or in the open glades and clearings of the forest. Now, of all the trees which composed these woods the oak appears to have been both the commonest and the most useful. The proof of this is drawn partly from the statements of classical writers, partly from the remains of ancient villages built on piles in lakes and marshes, and partly from the oak forests which have been found embedded in peat-bogs.

These bogs, which attain their greatest development in Northern Europe, but are met with also in the central and southern parts of the Continent, have preserved as in a museum the trees and plants which sprang up and flourished after the end of the glacial epoch. The great peat-bogs of Ireland shew that there was a time when vast woods of oak and yew covered the country, the oak growing on the hills up to a height of four hundred feet or thereabouts above the sea, while at higher levels deal was the prevailing timber. Human relics have often been discovered in these Irish bogs, and ancient roadways made of oak have also come to light. In the peat-bog near Abbeville, in the valley of the Somme, trunks of oak have been dug up fourteen feet thick, a diameter rarely met with outside the tropics in the old Continent.

Unequivocal proof of the prevalence of the oak and its usefulness to man in early times is furnished by the remains of the pile villages which have been discovered in many of the lakes of Europe. In the British Islands, Central Europe and the Po Valley the piles and the platforms on which these crannogs or lake dwellings rested appear to have been often of oak, though fir, birch, and other trees were sometimes used in their construction. Moreover, the old classical tradition that men lived upon acorns before they learned to till the ground may very well be founded on fact. Indeed acorns were still an article of diet in some parts of southern Europe within historical times. Speaking of the prosperity of the righteous, Hesiod declares that for them the earth bears much substance, and the oak on the mountains puts forth acorns. According to Strabo, the mountaineers of Spain subsisted on acorn bread for two-thirds of the year; and in that country acorns were served up as a second course even at the meals of the well-to-do. In the same regions the same practice has survived to modern times. The commonest and finest oak of modern Greece is the *Quercus Aegilops*, with a beautiful crown of leaves, and the peasants eat its acorns both roasted and raw. The sweeter acorns of the *Quercus Ballota* also

serve them as food, especially in Arcadia. In
Spain people eat the acorns of the evergreen oak
(*Quercus Ilex*) which are known as *bellotas*, and
are said to be much larger and more succulent
than the produce of the British oak. The
duchess in *Don Quixote* writes to Sancho's wife
to send her some of them. But oaks are now few
and far between in La Mancha.

Thus we may conclude that the primitive
Aryans of Europe lived among oak woods, used
oak sticks for the lighting of their fires, and oak
timber for the construction of their villages,
their roads, their canoes, fed their swine on
acorns, and themselves subsisted in part on the
same simple diet. No wonder, then, if the tree
from which they received so many benefits
should play an important part in their religion,
and should be invested with a sacred character.
We have seen that the worship of trees has been
world-wide, and that, beginning with a simple
reverence and dread of the tree as itself animated
by a powerful spirit, it has gradually grown into
a cult of tree gods and tree goddesses, who with
the advance of thought become more and more
detached from their old home in the trees, and
assume the character of sylvan deities and
powers of fertility in general, to whom the husbandman looks not merely for the prosperity
of his crops, but for the fecundity of his cattle
and his women. But it is to be borne in mind that
while all oaks were probably the object of superstitious awe, so that the felling of any of them for
timber or firewood would be attended with
ceremonies designed to appease the injured spirit
of the tree, only certain particular groves or
individual oaks would in general receive that
measure of homage which we should term worship. The reasons which led men to venerate
some trees more than others might be various.
We know, for example, that with the Druids the
growth of mistletoe on an oak was a sign that the
tree was especially sacred; and the rarity of this
feature – for mistletoe does not commonly grow

Nature worship: water
Water and springs are among the many aspects of nature
to have inspired religious veneration.
TOP. The medicinal qualities of the springs at Bath were
known in Roman times. Gorgon's head from the temple
of Sulis Minerva, deity of the hot springs at Bath. Roman
Museum, Bath
ABOVE. Bath was still a well-known spa in 18th-century
England, although the springs were no longer revered as
a manifestation of divinity. Satirist's view of patients at
Bath. Victoria Art Gallery. Photos: Bath City Council

on oaks – would enhance the sanctity and mystery of the tree. For it is the strange, the wonderful, the rare, not the familiar and commonplace, which excites the religious emotions of mankind.

The worship of the oak tree or of the oak god appears to have been shared by all the branches of the Aryan stock in Europe. Both Greeks and Italians associated the tree with their highest god, Zeus or Jupiter, the divinity of the sky, the rain, and the thunder. Zeus was the god to whom the Greeks regularly prayed for rain. Nothing could be more natural; for often, though not always, he had his seat on the mountains where the clouds gather and the oaks grow. On the Acropolis at Athens there was an image of Earth praying to Zeus for rain. And in time of drought the Athenians themselves prayed, 'Rain, rain, O dear Zeus, on the cornland of the Athenians and on the plains.' In ancient Italy every oak was sacred to Jupiter, the Italian counterpart of Zeus; and on the Capitol at Rome the god was worshipped as the deity not merely of the oak, but of the rain and the thunder.

When we pass from southern to central Europe we still meet with the great god of the oak and the thunder among the barbarous Aryans who dwelt in the vast primaeval forests. Thus among the Celts of Gaul the Druids esteemed nothing more sacred than the mistletoe and the oak on which it grew; they chose groves of oaks for the scene of their solemn service, and they performed none of their rites without oak leaves. 'The Celts', says a Greek writer, 'worship Zeus, and the Celtic image of Zeus is a tall oak.'

In the religion of the ancient Germans the veneration for sacred groves seems to have held the foremost place, and according to Grimm the chief of their holy trees was the oak. It appears to have been especially dedicated to the god of thunder, Donar or Thunar, the equivalent of the Norse Thor; for a sacred oak near Geismar, in Hesse, which Boniface cut down in the eighth

century, went among the heathen by the name of Jupiter's oak (*robur Jovis*), which in old German would be *Donares eih*, 'the oak of Donar'. That the Teutonic thunder god Donar, Thunar, Thor was identified with the Italian thunder god Jupiter appears from our word Thursday, Thunar's day, which is merely a rendering of the Latin *dies Jovis*. Thus among the ancient Teutons, as among the Greeks and Italians, the god of the oak was also the god of the thunder. Moreover, he was regarded as the great fertilising power, who sent rain and caused the earth to bear fruit; for Adam of Bremen tells us that 'Thor presides in the air; he it is who rules thunder and lightning, wind and rains, fine weather and crops'. In these respects, therefore, the Teutonic thunder god again resembled his southern counterparts Zeus and Jupiter. And like them Thor appears to have been the chief god of the pantheon; for in the great temple at Upsala his image occupied the middle place between the images of Odin and Frey, and in oaths by this or other Norse trinities he was always the principal deity invoked.

As might have been expected, the ancient worship of the oak in Europe has left its print in popular custom and superstition down to modern times. Thus in the French department of Maine it is said that solitary oak-trees in the fields are still worshipped, though the priests have sought to give the worship a Christian colour by hanging images of saints on the trees. In various parts of Lower Saxony and Westphalia, as late as the first half of the nineteenth century, traces survived of the sanctity of certain oaks, to which the people paid a half-heathenish, half-Christian worship. On the rivulet Micksy, between the governments of Pskov and Livonia in Russia, there stood a stunted, withered, but holy oak, which received the homage of the neighbouring peasantry down at least to 1874. An eye-witness has described the ceremonies. He found a great crowd of people, chiefly Esthonians of the Greek Church, assembled with their families about the tree, all dressed in gala costume. Some of them had brought wax candles and were fastening them about the trunk and in the branches. Soon a priest arrived, and, having donned his sacred robes, proceeded to sing a canticle, such as is usually sung in the Orthodox Church in honour of saints. But instead of saying as usual, 'Holy saint, pray the Lord for us', he said, 'Holy Oak Hallelujah, pray for us.' Then he incensed the tree all round. During the service the tapers on the oak were lighted, and the people, throwing themselves on the ground, adored the holy tree. When the pastor had retired, his flock remained till late at night, feasting, drinking, dancing, and lighting fresh tapers on the oak, till everybody was drunk and the proceedings ended in an orgy. We thus conclude that a god of the oak, the thunder, and the rain was worshipped of old by all the main branches of the Aryan stock in Europe, and was indeed the chief deity of their pantheon.

We can now apply our results to the priest at Nemi, the King of the Wood. In the classical period of Greek and Latin antiquity the reign of kings was for the most part a thing of the past; yet the stories of their lineage, titles, and pretensions suffice to prove that they too claimed to rule by divine right and to exercise superhuman powers. Hence we may without undue temerity assume that the King of the Wood at Nemi, though shorn in later times of his glory and fallen on evil days, represented a long line of sacred kings who had once received not only the homage but the adoration of their subjects in return for the manifold blessings which they were supposed to dispense. What little we know of the functions of Diana in the Arician grove seems to prove that she was here conceived as a goddess of fertility, and particularly as a divinity of childbirth. It is reasonable, therefore, to suppose that in the discharge of these important duties she was assisted by her priest, the two

figuring as King and Queen of the Wood in a solemn marriage, which was intended to make the earth gay with the blossoms of spring and the fruits of autumn, and to gladden the hearts of men and women with healthful offspring.

If the priest of Nemi posed not merely as a king, but as a god of the grove, we have still to ask, What deity in particular did he personate? The answer of antiquity is that he represented Virbius, the consort or lover of Diana. But this does not help us much, for of Virbius we know little more than the name. A clue to the mystery is perhaps supplied by the Vestal fire which burned in the grove. For the perpetual holy fires of the Aryans in Europe appear to have been commonly kindled and fed with oak-wood, and in Rome itself, not many miles from Nemi, the fuel of the Vestal fire consisted of oaken sticks or logs, which in early days the holy maidens doubtless gathered or cut in the coppices of oak that once covered the Seven Hills. But the ritual of the various Latin towns seems to have been marked by great uniformity; hence it is reasonable to conclude that wherever in Latium a Vestal fire was maintained, it was fed, as at Rome, with wood of the sacred oak. If this was so at Nemi, it becomes probable that the hallowed grove there consisted of a natural oak-wood, and that therefore the tree which the King of the Wood had to guard at the peril of his life was itself an oak; indeed it was from an evergreen oak, according to Virgil, that Aeneas plucked the Golden Bough. Now the oak was the sacred tree of Jupiter, the supreme god of the Latins. Hence it follows that the King of the Wood, whose life was bound up in a fashion with an oak, personated no less a deity than Jupiter himself. At least the evidence, slight as it is, seems to point to this conclusion. It would then appear that Virbius, with whom legend identified the priest, was nothing but a local form of Jupiter, god of the sky, the thunder, and the oak. If my analysis of this great divinity is correct, the

Nature worship: fire
In many cultures, fires are symbols of holiness and
spiritual power. Frazer thought that veneration of fires
was conditioned by a belief in their fecundating and
purificatory properties. This idea he associated with the
holiness of the oak, which was the chief source of tinder
for fires throughout prehistoric Europe.
TOP. Zoroastrians still hold fires to be the primary
manifestation of good, and the lifegiving power they
attribute to fire is reflected in ritual and taboo. Ancient
fire altars, Naksh-i-Rustam, Iran. Photo: Robert Harding
Associates, London
ABOVE. In India, fire was associated with spiritual
strength. This 15th-century Jain painting shows the ritual
of the 'Penanace of the Five Fires': a devotee sits in the
midst of four fires, the fifth being the sun, and absorbs
their spiritual powers. Courtesy Museum of Fine Arts,
Boston

original element in his composite nature was the
oak. It was fitting, therefore, that his human
representative at Nemi should dwell, as we have
seen reason to believe he did, in an oak grove.
His title of King of the Wood clearly indicates
the sylvan character of the deity whom he served;
and since he could only be assailed by him who
had plucked the bough of a certain tree in the
grove, his own life might be said to be bound up
with that of the sacred tree. Thus he not only
served but embodied the great Aryan god of the
oak; and as an oak-god he would mate with the
oak-goddess, whether she went by the name of
Egeria or Diana. Their union, however con-
summated, would be deemed essential to the
fertility of the earth and the fecundity of man
and beast. Further, as the oak-god had grown
into a god of the sky, the thunder, and the rain,
so his human representative would be required,
like many other divine kings, to cause the clouds
to gather, the thunder to peal, and the rain to
descend in due season, that the fields and orchards
might bear fruit and the pastures be covered
with luxuriant herbage. The reputed possessor of
powers so exalted must have been a very important personage; and the remains of buildings and
of votive offerings which have been found on
the site of the sanctuary combine with the testi-
mony of classical writers to prove that in later
times it was one of the greatest and most
popular shrines in Italy. Even in the old days
when the champaign country around was still
parcelled out among the petty tribes who composed the Latin League, the sacred grove is
known to have been an object of their common
reverence and care. And just as the kings of
Cambodia used to send offerings to the mystic
kings of Fire and Water far in the dim depths of
the tropical forest, so, we may well believe, from
all sides of the broad Latian plain the eyes and
footsteps of Italian pilgrims turned to the quarter
where, standing sharply out against the faint
blue line of the Apennines or the deeper blue of
the distant sea, the Alban Mountain rose before
them, the home of the mysterious priest of
Nemi, the King of the Wood. There, among the
green woods and beside the still waters of the
lonely hills, the ancient Aryan worship of the
god of the oak, the thunder, and the dripping sky
lingered in its early, almost Druidical form, long
after a great political and intellectual revolution
had shifted the capital of Latin religion from the
forest to the city, from Nemi to Rome.

Part 2. Taboo and the Perils of the Soul

We now know that the title King of the Wood was no mere empty form, but points to a time in remote antiquity when Diana's priest would have performed magical and kingly functions. Since such kings were thought to ensure good weather and the fertility of fields and animals, the manner of their living and dying was of paramount importance to their subjects. Therefore Frazer looks at ways of ensuring that the king will survive, dealing first with the dangers that threaten life (perils of the soul), and secondly with ways of overcoming them (taboo).

Many of the dangers to be overcome operate on the same principle as contagious magic, except that they do not have a human author. Taboos are designed to maintain life by preventing the action of contagion or contagious magic. In the case of a king, taboo preserves his life for the benefit of society, but at the same time it protects society from emanations of the king's magical power that might affect it on the principle of contagion. The force of taboo is thus two-edged. The individual, be he king or commoner, takes precautions to protect himself, and these same precautions simultaneously protect his neighbour and society at large.

Taboo is a set of rules prescribing actions and omissions that are designed to maintain life. In conformity with such rules, the dress of the Touareg may be designed to preserve the soul from contamination by the outside world. Granada Television Limited, *Disappearing World*

1. The Burden of Royalty

At a certain stage of early society the king or priest is often thought to be endowed with supernatural powers or to be an incarnation of a deity, and consistently with this belief the course of nature is supposed to be more or less under his control, and he is held responsible for bad weather, failure of the crops, and similar calamities. To some extent it appears to be assumed that the king's power over nature, like that over his subjects and slaves, is exerted through definite acts of will; and therefore if drought, famine, pestilence, or storms arise, the people attribute the misfortune to the negligence or guilt of their king, and punish him accordingly with stripes and bonds, or, if he remains obdurate, with deposition and death. Sometimes, however, the course of nature, while regarded as dependent on the king, is supposed to be partly independent of his will. His person is considered, if we may express it so, as the dynamical centre of the universe, from which lines of force radiate to all quarters of the heaven; so that any motion of his – the turning of his head, the lifting of his hand – instantaneously affects and may seriously disturb some part of nature. He is the point of support on which hangs the balance of the world, and the slightest irregularity on his part may overthrow the delicate equipoise. The greatest care must, therefore, be taken both by and of him; and his whole life, down to its minutest details, must be so regulated that no act of his, voluntary or involuntary, may disarrange or upset the established order of nature. Of this class of monarchs the Mikado or Dairi, the spiritual emperor of Japan, is or rather used to be a typical example. He is an incarnation of the sun goddess, the deity who rules the universe, gods and men included; once a year all the gods wait upon him and spend a month at his court. During that month, the name of which means 'without gods', no one frequents the temples, for they are believed to be deserted. The Mikado receives from his people and assumes in his official proclamations and decrees the title of 'manifest or incarnate deity' (*Akitsu Kami*) and he claims a general authority over the gods of Japan. For example, in an official decree of the year 646 the emperor is described as 'the incarnate god who governs the universe'.

In the West African kingdom of Congo there was a supreme pontiff called Chitomé or Chitombé, whom the negroes regarded as a god on earth and all-powerful in heaven. Hence before they would taste the new crops they offered him the first-fruits, fearing that manifold misfortunes would befall them if they broke this rule. When he left his residence to visit other places within his jurisdiction, all married people had to observe strict continence the whole time he was out; for it was supposed that any act of incontinence would prove fatal to him. And if he were to die a natural death, they thought that the world would perish, and the earth, which he alone sustained by his power and merit, would immediately be annihilated. Similarly in Humbe, a kingdom of Angola, the incontinence of young people under the age of puberty used to be a capital crime, because it was believed to entail the death of the king within the year. Of late the death penalty has been commuted for a fine of ten oxen inflicted on each of the culprits. This commutation has attracted thousands of dissolute youths to Humbe from the neighbouring tribes, among whom the old penalty is still rigorously exacted.

Wherever, as in Japan and West Africa, it is supposed that the order of nature, and even the existence of the world, is bound up with the life of the king or priest, it is clear that he must be regarded by his subjects as a source both of infinite blessing and of infinite danger. On the one hand, the people have to thank him for the rain and sunshine which foster the fruits of the earth, for the wind which brings ships to their coasts, and even for the solid ground beneath their feet. But what he gives he can refuse; and so close is the dependence of nature on his person, so delicate the balance of the system of forces whereof he is the centre, that the least irregularity on his part may set up a tremor which shall shake the earth to its foundations. And if nature may be disturbed by the slightest involuntary act of the king, it is easy to conceive the convulsion which his death might provoke. The natural death of the Chitomé, as we have seen, was thought to entail the destruction of all things. Clearly, therefore, out of a regard for their own safety, which might be imperilled by any rash act of the king, and still more by his death, the people will exact of their king or priest a strict conformity to those rules, the observance of which is deemed necessary for his own preservation, and consequently for the preservation of his people and the world. The idea that early kingdoms are despotisms in which the people exist only for the sovereign, is wholly inapplicable to the monarchies we are considering. On the contrary, the sovereign in them exists only for his subjects; his life is only valuable so long as he discharges the duties of his position by ordering the course of nature for his people's benefit. So soon as he fails to do so, the care, the devotion, the religious homage which they had hitherto lavished on him cease and are changed into hatred and contempt; he is dismissed ignominiously, and may be thankful if he escapes with his life. Worshipped as a god one day, he is killed as a criminal the next. But in this changed behaviour of the people there is nothing capricious or inconsistent. On the contrary, their conduct is entirely of a piece. If their king is their god, he is or should be also their preserver; and if he will not preserve them, he must make room for another who will. So long, however, as he answers their expectations, there is no limit to the care which they take of him, and which they compel him to take of himself. A king of this sort lives hedged in by a ceremonious etiquette, a network of prohibitions and observations, of which the intention is not to contribute to his dignity, much less to his comfort, but to restrain him from conduct which, by disturbing the harmony of nature, might involve himself, his people, and the universe in one common catastrophe.

Of the taboos imposed on priests we may see a striking example in the rules of life prescribed for the Flamen Dialis at Rome, who has been interpreted as a living image of Jupiter, or a human embodiment of the sky-spirit. They were such as the following: The Flamen Dialis might not ride or even touch a horse, nor see an army under arms, nor wear a ring which was not broken, nor have a knot on any part of his garments; no fire except a sacred fire might be taken out of his house; he might not touch wheaten flour or leavened bread; he might not touch or even name a goat, a dog, raw meat, beans, and ivy; he might not walk under a vine; the feet of his bed

The divine order of the universe

OPPOSITE. Cosmic form of the Hindu god Vishnu, who, as god encompassing all things, revealed himself to the hero Arjuna to strengthen him in his war against evil, both human and cosmic. The picture shows Arjuna's vision of Vishnu. Painting from west Rajasthan, c. 1800, Gulbenkian Museum of Oriental Art, Durham

The king as pivot of the universe

OPPOSITE. The cloak of the Emperor Henry II of Germany, 11th century (detail), showing sun, moon and constellations. The wearer stands at the centre of the revolving heavens. Cathedral Treasure, Diözesanmuseum, Bamberg

ABOVE. Chinese symbolism clothed the Emperor in an image of the world. The dragon robe of the Emperor Hsuan Tsung (1821–50) shows symbols of heaven and earth, of the elements and animate nature, as well as of the imperial powers of judging and punishing. Gulbenkian Museum of Oriental Art, Durham

had to be daubed with mud; his hair could be cut only by a free man and with a bronze knife, and his hair and nails when cut had to be buried under a lucky tree; he might not touch a dead body nor enter a place where one was burned; he might not see work being done on holy days; he might not be uncovered in the open air; if a man in bonds were taken into his house, the captive had to be unbound and the cords had to be drawn up through a hole in the roof and so let

down into the street. His wife, the Flaminica, had to observe nearly the same rules, and others of her own besides. She might not ascend more than three steps of the kind of staircase called Greek; at a certain festival she might not comb her hair; the leather of her shoes might not be made from a beast that had died a natural death, but only from one that had been slain or sacrificed; if she heard thunder she was tabooed till she had offered an expiatory sacrifice.

Man and the cosmos

The king is the pivot of the universe, but what is
true of him is true in principle of every human being.
BELOW. Figure of a man with the signs of the zodiac,
showing their influence on the parts of the body.
Medieval manuscript, MS Ashmole 370, fol. 28v, Bodleian
Library, Oxford

BELOW. Aztec painting of a man and the signs that govern
the body. Kingsborough, *Antiquities of Mexico*, 1830–48,
Bodleian Library, Oxford

BOTTOM. Dürer applied the idea of the harmony between
man and the cosmos to the proportions of the human
figure. *Dresden Sketchbook*, MS R147, fol. 112V, Sächsische
Landesbibliothek, Dresden

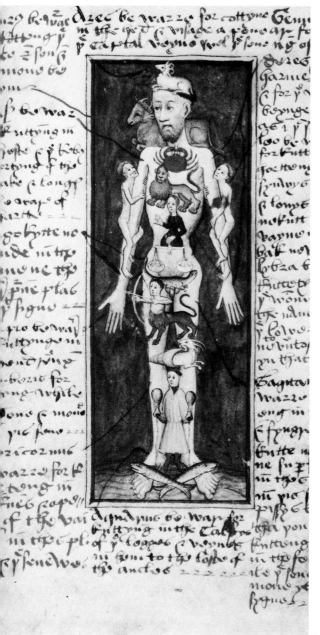

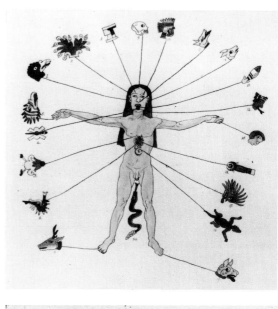

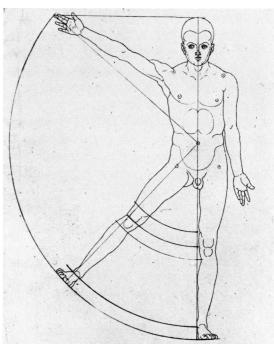

2. The Perils of the Soul

The foregoing examples have taught us that the office of a sacred king or priest is often hedged in by a series of burdensome restrictions or taboos, of which a principal purpose appears to be to preserve the life of the divine man for the good of his people. But if the object of the taboos is to save his life, the question arises, How is their observance supposed to effect this end? To understand this we must know the nature of the danger which threatens the king's life, and which it is the intention of these curious restrictions to guard against. We must, therefore, ask: What does early man understand by death? To what causes does he attribute it? And how does he think it may be guarded against?

As the savage commonly explains the processes of inanimate nature by supposing that they are produced by living beings working in or behind the phenomena, so he explains the phenomena of life itself. If an animal lives and moves, it can only be, he thinks, because there is a little animal inside which moves it: if a man lives and moves, it can only be because he has a little man or animal inside who moves him. The animal inside the animal, the man inside the man, is the soul. And as the activity of an animal or man is explained by the presence of the soul, so the repose of sleep or death is explained by its absence; sleep or trance being the temporary, death being the permanent absence of the soul. Hence if death be the permanent absence of the soul, the way to guard against it is either to prevent the soul from leaving the body, or, if it does depart, to ensure that it shall return. The precautions adopted by savages to secure one or other of these ends take the form of certain prohibitions or taboos, which are nothing but rules

intended to ensure either the continued presence or the return of the soul. In short, they are life preservers or life-guards.

So exact, according to some people, is the resemblance of the mannikin to the man, in other words, of the soul to the body, that, as there are fat bodies and thin bodies, so there are fat souls and thin souls; as there are heavy bodies and light bodies, long bodies and short bodies, so there are heavy souls and light souls, long souls and short souls. People in the Punjab who tattoo themselves accordingly believe that at death the soul, 'the little entire man or woman' inside the mortal frame, will go to heaven blazoned with the same tattoo patterns which adorned the body in life. Sometimes, however, as we shall see, the human soul is conceived not in human but in animal form. The soul is commonly supposed to escape by the natural openings of the body, especially the mouth and nostrils. Popular expressions in the language of civilised peoples, such as to have one's heart in one's mouth, or the soul on the lips or in the nose, shew how natural is the idea that the life or soul may escape by the mouth or nostrils.

Often the soul is conceived as a bird ready to take flight. This conception has probably left traces in most languages, and it lingers as a metaphor in poetry. But what is metaphor to a modern European poet was sober earnest to his savage ancestor, and is still so to many people. Thus in Java when a child is placed on the ground for the first time (a moment which uncultured people seem to regard as especially dangerous), it is put in a hen-coop and the mother makes a clucking sound, is if she were calling hens. Similarly in the district of Sintang in West

Borneo, if any one has had a great fright, or escaped a serious peril, or comes back after a long and dangerous journey, or has taken a solemn oath, the first thing that his relations or friends do is to strew yellow rice on his head, mumbling, 'Cluck! cluck! soul!' (*koer, koer semangat*).

The soul of a sleeper is supposed to wander away from his body and actually to visit the places, to see the persons, and to perform the acts of which he dreams. The Indians of the Gran Chaco are often heard to relate the most incredible stories as things which they have themselves seen and heard; hence strangers who do not know them intimately say in their haste that these Indians are liars. In point of fact the Indians are firmly convinced of the truth of what they relate; for these wonderful adventures are simply their dreams, which they do not distinguish from waking realities.

Now the absence of the soul in sleep has its dangers, for if from any cause the soul should be permanently detained away from the body, the person thus deprived of the vital principle must die. Many causes may detain the sleeper's soul. Thus, his soul may meet the soul of another sleeper and the two souls may fight; if a Guinea negro wakens with sore bones in the morning, he thinks that his soul has been thrashed by another soul in sleep. Or it may meet the soul of a person just deceased and be carried off by it; hence in the Aru Islands the inmates of a house will not sleep the night after a death has taken place in it, because the soul of the deceased is supposed to be still in the house and they fear to meet it in a dream.

But in order that a man's soul should quit his body, it is not necessary that he should be asleep. It may quit him in his waking hours, and then sickness, insanity, or death will be the result. Thus a man of the Wurunjeri tribe in Victoria lay at his last gasp because his spirit (*murup*) had departed from him. A medicine-man went in pursuit and caught the spirit by the middle just as it was about to plunge into the sunset glow, which is the light cast by the souls of the dead as they pass in and out of the underworld, where the sun goes to rest. Having captured the vagrant spirit the doctor brought it back under his opossum rug, laid himself down on the dying man, and put the soul back into him, so that after a time he revived.

The departure of the soul is not always voluntary. It may be extracted from the body against its will by ghosts, demons, or sorcerers. Hence, when a funeral is passing the house, the Karens of Burma tie their children with a special kind of string to a particular part of the house, lest the souls of the children should leave their bodies and go into the corpse which is passing. The children are kept tied in this way until the corpse is out of sight. At the funeral itself, adults will take precautions to prevent their souls being buried with the corpse. In one of the New Hebrides a ghost will sometimes impound the souls of trespassers within a magic fence in his garden, and will only consent to pull up the fence and let the souls out on receiving an unqualified apology and a satisfactory assurance that no personal disrespect was intended.

Often the abduction of a man's soul is set down to demons. The Annamites believe that when a man meets a demon and speaks to him, the demon inhales the man's breath and soul. In the Moluccas when a man is unwell it is thought that some devil has carried away his soul to the tree, mountain, or hill where he (the devil) resides. A sorcerer having pointed out the devil's abode, the friends of the patient carry thither cooked rice, fruit, fish, raw eggs, a hen, a chicken, a silken robe, gold, armlets, and so forth. Having set out the food in order they pray, saying: 'We come to offer to you, O devil, this offering of food, clothes, gold, and so on; take it and release the soul of the patient for whom we pray. Let it return to his body, and he who now is sick shall be made whole.' Then they

Perils of the soul: preventing the soul from leaving the body

TOP. Silver padlock from Shanghai, used to prevent a child's soul from leaving the body. Pitt Rivers Museum, University of Oxford

ABOVE. Bapedi woman and child. The medicine bag hanging from the woman's neck is for the protection of the child's soul. Duggan-Cronin Gallery, Alexander McGregor Memorial Museum, Kimberley

eat a little and let the hen loose as a ransom for the soul of the patient; also they put down the raw eggs; but the silken robe, the gold, and the armlets they take home with them. As soon as they are come to the house they place a flat bowl containing the offerings which have been brought back at the sick man's head, and say to him: 'Now is your soul released, and you shall fare well and live to grey hairs on the earth.'

Again, souls may be extracted from their bodies or detained on their wanderings not only by ghosts and demons but also by men, especially by sorcerers. In Fiji, if a criminal refused to confess, the chief sent for a scarf with which 'to catch away the soul of the rogue'. At the sight or even at the mention of the scarf the culprit generally made a clean breast. For if he did not, the scarf would be waved over his head till his soul was caught in it, when it would be carefully folded up and nailed to the end of a chief's canoe; and for want of his soul the criminal would pine and die.

But the spiritual dangers I have enumerated are not the only ones which beset the savage. Often he regards his shadow or reflection as his soul, or at all events as a vital part of himself, and as such it is necessarily a source of danger to him. For if it is trampled upon, struck, or stabbed, he will feel the injury as if it were done to his person; and if it is detached from him entirely (as he believes that it may be) he will die. In the island of Wetar there are magicians who can make a man ill by stabbing his shadow with a pike or hacking it with a sword. After Sankara had destroyed the Buddhists in India, it is said that he journeyed to Nepaul, where he had some difference of opinion with the Grand Lama. To prove his supernatural powers, he soared into the air. But as he mounted up, the Grand Lama, perceiving his shadow swaying and wavering on the ground, struck his knife into it and down fell Sankara and broke his neck.

The natives of Nias tremble at the sight of a

rainbow, because they think it is a net spread by a powerful spirit to catch their shadows. At a funeral in China, when the lid is about to be placed on the coffin, most of the bystanders, with the exception of the nearest kin, retire a few steps or even retreat to another room, for a person's health is believed to be endangered by allowing his shadow to be enclosed in a coffin. And when the coffin is about to be lowered into the grave most of the spectators recoil to a little distance lest their shadows should fall into the grave and harm should thus be done to their persons. The geomancer and his assistants stand on the side of the grave which is turned away from the sun; and the grave-diggers and coffin-bearers attach their shadows firmly to their persons by tying a strip of cloth tightly round their waists.

Nowhere, perhaps, does the equivalence of the shadow to the life or soul come out more clearly than in some customs practised to this day in south-eastern Europe. In modern Greece, when the foundation of a new building is being laid, it is the custom to kill a cock, a ram, or a lamb, and to let its blood flow on the foundation-stone, under which the animal is afterwards buried. The object of the sacrifice is to give strength and stability to the building. But sometimes, instead of killing an animal, the builder entices a man to the foundation-stone, secretly measures his body, or a part of it, or his shadow, and buries the measure under the foundation-stone; or he lays the foundation-stone upon the man's shadow. It is believed that the man will die within the year. In the island of Lesbos it is deemed enough if the builder merely casts a stone at the shadow of a passer-by; the man whose shadow is thus struck will die, but the building will be solid.

As some peoples believe a man's soul to be in his shadow, so other (or the same) peoples believe it to be in his reflection in water or a mirror. Thus 'the Andamanese do not regard their

Perils of the soul: the soul as a reflection
Bar Kafari of Tani, Sierra Leone, in the regalia of a Temne paramount chief. He may never see his own likeness; thus when crossing rivers he must wrap his head to prevent the escape of his soul. Pitt Rivers Museum, University of Oxford. Photo: Rattray

shadows but their reflections [in any mirror] as their souls.' According to one account, some of the Fijians thought that man has two souls, a light one and a dark one; the dark one goes to Hades, the light one is his reflection in water or a mirror. When the Motumotu of New Guinea first saw their likenesses in a looking-glass they thought that their reflections were their souls.

3. Tabooed Acts and Persons

So much for the primitive conceptions of the soul and the dangers to which it is exposed. These conceptions are not limited to one people or country; with variations of detail they are found all over the world, and survive in modern Europe. Beliefs so deep-seated and so widespread must necessarily have contributed to shape the mould in which the early kingship was cast. For if every person was at such pains to save his own soul from the perils which threatened it on so many sides, how much more carefully must *he* have been guarded upon whose life hung the welfare and even the existence of the whole people, and whom therefore it was the common interest of all to preserve? Therefore we should expect to find the king's life protected by a system of precautions or safeguards still more numerous and minute than those which in primitive society every man adopts for the safety of his own soul. Now in point of fact the life of the early kings is regulated, as we have seen and shall see more fully presently, by a very exact code of rules. May we not then conjecture that these rules are in fact the very safeguards which we should expect to find adopted for the protection of the king's life? An examination of the rules themselves confirms this conjecture. For from this it appears that some of the rules observed by the kings are identical with those observed by private persons out of regard for the safety of their souls; and even of those which seem peculiar to the king, many, if not all, are most readily explained on the hypothesis that they are nothing but safeguards or lifeguards of the king.

As the object of the royal taboos is to isolate the king from all sources of danger, their general effect is to compel him to live in a state of seclusion, more or less complete, according to the number and stringency of the rules he observes. Now of all sources of danger none are more dreaded by the savage than magic and witchcraft, and he suspects all strangers of practising these black arts. To guard against the baneful influence exerted voluntarily or involuntarily by strangers is therefore an elementary dictate of savage prudence. Hence before strangers are allowed to enter a district, or at least before they are permitted to mingle freely with the inhabitants, certain ceremonies are often performed by the natives of the country for the purpose of disarming the strangers of their magical powers, of counteracting the baneful influence which is believed to emanate from them, or of disinfecting, so to speak, the tainted atmosphere by which they are supposed to be surrounded. Thus, when the ambassadors sent by Justin II, Emperor of the East, to conclude a peace with the Turks had reached their destination, they were received by shamans, who subjected them to a ceremonial purification for the purpose of exorcising all harmful influence. Having deposited the goods brought by the ambassadors in an open place, these wizards carried burning branches of incense round them, while they rang a bell and beat on a tambourine, snorting and falling into a state of frenzy in their efforts to dispel the powers of evil. Afterwards they purified the ambassadors themselves by leading them through the flames. In the island of Nanumea (South Pacific) strangers from ships or from other islands were not allowed to communicate with the people until they all, or a few as representatives of the rest, had been taken to each of the four temples in the island, and prayers offered that the god would avert any disease or treachery which these strangers might have brought with them. Meat offerings were also laid upon the altars, accompanied by songs and dances in honour of the god. While these ceremonies were going on, all the people except the priests and their attendants kept out of sight.

The fear entertained of alien visitors is often mutual. Entering a strange land the savage feels that he is treading enchanted ground, and he takes steps to guard against the demons that haunt it and the magical arts of its inhabitants. Thus on going to a strange land the Maoris of New Zealand used to perform a ceremony called *Uruura-whenua*. 'This is a ceremony performed by a person who, for the first time, ascends a mountain, crosses a lake, or enters a district never before traversed by him. The term implies "to enter or become of the land". It is an offering to the spirits of the strange land. It is generally performed at a tree or rock situated on the trail by which travellers pass into the district. Every person on passing such places for the first time would pluck a twig or piece of fern and cast it at the base of the tree or stone, at the same time repeating a short invocation to the spirits of the land. After passing on such a person would never look back towards the tree; it would be an evil omen were he to do so.'

Furthermore, it is thought that a man who has been on a journey may have contracted some magic evil from the strangers with whom he has been brought into contact. Hence, on returning home, before he is readmitted to the society of his tribe and friends, he has to undergo certain purificatory ceremonies. A story is told of a Navajo Indian who, after long wanderings, returned to his own people. When he came within sight of his house, his people made him stop and told him not to approach nearer till they had summoned a shaman. When the shaman

Tabooed persons
The life of the king is protected by walls and gateways from the material and spiritual dangers of the outside world.
TOP. The guarded palace gate of the Oba. Benin bronze plaque, late 16th century, British Museum, London
ABOVE. Buckingham Palace, London. Barnaby's Picture Library. Photo: Bill Coward

was come 'ceremonies were performed over the returned wanderer, and he was washed from head to foot, and dried with corn-meal; for thus do the Navajo treat all who return to their homes from captivity with another tribe, in order that all alien substances and influences may be removed from them. When he had been thus purified he entered the house, and his people embraced him and wept over him.'

When precautions like these are taken on behalf of the people in general against the malignant influence supposed to be exercised by strangers, it is no wonder that special measures are adopted to protect the king from the same insidious danger. In the middle ages the envoys who visited a Tartar Khan were obliged to pass between two fires before they were admitted to his presence, and the gifts they brought were also carried between the fires. The reason assigned for the custom was that the fire purged away any magic influence which the strangers might mean to exercise over the Khan. When subject chiefs come with their retinues to visit Kalamba (the most powerful chief of the Bashilange in the Congo Basin) for the first time or after being rebellious, they have to bathe, men and women together, in two brooks on two successive days, passing the nights under the open sky in the market-place. After the second bath they proceed, entirely naked, to the house of Kalamba, who makes a long white mark on the breast and forehead of each of them. Then they return to the market-place and dress, after which they undergo the pepper ordeal. Pepper is dropped into the eyes of each of them, and while this is being done the sufferer has to make a confession of all his sins, to answer all questions that may be put to him, and to take certain vows. This ends the ceremony, and the strangers are now free to take up their quarters in the town for as long as they choose to remain.

In the opinion of savages the acts of eating and drinking are attended with special danger; for at these times the soul may escape from the mouth, or be extracted by the magic arts of an enemy present. Among the Ewe-speaking peoples of the Slave Coast 'the common belief seems to be that the indwelling spirit leaves the body and returns to it through the mouth; hence, should it have gone out, it behoves a man to be careful about opening his mouth, lest a homeless spirit should take advantage of the opportunity and enter his body. This, it appears, is considered most likely to take place while the man is eating.' Precautions are therefore taken to guard against these dangers, particularly if the person to be protected is a king.

Again, magic mischief may be wrought upon a man through the remains of the food he has partaken of, or the dishes out of which he has eaten. On the principles of sympathetic magic a real connexion continues to subsist between the food which a man has in his stomach and the refuse of it which he has left untouched, and hence by injuring the refuse you can simultaneously injure the eater.

The Mikado's food was cooked every day in new pots and served up in new dishes; both pots and dishes were of common clay, in order that they might be broken or laid aside after they had been once used. They were generally broken, for it was believed that if any one else ate his food out of these sacred dishes, his mouth and throat would become swollen and inflamed. The same ill effect was thought to be experienced by any one who should wear the Mikado's clothes without his leave; he would have swellings and pains all over his body. In Fiji there is a special name (*kana lama*) for the disease supposed to be caused by eating out of a chief's dishes or wearing his clothes.

In the evil effects thus supposed to follow upon the use of the vessels or clothes of the Mikado and a Fijian chief we see that other side of the god-man's character to which attention has been already called. The divine person is a source of danger as well as of blessing; he must not only be guarded, he must also be guarded against. His sacred organism, so delicate that a touch may disorder it, is also, as it were, electrically charged with a powerful magical or spiritual force which may discharge itself with fatal effect on whatever comes in contact with it. Accordingly the isolation of the man-god is quite as necessary for the safety of others as for his own. His magical virtue is in the strictest sense of the word contagious: his divinity is a fire, which, under proper restraints, confers endless blessings, but, if rashly touched or allowed to break bounds, burns and destroys what it touches. Hence the disastrous effects supposed to attend a breach of taboo; the offender has thrust his hand into the divine fire, which shrivels up and consumes him on the spot. In Tonga it was believed that if any one fed himself with his own hands after touching the sacred person of a superior chief or anything that belonged to him, he would swell up and die; the sanctity of the chief, like a virulent poison, infected the hands of his inferior, and, being communicated through them to the food, proved fatal to the eater.

In New Zealand the dread of the sanctity of chiefs was at least as great as in Tonga. Their ghostly power, derived from an ancestral spirit or *atua*, diffused itself by contagion over everything they touched, and could strike dead all who rashly or unwittingly meddled with it. For instance, it once happened that a New Zealand chief of high rank and great sanctity had left the remains of his dinner by the wayside. A slave, a stout, hungry fellow, coming up after the chief had gone, saw the unfinished dinner, and ate it up without asking questions. Hardly had he finished when he was informed by a horror-stricken spectator that the food of which he had eaten was the chief's. 'I knew the unfortunate delinquent well. He was remarkable for courage, and had signalised himself in the wars of the

The power of the ancestors
LEFT. Ashanti youth offering a fowl to the spirit of his father. Pitt Rivers Museum, University of Oxford. Photo: Rattray
RIGHT. Ancestor figure from Easter Island. British Museum, London

tribe,' but 'no sooner did he hear the fatal news than he was seized by the most extraordinary convulsions and cramp in the stomach, which never ceased till he died, about sundown the same day'.

Thus regarding his sacred chiefs and kings as charged with a mysterious spiritual force which so to say explodes at contact, the savage naturally ranks them among the dangerous classes of society, and imposes upon them the same sort of restraints that he lays on manslayers, menstruous women, and other persons whom he looks upon with a certain fear and horror. For example, sacred kings and priests in Polynesia were not allowed to touch food with their hands, and had therefore to be fed by others; and their vessels, garments, and other property might not be used by others on pain of disease and death. Now precisely the same observances are exacted by some savages from girls at their first menstruation, women after childbirth and homicides.

In general, we may say that the prohibition to use the vessels, garments, and so on of certain persons, and the effects supposed to follow an infraction of the rule, are exactly the same whether the persons to whom the things belong are sacred or what we might call unclean and polluted. As the garments which have been touched by a sacred chief kill those who handle them, so do the things which have been touched by a menstruous woman. In Uganda the pots which a woman touches while the impurity of childbirth or of menstruation is on her should be destroyed; spears and shields defiled by her touch are not destroyed but only purified. No Esquimaux of Alaska will willingly drink out of the same cup or eat out of the same dish that has been used by a woman at her confinement until it has been purified by certain incantations. Amongst some of the Indians of North America, women at menstruation are forbidden to touch men's utensils, which would be so defiled by their touch that their subsequent use would be attended by certain mischief or misfortune.

Once more, warriors are conceived by the savage to move, so to say, in an atmosphere of spiritual danger which constrains them to practise a variety of superstitious observances quite different in their nature from those rational precautions which, as a matter of course, they adopt against foes of flesh and blood. The general effect of these observances is to place the warrior, both before and after victory, in the same state of seclusion or spiritual quarantine in which, for his own safety, primitive man puts his human gods and other dangerous characters. Thus when the Maoris went out on the war-path they were sacred or taboo in the highest degree, and they and their friends at home had to observe strictly many curious customs over and above the numerous taboos of ordinary life. Similarly, when the Israelites marched forth to war they were bound by certain rules of ceremonial purity identical with rules observed by Maoris and Australian black-fellows on the war-path. The vessels they used were sacred, and they had to practise continence and a custom of personal cleanliness of which the original motive, if we may judge from the avowed motive of savages who conform to the same custom, was a fear lest the enemy should obtain the refuse of their persons, and thus be enabled to work their destruction by magic. Among some Indian tribes of North America a young warrior in his first campaign had to conform to certain customs, of which two were identical with the observances imposed by the same Indians on the girls at their first menstruation: the vessels he ate and drank out of might be touched by no other person, and he was forbidden to scratch his head or any other part of his body with his fingers; if he could not help scratching himself, he had to do it with a stick. The latter rule, like the one which forbids a tabooed person to feed himself with his own fingers, seems to rest on the supposed sanctity or pollution, whichever we choose to call it, of the tabooed hands. Moreover among these Indian tribes the men on the war-path had always to sleep at night with their faces turned towards their own country; however uneasy the posture they might not change it. They might not sit upon the bare ground, nor wet their feet, nor walk on a beaten path if they could help it; when they had no choice but to walk on a path, they sought to counteract the ill effect of doing so by doctoring their legs with certain medicines or charms which they carried with them for the purpose. The vessels out of which the warriors ate their food were commonly small bowls of wood or birch bark, with marks to distinguish the two sides; in marching from home the Indians invariably drank out of one side of the bowl, and in returning they drank out of the other. When on their way home they came within a day's march of the village, they hung up all their bowls on trees, or threw them away on the prairie, doubtless to prevent their sanctity or defilement from being communicated with disastrous effects to their friends, just as the vessels and clothes of the sacred Mikado, of women at childbirth and menstruation, of boys at circumcision, and of persons defiled by contact with the dead are destroyed or laid aside for a similar reason.

If the reader still doubts whether the rules of conduct which we have just been considering are based on superstitious fears or dictated by a rational prudence, his doubts will probably be dissipated when he learns that rules of the same sort are often imposed even more stringently on warriors after the victory has been won and when all fear of the living corporeal foe is at an end. In such cases one motive for the inconvenient restrictions laid on the victors in their hour of triumph is probably a dread of the angry ghosts of the slain; and that the fear of the vengeful ghosts does influence the behaviour of the slayers is often expressly affirmed. The general effect of the taboos laid on sacred chiefs, mourners, women at childbirth, men on the warpath, and so on, is to seclude or isolate the tabooed persons from ordinary society, this effect being attained by a variety of rules, which oblige the men or women to live in separate huts or in the open air, to shun the commerce of the sexes, to avoid the use of vessels employed by others, and so forth. Now the same effect is produced by similar means in the case of victorious warriors, particularly such as have actually shed the blood of their enemies.

Among the primitive natives of the Andaman Islands if a man kills another in a fight between

Both dangers and blessings emanate from the dead
TOP. The ghost of a man appears to his wife, who had murdered him. Print by Hokusai, British Museum, London
ABOVE. The dead in India have an intimate connection with the crops. At Mannemgolu, 'at the time of the taking out of the seed' in 1944, the ghost of a man called Jamburu visited his widow in a dream. He instructed her to draw a picture of his house and possessions in the land of the dead in order to safeguard her crops. V. Elwin, *The Tribal Art of Middle India*, 1951, Oxford University Press, Indian Branch

two villages, or in a private quarrel, he leaves his village and goes to live by himself in the jungle, where he must stay for some weeks, or even months. His wife, and one or two of his friends may live with him or visit him and attend to his wants. For some weeks the homicide must observe a rigorous taboo. He may not handle a bow or arrow. He may not feed himself or touch any food with his hands, but must be fed by his wife or a friend. He must keep his neck and upper lip covered with red paint, and must wear plumes of shredded *Tetrathera* wood in his belt before and behind, and in his necklace at the back of his neck. If he breaks any of these rules it is supposed that the spirit of the man he has killed will cause him to be ill. At the end of a few weeks the homicide undergoes a sort of purification ceremony. His hands are first rubbed with white clay and then with red paint. After this he may wash his hands and may then feed himself with his hands and may handle bows and arrows. He retains the plumes of shredded wood for a year or so.

Among the Natchez of North America young braves who had taken their first scalps were obliged to observe certain rules of abstinence for six months. They might not sleep with their wives nor eat flesh; their only food was fish and hasty-pudding. If they broke these rules, they believed that the soul of the man they had killed would work their death by magic, that they would gain no more successes over the enemy, and that the least wound inflicted on them would prove mortal. When a Choctaw had killed an enemy and taken his scalp, he went into mourning for a month, during which he might not comb his hair, and if his head itched he might not scratch it except with a little stick which he wore fastened to his wrist for the purpose. This ceremonial mourning for the enemies they had slain was not uncommon among the North American Indians. Thus the Dacotas, when they had killed a foe, unbraided their hair,

blackened themselves all over, and wore a small knot of swan's down on the top of the head. 'They dress as mourners yet rejoice.' A Thompson River Indian of British Columbia, who had slain an enemy, used to blacken his own face, lest his victim's ghost should blind him. When the Osages have mourned over their own dead, 'they will mourn for the foe just as if he was a friend'. Among the Esquimaux of Chesterfield Inlet, 'it is the custom that when an Esquimaux kills a person, he must not handle rocks for a certain time, and he must eat only straight meat, and when he eats, he must be under some shelter from the sun. Ouang-Wak was made to observe these customs, and did so while I was there. This was proof that Ouang-Wak killed these two men.'

Thus we see that warriors who have taken the life of a foe in battle are temporarily cut off from free intercourse with their fellows, and especially with their wives, and must undergo certain rites of purification before they are readmitted to society. Now if the purpose of their seclusion and of the expiatory rites which they have to perform is, as we have been led to believe, no other than to shake off, frighten, or appease the angry spirit of the slain man, we may safely conjecture that the similar purification of homicides and murderers, who have imbrued their hands in the blood of a fellow-tribesman, had at first the same significance, and that the idea of a moral or spiritual regeneration symbolised by the washing, the fasting, and so on, was merely a later interpretation put upon the old custom by men who had outgrown the primitive modes of thought in which the custom originated.

In savage society the hunter and the fisherman have often to observe rules of abstinence and to submit to ceremonies of purification of the same sort as those which are obligatory on the warrior and the manslayer; and though we cannot in all cases perceive the exact purpose which these rules and ceremonies are supposed to serve, we

The consequences of breaking a taboo
Both traditional and modern societies segregate those
who break taboos.

A man becomes a hartebeest after killing one. Bushman
rock painting, from South Africa. Copy by G. Stow,
1868, Bodleian Library, Oxford

may with some probability assume that, just as
the dread of the spirits of his enemies is the main
motive for the seclusion and purification of the
warrior who hopes to take or has already taken
their lives, so the huntsman or fisherman who
complies with similar customs is principally
actuated by a fear of the spirits of the beasts,
birds, or fish which he has killed or intends to
kill. For the savage commonly conceives animals
to be endowed with souls and intelligences like
his own, and hence he naturally treats them
with similar respect. Just as he attempts to
appease the ghosts of the men he has slain, so he
essays to propitiate the spirits of the animals he
has killed. The taboos observed by the hunter
and the fisherman before or during the hunting
and fishing seasons are analogous to those observed by warriors and comprise abstinence from
sleep, from food and drink, from commerce
with women as well as other bodily disciplines.
In general it appears to be supposed that the evil
effect of breaking such taboos is not so much that
it weakens the hunter or fisher, as that, for some
reason or other, it offends the animals, who in
consequence will not suffer themselves to be
caught.

precautions for maintaining the men in health and strength to do their work, it is obvious that the observance of these abstinences or taboos after the work is done, that is, when the game is killed and the fish caught, must be wholly superfluous, absurd, and inexplicable. But these taboos often continue to be enforced or even increased in stringency after the death of the animals, in other words, after the hunter or fisher has accomplished his object by making his bag or landing his fish. The rationalistic theory of them therefore breaks down entirely; the hypothesis of superstition is clearly the only one open to us.

We have a native explanation of the taboos enjoined on hunters and fishers after the animals have been killed. It comes from the Central Esquimaux and sets down what may be called the spiritual basis of taboo. The goddess Sedna, the mother of the sea-mammals, may be considered to be the chief deity of the central Esquimaux. She is supposed to bear supreme sway over the destinies of mankind, and almost all the observances of these tribes have for their object to retain her good will or appease her anger. Her home is in the lower world, where she dwells in a house built of stone and whale-ribs. The souls of seals, ground seals, and whales are believed to proceed from her house. After one of these animals has been killed, its soul stays with the body for three days. Then it goes back to Sedna's abode, to be sent forth again by her. If, during the three days that the soul stays with the body, any taboo or proscribed custom is violated, the violation (*pitssēte*) becomes attached to the animal's soul, and causes it pain. The soul strives in vain to free itself of these attachments, but is compelled to take them down to Sedna. The attachments, in some manner not explained, make her hands sore, and she punishes the people who are the cause of her pains by sending to them sickness, bad weather, and starvation. If, on the other hand, all taboos have

Holloway Prison, London. Photo: John Topham Picture Library

If the taboos or abstinences observed by hunters and fishermen before and during the chase are dictated, as we have seen reason to believe, by superstitious motives, and chiefly by a dread of offending or frightening the spirits of the creatures whom it is proposed to kill, we may expect that the restraints imposed after the slaughter has been perpetrated will be at least as stringent, the slayer and his friends having now the added fear of the angry ghosts of his victims before their eyes. Whereas on the hypothesis that the abstinences in question, including those from food, drink, and sleep, are merely salutary

been observed, the sea-animals will allow them- selves to be caught; they will even come to meet the hunter. The object of the innumerable taboos that are in force after the killing of these sea-animals, therefore, is to keep their souls free from attachments that would hurt their souls as well as Sedna.

In these taboos we seem to see a system of animism in the act of passing into religion. The rules themselves bear the clearest traces of having originated in a doctrine of souls, and of being determined by the supposed likes and dislikes, sympathies and antipathies of the various classes of spirits toward each other. But above and be- hind the souls of men and animals has grown up the overshadowing conception of a powerful goddess who rules them all, so that the taboos come more and more to be viewed as a means of propitiating her rather than as merely adapted to suit the tastes of the souls themselves. Thus the standard of conduct is shifted from a natural to a supernatural basis: the supposed wish of the deity or, as we commonly put it, the will of God, tends to supersede the wishes, real or imaginative, of purely natural beings as the measure of right and wrong. The old savage taboos, resting on a theory of the direct relations of living creatures to each other, remain in substance unchanged, but they are outwardly transformed into ethical precepts with a religious or supernatural sanction.

It seems not improbable that in our own rules of conduct, in what we call the common decencies of life as well as in the weightier matters of morality, there may survive not a few old savage taboos which, masquerading as an expression of the divine will or draped in the flowing robes of a false philosophy, have maintained their credit long after the crude ideas out of which they sprang have been discarded by the progress of thought and knowledge; while on the other hand many ethical precepts and social laws, which now rest firmly on a solid basis of utility, may at first have drawn some portion of their sanctity from the same ancient system of superstition. For example, we can hardly doubt that in primitive society the crime of murder derived much of its horror from a fear of the angry ghost of the murdered man. Thus superstition may serve as a convenient crutch to morality till she is strong enough to throw away the crutch and walk alone. To judge by the legislation of the Pentateuch the ancient Semites appear to have passed through a course of moral evolution not unlike that which we can still detect in process among the Esqui- maux of Baffin Land. Some of the old laws of Israel are clearly savage taboos of a familiar type thinly disguised as commands of the deity. This disguise is indeed a good deal more perfect in Palestine than in Baffin Land, but in substance it is the same. Among the Esquimaux it is the will of Sedna; among the Israelites it is the will of Jehovah.

Perils of the soul
Both perils and powers can emanate from the same object. The loss of a person's hair may endanger his life, but, conversely, power may be acquired by the removal of hair.
OPPOSITE. The Buddha is seen severing a hair tuft when renouncing his princely existence to become an ascetic. Tibetan Temple Banner, 18th century, Musée Guimet, Paris. Photo: Musées Nationaux

4. Our Debt to the Savage

It would be easy to extend the list of royal and priestly taboos, but the instances collected in the preceding pages may suffice as specimens. To conclude this part of our subject it only remains to state summarily the general conclusions to which our enquiries have thus far conducted us. We have seen that in savage or barbarous society there are often found men to whom the superstition of their fellows ascribes a controlling influence over the general course of nature. Such men are accordingly adored and treated as gods. Whether these human divinities also hold temporal sway over the lives and fortunes of their adorers, or whether their functions are purely spiritual and supernatural, in other words, whether they are kings as well as gods or only the latter, is a distinction which hardly concerns us here. Their supposed divinity is the essential fact with which we have to deal. In virtue of it they are a pledge and guarantee to their worshippers of the continuance and orderly succession of those physical phenomena upon which mankind depends for subsistence. Naturally, therefore, the life and health of such a god-man are matters of anxious concern to the people whose welfare and even existence are bound up with his; naturally he is constrained by them to conform to such rules as the wit of early man has

devised for averting the ills to which flesh is heir, including the last ill, death. These rules, as an examination of them has shewn, are nothing but the maxims with which, on the primitive view, every man of common prudence must comply if he would live long in the land. But while in the case of ordinary men the observance of the rules is left to the choice of the individual, in the case of the god-man it is enforced under penalty of dismissal from his high station, or even of death. For his worshippers have far too great a stake in his life to allow him to play fast and loose with it. Therefore all the quaint superstitions, the old-world maxims, the venerable saws which the ingenuity of savage philosophers elaborated long ago, and which old women at chimney corners still impart as treasures of great price to their descendants gathered round the cottage fire on winter evenings – all these antique fancies clustered, all these cobwebs of the brain were spun about the path of the old king, the human god, who, immeshed in them like a fly in the toils of a spider, could hardly stir a limb for the threads of custom, 'light as air but strong as links of iron', that crossing and recrossing each other in an endless maze bound him fast within a network of observances from which death or deposition alone could release him.

Thus to students of the past the life of the old kings and priests teems with instruction. In it was summed up all that passed for wisdom when the world was young. It was the perfect pattern after which every man strove to shape his life; a faultless model constructed with rigorous accuracy upon the lines laid down by a barbarous philosophy. Crude and false as that philosophy

The perils of the soul: the soul as a reflection
The ancient Greeks regarded it as an omen of death if a man should dream of seeing himself reflected in water, because the soul may be drawn from the body by water spirits. This idea is echoed in the myth of the beautiful Narcissus, who fell in love with his own fair image and died through gazing at it in a pool of water.
OPPOSITE. Narcissus, by Caravaggio, Palazzo Barberini, Rome. Photo: Scala

may seem to us, it would be unjust to deny it the merit of logical consistency. Starting from a conception of the vital principle as a tiny being or soul existing in, but distinct and separable from, the living being, it deduces for the practical guidance of life a system of rules which in general hangs well together and forms a fairly complete and harmonious whole. The flaw – and it is a fatal one – of the system lies not in its reasoning, but in its premises; in its conception of the nature of life, not in any irrelevancy of the conclusions which it draws from that conception. But to stigmatise these premises as ridiculous because we can easily detect their falseness, would be ungrateful as well as unphilosophical. We stand upon the foundation reared by the generations that have gone before, and we can but dimly realise the painful and prolonged efforts which it has cost humanity to struggle up to the point, no very exalted one after all, which we have reached. Our gratitude is due to the nameless and forgotten toilers, whose patient thought and active exertions have largely made us what we are. The amount of new knowledge which one age, certainly which one man, can add to the common store is small, and it argues stupidity or dishonesty, besides ingratitude, to ignore the heap while vaunting the few grains which it may have been our privilege to add to it. There is indeed little danger at present of undervaluing the contributions which modern times and even classical antiquity have made to the general advancement of our race. But when we pass these limits, the case is different. Contempt and ridicule or abhorrence and denunciation are too often the only recognition vouchsafed to the savage and his ways. Yet of the benefactors whom we are bound thankfully to commemorate, many, perhaps most, were savages. For when all is said and done our resemblances to the savage are still far more numerous than our differences from him; and what we have in common with him, and deliberately retain as true and useful, we owe to our savage forefathers who slowly acquired by experience and transmitted to us by inheritance those seemingly fundamental ideas which we are apt to regard as original and intuitive. We are like heirs to a fortune which has been handed down for so many ages that the memory of those who built it up is lost, and its possessors for the time being regard it as having been an original and unalterable possession of their race since the beginning of the world. But reflection and enquiry should satisfy us that to our predecessors we are indebted for much of what we thought most our own, and that their errors were not wilful extravagances or the ravings of insanity, but simply hypotheses, justifiable as such at the time when they were propounded, but which a fuller experience has proved to be inadequate. It is only by the successive testing of hypotheses and rejection of the false that truth is at last elicited. After all, what we call truth is only the hypothesis which is found to work best. Therefore in reviewing the opinions and practices of ruder ages and races we shall do well to look with leniency upon their errors as inevitable slips made in the search for truth, and to give them the benefit of that indulgence which we ourselves may one day stand in need of: *cum excusatione itaque veteres audiendi sunt.*

Part 3. The Dying God

Frazer explains more precisely the link between nature and the king by using the examples of kings who were in some way identified with gods and were therefore regarded as part of nature and its pivot.

Taboo and the Perils of the Soul *was concerned with the survival of kings in general; now we look at the king's death when, like the King of the Wood, he is seen as a man in the guise of a god. A feeble or old king will not be able to perform his proper functions of safeguarding the course of nature, because, on the principle of contagion, his feebleness will threaten nature's fertility. Therefore, he must give way to a successor who, by killing him, demonstrates his own better ability to perform the duties of kingship. In this same context, Frazer also deals with the principle of imitation: the King of the Wood is the human representative of the god of the oak, and his death at the hands of his successor reflects the order of nature, the death and revival of vegetation, and ensures its continuance:* le roi est mort, vive le roi.

The Holy Face of Christ, who died and rose again, on the kerchief of Veronica. Veronica was one of the women who walked with Christ on the Way of the Cross; she wiped his face with her handkerchief, and the divine countenance remained imprinted on the cloth. This story is a reminder to Christians both of the death of Christ, and of his resurrection and continuing saving power. Painting by El Greco, Museo Santa Cruz, Toledo. Photo: MAS

1. The Mortality of the Gods

At an early stage of his intellectual development man deems himself naturally immortal, and imagines that were it not for the baleful arts of sorcerers, who cut the vital thread prematurely short, he would live for ever. The illusion, so flattering to human wishes and hopes, is still current among many savage tribes at the present day, and it may be supposed to have prevailed universally in that Age of Magic which appears to have everywhere preceded the Age of Religion. But in time the sad truth of human mortality was borne in upon our primitive philosopher with a force of demonstration which no prejudice could resist and no sophistry dissemble. Among the manifold influences which combined to wring from him a reluctant assent to the necessity of death must be numbered the growing influence of religion, which by exposing the vanity of magic and of all the extravagant pretensions built on it gradually lowered man's proud and defiant attitude towards nature, and taught him to believe that there are mysteries in the universe which his feeble intellect can never fathom, and forces which his puny hands can never control. Thus more and more he learned to bow to the inevitable and to console himself for the brevity and the sorrows of life on earth by the hope of a blissful eternity hereafter. But if he reluctantly acknowledged the existence of beings at once superhuman and supernatural, he was as yet far from suspecting the width and the depth of the gulf which divided him from them. The gods with whom his imagination now peopled the darkness of the unknown were indeed admitted by him to be his superiors in knowledge and in power, in the joyous splendour of their life and in the length of its duration.

But, though he knew it not, these glorious and awful beings were merely, like the spectre of the Brocken, the reflections of his own diminutive personality exaggerated into gigantic proportions by distance and by the mists and clouds of ignorance upon which they were cast. Man in fact created gods in his own likeness and being himself mortal he naturally supposed his creatures to be in the same sad predicament. Thus the Greenlanders believed that a wind could kill their most powerful god, and that he would certainly die if he touched a dog. When they heard of the Christian God, they kept asking if he never died, and being informed that he did not, they were much surprised, and said that he must be a very great god indeed.

The great gods of Egypt themselves were not exempt from the common lot. They too grew old and died. For like men they were composed of body and soul, and like men were subject to all the passions and infirmities of the flesh. Their bodies, it is true, were fashioned of more ethereal mould, and lasted longer than ours, but they could not hold out for ever against the siege of time. Age converted their bones into silver, their flesh into gold, and their azure locks into lapis-lazuli. When their time came, they passed away from the cheerful world of the living to reign as dead gods over dead men in the melancholy world beyond the grave. Even their souls, like those of mankind, could only endure after death so long as their bodies held together; and hence it was as needful to preserve the corpses of the gods as the corpses of common folk, lest with the divine body the divine spirit should also come to an untimely end. The high gods of Babylon also, though they appeared to their worshippers only in dreams and visions, were conceived to be human in their bodily shape, human in their passions, and human in their fate; for like men they were born into the world, and like men they loved and fought and died.

One of the most famous stories of the death of a god is told by Plutarch. It runs thus. In the reign of the emperor Tiberius a certain schoolmaster named Epitherses was sailing from Greece to Italy. The ship in which he had taken his passage was a merchantman and there were many other passengers on board. At evening,

Man and the universe
The stars were once thought to predict the destinies of empires and the birth and death of kings; now they reveal scientific truths.
TOP. A comet presages the conquest of Mexico by the Spaniards. Michoacán Codex, 15th century, Escorial
ABOVE. Sirius, the star of the Egyptian goddess Isis, seen through a modern telescope, three exposures. Lick Observatory Photograph

when they were off the Echinadian Islands, the wind died away, and the vessel drifted close in to the island of Paxos. Most of the passengers were awake and many were still drinking wine after dinner, when suddenly a voice hailed the ship from the island, calling upon Thamus. The crew and passengers were taken by surprise, for though there was an Egyptian pilot named Thamus on board, few knew him even by name. Twice the cry was repeated, but Thamus kept silence. However, at the third call he answered, and the voice from the shore, now louder than ever, said, 'When you are come to Palodes, announce that the Great Pan is dead.' Astonishment fell upon all, and they consulted whether it would be better to do the bidding of the voice or not. At last Thamus resolved that, if the wind held, he would pass the place in silence, but if it dropped when they were off Palodes he would give the message. Well, when they were come to Palodes, there was a great calm; so Thamus standing in the stern and looking towards the land cried out, as he had been bidden, 'The Great Pan is dead.' The words had hardly passed his lips when a loud sound of lamentation broke on their ears, as if a multitude were mourning.

Stories of the same kind found currency in western Asia down to the Middle Ages. An Arab writer relates that in the year 1063 or 1064 AD, in the reign of the caliph Caiem, a rumour went abroad through Bagdad, which soon spread all over the province of Irac, that some Turks out hunting in the desert had seen a black tent, where many men and women were beating their faces and uttering loud cries, as it is the custom to do in the East when some one is dead. And among the cries they distinguished these words, 'The great King of the Jinn is dead, woe to this country!' In consequence of this a mysterious threat was circulated from Armenia to Chuzistan that every town which did not lament the dead King of the Jinn should utterly perish.

2. The Killing of the Divine King

Kings Killed when their Strength Fails

If the high gods, who dwell remote from the fret and fever of this earthly life, are yet believed to die at last, it is not to be expected that a god who lodges in a frail tabernacle of flesh should escape the same fate, though we hear of African kings who have imagined themselves immortal by virtue of their sorceries. Now primitive peoples, as we have seen, sometimes believe that their safety and even that of the world is bound up with the life of one of these god-men or human incarnations of the divinity. Naturally, therefore, they take the utmost care of his life, out of a regard for their own. But no amount of care and precaution will prevent the man-god from growing old and feeble and at last dying. His worshippers have to lay their account with this sad necessity and to meet it as best they can. The danger is a formidable one; for if the course of nature is dependent on the man-god's life, what catastrophes may not be expected from the gradual enfeeblement of his powers and their final extinction in death? There is only one way of averting these dangers. The man-god must be killed as soon as he shews symptoms that his powers are beginning to fail, and his soul must be transferred to a vigorous successor before it has been seriously impaired by the threatened decay. The advantages of thus putting the man-god to death instead of allowing him to die of old age and disease are, to the savage, obvious enough. For if the man-god dies what we call a natural death, it means, according to the savage, that his soul has either voluntarily departed from his body and refuses to return, or more commonly that it has been extracted, or at least detained in its wanderings, by a demon or sorcerer. In any of these cases the soul of the man-god is lost to his worshippers; and with it their prosperity is gone and their very existence endangered. Even if they could arrange to catch the soul of the dying god as it left his lips or his nostrils and so transfer it to a successor, this would not effect their purpose; for, dying of disease, his soul would necessarily leave his body in the last stage of weakness and exhaustion, and so enfeebled it would continue to drag out a languid, inert existence in any body to which it

Killing the king when his strength fails
The Greek king Oenomaus was defeated in a chariot race by his daughter's suitor Pelops. On this Roman sarcophagus, he falls from his chariot and dies, while his charioteer drives on. Vatican Museum, Rome. Photo: Alinari

might be transferred. Whereas by slaying him his worshippers could, in the first place, make sure of catching his soul as it escaped and transferring it to a suitable successor; and, in the second place, by putting him to death before his natural force was abated, they would secure that the world should not fall into decay with the decay of the man-god. Every purpose, therefore, was answered, and all dangers averted by thus killing the man-god and transferring his soul, while yet at its prime, to a vigorous successor.

The mystic kings of Fire and Water in Cambodia are not allowed to die a natural death. Hence when one of them is seriously ill and the elders think that he cannot recover, they stab him to death. The people of Congo believed, as we have seen, that if their pontiff the Chitomé were to die a natural death, the world would perish, and the earth, which he alone sustained by his power and merit, would immediately be annihilated. Accordingly when he fell ill and seemed likely to die, the man who was destined to be his successor entered the pontiff's house with a rope or a club and strangled or clubbed him to death. The Ethiopian kings of Meroe were worshipped as gods; but whenever the priests chose, they sent a messenger to the king, ordering him to die, and alleging an oracle of the gods as their authority for the command. This command the kings always obeyed down to the reign of Ergamenes, a contemporary of Ptolemy II, King of Egypt. Having received a Greek education which emancipated him from the superstitions of his countrymen, Ergamenes ventured to disregard the command of the priests, and, entering the Golden Temple with a body of soldiers, put the priests to the sword.

A custom of putting their divine kings to death at the first symptoms of infirmity or old age prevailed until lately, if indeed it is even now extinct and not merely dormant, among the Shilluk of the White Nile. The country of the Shilluk is almost entirely in grass, hence the

The king as incarnate deity
Each Shilluk king is the bearer of the spirit of the divine ancestor Nyakang. Ayang Anei Kur of the Shilluks at his investiture. Granada Television Limited, *Disappearing World*

principal wealth of the people consists in their flocks and herds, but they also grow a considerable quantity of the species of millet which is known as durra. But though the Shilluk are mainly a pastoral people, they are not nomadic, but live in many settled villages. The tribe at present numbers about forty thousand souls, and is governed by a single king (*ret*), whose residence is at Fashoda. His subjects take great care of him, and hold him in much honour.

The reverence which the Shilluk pay to their king appears to arise chiefly from the conviction that he is a reincarnation of the spirit of Nyakang, the semi-divine hero who founded the dynasty and settled the tribe in their present territory, to which he is variously said to have conducted them either from the west or from the south. Tradition has preserved the pedigree of the kings from Nyakang to the present day.

The Shilluk about Kodok (Fashoda) think of Nyakang as having been a man in appearance and physical qualities, though unlike his royal descendants of more recent times he did not die but simply disappeared. His holiness is manifested especially by his relation to Jŭok, the great god of the Shilluk, who created man and is responsible for the order of nature. Jŭok is formless and invisible and like the air he is everywhere at once. He is far above Nyakang and men alike, but he is not worshipped directly, and it is only through the intercession of Nyakang, whose favour the Shilluk secure by means of sacrifices, that Jŭok can be induced to send the needed rain for the cattle and the crops. In his character of rain-giver Nyakang is the great benefactor of the Shilluk. The religion of the Shilluk at the present time consists mainly of the worship paid to this semi-divine hero, the traditionary ancestor of their kings. There seems to be no reason to doubt that the traditions concerning him are substantially correct; in all probability he was simply a man whom the superstition of his fellows in his own and subsequent ages has raised to the rank of a deity. No less than ten shrines are dedicated to his worship; the three most famous are at Fashoda, Akurwa, and Fenikang. All the shrines of Nyakang are called graves of Nyakang (*kengo Nyakang*), though it is well known that nobody is buried there. Two great ceremonies are annually performed at the shrines of Nyakang: one of them is intended to ensure the fall of rain, the other is celebrated at harvest.

It is a fundamental article of the Shilluk creed that the spirit of the divine or semi-divine Nyakang is incarnate in the reigning king, who is accordingly himself invested to some extent with the character of a divinity. But while the Shilluk hold their kings in high, indeed religious reverence and take every precaution against their accidental death, nevertheless they cherish 'the conviction that the king must not be allowed to become ill or senile, lest with his diminishing vigour the cattle should sicken and fail to bear their increase, the crops should rot in the fields, and man, stricken with disease, should die in ever increasing numbers'. To prevent these calamities it used to be the regular custom with the Shilluk to put the king to death whenever he shewed signs of ill-health or failing strength. One of the fatal symptoms of decay was taken to be an incapacity to satisfy the sexual passions of his wives, of whom he has very many, distributed in a large number of houses at Fashoda.

The Shilluk king was liable to be killed with due ceremony at the first symptoms of incipient decay; moreover, even while he was yet in the prime of health and strength he might be attacked at any time by a rival and have to defend his crown in a combat to the death. According to the common Shilluk tradition any son of a king had the right thus to fight the king in possession and, if he succeeded in killing him, to reign in his stead. The combat would usually take place at night and in grim silence, broken only by the clash of spears and shields, for it was a point of honour with the king not to call the herdsmen to his assistance.

When the king did not perish in single combat, but was put to death on the approach of sickness or old age, it became necessary to find a successor for him. Apparently the successor was chosen by the most powerful chiefs from among the princes (*niǎret*), the sons either of the late king or of one of his predecessors. An important part of the solemnities attending the accession of a Shilluk king appears to be intended to convey to the new monarch the divine spirit of Nyakang, which has been transmitted from the founder of the dynasty to all his successors on the throne.

Like Nyakang himself, their founder, each of the Shilluk kings after death is worshipped at a shrine, which is erected over his grave, and the grave of a king is always in the village where he was born. The tomb-shrine of a king resembles the shrine of Nyakang, consisting of a few huts enclosed by a fence; one of the huts is built over the king's grave, the others are occupied by the guardians of the shrine. Indeed the shrines of Nyakang and the shrines of the kings are scarcely to be distinguished from each other, and the religious rituals observed at all of them are identical in form and vary only in matters of detail, the variations being due apparently to the far greater sanctity attributed to the shrines of Nyakang. The harvest ceremony which is performed at the shrines of Nyakang is usually, though not necessarily, performed also at the grave-shrines of the kings; and, lastly, sick folk send animals to be sacrificed as offerings on their behalf at the shrines of the kings just as they send them to the shrines of Nyakang.

In general the principal element in the religion of the Shilluk would seem to be the worship which they pay to their sacred or divine kings, whether dead or alive. These are believed to be animated by a single divine spirit, which has been transmitted from the semi-mythical, but probably in substance historical, founder of the dynasty through all his successors to the present day. Yet the divine spirit is clearly not thought of as congenital in the members of the royal house; it is only conveyed to each king on his accession by means of a mysterious object called Nyakang, in which the holy spirit of Nyakang may be supposed to reside. Hence, regarding their kings as incarnate divinities on whom the welfare of men, of cattle, and of the corn implicitly depends, the Shilluk naturally pay them the greatest respect and take every care of them; and however strange it may seem to us, their custom of putting the divine king to death as soon as he shews signs of ill-health or failing strength springs directly from their profound veneration for him and from their anxiety to preserve him, or rather the divine spirit by which he is animated, in the most perfect state of efficiency: nay, we may go further and say that their practice of regicide is the best proof they can give of the high regard in which they hold their kings.

On the whole the theory and practice of the divine kings of the Shilluk correspond very nearly to the theory and practice of the priests of Nemi, the Kings of the Wood, if my view of the latter is correct. In both we see a series of divine kings on whose life the fertility of men, of cattle, and of vegetation is believed to depend, and who are put to death, whether in single combat or otherwise, in order that their divine spirit may be transmitted to their successors in full vigour, uncontaminated by the weakness and decay of sickness or old age, because any such degeneration on the part of the king would, in the opinion of his worshippers, entail a corresponding degeneration on mankind, on cattle, and on the crops.

The Dinka are a congeries of independent tribes in the valley of the White Nile, whose territory, lying mostly on the eastern bank of the river and stretching from the sixth to the twelfth degree of North Latitude, has been estimated to comprise between sixty and seventy thousand square miles.

In spite, or rather in virtue, of the high honour in which he is held, no Dinka rain-maker is allowed to die a natural death of sickness or old age; for the Dinka believe that if such an untoward event were to happen, the tribe would suffer from disease and famine, and the herds would not yield their increase. So when a rain-maker feels that he is growing old and infirm, he tells his children that he wishes to die. Among the Agar Dinka a large grave is dug and the rain-maker lies down in it on his right side with his head resting on a skin. He is surrounded by his friends and relatives, including his younger children; but his elder children are not allowed to approach the grave lest in their grief and despair they should do themselves a bodily injury. For many hours, generally for more than a day, the rain-maker lies without eating or drinking. From time to time he speaks to the people, recalling the past history of the tribe, reminding them how he has ruled and advised them, and instructing them how they are to act in the future. Then, when he has concluded his admonition, he tells them that it is finished and bids them cover him up. So the earth is thrown down on him as he lies in the grave, and he soon dies of suffocation. As soon as a rain-maker is killed, his valuable spirit is supposed to pass to a suitable successor, whether a son or other near blood relation.

Kings Killed at the End of a Fixed Term

In the cases hitherto described, the divine king or priest is suffered by his people to retain office until some outward defect, some visible symptom of failing health or advancing age, warns them that he is no longer equal to the discharge of his divine duties; but not until such symptoms have made their appearance is he put to death. Some peoples, however, appear to have thought it unsafe to wait for even the slightest symptom of decay and have preferred to kill the king while he was still in the full vigour of life. Accordingly, they have fixed a term beyond which he might not reign, and at the close of which he must die, the term fixed upon being short enough to exclude the probability of his degenerating physically in the interval. In some parts of southern India the period fixed was twelve years. Thus, according to an old traveller in the province of Quilacare, about twenty leagues to the north-east of Cape Comorin, 'there is a Gentile house of prayer, in which there is an idol which they hold in great account, and every twelve years they celebrate a great feast to it, whither all the Gentiles go as to a jubilee. This temple possesses many lands and much revenue: it is a very great affair. This province has a king over it, who has not more than twelve years to reign from jubilee to jubilee. His

manner of living is in this wise, that is to say: when the twelve years are completed, on the day of this feast there assemble together innumerable people, and much money is spent in giving food to Bramans. The king has a wooden scaffolding made, spread over with silken hangings: and on that day he goes to bathe at a tank with great ceremonies and sound of music, after that he comes to the idol and prays to it, and mounts on to the scaffolding, and there before all the people he takes some very sharp knives, and begins to cut off his nose, and then his ears, and his lips, and all his members, and as much flesh off himself as he can; and he throws it away very hurriedly until so much of his blood is spilled that he begins to faint, and then he cuts his throat himself. And he performs this sacrifice to the idol, and whoever desires to reign over twelve years and undertake this martyrdom for love of the idol, has to be present looking on at this: and from that place they raise him up as king.'

When kings were bound to suffer death on the expiration of a fixed term of years, it was natural that they should seek to delegate the painful duty, along with some of the privileges of sovereignty, to a substitute who should suffer vicariously in their stead. The delegation of the duty of dying for his country was perhaps practised by the sultans of Java. At least such a custom would explain a strange scene which was witnessed at the court of one of these sultans by the famous traveller Ibn Batuta, a native of Tangier, who visited the East Indies in the first half of the fourteenth century. He says: 'During my audience with the Sultan I saw a man who held in his hand a knife like that used by a grape-gleaner. He placed it on his own neck and spoke for a long time in a language which I did not understand. After that he seized the knife with both hands at once and cut his throat. His head fell to the ground, so sharp was the blade and so great the force with which he used it. I remained dumbfounded at his behaviour,

Burning individuals for the good of their fellows
The peoples of the ancient Near East practised human
sacrifice by fire; the Old Testament story of the three
young men in the fiery furnace echoes this tradition, but
now with a message of personal salvation. Christian
sarcophagus, Vatican, Rome. Photo: PCAS, Rome

King Croesus of Lydia, burned for the good of his
subjects. A subsequent version of the story, modifying its
original meaning, relates that Croesus was to be burned
by his conqueror Cyrus. Greek amphora, Louvre, Paris.
Photo: Musées Nationaux

but the Sultan said to me, "Does any one do
like that in your country?" I answered, "Never
did I see such a thing." He smiled and replied,
"These people are our slaves, and they kill
themselves for love of us." Then he commanded
that they should take away him who had slain
himself and should burn him. The Sultan's
officers, the grandees, the troops, and the
common people attended the cremation. The
sovereign assigned a liberal pension to the
children of the deceased, to his wife, and to
his brothers; and they were highly honoured because of his conduct. A person, who was present
at the audience when the event I have described
took place, informed me that the speech made
by the man who sacrificed himself set forth his
devotion to the monarch. He said that he wished

to immolate himself out of affection for the
sovereign, as his father had done for love of the
prince's father, and as his grandfather had done
out of regard for the prince's grandfather.' We
may conjecture that formerly the sultans of Java,
like the kings of Quilacare, were bound to cut
their own throats at the end of a fixed term of
years, but that at a later time they deputed the
painful, though glorious, duty of dying for their
country to the members of a certain family, who
received by way of recompense ample provi-
sion during their life and a handsome funeral at
death.

There are some grounds for believing that the
reign of many ancient Greek kings was limited
to eight years, or at least that at the end of every
period of eight years a new consecration, a fresh

outpouring of the divine grace, was regarded as necessary in order to enable them to discharge their civil and religious duties. Thus it was a rule of the Spartan constitution that every eighth year the ephors should choose a clear and moonless night and sitting down observe the sky in silence. If during their vigil they saw a meteor or shooting star, they inferred that the king had sinned against the deity, and they suspended him from his functions until the Delphic or Olympic oracle should reinstate him in them. This custom, which has all the air of great antiquity, was not suffered to remain a dead letter even in the last period of the Spartan monarchy; for in the third century before our era a king, who had rendered himself obnoxious to the reforming party, was actually deposed on various trumped-up charges, among which the allegation that the ominous sign had been seen in the sky took a prominent place. This was the attenuated survival of an institution which may once have had great significance, and it throws an important light on the restrictions and limitations anciently imposed by religion on the Dorian kingship. What exactly was the import of a meteor in the opinion of the old Dorians we can hardly hope to determine; one thing only is clear, they regarded it as a portent of so ominous and threatening a kind that its appearance under certain circumstances justified and even required the deposition of their king. This exaggerated dread of so simple a natural phenomenon is shared by many savages at the present day; and we shall hardly err in supposing that the Spartans inherited it from their barbarous ancestors, who may have watched with consternation, on many a starry night among the woods of Germany, the flashing of a meteor through the sky.

At Babylon, within historical times, the tenure of the kingly office was in practice lifelong, yet in theory it would seem to have been merely annual. For every year at the festival of Zagmuk the king had to renew his power by seizing the

Royal succession
The dead king's spirit passes to his successor, through kinship or through the royal insignia.
ABOVE. A magician points to the son of the Benin king. Benin bronze plaque, late 16th century, British Museum, London

hands of the image of Marduk in his great temple of Esagil at Babylon. Even when Babylon passed under the power of Assyria, the monarchs of that country were expected to legalise their claim to the throne every year by coming to Babylon and performing the ancient ceremony at the New Year festival, and some of them found the obligation so burdensome that rather than discharge it they renounced the title of king altogether and contented themselves with the humbler one of governor. Further, it would appear that in remote times, though not within the historical period, the kings of Babylon or their barbarous predecessors forfeited not merely their crown but their life at the end of a year's tenure of office. At least this is the conclusion to which the following evidence seems to point. According to the historian Berosus, who as a Babylonian priest spoke with ample

Gold pectoral disk worn by the Ashanti kings, 19th century, British Museum, London

The Crown of England, copied in the time of Charles II from the ancient crown worn by Edward the Confessor, and used at the coronation of every monarch since.
Photo: John Topham Picture Library

knowledge, there was annually celebrated in Babylon a festival called the Sacaea. It began on the sixteenth day of the month Lous, and lasted for five days. During these five days masters and servants changed places, the servants giving orders and the masters obeying them. A prisoner condemned to death was dressed in the king's robes, seated on the king's throne, allowed to issue whatever commands he pleased, to eat, drink, and enjoy himself, and to lie with the king's concubines. But at the end of the five days he was stripped of his royal robes, scourged, and hanged or impaled. During his brief term of office he bore the title of Zoganes.

If at Babylon before the dawn of history the king himself used to be slain at the festival of the Sacaea, it is natural to suppose that the Sacaea was no other than Zagmuk or Zakmuk, the great New Year festival at which down to his-

torical times the king's power had to be formally renewed by a religious ceremony in the temple of Marduk. A reminiscence of Zagmuk seems to linger in the belief of the Yezidis that on New Year's day God sits on his throne arranging the decrees for the coming year, assigning to dignitaries their various offices, and delivering to them their credentials under his signature and seal.

The view that at Babylon the condemned prisoner who wore the royal robes was slain as a substitute for the king may be supported by the practice of West Africa, where at the funeral of a king slaves used sometimes to be dressed up as ministers of state and then sacrificed in that character instead of the real ministers, their masters, who purchased for a sum of money the privilege of thus dying by proxy. Such vicarious sacrifices were witnessed by Catholic mission-

aries at Porto Novo on the Slave Coast. The
Banyoro or Bakitara of Uganda used to practise
a remarkable custom which seems to indicate
that down to recent times they practised a similar custom of limiting to a single year the tenure
of the king's office and life. The custom is thus
described by Canon Roscoe. 'At or about the
time of year when the king had been buried, the
reigning king told *Bamuroga* to prepare a feast
for the departed king. *Bamuroga* chose a poor
man of the Babito clan to impersonate the dead
king, and the man so chosen lived in regal state
in the king's tomb and was called by the name of
the monarch he represented, for he was said to be
the old king revived. He lived in the tomb, was
feasted and honoured, and had full use of the
women of the tomb, the widows of the old king.
The king sent him presents and he sent his blessing to the king, the country, and the cattle. He
distributed gifts of cows belonging to the king as
he pleased, and for eight days lived like a king.
When the ninth day came he was taken away to
the back of the tomb and strangled, and no one
heard anything more about him. This was an
annual ceremony.' It seems probable that this
mock king who held office for eight days every
year was a substitute for the king himself, who
thus died every year in the person of his deputy.
In earlier times the king may have had no choice
but to die every year in his own person, at the
end of a brief reign of a single year.

'The worshipful animals'
The association between men and animals may have
developed out of the belief in the transmigration of souls.
In many cultures, the souls of dead kings in particular are
thought to migrate into animals, and sometimes living
kings may be embodied in them. A trace of this idea
survives in European heraldry.
TOP. The Emperor Henry VI of Germany, with eagle
blazon. Manessische Liederhandschrift, 14th century,
Cod. Pal. Germ. 848 fol. 6R, Universitätsbibliothek,
Heidelberg
RIGHT. The British lion and unicorn on the gates of
Buckingham Palace. Photo: Derrick Witty

3. Alternatives to Killing the King

Temporary Kings

In some places the modified form of the old custom of regicide which appears to have prevailed at Babylon has been further softened down. The king still abdicates annually for a short time and his place is filled by a more or less nominal sovereign; but at the close of his short reign the latter is no longer killed, though sometimes a mock execution still survives as a memorial of the time when he was actually put to death. In the month of Méac (February) the king of Cambodia annually abdicated for three days. During this time he performed no act of authority, he did not touch the seals, he did not even receive the revenues which fell due. In his stead there reigned a temporary king called Sdach Méac, that is, King February. The office of temporary king was hereditary in a family distantly connected with the royal house, the sons succeeding the fathers and the younger brothers the elder brothers, just as in the succession to the real sovereignty. On a favourable day fixed by the astrologers the temporary king was conducted by the mandarins in triumphal procession. He rode one of the royal elephants, seated in the royal palanquin, and escorted by soldiers who, dressed in appropriate costumes, represented the neighbouring peoples of Siam, Annam, Laos, and so on. In place of the golden crown he wore a peaked white cap, and his regalia, instead of being of gold encrusted with diamonds, were of rough wood. After paying homage to the real king, from whom he received the sovereignty for three days, together with all the revenues accruing during that time (though this last custom has been omitted for some time), he moved in procession round the palace and through the streets of the capital. On the third day, after the usual procession, the temporary king gave orders that the elephants should trample under foot the 'mountain of rice', which was a scaffold of bamboo surrounded by sheaves of rice. The people gathered up the rice, each man taking home a little with him to secure a good harvest. Some of it was also taken to the king, who had it cooked and presented to the monks.

In Siam on the sixth day of the moon in the sixth month (the end of April) a temporary king is appointed, who for three days enjoys the royal prerogatives, the real king remaining shut up in his palace. This temporary king sends his numerous satellites in all directions to seize and confiscate whatever they can find in the bazaar and open shops; even the ships and junks which arrive in harbour during the three days are forfeited to him and must be redeemed. He goes to a field in the middle of the city, whither they bring a gilded plough drawn by gaily-decked oxen. After the plough has been anointed and the oxen rubbed with incense, the mock king traces nine furrows with the plough, followed by aged dames of the palace scattering the first seed of the season. As soon as the nine furrows are drawn, the crowd of spectators rushes in and scrambles for the seed which has just been sown, believing that, mixed with the seed-rice, it will ensure a plentiful crop. Then the oxen are unyoked, and rice, maize, sesame, sago, bananas, sugar-cane, melons, and so on, are set before them; whatever they eat first will, it is thought, be dear in the year following, though some people interpret the omen in the opposite sense. During this time the temporary king stands leaning against a tree with his right foot resting on his left knee. From standing thus on one foot he is popularly known as King Hop; but his official title is Phaya Phollathep, 'Lord of the Heavenly Hosts'. He is a sort of Minister of Agriculture; all disputes about fields, rice, and so forth, are referred to him. There is moreover another ceremony in which he personates the king. It takes place in the second month (which falls in the cold season) and lasts three days. He is conducted in procession to an open place opposite the Temple of the Brahmans, where there are a number of poles dressed like May-poles, upon which the Brahmans swing. All the while that they swing and dance, the Lord of the Heavenly Hosts has to stand on one foot upon a seat which is made of bricks plastered over, covered with a white cloth, and hung with tapestry. He is supported by a wooden frame with a gilt canopy, and two Brahmans stand one on each side of him. The dancing Brahmans carry buffalo horns with which they draw water from a large copper caldron and sprinkle it on the spectators; this is supposed to bring good luck, causing the people to dwell in peace and quiet, health and prosperity. The time during which the Lord of the Heavenly Hosts has to stand on one foot is about three hours. This is thought 'to prove the dispositions of the Devattas and spirits'. If he lets his foot down 'he is liable to forfeit his property and have his family enslaved by the king; as it is believed to be a bad omen, portending destruction to the state, and instability to the throne. But if he stands firm he is believed to have gained a victory over evil spirits, and he has moreover the privilege, ostensibly at least, of seizing any ship which may enter the harbour during these three days, and taking its contents, and also of entering any open shop in the town and carrying away what he chooses.' Such were the duties and privileges of the Siamese King Hop down to about the middle of the nineteenth century or later.

Some points about these temporary kings deserve to be specially noticed before we pass to the next branch of the evidence. In the first place, the examples shew clearly that it is especially the divine or magical functions of the king which are transferred to his temporary substitute. This appears from the belief that by keeping up his foot the temporary king of Siam gained a victory over the evil spirits, whereas by letting it down he imperilled the existence of the state. Again, the Cambodian ceremony of trampling down the 'mountain of rice', and the Siamese ceremony of opening the ploughing and sowing, are charms to produce a plentiful harvest, as appears from the belief that those who carry home some of the trampled rice, or of the seed sown, will thereby secure a good crop. Moreover, when the Siamese representative of the king is guiding the plough, the people watch him anxiously, not to see whether he drives a straight furrow, but to mark the exact point on his leg to which the skirt of his silken robe reaches; for on that is supposed to hang the state of the weather and the crops during the ensuing season. If the Lord of the Heavenly Hosts hitches up his garment above his knee, the weather will be wet and heavy rains will spoil the harvest. If he lets it trail to his ankle, a drought will be the consequence. But fine weather and heavy crops will follow if the hem of his robe hangs exactly half-way down the calf of his leg. So closely is the course of nature, and with it the weal or woe of the people, dependent on the minutest act or gesture of the king's representative. But the task of making the crops grow, thus deputed to the temporary kings, is one of the magical functions regularly supposed to be discharged by kings in primitive society. The rule that the mock king must stand on one foot upon a raised seat in the rice-field was perhaps originally meant as a charm to make the crop grow high.

We have seen how the temporary king is appointed annually in accordance with a regular custom. But in other cases the appointment is made only to meet a special emergency, such as to relieve the real king from some actual or threatened evil by diverting it to a substitute, who takes his place on the throne for a short time. The history of Persia furnishes instances of such occasional substitutes for the Shah. One instance concerns Shah Abbas the Great, the most eminent of all the kings of Persia, who reigned from 1586 to 1628 AD; he was warned by his astrologers in the year 1591 that a serious danger impended over him, and attempted to avert the omen by abdicating the throne and appointing a certain unbeliever named Yusoofee, probably a Christian, to reign in his stead. The substitute was accordingly crowned, and for three days, if we may trust the Persian historians, he enjoyed not only the name and the state but the power of the king. At the end of his brief reign he was put to death: the decree of the stars was fulfilled by this sacrifice; and Abbas, who reascended his throne in a most propitious hour, was promised by his astrologers a long and glorious reign.

Sacrifice of the King's Son

A point to notice about the temporary kings described above is that in Cambodia they come of a stock which is believed to be akin to the royal family. If the view here taken of the origin of these temporary kingships is correct, we can easily understand why the king's substitute should sometimes be of the same race as the king. When the king first succeeded in getting the life of another accepted as a sacrifice instead of his own, he would have to shew that the death of that other would serve the purpose quite as well as his own would have done. Now it was as a god or demigod that the king had to die; therefore the substitute who died for him had to be invested, at least for the occasion, with the divine attributes of the king. This, as we have just seen, was certainly the case with the temporary kings

of Siam and Cambodia; they were invested with the supernatural functions, which in an earlier stage of society were the special attributes of the king. But no one could so well represent the king in his divine character as his son, who might be supposed to share the divine afflatus of his father. No one, therefore, could so appropriately die for the king and, through him, for the whole people, as the king's son.

According to tradition, Aun or On, King of Sweden, sacrificed nine of his sons to Odin at Upsala in order that his own life might be spared. After he had sacrificed his second son he received from the god an answer that he should live so long as he gave him one of his sons every ninth year. When he had sacrificed his seventh son, he still lived, but was so feeble that he could not walk but had to be carried in a chair. Then he offered up his eighth son, and lived nine years more, lying in his bed. After that he sacrificed his ninth son, and lived another nine years, but so that he drank out of a horn like a weaned child. He now wished to sacrifice his only remaining son to Odin, but the Swedes would not allow him. So he died and was buried in a mound at Upsala.

A similar custom obtained among some Chagga chiefs on Mount Kilimanjaro in East Africa. About them we are told that 'it is said that formerly when a chief was seriously ill he would first sacrifice animals in great numbers to his own ancestors, then to the ancestors of those chiefs who had been vanquished and killed, and finally to the ancestors of all those whom he had killed in war. The great Chief Rongoma even sacrificed his own first-born son to Ruwa, and the same is told of other chiefs in olden days.'

Among the Semites of Western Asia the king, in a time of national danger, sometimes gave his own son to die as a sacrifice for the people. Thus Philo of Byblus, in his work on the Jews, says: 'It was an ancient custom in a crisis of great danger that the ruler of a city or nation should give his beloved son to die for the whole people, as a ransom offered to the avenging demons; and the children thus offered were slain with mystic rites. So Cronus, whom the Phoenicians call Israel, being king of the land and having an only-begotten son called Jeoud (for in the Phoenician tongue Jeoud signifies "only-begotten"), dressed him in royal robes and sacrificed him upon an altar in a time of war, when the country was in great danger from the enemy.' When the king of Moab was besieged by the Israelites and hard beset, he took his eldest son, who should have reigned in his stead, and offered him for a burnt offering on the wall.

But amongst the Semites the practice of sacrificing their children was not confined to kings. In times of great calamity, such as pestilence, drought, or defeat in war, the Phoenicians used to sacrifice one of their dearest to Baal. 'Phoenician history', says an ancient writer, 'is full of such sacrifices.' Infants were publicly sacrificed by the Carthaginians down to the proconsulate of Tiberius, who crucified the priests on the trees beside their temples. Yet the practice still went on secretly in the lifetime of Tertullian.

Among the Canaanites or aboriginal inhabitants of Palestine, whom the invading Israelites conquered but did not exterminate, the grisly custom of burning their children in honour of Baal or Moloch seems to have been regularly practised. When the Hebrew annalist has recorded how Shalmaneser, king of Assyria, besieged Samaria for three years and took it and carried Israel away into captivity, he explains that this was a divine punishment inflicted on his people for having fallen in with the evil ways of the Canaanites. They had built high places in all their cities, and set up pillars and sacred poles (*asherim*) upon every high hill and under every green tree; and there they burnt incense after the manner of the heathen. 'And they forsook all the commandments of the Lord their God, and made them molten images, even two calves, and

Sacrificing the king's firstborn son
New light was shed on the Old Testament stories by early ethnographers, who witnessed similar practices in other parts of the world.
ABOVE. Abraham is prevented by the angel of the Lord from sacrificing Isaac, his firstborn son. Facsimile of Guaman Poma de Ayala, *Nueva Corónica* (c. 1615), Institut d'Ethnologie, Paris

made an Asherah, and worshipped all the host of heaven, and served Baal. And they caused their sons and their daughters to pass through the fire, and used divination and enchantments.'

We may thus safely infer that a custom of allowing a king to kill his son, as a substitute or

Sacrifice of the king's first male child in Florida,
witnessed by European travellers. De Bry, *America*, 1599,
Bodleian Library, Oxford

vicarious sacrifice for himself, would be in no
way exceptional or surprising, at least in Semitic
lands, where indeed religion seems at one time to
have recommended or enjoined every man, as a
duty that he owed to his god, to take the life of
his eldest son. And it would be entirely in accordance with analogy if, long after the barbarous
custom had been dropped by others, it continued to be observed by kings, who remain in
many respects the representatives of a vanished
world, solitary pinnacles that topple the rising
waste of waters under which the past lies buried.

4. The Killing of the Tree-Spirit

The Whitsuntide Mummers

It remains to ask what light the custom of killing the divine king or priest sheds upon the special subject of our enquiry. In the first part of this work we saw reason to suppose that the King of the Wood at Nemi was regarded as an incarnation of a tree-spirit or of the spirit of vegetation, and that as such he would be endowed, in the belief of his worshippers, with a magical power of making the trees to bear fruit, the crops to grow, and so on. His life must therefore have been held very precious by his worshippers, and was probably hedged in by a system of elaborate precautions or taboos like those by which, in so many places, the life of the man-god has been guarded against the malignant influence of demons and sorcerers. But we have seen that the very value attached to the life of the man-god necessitates his violent death as the only means of preserving it from the inevitable decay of age. The same reasoning would apply to the King of the Wood; he, too, had to be killed in order that the divine spirit, incarnate in him, might be transferred in its integrity to his successor. The rule that he held office till a stronger should slay him might be supposed to secure both the preservation of his divine life in full vigour and its transference to a suitable successor as soon as that vigour began to be impaired. For so long as he could maintain his position by the strong hand, it might be inferred that his natural force was not abated; whereas his defeat and death at the hands of another proved that his strength was beginning to fail and that it was time his divine life should be lodged in a less dilapidated tabernacle. This explanation of the rule that the King of the Wood had to be slain by

his successor at least renders that rule perfectly intelligible. It is strongly supported by the theory and practice of the Shilluk, who put their divine king to death at the first signs of failing health, lest his decrepitude should entail a corresponding failure of vital energy on the corn, the cattle, and men. Moreover, it is countenanced by the analogy of the Chitomé, upon whose life the existence of the world was supposed to hang, and who was therefore slain by his successor as soon as he shewed signs of breaking up.

We may conjecture that the King of the Wood was formerly put to death at the expiry of a fixed term, without being allowed a chance for his life; this will be confirmed if evidence can be adduced of a custom of periodically killing his counterparts, the human representatives of the tree-spirit, in Northern Europe. Now in point of fact such a custom has left unmistakable traces of itself in the rural festivals of the peasantry. The most instructive of the numerous mimic executions of the tree-spirit which could be cited is the following Bohemian one. In some places of the Pilsen district (Bohemia) on Whit-Monday the King is dressed in bark, ornamented with flowers and ribbons; he wears a crown of gilt paper and rides a horse, which is also decked with flowers. Attended by a judge, an executioner, and other characters, and followed by a train of soldiers, all mounted, he rides to the village square, where a hut or arbour of green boughs has been erected under the May-trees, which are firs, freshly cut, peeled to the top, and dressed with flowers and ribbons. After the dames and maidens of the village have been criticised and a frog beheaded, the cavalcade rides to a place previously determined upon, in a straight, broad street. Here they draw up in two lines and the King takes to flight. He is given a short start and rides off at full speed, pursued by the whole troop. If they fail to catch him he remains King for another year, and his companions must pay his score at the ale-house in the evening. But if they overtake and catch him he is scourged with hazel rods or beaten with the wooden swords and compelled to dismount. Then the executioner asks, 'Shall I behead this King?' The answer is given, 'Behead him'; the executioner brandishes his axe, and with the words, 'One, two, three, let the King headless be!' he strikes off the King's crown. Amid the loud cries of the bystanders the King sinks to the ground; then he is laid on a bier and carried to the nearest farmhouse.

It is impossible not to recognise representatives of the tree-spirit or spirit of vegetation, as he is supposed to manifest himself in spring, in personages who, like the Bohemian May-king, are slain in mimicry. The bark, leaves, and flowers in which the actors are dressed, and the season of the year at which they appear, shew that they belong to the same class as the representatives of the vernal spirit of vegetation which we examined in the first part of this work. But if these personages represent, as they certainly do, the spirit of vegetation in spring, the question arises, Why kill them? What is the object of slaying the spirit of vegetation at any time and above all in spring, when his services are most wanted? The only probable answer to this question seems to be given in the explanation already proposed of the custom of killing the divine king or priest. The divine life, incarnate in a material and mortal body, is liable to be tainted and corrupted by the weakness of the frail medium in which it is for a time enshrined; and if it is to be saved from the increasing enfeeblement which it must necessarily share with its human incarnation as he advances in years, it must be detached from him before, or at least as soon as, he exhibits signs of decay, in order to be

transferred to a vigorous successor. This is done by killing the old representative of the god and conveying the divine spirit from him to a new incarnation. The killing of the god, that is, of his human incarnation, is therefore merely a necessary step to his revival or resurrection in a better form. Thus the killing of the representative of the tree-spirit in spring is regarded as a means to promote and quicken the growth of vegetation.

The points of similarity between North European personages of this type and the subject of our enquiry – the King of the Wood or priest of Nemi – are sufficiently striking. In these northern maskers we see kings, whose dress of bark and leaves, along with the hut of green boughs and the fir-trees under which they hold their court, proclaim them unmistakably as, like their Italian counterpart, Kings of the Wood. Like him they die a violent death, but like him they may escape from it for a time by their bodily strength and agility. The life of the god-man is prolonged on condition of his shewing, in a severe physical contest of fight or flight, that his bodily strength is not decayed, and that, therefore, the violent death, which sooner or later is inevitable, may for the present be postponed. One more point of resemblance may be noted between the Italian King of the Wood and his northern counterparts. In Saxony and Thüringen the representative of the tree-spirit, after being killed, is brought to life again by a doctor. This is exactly what legend affirmed to have happened to the first King of the Wood at Nemi, Hippolytus or Virbius, who after he had been killed by his horses was restored to life by the physician Aesculapius. Such a legend tallies well with the theory that the slaying of the King of the Wood was only a step to his revival or resurrection in his successor.

Mock Human Sacrifices

In the preceding discussion it has been assumed that the mock killing of the King in North

European folk-custom is a modern substitute for an ancient custom of killing him in earnest. Those who best know the tenacity of life possessed by folk-custom and its tendency, with the growth of civilisation, to dwindle from solemn ritual into mere pageant and pastime, will be least likely to question the truth of this assumption. That human sacrifices were commonly offered by the ancestors of the civilised races of North Europe, Celts, Teutons, and Slavs, is certain. It is not, therefore, surprising that the modern peasant should do in mimicry what his forefathers did in reality. We know as a matter of fact that in other parts of the world mock human sacrifices have been substituted for real ones. Thus in Minahassa, a district of Celebes, human victims used to be regularly sacrificed at certain festivals, but through Dutch influence the custom was abolished and a sham sacrifice substituted for it. Captain Bourke was informed by an old chief that the Indians of Arizona used to offer human sacrifices at the Feast of Fire when the days are shortest. The victim had his throat cut, his breast opened, and his heart taken out by one of the priests. This custom was abolished by the Mexicans, but for a long time afterwards a modified form of it was secretly observed as follows. The victim, generally a young man, had his throat cut, and blood was allowed to flow freely; but the medicine-men sprinkled 'medicine' on the gash, which soon healed up, and the man recovered. So in the ritual of Artemis at Halae in Attica, a man's throat was cut and the blood allowed to gush out, but he was not killed.

Sometimes the pretended sacrifice is carried out, not on a living person, but on an effigy. At the City of the Sun in ancient Egypt three men used to be sacrificed every day, after the priests had stripped and examined them, like calves, to see whether they were without blemish and fit for the altar. But King Amasis ordered waxen images to be substituted for the human victims.

An Indian law-book, the *Calica Puran*, prescribes that when the sacrifice of lions, tigers, or human beings is required, an image of a lion, tiger, or man shall be made with butter, paste, or barley meal, and sacrificed instead. Some of the Gonds of India formerly offered human sacrifices; they now sacrifice straw-men, which are found to answer the purpose just as well.

Burying the Carnival, Carrying out Death and Bringing in Summer

Thus far I have offered an explanation of the rule which required that the priest of Nemi should be slain by his successor. The explanation claims to be no more than probable; our scanty knowledge of the custom and of its history forbids it to be more. At the same time, it is nonetheless possible to clear up some obscurities which still remain, and to answer some objections which may have suggested themselves to the reader.

We start from the point at which we left off – the spring customs of European peasantry. Besides the ceremonies already described there are two kindred sets of observances in which the simulated death of a divine or supernatural being is a conspicuous feature. In one of them the being whose death is dramatically represented is a personification of the Carnival; in the other it is Death himself. The former ceremony falls naturally at the end of the Carnival, either on the last day of that merry season, namely Shrove Tuesday, or on the first day of Lent, namely Ash Wednesday.

At Lerida, in Catalonia, the funeral of the Carnival was witnessed by an English traveller in 1877. On the last Sunday of the Carnival a grand procession of infantry, cavalry, and maskers of many sorts, some on horseback and some in carriages, escorted the grand car of His Grace Pau Pi, as the effigy was called, in triumph through the principal streets. For three days the revelry ran high, and then at midnight on the last day of the Carnival the same procession

Swinging to purify the air and make the crops grow high
Santal men swinging in pairs for the good of the crops at the Pata festival. Photo: W.G. Archer

Swinging is also a central motif of the exemplary love between the Hindu god Krishna, and his human beloved Radha. Jaipur painting, mid-17th century (detail). Courtesy Museum of Fine Arts, Boston

again wound through the streets, but under a different aspect and for a different end. The triumphal car was exchanged for a hearse, in which reposed the effigy of his dead Grace: a troop of maskers, who in the first procession had played the part of Students of Folly with many a merry quip and jest, now, robed as priests and bishops, paced slowly along holding aloft huge lighted tapers and singing a dirge. On reaching the principal square the procession halted, a burlesque funeral oration was pronounced over the defunct Pau Pi, and the lights were extinguished. Immediately the devil and his angels darted from the crowd, seized the body and fled away with it, hotly pursued by the whole multitude, yelling, screaming, and cheering. Naturally the fiends were overtaken and dispersed; and the sham corpse, rescued from their clutches, was laid in a grave that had been made ready for its reception. Thus the Carnival of 1877 at Lerida died and was buried.

In some German villages of Moravia, as in Jassnitz and Seitendorf, the young folk assemble on the third Sunday in Lent and fashion a strawman, who is generally adorned with a fur cap and a pair of old leathern hose, if such are to be had. The effigy is then hoisted on a pole and carried by the lads and lasses out into the open fields. On the way they sing a song, in which it is said that they are carrying Death away and bringing dear Summer into the house, and with Summer the May and the flowers. On reaching an appointed place they dance in a circle round the effigy with loud shouts and screams, then suddenly rush at it and tear it to pieces with their hands. Lastly, the pieces are thrown together in a heap, the pole is broken, and fire is set to the whole. While it burns the troop dances merrily round it, rejoicing at the victory won by Spring; and when the fire has nearly died out they go to the householders to beg for a present of eggs wherewith to hold a feast, taking care to give as a reason for the request that they have carried Death out and away.

So far, the return of Spring, Summer, or Life, as a sequel to the expulsion of Death, is only implied or at most announced. In other ceremonies it is plainly enacted. Thus in some parts of Bohemia the effigy of Death is drowned by being thrown into the water at sunset; then the girls go out into the wood and cut down a young tree with a green crown, hang a doll dressed as a woman on it, deck the whole with green, red, and white ribbons, and march in procession with their *Líto* (Summer) into the village, collecting gifts and singing:

Death swims in the water,
Spring comes to visit us,
With eggs that are red,
With yellow pancakes.
We carried Death out of the village,
We are carrying Summer into the village.

In ceremonies of this type, Death is represented by the puppet which is thrown away, Summer or Life by the branches of trees which are brought back. But sometimes a new potency of life seems to be attributed to the image of Death itself, and by a kind of resurrection it becomes the instrument of the general revival. Thus in some parts of Lusatia women alone are concerned in carrying out Death, and suffer no male to meddle with it. Attired in mourning, which they wear the whole day, they make a puppet of straw, clothe it in a white shirt, and give it a broom in one hand and a scythe in the other. Singing songs and pursued by urchins throwing stones, they carry the puppet to the village boundary, where they tear it in pieces. Then they cut down a fine tree, hang the shirt on it, and carry it home singing.

Here we see that the Death whose demolition is represented in these ceremonies cannot be regarded as the purely destructive agent which we understand by Death. If the tree which is brought back as an embodiment of the reviving vegetation of spring is clothed in the shirt worn by the Death which has just been destroyed, the object certainly cannot be to check and counteract the revival of vegetation: it can only be to foster and promote it. Therefore the being which has just been destroyed – the so-called Death – must be supposed to be endowed with a vivifying and quickening influence, which it can communicate to the vegetable and even the animal world. This ascription of a life-giving virtue to the figure of Death is put beyond a doubt by the custom, observed in some places, of taking pieces of the straw effigy of Death and placing them in the fields to make the crops grow, or in the manger to make the cattle thrive.

We may fairly conjecture that the names Carnival, Death, and Summer are comparatively late and inadequate expressions for the beings personified or embodied in the customs with which we have been dealing. The very abstractness of the names bespeaks a modern origin; for the personification of times and seasons like the Carnival and Summer, or of an abstract notion like death, is hardly primitive. But the ceremonies themselves bear the stamp of a dateless antiquity; therefore we can hardly help supposing that in their origin the ideas which they embodied were of a more simple and concrete order. The notion of a tree, perhaps of a particular kind of tree (for some savages have no word for tree in general), or even of an individual tree, is sufficiently concrete to supply a basis from which by a gradual process of generalisation the wider idea of a spirit of vegetation might be reached. Again, the concrete notion of the dying tree or dying vegetation would by a similar process of generalisation glide into a notion of death in general; so that the practice of carrying out the dying or dead vegetation in spring, as a preliminary to its revival, would in time widen out into an attempt to banish Death in general from the village or district.

Part 4. Adonis

In The Dying God *Frazer dealt with the mortality of human kings, who, like the King of the Wood, impersonated a god – in his case Jupiter, god of the oak. He now examines the death of the gods themselves, who, thanks to their role as deities of vegetation, can also be exposed to this most human of all hazards. The story is told through the myth and cult of Adonis, a god of the ancient Mediterranean, whose annual death and resurrection was particularly associated with the death of nature in autumn and its revival in spring. The connection between Adonis and the King of the Wood is that both had to die to preserve the reproductive power of nature. But a further link is that, although themselves mortal, both were the partners of immortal goddesses. This partnership is fundamental because by imitation, the intercourse of the sexes ensures the fertility of nature. And the goddess who mourns the death of her lover and rejoices at his birth in spring mirrors the order of the seasons.*

Cybele, the mother of the gods, rides in a cart drawn by lions with her beloved Attis, whose death was annually mourned by the devotees of the divine pair. Cybele and Attis are shown surrounded by personifications of nature and the universe: the sun and moon in chariots; the zodiac and time (a serpent around an obelisk); the four seasons as children; the earth; the ocean and his consort; and spirits of vegetation. Roman silver platter from Parabiago, Pinacoteca di Brera, Milan. Photo: Hirmer Fotoarchiv

1. The Myth of Adonis

The spectacle of the great changes which annually pass over the face of the earth has powerfully impressed the minds of men in all ages, and stirred them to meditate on the causes of transformations so vast and wonderful. Their curiosity has not been purely disinterested; for even the savage cannot fail to perceive how intimately his own life is bound up with the life of nature, and how the same processes which freeze the stream and strip the earth of vegetation menace him with extinction. At a certain stage of development men seem to have imagined that the means of averting the threatened calamity were in their own hands, and that they could hasten or retard the flight of the seasons by magic art. Accordingly they performed ceremonies and recited spells to make the rain to fall, the sun to shine, animals to multiply, and the fruits of the earth to grow. In course of time the slow advance of knowledge, which has dispelled so many cherished illusions, convinced at least the more thoughtful portion of mankind that the alternations of summer and winter, of spring and autumn, were not merely the result of their own magical rites, but that some deeper cause, some mightier power, was at work behind the shifting scenes of nature. They now pictured to themselves the growth and decay of vegetation, the birth and death of living creatures, as effects of the waxing or waning strength of divine beings, of gods and goddesses, who were born and died, who married and begot children, on the pattern of human life.

Thus the old magical theory of the seasons was displaced, or rather supplemented, by a religious theory. For although men now attributed the annual cycle of change primarily to corresponding changes in their deities, they still thought that by performing certain magical rites they could aid the god, who was the principle of life, in his struggle with the opposing principle of death. They imagined that they could recruit his failing energies and even raise him from the dead. The ceremonies which they observed for this purpose were in substance a dramatic representation of the natural processes which they wished to facilitate; for it is a familiar tenet of magic that you can produce any desired effect by merely imitating it. And as they now explained the fluctuations of growth and decay, of reproduction and dissolution, by the marriage, the death, and the rebirth or revival of the gods, their religious or rather magical dramas turned in great measure on these themes. They set forth the fruitful union of the powers of fertility, the sad death of one at least of the divine partners, and his joyful resurrection. Thus a religious theory was blended with a magical practice. The combination is familiar in history. Indeed, few religions have ever succeeded in wholly extricating themselves from the old trammels of magic. The inconsistency of acting on two opposite principles, however it may vex the soul of the philosopher, rarely troubles the common man; indeed he is seldom even aware of it. His affair is to act, not to analyse the motives of his action. If mankind had always been logical and wise, history would not be a long chronicle of folly and crime.

Of the changes which the seasons bring with them, the most striking within the temperate zone are those which affect vegetation. The influence of the seasons on animals, though great, is not nearly so manifest. Hence it is natural that in the magical dramas designed to dispel winter and bring back spring the emphasis should be laid on vegetation, and that trees and plants should figure in them more prominently than beasts and birds. Yet the two sides of life, the vegetable and the animal, were not dissociated in the minds of those who observed the ceremonies. Indeed they commonly believed that the tie between the animal and the vegetable world was even closer than it really is; hence they often combined the dramatic representation of reviving plants with a real or a dramatic union of the sexes for the purpose of furthering at the same time and by the same act the multiplication of fruits, of animals, and of men. To them the principle of life and fertility, whether animal or vegetable, was one and indivisible. To live and to cause to live, to eat food and to beget children, these were the primary wants of men in the past, and they will be the primary wants of men in the future so long as the world lasts. Other things may be added to enrich and beautify human life, but unless these wants are first satisfied, humanity itself must cease to exist. These two things, therefore, food and children, were what men chiefly sought to procure by the performance of magical rites for the regulation of the seasons.

Nowhere, apparently, have these rites been more widely and solemnly celebrated than in the lands which border the Eastern Mediterranean. Under the names of Osiris, Tammuz, Adonis, and Attis, the peoples of Egypt and Western Asia represented the yearly decay and revival of life, especially of vegetable life, which they personified as a god who annually died and rose again from the dead. In name and detail the rites varied from place to place: in substance they were the same. The supposed death and resurrection of this oriental deity, a god of many names but of essentially one nature, is the subject of the present inquiry. We will take as our example of these cults that of Tammuz or Adonis.

The worship of Adonis was practised by the Semitic peoples of Babylonia and Syria, and the Greeks borrowed it from them as early as the seventh century before Christ. The true name of the deity was Tammuz: the appellation of Adonis is merely the Semitic *Adon*, 'lord', a title of honour by which his worshippers addressed him. In the Hebrew text of the Old Testament the same name Adonai, originally perhaps Adoni, 'my lord', is often applied to Jehovah. But the Greeks through a misunderstanding converted the title of honour into a proper name. While Tammuz or his equivalent Adonis enjoyed a wide and lasting popularity among peoples of the Semitic stock, there are grounds for thinking that his worship originated with a race of other blood and other speech, the Sumerians, who in the dawn of history inhabited the flat alluvial plain at the head of the Persian Gulf and created the civilization which was afterwards called Babylonian.

In the religious literature of Babylonia Tammuz appears as the youthful spouse or lover of Ishtar, the great mother goddess, the embodiment of the reproductive energies of nature. The references to their connexion with each other in myth and ritual are both fragmentary and obscure, but we gather from them that every year Tammuz was believed to die, passing away from the cheerful earth to the gloomy subterranean world, and that every year his divine mistress journeyed in quest of him 'to the land from which there is no returning, to the house of darkness, where dust lies on door and bolt'. During her absence the passion of love ceased to operate: men and beasts alike forgot to reproduce their kinds: all life was threatened with extinction. So intimately bound up with the goddess were the sexual functions of the whole animal kingdom that without her presence they could not be discharged. A messenger of the great god Ea was accordingly despatched to rescue the goddess on whom so much depended. The stern queen of

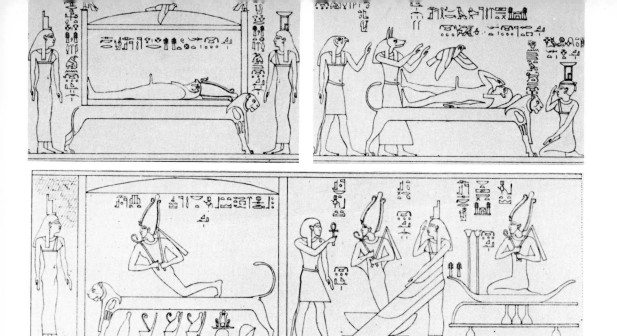

Death and resurrection of the gods: Osiris

Gods of vegetation in the ancient world, such as Osiris from Egypt, Adonis from Syria and Attis from Phrygia, were thought to die and return to life each year. The death and resurrection of the Egyptian god Osiris, carved in relief on the walls of the great temple of Denderah, assured worshippers of their own resurrection after death, and of the recurrence of seedtime and harvest.
A. Mariette-Bey, *Denderah*, 1873

the infernal regions, Allatu or Eresh-Kigal by name, reluctantly allowed Ishtar to be sprinkled with the Water of Life and to depart, in company probably with her lover Tammuz, that the two might return together to the upper world, and that with their return all nature might revive.

Laments for the departed Tammuz are contained in several Babylonian hymns, which liken him to plants that quickly fade. He is

A tamarisk that in the garden has drunk no water,
Whose crown in the field has brought forth no blossom.
A willow that rejoiced not by the watercourse,
A willow whose roots were torn up.
A herb that in the garden had drunk no water.

His death appears to have been annually mourned, to the shrill music of flutes, by men and women about midsummer in the month named after him, the month of Tammuz. The dirges were seemingly chanted over an effigy of the dead god, which was washed with pure water, anointed with oil, and clad in a red robe, while the fumes of incense rose into the air, as if to stir his dormant senses by their pungent fragrance and wake him from the sleep of death. In one of these dirges, inscribed *Lament of the Flutes for Tammuz*, we seem still to hear the voices of the singers chanting the sad refrain and to catch, like far-away music, the wailing notes of the flutes:

At his vanishing away she lifts up a lament,
　'Oh my child!' at his vanishing away she lifts up a lament;
'My Damu!' at his vanishing away she lifts up a lament.
　'My enchanter and priest!' at his vanishing away she lifts
　　up a lament,
At the shining cedar, rooted in a spacious place,
　In Eanna, above and below, she lifts up a lament.
Like the lament that a house lifts up for its master,
　　lifts she up a lament,
　Like the lament that a city lifts up for its lord,
　　lifts she up a lament.

Her lament is the lament for a herb that grows not in the bed,
　Her lament is the lament for the corn that grows
　　not in the ear.
Her chamber is a possession that brings not forth a possession,
　A weary woman, a weary child, forspent.

Attis
Attis with his attributes. The primitive stone knife in his left hand indicates his self-castration and death, while the fruits in his right are tokens of his annual revival. Roman statue, Museo Laterano, Rome. Photo: Anderson

Attis (left) as one of the four seasons on the sarcophagus of a married couple. The busts of the deceased couple are surrounded by the zodiac, which betokens life after death. Roman sarcophagus, 3rd century. Courtesy of the Dumbarton Oaks Collection, Washington, DC

Her lament is for a great river, where no willows grow,
   Her lament is for a field, where corn and herbs grow not.
Her lament is for a pool, where fishes grow not.
   Her lament is for a thicket of reeds, where no reeds grow.
Her lament is for woods, where tamarisks grow not.
   Her lament is for a wilderness where no cypresses [?] grow.
Her lament is for the depth of a garden of trees, where honey
    and wine grow not.
   Her lament is for meadows, where no plants grow.
Her lament is for a palace, where length of life grows not.

The tragical story and the melancholy rites of Adonis are better known to us from the descriptions of Greek writers than from the fragments of Babylonian literature or the brief reference of the prophet Ezekiel, who saw the women of Jerusalem weeping for Tammuz at the north gate of the temple. Mirrored in the glass of Greek mythology, the oriental deity appears as a comely youth beloved by Aphrodite. In his infancy the goddess hid him in a chest, which she gave in charge to Persephone, queen of the nether world. But when Persephone opened the chest and beheld the beauty of the babe, she refused to give him back to Aphrodite, though the goddess of love went down herself to hell to ransom her dear one from the power of the grave. The dispute between the two goddesses of love and death was settled by Zeus, who decreed that Adonis should abide with Persephone in the under world for one part of the year, and with Aphrodite in the upper world for another part. At last the fair youth was killed in hunting by a wild boar, or by the jealous Ares, who turned himself into the likeness of a boar in order to compass the death of his rival. Bitterly did Aphrodite lament her loved and lost Adonis. In this form of the myth, the contest between Aphrodite and Persephone for the possession of Adonis clearly reflects the struggle between Ishtar and Allatu in the land of the dead, while the decision of Zeus that Adonis is to spend one part of the year under ground and another part above ground is merely a Greek version of the annual disappearance and reappearance of Tammuz.

2. Adonis in Syria

The myth of Adonis was localized and his rites celebrated with much solemnity at Byblus on the coast of Syria and Paphos in Cyprus. Both were great seats of the worship of Aphrodite, or rather of her Semitic counterpart, Astarte; and of both, if we accept the legends, Cinyras, the father of Adonis, was king. Of the two cities Byblus was the more ancient; in historical times it ranked as a holy place, the religious capital of the country, the Mecca or Jerusalem of the Phoenicians. From the earliest to the latest times the city appears to have been ruled by kings, assisted perhaps by a senate or council of elders. The names of these kings suggest that they claimed affinity with their god Baal or Moloch, for Moloch is only a corruption of *melech*, that is 'king'. Such a claim at all events appears to have been put forward by many other Semitic kings. The early monarchs of Babylon, for instance, were worshipped as gods in their lifetime. In like manner the kings of Byblus may have assumed the style of Adonis; for Adonis was simply the divine Adon or 'lord' of the city, a title which hardly differs in sense from Baal ('master') and Melech ('king'). Some of the old Canaanite kings of Jerusalem appear to have played the part of Adonis in their lifetime, if we may judge from their names, Adoni-bezek and Adoni-zedek, which are divine rather than human titles. Thus we need not wonder that in later times the women of Jerusalem used to weep for Tammuz, that is, for Adonis, at the north gate of the temple.

But if Jerusalem had been from of old the seat of a dynasty of spiritual potentates or Grand Lamas, who held the keys of heaven and were revered far and wide as kings and gods in one, we can easily understand why the upstart David chose it for the capital of the new kingdom which he had won for himself at the point of the sword. The central position and the natural strength of the virgin fortress need not have been the only or the principal inducements which decided the politic monarch to transfer his throne from Hebron to Jerusalem. By serving himself heir to the ancient kings of the city he might reasonably hope to inherit their ghostly repute along with their broad acres, to wear their nimbus as well as their crown. The history of the Hebrew kings presents some features which may perhaps, without straining them too far, be interpreted as traces or relics of a time when they or their predecessors played the part of a divinity, and particularly of Adonis, the divine lord of the land. But whether identified with Adonis or not, the Hebrew kings certainly seem to have been regarded as in a sense divine, as representing and to some extent embodying Jehovah on earth. For the king's throne was called the throne of Jehovah; and the application of the holy oil to his head was believed to impart to him directly a portion of the divine spirit. Hence he bore the title of Messiah, which with its Greek equivalent, Christ, means no more than 'the Anointed One'. Thus when David had cut off the skirt of Saul's robe in the darkness of a cave where he was in hiding, his heart smote him for having laid sacrilegious hands upon *Adoni Messiah Jehovah*, 'my Lord the Anointed of Jehovah'.

The custom of anointing the king was also observed in various parts of Polynesia. Thus in Samoa 'Kings in ancient times were publicly proclaimed and recognized by anointing in the presence of a large assembly of chiefs and people. A sacred stone was consecrated as a throne, or, rather, stool (*scabellum*), on which the king stood, and a priest – who must also be a chief – called upon the gods to behold and bless the king, and pronounced denunciations against the people who failed to obey him. He then poured scented oil from a native bottle over the head, shoulders, and body of the king, and proclaimed his several titles and honours.'

Like other divine or semi-divine rulers the Hebrew kings were apparently held answerable for famine and pestilence. When a dearth, caused perhaps by a failure of the winter rains, had visited the land for three years, King David inquired of the oracle, which discreetly laid the blame not on him but on his predecessor Saul. The dead king was indeed beyond the reach of punishment, but his sons were not. So David had seven of them sought out, and they were hanged before the Lord at the beginning of barley harvest in spring: and all the long summer the mother of two of the dead men sat under the gallows-tree, keeping off the jackals by night and the vultures by day, till with the autumn the blessed rain came at last to wet their dangling bodies and fertilize the barren earth once more. Then the bones of the dead were taken down from the gibbet and buried in the sepulchre of their fathers.

In the days of the Hebrew monarchy the king was apparently credited with the power of making sick and making whole. Thus the king of Syria sent a leper to the king of Israel to be healed by him, just as scrofulous patients used to fancy that they could be cured by the touch of a French or English king. However, the Hebrew monarch, with more sense than has been shewn by his royal brothers in modern times, professed himself unable to work any such miracle. 'Am I God,' he asked, 'to kill and to make alive, that this man doth send unto me to recover a man of his leprosy?'

To this theory of the sanctity, nay the divinity of the Hebrew kings it may be objected that few traces of it survive in the historical books of the Bible. But the force of the objection is weakened by a consideration of the time and the circumstances in which these books assumed their final shape. The great prophets of the eighth and the seventh centuries (BC) by the spiritual ideals and ethical fervour of their teaching had wrought a religious and moral reform perhaps unparalleled in history. Under their influence an austere monotheism had replaced the old sensuous worship of the natural powers: a stern Puritanical spirit, an unbending rigour of mind, had succeeded to the old easy supple temper with its weak compliances, its wax-like impressionability, its proclivities to the sins of the flesh. And the moral lessons which the prophets inculcated were driven home by the political events of the time, above all by the ever-growing pressure of the great Assyrian empire on the petty states of Palestine.

It was in this period of national gloom and despondency that the two great reformations of Israel's religion were accomplished, the first by king Hezekiah, the second a century later by king Josiah. We need not wonder then that the reformers who in that and subsequent ages composed or edited the annals of their nation should have looked as sourly on the old unreformed paganism of their forefathers as the fierce zealots of the Commonwealth looked on the far more innocent pastimes of Merry England; and that in their zeal for the glory of God they should have blotted many pages of history lest they should perpetuate the memory of practices to which they traced the calamities of their country.

But if Semitic kings in general and the kings of Byblus in particular often assumed the style of Baal or Adonis, it follows that they may have mated with the goddess, the Baalath or Astarte of the city. Certainly we hear of kings of Tyre and Sidon who were priests of Astarte. Now to the agricultural Semites the Baal or god of a land was the author of all its fertility; he it was who produced the corn, the wine, the figs, the oil, and the flax, by means of his quickening waters, which in the arid parts of the Semitic world are oftener springs, streams, and underground flow than the rains of heaven. 'The Baal was conceived as the male principle of reproduction, the husband of the land which he fertilised.' So far, therefore, as the Semite personified the reproductive energies of nature as male and female, as a Baal and a Baalath, he appears to have identified the male power especially with water and the female especially with earth. On this view plants and trees, animals and men, are the offspring or children of the Baal and Baalath.

If, then, at Byblus and elsewhere, the Semitic king was allowed, or rather required, to personate the god and marry the goddess, the intention of the custom can only have been to ensure the fertility of the land and the increase of men and cattle by means of homoeopathic magic. There is reason to think that a similar custom was observed from a similar motive in other parts of the ancient world, and particularly at Nemi, where both the male and the female powers, the Dianus and Diana, were in one aspect of their nature personifications of the life-giving waters.

As for the people of Byblus, they shaved their heads in the annual mourning for Adonis. Women who refused to sacrifice their hair had to give themselves up to strangers on a certain day of the festival, and the money which they thus earned was devoted to the goddess. This custom may have been a mitigation of an older rule which at Byblus as elsewhere formerly compelled every woman without exception to sacrifice her virtue in the service of religion. We are told that in Lydia all girls were obliged to prostitute themselves in order to earn a dowry; but we may suspect that the real motive of the custom was devotion rather than economy. The suspicion is confirmed by a Greek inscription found at Tralles in Lydia, which proves that the practice of religious prostitution survived in that country as late as the second century of our era. It records of a certain woman, Aurelia Aemilia by name, not only that she herself served the god in the capacity of a harlot at his express command, but that her mother and other female ancestors had done the same before her; and the publicity of the record, engraved on a marble column which supported a votive offering, shows that no stain attached to such a life and such a parentage. In Armenia the noblest families dedicated their daughters to the service of the goddess Anaitis in her temple at Acilisena, where the damsels acted as prostitutes for a long time before they were given in marriage. Nobody scrupled to take one of the girls to wife when her period of service was over.

In Cyprus, where Adonis was also worshipped, it appears that before marriage all women were formerly obliged by custom to prostitute themselves to strangers at the sanctuary of the goddess, whether she went by the name of Aphrodite, Astarte, or what not. Similar customs prevailed in many parts of Western Asia. Whatever its motive, the practice was clearly regarded, not as an orgy of lust, but as a solemn religious duty performed in the service of that great Mother Goddess of Western Asia whose name varied, while her type remained constant, from place to place. Thus at Babylon every woman, whether rich or poor, had once in her life to submit to the embraces of a stranger at the temple of Mylitta, that is, of Ishtar or Astarte, and to dedicate to the goddess the wages earned by this sanctified harlotry. The sacred precinct was crowded with women waiting to

The mortality of the gods
The Egyptian pharaoh was the son of a god, and yet was mortal like other men. Age converted the bones of the gods 'into silver, their flesh into gold, and their azure locks into lapis-lazuli'. (Frazer, above page 100) OPPOSITE. The throne of the young pharaoh Tutankhamen hints at this transformation in death. Photo: GRL/F.L. Kenett

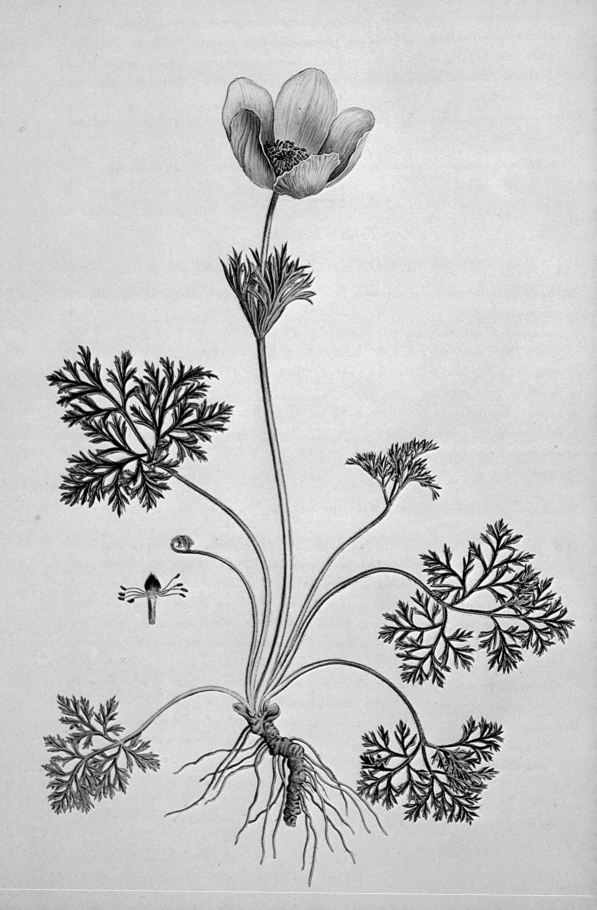

Nature reflects the life and death of the gods
OPPOSITE. Spring flowers spoke to the ancients of the resurrection of their gods, while the fading of the same flowers reminded them of their death. The Scarlet Anemone (*Anemone coronaria*) received its colour from the blood of Adonis. *Flora Graeca Sibthorpiana*, VI, 1826
ABOVE. The poppy, *Papaver rhoeas*, which grows all over the Mediterranean world, once reminded initiates of the spilt blood of their gods. Curtis, *Flora Londinensis* 1798. Courtesy of the Sherardian Professor of Botany, University of Oxford

Amorites, that she who was about to marry should sit in fornication seven days by the gate.'

A great Mother Goddess, the personification of all the reproductive energies of nature, was worshipped under different names but with a substantial similarity of myth and ritual by many peoples of Western Asia; associated with her was a lover, or rather series of lovers, divine yet mortal, with whom she mated year by year, their commerce being deemed essential to the propagation of animals and plants, each in their several kind; and further, that the fabulous union of the divine pair was simulated and, as it were, multiplied on earth by the real, though temporary, union of the human sexes at the sanctuary of the goddess for the sake of thereby ensuring the fruitfulness of the ground and the increase of man and beast.

The last king of Byblus bore the ancient name of Cinyras, and was beheaded by Pompey the Great for his tyrannous excesses. His legendary namesake Cinyras is said to have founded a sanctuary of Aphrodite, that is, of Astarte, at a place on Mount Lebanon, distant a day's journey from the capital. The spot was probably Aphaca, at the source of the river Adonis, half-way between Byblus and Baalbec; for at Aphaca there was a famous grove and sanctuary of Astarte which Constantine destroyed on account of the flagitious character of the worship. It was here that, according to the legend, Adonis met Aphrodite for the first or the last time, and here his mangled body was buried. Every year, in the belief of his worshippers, Adonis was wounded to death on the mountains, and every year the face of nature itself was dyed with his sacred blood. So year by year the Syrian damsels lamented his untimely fate, while the red anemone, his flower, bloomed among the cedars of Lebanon, and the river ran red to the sea, fringing the winding shores of the blue Mediterranean, whenever the wind set inshore, with a sinuous band of crimson.

observe the custom. Some of them had to wait there for years. At Heliopolis or Baalbec in Syria, famous for the imposing grandeur of its ruined temples, the custom of the country required that every maiden should prostitute herself to a stranger at the temple of Astarte, and matrons as well as maids testified their devotion to the goddess in the same manner. The emperor Constantine abolished the custom, destroyed the temple, and built a church in its stead. In Phoenician temples women prostituted themselves for hire in the service of religion, believing that by this conduct they propitiated the goddess and won her favour. 'It was a law of the

3. Adonis Then and Now

The Ritual of Adonis

Thus far we have dealt with the myth of Adonis and the legends which associated him with Byblus. A discussion of these legends led us to the conclusion that among Semitic peoples in early times, Adonis, the divine lord of the city, was often personated by priestly kings. At the same time, it may be suggested that the death of Adonis, annually mourned, reflects an ancient custom of putting the king to death every year to reinvigorate the life of nature.

From the legends, we now pass to the ritual of Adonis, knowledge of which is to be derived mainly from Greek authors who saw what they describe; and it applies to ages in which the growth of humane feeling had softened some of the harsher features of the worship.

At the festivals of Adonis, which were held in Western Asia and in Greek lands, the death of the god was annually mourned, with a bitter wailing, chiefly by women; images of him, dressed to resemble corpses, were carried out as to burial and then thrown into the sea or into springs; and in some places his revival was celebrated on the following day. At Alexandria images of Aphrodite and Adonis were displayed on two couches; beside them were set ripe fruits of all kinds, cakes, plants growing in flower-pots, and green bowers twined with anise. The marriage of the lovers was celebrated one day, and on the morrow women attired as mourners, with streaming hair and bared breasts, bore the image of the dead Adonis to the sea-shore and committed it to the waves. Yet they sorrowed not without hope, for they sang that the lost one would come back again.

In Attica the festival fell at the height of summer. For the fleet which Athens fitted out against Syracuse, and by the destruction of which her power was permanently crippled, sailed at midsummer, and by an ominous coincidence the sombre rites of Adonis were being celebrated at the very time. As the troops marched down to the harbour to embark, the streets through which they passed were lined with coffins and corpse-like effigies, and the air was rent with the noise of women wailing for the dead Adonis. The circumstance cast a gloom over the sailing of the most splendid armament that Athens ever sent to sea. Many ages afterwards, when the Emperor Julian made his first entry into Antioch, he found in like manner the gay, the luxurious capital of the East plunged in mimic grief for the annual death of Adonis: and if he had any presentiment of coming evil, the voices of lamentation which struck upon his ear must have seemed to sound his knell.

The character of Tammuz or Adonis as a corn-spirit comes out plainly in an account of his festival given by an Arabic writer of the tenth century. In describing the rites and sacrifices observed at the different seasons of the year by the heathen Syrians of Harran, he says: 'Tammuz (July). In the middle of this month is the festival of el-Bûgât, that is, of the weeping women, and this is the Tâ-uz festival, which is celebrated in honour of the god Tâ-uz. The women bewail him, because his lord slew him so cruelly, ground his bones in a mill, and then scattered them to the wind. The women [during this festival] eat nothing which has been ground in a mill, but limit their diet to steeped wheat, sweet vetches, dates, raisins, and the like.'

This concentration, so to say, of the nature of

Adonis upon the cereal crops is characteristic of the stage of culture reached by his worshippers in historical times. They had left the nomadic life of the wandering hunter and herdsman far behind them; for ages they had been settled on the land, and had depended for their subsistence mainly on the products of tillage. The berries and roots of the wilderness, the grass of the pastures, which had been matters of vital importance to their ruder forefathers, were now of little moment to them: more and more their thoughts and energies were engrossed by the staple of their life, the corn; more and more accordingly the propitiation of the deities of fertility in general and of the corn-spirit in particular tended to become the central feature of their religion. The aim they set before themselves in celebrating the rites was thoroughly practical. It was no vague poetical sentiment which prompted them to hail with joy the rebirth of vegetation and to mourn its decline. Hunger, felt or feared, was the mainspring of the worship of Adonis.

It has been suggested that the mourning for Adonis was essentially a harvest rite designed to propitiate the corn-god, who was then either perishing under the sickles of the reapers, or being trodden to death under the hoofs of the oxen on the threshing-floor.

Thus interpreted the death of Adonis is not the natural decay of vegetation in general under the summer heat or the winter cold; it is the violent destruction of the corn by man, who cuts it down on the field, stamps it to pieces on the threshing-floor, and grinds it to powder in the mill. That this was indeed the principal aspect in which Adonis presented himself in later times to the agricultural peoples of the Levant, may be admitted; but whether from the beginning he had been the corn and nothing but the corn, may be doubted. At an earlier period he may have been to the herdsman, above all, the tender herbage which sprouts after rain, offering rich pasture to the lean and hungry cattle. Earlier still he may

have embodied the spirit of the nuts and berries which the autumn woods yield to the savage hunter and his squaw. And just as the husbandman must propitiate the spirit of the corn which he consumes, so the herdsman must appease the spirit of the grass and leaves which his cattle munch, and the hunter must soothe the spirit of the roots which he digs, and of the fruits which he gathers from the bough.

There is reason to think that in early times Adonis was sometimes personated by a living man who died a violent death in the character of the god. Further, there is evidence which goes to show that among the agricultural peoples of the Eastern Mediterranean, the corn-spirit, by whatever name he was known, was often represented, year by year, by human victims slain on the harvest-field. If that was so, it seems likely that the propitiation of the corn-spirit would tend to fuse to some extent with the worship of the dead. For the spirits of these victims might be thought to return to life in the ears which they had fattened with their blood, and to die a second death at the reaping of the corn.

I sometimes think that never blows so red
The Rose as where some buried Caesar bled;
　　That every Hyacinth the Garden wears
Dropt in her Lap from some once lovely Head.

And this reviving Herb whose tender Green
Fledges the River-Lip on which we lean –
　　Ah, lean upon it lightly, for who knows
From what once lovely Lip it springs unseen?

The Gardens of Adonis

Perhaps the best proof that Adonis was a deity of vegetation, and especially of the corn, is furnished by the gardens of Adonis, as they were called. These were baskets or pots filled with earth, in which wheat, barley, lettuces, fennel, and various kinds of flowers were sown and tended for eight days, chiefly or exclusively by women. Fostered by the sun's heat, the plants shot up rapidly, but having no root they withered as rapidly away, and at the end of eight days were

Viola odorata

Flowers in ritual and myth

ABOVE. The violet, *Viola odorata*, was used to decorate the processional tree carried during the Roman spring mourning rites for the god Attis. Curtis, *Flora Londinensis*, 1835

RIGHT. The hyacinth, *Hyacinthus romanus*. The ancients read in its petals the letters AI, which spell the wailing cry uttered for the death of the young Hyacinth, revered as a deity of vegetation at Sparta in Greece. *Flora Graeca Sibthorpiana*, IV, 1819. Photos: courtesy of the Sherardian Professor of Botany, University of Oxford

carried out with the images of the dead Adonis, and flung with them into the sea or into springs.

These gardens of Adonis are most naturally interpreted as representatives of Adonis or manifestations of his power; they represented him, true to his original nature, in vegetable form, while the images of him, with which they were carried out and cast into the water, portrayed him in his later human shape. All these Adonis ceremonies, if I am right, were originally intended as charms to promote the growth or revival of vegetation; and the principle by which they were supposed to produce this effect was homoeopathic or imitative magic. For ignorant people suppose that by mimicking the effect which they desire to produce they actually help to produce it; thus by sprinkling water they make rain, by lighting a fire they make sunshine, and so on. Similarly, by mimicking the growth of crops they hope to ensure a good harvest. The rapid growth of the wheat and barley in the gardens of Adonis was intended to make the corn shoot up; and the throwing of the gardens and of the images into the water was a charm to secure a due supply of fertilizing rain. The same, I take it, was the object of throwing the effigies of Death and the Carnival into water in the corresponding ceremonies of modern Europe. Certainly the custom of drenching with water a leaf-clad person, who undoubtedly personifies vegetation, is still resorted to in Europe for the express purpose of producing rain. Similarly the custom of throwing water on the last corn cut at harvest, or on the person who brings it home (a custom observed in Germany and France, and till quite lately in England and Scotland), is in some places practised with the avowed intent to procure rain for the next year's crops.

The opinion that the gardens of Adonis are essentially charms to promote the growth of vegetation, especially of the crops, and that they belong to the same class of customs as those spring and midsummer folk-customs of modern Europe which I have described elsewhere, does not rest for its evidence merely on the intrinsic probability of the case. Fortunately we are able to show that gardens of Adonis (if we may use the expression in a general sense) are still planted by European peasants at Midsummer.

In some parts of Bavaria it is customary to sow flax in a pot on the last three days of the Carnival; from the seed which grows best an omen is drawn as to whether the early, the middle, or the late sowing will produce the best crop. In Sardinia the gardens of Adonis are still planted in connexion with the great Midsummer

festival which bears the name of St John. At the end of March or on the first of April a young man of the village presents himself to a girl, and asks her to be his *comare* (gossip or sweetheart), offering to be her *compare*. The invitation is considered as an honour by the girl's family, and is gladly accepted. At the end of May the girl makes a pot of the bark of the cork-tree, fills it with earth, and sows a handful of wheat and barley in it. The pot being placed in the sun and often watered, the corn sprouts rapidly and has a good head by Midsummer Eve (St John's Eve, the twenty-third of June). The pot is then called *Erme* or *Nenneri*. On St John's Day the young man and the girl, dressed in their best, accompanied by a long retinue and preceded by children gambolling and frolicking, move in procession to a church outside the village. Here they break the pot by throwing it against the door of the church. Then they sit down in a ring on the grass and eat eggs and herbs to the music of flutes. Wine is mixed in a cup and passed round, each one drinking as it passes. Then they join hands and sing 'Sweethearts of St John' (*Compare e comare di San Giovanni*) over and over again, the flutes playing the while. When they tire of singing they stand up and dance gaily in a ring till evening.

In these midsummer customs of Sardinia it is possible that St John has replaced Adonis. We have seen that the rites of Tammuz or Adonis were commonly celebrated about midsummer; according to Jerome, their date was June. And besides their date and their similarity in respect of the pots of herbs and corn, there is another point of affinity between the two festivals, the heathen and the Christian. In both of them water plays a prominent part. At his midsummer festival in Babylon the image of Tammuz, whose name is said to mean 'true son of the deep water', was bathed with pure water: at his summer festival in Alexandria the image of Adonis, with that of his divine mistress Aphrodite, was

**Music and religion: the worshippers are imbued
with the spirit of their divinity**

Music and dance have often been employed as rituals to
aid men to draw closer to their gods. The whirling circles
of the dervishes imitate the motions of the heavens and
put the dancers into a cosmic relationship with Allah. The
music and dances of many South American Indian tribes
record and expound mythical events that influence the
lives of men.

Dancing dervishes, Rajput, Pahari painting, c.1740, Los
Angeles County Museum of Art. Formerly the Nasli and
Alice Heeramaneck Collection, Museum Associates
Purchase

committed to the waves; and at the midsummer
celebration in Greece the gardens of Adonis
were thrown into the sea or into springs. Now a
great feature of the midsummer festival associated with the name of St John is, or used to be
the custom of bathing in the sea, springs, rivers,
or the dew on Midsummer Eve or the morning
of Midsummer Day. Thus, for example, at
Naples there is a church dedicated to St John the
Baptist under the name of St John of the Sea
(*S. Giovan a mare*); and it was an old practice for
men and women to bathe in the sea on St John's
Eve, that is, on Midsummer Eve, believing that
thus all their sins were washed away. In the
Abruzzi water is still supposed to acquire certain
marvellous and beneficent properties on St
John's Night. They say that on that night the
sun and moon bathe in the water. Hence many

Patagonian dancers in the spring festival of the god Vita Uentra, spirit of good. Victorian engraving, Bodleian Library, Oxford

people take a bath in the sea or in a river at that season, especially at the moment of sunrise. At Marsala in Sicily there is a spring of water in a subterranean grotto called the Grotto of the Sibyl. Beside it stands a church of St John, which has been supposed to occupy the site of a temple of Apollo. On St John's Eve, the twenty-third of June, women and girls visit the grotto, and by drinking of the prophetic water learn whether

their husbands have been faithful to them in the year that is past, or whether they themselves will wed in the year that is to come. Sick people, too, imagine that by bathing in the water, drinking of it, or ducking thrice in it in the name of the Trinity, they will be made whole.

It may perhaps be suggested that this widespread custom of bathing in water or dew on Midsummer Eve or Midsummer Day is purely Christian in origin, having been adopted as an appropriate mode of celebrating the day dedicated to the Baptist. But in point of fact the custom is older than Christianity, for it was denounced and forbidden as a heathen practice by Augustine, and to this day it is practised at midsummer by the Mohammedan peoples of North Africa. We may conjecture that the Church, unable to put down this relic of paganism, followed its usual policy of accommodation by bestowing on the rite a Christian name and acquiescing, with a sigh, in its observance. And casting about for a saint to supplant a heathen patron of bathing, the Christian doctors could hardly have hit upon a more appropriate successor than St John the Baptist.

In this connexion a well-known statement of Jerome may not be without significance. He tells us that Bethlehem, the traditionary birthplace of the Lord, was shaded by a grove of that still older Syrian Lord, Adonis, and that where the infant Jesus had wept, the lover of Venus was bewailed. Though he does not expressly say so, Jerome seems to have thought that the grove of Adonis had been planted by the heathen after the birth of Christ for the purpose of defiling the sacred spot. In this he may have been mistaken. If Adonis was indeed, as I have argued, the spirit of the corn, a more suitable name for his dwelling-place could hardly be found than Bethlehem, 'the House of Bread', and he may well have been worshipped there at his House of Bread long ages before the birth of Him who said, 'I am the bread of life'.

Part 5. Spirits of the Corn

We have learned that the death of the King of the Wood was necessary to ensure the fertility of nature. The death and resurrection of Adonis performed this task by the principle of imitation. Frazer now explains this principle in greater detail in the persons of the two Greek corn-goddesses, who not only stood for the corn but were the corn. Demeter, the mother, is last year's old corn and her daughter Persephone is the new corn of this year. The myth of these two goddesses, which tells of Persephone's annual death and her mother's mourning, is, therefore, not merely a parable but a historical account of seedtime and harvest. Analogies to it are found in harvest customs the world over.

Since the divinity is the corn, we can conclude that when the corn is eaten, it is a sacrament, because the divinity is eaten. If we view the King of the Wood as an embodiment of vegetation, a possible analogy to this custom existed at Nemi, where human-shaped loaves were ceremonially consumed. These loaves could, in a former age, have stood for the king, who, like other personifications of the crops that have been considered, may originally have been killed every year at harvest.

Greek myth told of the triumphal progress of Dionysus, god of the vine and of ecstasy; the god travelled to the edge of the known world and won mankind to his worship and the cultivation of vines. Dionysus was killed by the Titans, creatures of an earlier epoch, who mangled his body as the grape is mangled to extract its juice for wine. Hence, later in antiquity, the triumph of Dionysus was understood as a sign of the afterlife and was therefore often depicted on sarcophagi.

The triumphal progress of Dionysus with the four seasons. Roman sarcophagus, Staatliche Kunstsammlungen, Kassel

1. Demeter and Persephone

In the preceding part of this work we saw that in antiquity the civilised nations of western Asia pictured to themselves the changes of the seasons, and particularly the annual growth and decay of vegetation, as episodes in the life of a god, whose mournful death and happy resurrection they celebrated with dramatic rites of alternate lamentation and rejoicing. But if the celebration was in form dramatic, it was in substance magical; that is to say, it was intended, on the principles of sympathetic magic, to ensure the vernal regeneration of plants and the multiplication of animals, which had seemed to be menaced by the inroads of winter. In the ancient world, however, such ideas and such rites were by no means confined to the Near East, but were shared by the races of livelier fancy and more mercurial temperament who inhabited the shores and islands of the Aegean. We need not, with some enquirers in ancient and modern times, suppose that these Western peoples borrowed from the older civilisation of the Orient the conception of the Dying and Reviving God, together with the solemn ritual, in which that conception was dramatically set forth before the eyes of the worshippers. More probably the resemblance which may be traced in this respect between the religions of the East and the West is no more than what we commonly, though incorrectly, call a fortuitous coincidence, the effect of similar causes acting alike on the similar constitution of the human mind in different countries and under different skies. The Greek had no need to journey into far countries to learn the vicissitudes of the seasons, to mark the fleeting beauty of the damask rose, the transient glory of the golden corn, the passing splendour of the purple grapes. Year by year in his own beautiful land he beheld, with natural regret, the bright pomp of summer fading into the gloom and stagnation of winter, and year by year he hailed with natural delight the outburst of fresh life in spring. Accustomed to personify the forces of nature, to tinge her cold abstractions with the warm hues of imagination, to clothe her naked realities with the gorgeous drapery of a mythic fancy, he fashioned for himself a train of gods and goddesses, of spirits and elves, out of the shifting panorama of the seasons, and followed the annual fluctuations of their fortunes with alternate emotions of cheerfulness and dejection, which he expressed in the form of ritual and myth. One such myth is that of Demeter and Persephone.

The oldest literary document which narrates it is the beautiful Homeric *Hymn to Demeter*, which critics assign to the seventh century before our era. The object of the poem is to explain the origin of the Eleusinian mysteries, and the complete silence of the poet as to Athens and the Athenians, who in after ages took a conspicuous part in the festival, renders it probable that the hymn was composed in the far off time when Eleusis was still a petty independent state, and before the stately procession of the Mysteries had begun to defile, in bright September days, over the low chain of barren rocky hills which divides the flat Eleusinian cornland from the more spacious olive-clad expanse of the Athenian plain. Be that as it may, the hymn reveals to us the conception which the writer entertained of the character and functions of the two goddesses: their natural shapes stand out sharply enough under the thin veil of poetical imagery.

Dionysus, god of wine and ecstasy
This Greek cylix of the 6th century BC, shows Dionysus sailing across the sea to his temple at Delphi. Staatliche Antikensammlungen und Glyptothek, Munich. Photo: C.H. Krüger Moessner

The corn-maiden
The world of the living and the crops above ground and the world of the dead and the sleeping seeds beneath it: Persephone and Pluto, gods of the underworld and of the crops. Reggio Museum, Italy. Photo: Hirmer Fotoarchiv

The youthful Persephone, so runs the tale, was gathering roses and lilies, crocuses and violets, hyacinths and narcissuses in a lush meadow, when the earth gaped and Pluto, lord of the Dead, issuing from the abyss carried her off on his golden car to be his bride and queen in the gloomy subterranean world. Her sorrowing mother Demeter, with her yellow tresses veiled in a dark mourning mantle, sought her over land and sea, and learning from the Sun her daughter's fate she withdrew in high dudgeon from the gods and took up her abode at Eleusis, where she presented herself to the king's daughters in the guise of an old woman, sitting sadly under the shadow of an olive tree beside the Maiden's Well, to which the damsels had come to draw water in bronze pitchers for their father's house. In her wrath at her bereavement the goddess suffered not the seed to grow in the earth but kept it hidden under ground, and she vowed that never would she set foot on Olympus and never would she let the corn sprout till her lost

daughter should be restored to her. Vainly the oxen dragged the ploughs to and fro in the fields; vainly the sower dropped the barley seed in the brown furrows; nothing came up from the parched and crumbling soil. Even the Rarian plain near Eleusis, which was wont to wave with yellow harvests, lay bare and fallow. Mankind would have perished of hunger and the gods would have been robbed of the sacrifices which were their due, if Zeus in alarm had not commanded Pluto to disgorge his prey, to restore his bride Persephone to her mother Demeter. The grim lord of the Dead smiled and obeyed, but before he sent back his queen to the upper air on a golden car, he gave her the seed of a pomegranate to eat, which ensured that she would return to him. But Zeus stipulated that henceforth Persephone should spend two thirds of every year with her mother and the gods in the upper world and one third of the year with her husband in the nether world, from which she was to return year by year when the earth was

theme which the poet set before himself in composing this hymn was to describe the traditional foundation of the Eleusinian mysteries by the goddess Demeter. The revelation of the mysteries is the triumphal close of the piece. Amongst the rites as to which the poet thus drops significant hints are the preliminary fast of the candidates for initiation, the torchlight procession, the all-night vigil, the sitting of the candidates, veiled and in silence, on stools covered with sheepskins, the use of scurrilous language, the breaking of ribald jests, and the solemn communion with the divinity by participation in a draught of barley-water from a holy chalice.

But there is yet another and a deeper secret of the mysteries which the author of the poem appears to have divulged under cover of his narrative. He tells us how, as soon as Demeter had transformed the barren brown expanse of the Eleusinian plain into a field of golden grain, she gladdened the eyes of Triptolemus and the other Eleusinian princes by shewing them the growing or standing corn. When we compare this part of the story with the statement of a Christian writer of the second century, Hippolytus, that the very heart of the mysteries consisted in shewing to the initiated a reaped ear of corn, we can hardly doubt that the poet of the hymn was well acquainted with this solemn rite, and that he deliberately intended to explain its origin in precisely the same way as he explained other rites of the mysteries, namely by representing Demeter as having set the example of performing the ceremony in her own person. Thus myth and ritual mutually explain and confirm each other.

In the Homeric Hymn to Demeter, the figures of the two goddesses, the mother and the daughter, resolve themselves into personifications of the corn. Persephone, the goddess who spends three or, according to another version of the myth, six months of every year with the dead under ground and the remainder of the year

The origin of agriculture
Demeter and Persephone send Triptolemus on a winged chariot to teach the cultivation of cereals to mankind. Athenian skyphos by Makron and Hieron, British Museum, London

gay with spring flowers. Gladly the daughter then returned to the sunshine, gladly her mother received her and fell upon her neck; and in her joy at recovering the lost one Demeter made the corn to sprout from the clods of the ploughed fields and all the broad earth to be heavy with leaves and blossoms. And straightway she went and shewed this happy sight to the princes of Eleusis, to Triptolemus, Eumolpus, Diocles, and to the king Celeus himself, and moreover she revealed to them her sacred rites and mysteries. Blessed, says the poet, is the mortal man who has seen these things, but he who has had no share of them in life will never be happy in death when he has descended into the darkness of the grave. So the two goddesses departed to dwell in bliss with the gods on Olympus; and the bard ends the hymn with a pious prayer to Demeter and Persephone that they would be pleased to grant him a livelihood in return for his song.

It has been generally recognised, and indeed it seems scarcely open to doubt, that the main

with the living above ground; in whose absence the barley seed is hidden in the earth and the fields lie bare and fallow; on whose return in spring to the upper world the corn shoots up from the clods and the earth is heavy with leaves and blossoms – this goddess can surely be nothing else than a mythical embodiment of the vegetation, and particularly of the corn, which is buried under the soil for some months of every winter and comes to life again, as from the grave, in the sprouting cornstalks and the opening flowers and foliage of every spring. And if the daughter goddess was a personification of the young corn of the present year, the mother goddess may be understood to be a personification of the old corn of last year, which has given birth to the new crops.

The Greek husbandman prayed to Demeter when he committed the seed, with anxious forebodings, to the furrows, and after he had reaped the harvest and brought back the yellow sheaves with rejoicing to the threshing-floor, he paid the bountiful goddess her dues in the form of a thank-offering of golden grain. Theocritus has painted for us in glowing colours a picture of a rustic harvest-home, as it fell on a bright autumn day some two thousand years ago in the little Greek island of Cos. The poet tells us how he went with two friends from the city to attend a festival given by farmers, who were offering first-fruits to Demeter from the store of barley with which she had filled their barns. 'All things', says the poet, 'smelt of summer, but smelt of autumn too.' Indeed the day was really autumnal; for a goat-herd who met the friends on their way to the rural merry-making, asked them whether they were bound for the treading of the grapes in the wine-presses. Later, couched on soft beds of fragrant lentisk they passed the sultry hours singing ditties alternately, while a rustic image of Demeter, to whom the honours of the day were paid, stood smiling beside a heap of yellow grain on the threshing-floor, with corn-stalks and poppies in her hands. The day immortalised by Theocritus was one of those autumn days of great heat and effulgent beauty which in Greece may occur at any time up to the very verge of winter.

Thus we may infer that in the rural districts of ancient Greece farmers offered their first-fruits of the barley harvest to Demeter in autumn about the time when the grapes were being trodden in the wine-presses and the ripe apples and pears littered the ground in the orchards. The Greek offering of first-fruits took place so late in the year because it was prompted not so much by gratitude for past favours as by a shrewd eye to favours to come, and perhaps this interpretation of the custom does no serious injustice to the cool phlegmatic temper of the bucolic mind, which is more apt to be moved by considerations of profit than by sentiment. In Greece, the summer is practically rainless, and during the long months of heat and drought the cultivation of the two ancient cereals, barley and wheat, is at a standstill. The first rains of autumn fall about the middle of October, and that was the Greek farmer's great time for ploughing and sowing. Hence we should expect him to make his offering of first-fruits to the Corn Goddess shortly before he ploughed and sowed, and this expectation is entirely confirmed by the date which we have inferred for the offering from the evidence of Theocritus. Thus the sacrifice of barley to Demeter in the autumn would seem to have been not so much a thank-offering as a bribe judiciously administered to her at the very moment of all the year when her services were most urgently wanted.

When with the progress of civilisation a number of petty agricultural communities have merged into a single state dependent for its subsistence mainly on the cultivation of the ground, it commonly happens that, though every farmer continues to perform for himself the simple old rites designed to ensure the blessing of the gods on his crops, the government undertakes to celebrate similar, though more stately and elaborate, rites on behalf of the whole people, lest the neglect of public worship should draw down on the country the wrath of the offended deities. Hence it comes about that, for all their pomp and splendour, the national festivals of such states are often merely magnified and embellished copies of homely rites and uncouth observances carried out by rustics in the open fields, in barns, and on threshing-floors. In ancient Egypt the religion of Isis and Osiris furnishes examples of solemnities which have been thus raised from the humble rank of rural festivities to the dignity of national celebrations; and in ancient Greece a like development may be traced in the religion of Demeter. If the Greek ploughman prayed to Demeter and Underground Zeus for a good crop before he put his hand to the plough in autumn, the authorities of the Athenian state celebrated about the same time and for the same purpose a public festival of Demeter at Eleusis. It was called the Proerosia, which signifies 'Before the Ploughing'; and as the festival was dedicated to her, Demeter herself bore the name of Proerosia.

Just as the ploughman's prayer to Demeter, before he drove the share through the clods of the field, was taken up and reverberated, so to say, with a great volume of sound in the public prayers which the Athenian state annually offered to the goddess before the ploughing on behalf of the whole world, so the simple first-fruits of barley, presented to the rustic Demeter under the dappled shade of rustling poplars and elms on threshing-floors in Cos, were repeated year by year on a grander scale in the first-fruits of the barley and wheat harvest, which were presented to the Corn Mother and the Corn Maiden at Eleusis, not merely by every husband-man in Attica, but by all the allies and subjects of Athens far and near, and even by many free Greek communities beyond the sea. Offerings

continued to be brought to Eleusis until the end of paganism, long after the Athenian Empire had fallen. The festival was called Haloa, or Festival of the Threshing-floor. The Festival of the Threshing-floor took place in December and thus was quite distinct from the actual threshing of the corn. It is said to have included certain mystic rites performed by women alone, who feasted and quaffed wine, while they broke filthy jests on each other and exhibited cakes baked in the form of the male and female organs of generation. We may suppose that these indecencies, like certain obscenities which seem to have formed part of the Great Mysteries at Eleusis, were no mere wanton outbursts of licentious passion, but were deliberately practised as rites calculated to promote the fertility of the ground by means of homoeopathic or imitative magic.

Other festivals held at Eleusis in honour of Demeter and Persephone were known as the Green Festival and the Festival of the Cornstalks. Of the manner of their celebration we know nothing except that they comprised sacrifices, which were offered to Demeter and Persephone. But their names suffice to connect the two festivals with the green and the standing corn.

Part of the religious drama performed in the mysteries of Eleusis may have been a marriage between the sky-god Zeus and the corn-goddess Demeter, represented by the hierophant and the priestess of the goddess respectively. The story of this marriage was known to Homer, for in the list of beauties to whom he makes Zeus, in a burst of candour, confess that he had lost his too susceptible heart, there occurs the name of 'the fair-haired Queen Demeter'; and in another passage the poet represents the jealous god smiting with a thunderbolt the favoured lover with whom the goddess had forgotten her dignity among the furrows of a fallow field. Moreover, according to one tradition, Dionysus himself was the offspring of the intrigue between Zeus and Demeter. But at the same time, there is reason to suppose that the sacred marriage took place not between Demeter and Zeus, but between Persephone and Pluto, brother of Zeus and god of the Underworld. We are told that at these rites the worshippers looked up to the sky and cried 'Rain!' and then looked down at the earth and cried 'Conceive!' Nothing could be more appropriate at a marriage of the Sky God and the Earth or Corn Goddess than such invocations to the heaven to pour down rain and to the earth or the corn to conceive seed under the fertilising shower; in Greece no time could well be more suitable for the utterance of such prayers than just at the date when the Great Mysteries of Eleusis were celebrated, at the end of the long drought of summer and before the first rains of autumn.

Different both from the Great Mysteries and the offerings of first-fruits at Eleusis were the games which were celebrated there on a great scale once in every four years and on a less scale once in every two years. These games included athletic and musical contests, a horserace, and a competition which bore the name of the Ancestral or Hereditary Contest, and which accordingly may well have formed the original kernel of the games.

So far as the scanty evidence at our disposal permits us to judge, the Eleusinian games, like the Eleusinian Mysteries, would seem to have been primarily concerned with Demeter and Persephone as goddesses of the corn. At least that is expressly affirmed by the old scholiast on Pindar and it is borne out by the practice of rewarding the victors with measures of barley. Perhaps the Ancestral Contest, which may well have formed the original nucleus of the games, was a contest between the reapers on the sacred Rarian plain to see who should finish his allotted task before his fellows. For success in such a contest no prize could be more appropriate than a measure of the sacred barley which the vic-

torious reaper had just cut on the barley-field. Similar contests between reapers have been common on the harvest fields of modern Europe, and it will appear that such competitions are not purely athletic; their aim is not simply to demonstrate the superior strength, activity, and skill of the victors; it is to secure for the particular farm the possession of the blooming young Corn-maiden of the present year, conceived as the embodiment of the vigorous grain, and to pass on to laggard neighbours the aged Corn-mother of the past year, conceived as an embodiment of the effete and outworn energies of the corn. May it not have been so at Eleusis? may not the reapers have vied with each other for possession of the young corn-spirit

Nature and culture
The Taoists of China possessed an extensive lore about the sacred properties of plants. Here, Chinese immortals enjoy the gifts of nature and watch the arrival of Lao Tsin, god of immortality, on a crane. The pine, the plum, and the bamboo are symbols of longevity. Bronze and lacquer box, 16th to 17th century, British Museum, London

Persephone and for avoidance of the old corn-spirit Demeter? may not the prize of barley, which rewarded the victor in the Ancestral Contest, have been supposed to house in the ripe ears no less a personage than the Corn-maiden Persephone herself?

If we adhere to the evidence of the ancients themselves in regard to the rites of Eleusis, including under that general term the Great Mysteries, the games, the Festival before Ploughing (*proerosia*), the Festival of the Threshing-floor, the Green Festival, the Festival of the Cornstalks, and the offerings of first-fruits, we shall probably incline to agree with the most learned of ancient antiquaries, the Roman Varro, who, to quote Augustine's report of his opinion, 'interpreted the whole of the Eleusinian mysteries as relating to the corn which Ceres (Demeter) had discovered, and to Proserpine (Persephone), whom Pluto had carried off from her. And Proserpine herself, he said, signifies the fecundity of the seeds, the failure of which at a certain time had caused the earth to mourn for barrenness, and therefore had given rise to the opinion that the daughter of Ceres, that is fecundity itself, had been ravished by Pluto and detained in the nether world; and when the dearth had been publicly mourned and fecundity had returned once more, there was gladness at the return of Proserpine and solemn rites were instituted accordingly. After that he says', continues Augustine, reporting Varro, 'that many things were taught in her mysteries which had no reference but to the discovery of the corn.'

In these mysteries, the thought of the seed buried in the earth in order to spring up to new and higher life readily suggested a comparison with human destiny, and strengthened the hope that for man too the grave may be but the beginning of a better and happier existence in some brighter world unknown. This simple and natural reflection seems perfectly sufficient to explain the association of the Corn Goddess at Eleusis with the mystery of death and the hope of a blissful immortality. For that the ancients regarded initiation in the Eleusinian mysteries as a key to unlock the gates of Paradise appears to be proved by the allusions which well-informed writers among them drop to the happiness in store for the initiated hereafter. The Greeks, like ourselves, with death before them and a great love of life in their hearts, did not stop to weigh with too nice a hand the arguments that told for and against the prospect of human immortality. The reasoning that satisfied Saint Paul and has brought comfort to untold thousands of sorrowing Christians, standing by the deathbed or the open grave of their loved ones, was good enough to pass muster with ancient pagans, when they too bowed their heads under the burden of grief, and, with the taper of life burning low in the socket, looked forward into the darkness of the unknown. Therefore we do no indignity to the myth of Demeter and Persephone – one of the few myths in which the sunshine and clarity of the Greek genius are crossed by the shadow and mystery of death – when we trace its origin to some of the most familiar, yet eternally affecting aspects of nature, to the melancholy gloom and decay of autumn and to the freshness, the brightness, and the verdure of spring.

2. The Corn-Mother and the Corn-Maiden in Europe and Beyond

The Corn-Mother in Europe

We have found reasons for identifying Demeter as the Corn-mother, and of the two species of corn associated with her in Greek religion, namely barley and wheat, the barley has perhaps the better claim to be her original element; for not only would it seem to have been the staple food of the Greeks in the Homeric age, but there are grounds for believing that it is one of the oldest, if not the very oldest, cereal cultivated by the Aryan race. Certainly the use of barley in the religious ritual of the ancient Hindoos as well as of the ancient Greeks furnishes a strong argument in favour of the great antiquity of its cultivation, which is known to have been practised by the lake-dwellers of the Stone Age in Europe.

Analogies to the Corn-mother or Barley-mother of ancient Greece have been collected in great abundance from the folk-lore of modern Europe. The following may serve as specimens.

In Germany the corn is very commonly personified under the name of the Corn-mother who plays an important part in harvest customs. She is believed to be present in the handful of corn which is left standing last on the field; and with the cutting of this last handful she is caught, or driven away, or killed. In the first of these cases, the last sheaf is carried joyfully home and honoured as a divine being. It is placed in the barn, and at threshing the corn-spirit appears again.

In Russia, as elsewhere, the last sheaf is often shaped and dressed as a woman, and carried with dance and song to the farmhouse. Out of the last sheaf the Bulgarians make a doll which they call the Corn-queen or Corn-mother; it is dressed in a woman's shirt, carried round the village, and then thrown into the river in order to secure plenty of rain and dew for the next year's crop. Or it is burned and the ashes strewn on the fields, doubtless to fertilise them. The name Queen, as applied to the last sheaf, has its analogies in central and northern Europe. Milton must have been familiar with the custom of the Harvest Queen, for in *Paradise Lost* he says:

> Adam the while
> Waiting desirous her return, had wove
> Of choicest flow'rs a garland to adorn
> Her tresses, and her rural labours crown,
> As reapers oft are wont their harvest-queen.

Often customs of this sort are practised, not on the harvest-field but on the threshing-floor. The spirit of the corn, fleeing before the reapers as they cut down the ripe grain, quits the reaped corn and takes refuge in the barn, where it appears in the last sheaf threshed, either to perish under the blows of the flail or to flee thence to the still unthreshed corn of a neighbouring farm. Thus the last corn to be threshed is called the Mother-Corn or the Old Woman. Sometimes the person who gives the last stroke with the flail is called the Old Woman, and is wrapt in the straw of the last sheaf, or has a bundle of straw fastened on his back.

Gods of death and vegetation: Osiris

Primitive thought sees a connection between the dead who are laid into the ground, and vegetation, which rises from it. Thus Osiris, the Egyptian king of the dead, is also a divinity of vegetation, and as such can be represented with green skin.

OPPOSITE. The green Osiris, with the insignia of a ruler over the living, is enthroned as king of the dead. *Theban Book of the Dead, c.*1250 BC, British Museum, London

In some parts of Sweden, when a stranger woman appears on the threshing-floor, a flail is put round her body, stalks of corn are wound round her neck, a crown of ears is placed on her head, and the threshers call out, 'Behold the Corn-woman'. Here the stranger woman, thus suddenly appearing, is taken to be the corn-spirit who has just been expelled by the flails from the corn-stalks. In other cases the farmer's wife represents the corn-spirit. Thus in the Commune of Saligné, Canton de Poiret (Vendée), the farmer's wife, along with the last sheaf, is tied up in a sheet, placed on a litter, and carried to the threshing machine, under which she is shoved. Then the woman is drawn out and the sheaf is threshed by itself, but the woman is tossed in the sheet, as if she were being winnowed. It would be impossible to express more clearly the identification of the woman with the corn than by this graphic imitation of threshing and winnowing her.

Generally, the spirit of the ripe corn is regarded as old, or at least as of mature age. Hence the names of Mother, Grandmother, Old Woman, and so forth. But in other cases the corn-spirit is conceived as young. Thus at Saldern, near Wolfenbuttel, when the rye has been reaped, three sheaves are tied together with a rope so as to make a puppet with the corn ears for a head. This puppet is called the Maiden or the Corn-maiden (*Kornjunfer*). Sometimes the corn-spirit is conceived as a child who is separated from its mother by the stroke of the sickle. This last view appears in the Polish custom of calling out to the man who cuts the last handful of corn, 'You have cut the navel-string'. In some

districts of West Prussia the figure made out of the last sheaf is called the Bastard, and a boy is wrapt up in it. The woman who binds the last sheaf and represents the Corn-mother is told that she is about to be brought to bed; she cries like a woman in travail, and an old woman in the character of grandmother acts as midwife. At last a cry is raised that the child is born; whereupon the boy who is tied up in the sheaf whimpers and squalls like an infant. The grandmother wraps a sack, in imitation of swaddling bands, round the pretended baby, who is carried joyfully to the barn, lest he should catch cold in the open air. In other parts of North Germany the last sheaf, or the puppet made out of it, is called the Child, the Harvest-child, and so on, and they call out to the woman who binds the last sheaf, 'You are getting the child'.

A somewhat maturer but still youthful age is assigned to the corn-spirit by the appellations of Bride, Oats-bride, and Wheat-bride, which in Germany are sometimes bestowed both on the last sheaf and on the woman who binds it. At wheat-harvest near Müglitz, in Moravia, a small portion of the wheat is left standing after all the rest has been reaped. This remnant is then cut, amid the rejoicing of the reapers, by a young girl who wears a wreath of wheaten ears on her head and goes by the name of the Wheat-bride. It is supposed that she will be a real bride that same year.

Sometimes the idea implied by the name of Bride is worked out more fully by representing the productive powers of vegetation as bride and bridegroom. In Austrian Silesia the ceremony of 'the Wheat-bride' is celebrated by the young people at the end of the harvest. The woman who bound the last sheaf plays the part of the Wheat-bride, wearing the harvest-crown of wheat ears and flowers on her head. Thus adorned, standing beside her Bridegroom in a waggon and attended by bridesmaids, she is drawn by a pair of oxen, in full imitation of a

The omnipresence of demons
OPPOSITE. A demon of disease, flanked by attendants, holds his victim, ready to devour him. Wooden painted image from Ceylon, 19th century. The Royal Pavilion, Art Gallery and Museums, Brighton

marriage procession, to the tavern, where the dancing is kept up till morning. Somewhat later in the season the wedding of the Oats-bride is celebrated with the like rustic pomp. About Neisse, in Silesia, an Oats-king and an Oats-queen, dressed up as a bridal pair, are seated on a harrow and drawn by oxen into the village.

The harvest customs just described are strikingly analogous to the spring customs which we reviewed in the first part of this work. (1) As in the spring customs the tree-spirit is represented both by a tree and by a person, so in the harvest customs the corn-spirit is represented both by the last sheaf and by the person who cuts or binds or threshes it. The equivalence of the person to the sheaf is shewn by giving him or her the same name as the sheaf; by wrapping him or her in it; and by the rule observed in some places, that when the sheaf is called the Mother, it must be made up into human shape by the oldest married woman, but that when it is called the Maiden, it must be cut by the youngest girl. Here the age of the personal representative of the corn-spirit corresponds with that of the supposed age of the corn-spirit, just as the human victims offered by the Mexicans to promote the growth of the maize varied with the age of the maize. For in the Mexican, as in the European, custom the human beings were probably representatives of the corn-spirit rather than victims offered to it. (2) Again, the same fertilising influence which the tree-spirit is supposed to exert over vegetation, cattle, and even women is ascribed to the corn-spirit. Thus, its supposed influence on vegetation is shewn by the practice of taking some of the grain of the last sheaf (in which the corn-spirit is regularly supposed to be present), and scattering it among the young corn in spring or mixing it with the seed-corn. Its influence on animals is shewn by giving the last sheaf to a mare in foal, to a cow in calf, and to horses at the first ploughing. Lastly, its influence on women is indicated by the custom of delivering the Mother-sheaf, made into the likeness of a pregnant woman, to the farmer's wife; by the belief that the woman who binds the last sheaf will have a child next year; perhaps, too, by the idea that the person who gets it will soon be married.

Plainly, therefore, these spring and harvest customs are based on the same ancient modes of thought, and form parts of the same primitive heathendom, which was doubtless practised by our forefathers long before the dawn of history. No special class of persons and no special places are set exclusively apart for their performance; they may be performed by any one, master or man, mistress or maid, boy or girl; they are practised, not in temples or churches, but in the woods and meadows, beside brooks, in barns, on harvest fields and cottage floors. The supernatural beings whose existence is taken for granted in them are spirits rather than deities: their functions are limited to certain well-defined departments of nature: their names are general, like the Barley-mother, the Old Woman, the Maiden, not proper names like Demeter, Persephone, Dionysus. Their generic attributes are known, but their individual histories and characters are not the subject of myths. For they exist in classes rather than as individuals, and the members of each class are indistinguishable. For example, every farm has its Corn-mother, or its Old Woman, or its Maiden; but every Corn-mother is much like every other Corn-mother, and so with the Old Women and Maidens. Lastly, in these harvest as in the spring customs, the ritual is magical rather than propitiatory. This is shewn by throwing the Corn-mother into the river in order to secure rain and dew for the crops; by making the Old Woman heavy in order to get a heavy crop next year; by strewing grain from the last sheaf amongst the young crops in spring; and by giving the last sheaf to the cattle to make them thrive.

The corn-spirit in England and France
TOP. At Whalton, Northumberland, a 'kern baby' was raised in the fields after the last sheaf was cut, until the early 20th century. *Sir Benjamin Stone's Pictures*, 1906, Bodleian Library, Oxford
ABOVE. In France the last ears of corn were made into a 'plumette' and hung up in the house until the next harvest. Pitt Rivers Museum, University of Oxford

The Corn-Mother in Many Lands

European peoples, ancient and modern, have not been singular in personifying the corn as a mother goddess. The same simple idea has suggested itself to other agricultural races in distant parts of the world, and has been applied by them to other indigenous cereals than barley and wheat. If Europe has its Wheat-mother and its Barley-mother, America has its Maize-mother and the East Indies their Rice-mother. These personifications I will now illustrate, beginning with the American personification of the maize.

The Peruvian Mother of the Maize, consisting of a portion of maize attired in rich garments, was kept for a year in order that by her means the corn might grow and multiply. But lest her strength might not suffice to last till the next harvest, she was asked in the course of the year how she felt, and if she answered that she felt weak, she was burned and a fresh Mother of the Maize made, 'to the end the seed of maize may not perish'. Here, it may be observed, we have a strong confirmation of the explanation already given of the custom of killing the god, both periodically and occasionally. The Mother of the Maize was allowed, as a rule, to live through a year, that being the period during which her strength might reasonably be supposed to last unimpaired; but on any symptom of her strength failing she was put to death, and a fresh and vigorous Mother of the Maize took her place, lest the maize which depended on her for its existence should languish and decay.

An account of the ancient Mexican worship of the maize has been given us by the Franciscan monk Bernardino de Sahagun, who arrived in Mexico in 1529, only eight years after its conquest by the Spaniards, and devoted the remaining sixty-one years of his long life to labouring among the Indians for their moral and spiritual good. From him we learn some valuable particulars as to the worship of the Maize-goddess and the ceremonies observed by the Mexicans

Spirits of the maize from coastal Peru
Native to the Americas, maize has been a staple crop and divine power for many American societies.
LEFT. To this day 'mother maize' is venerated in the Andes. Mochica conopa pots representing maize deities,

*c.*500 AD, British Museum, London
RIGHT. Navajo sacred maize; sand painting used in a 20th-century ritual to ensure the wellbeing of man in the universe. Wheelwright Museum, Santa Fe, USA

for the purpose of ensuring a good crop of maize. The festival was the fourth of the Aztec year, and went by the name of the Great Vigil. It fell on a date which corresponds to the seventh of April. The name of the Maize-goddess was Chicome Couatl, and the Mexicans conceived and represented her in the form of a woman, red in face and arms and legs, wearing a paper crown dyed vermilion, and clad in garments of the hue of ripe cherries. No doubt the red colour of the goddess and her garments referred to the deep orange hue of the ripe maize; it was like the yellow hair of the Greek corn-goddess Demeter. She was supposed to make all kinds of maize, beans, and vegetables to grow. On the day of the festival the Mexicans sent out to the maize-fields and fetched from every field a plant of maize, which they brought to their houses and greeted as their maize-gods, setting them up in their dwellings, clothing them in garments, and placing food before them. And after sunset they carried the maize-plants to the temple of the Maize-goddess, where they snatched them from one another and fought and struck each other with them. Further, at this festival they brought to the

temple of the Maize-goddess the maize-cobs which were to be used in the sowing. The cobs were carried by three maidens in bundles of seven wrapt in red paper. One of the girls was small with short hair, another was older with long hair hanging down, and the third was full-grown with her hair wound round her head. Red feathers were gummed to the arms and legs of the three maidens and their faces were painted, probably to resemble the red Maize-goddess, whom they may be supposed to have personated at various stages of the growth of the corn. The maize-cobs which they brought to the temple of the Maize-goddess were called by the name of the Maize-god Cinteotl, and they were afterwards deposited in the granary and kept there as 'the heart of the granary' till the sowing time came round, when they were used as seed.

The eastern Indians of North America, who subsisted to a large extent by the cultivation of maize, generally conceived the spirit of the maize as a woman, and supposed that the plant itself had sprung originally from the blood drops or the dead body of the Corn Woman. In the sacred formulas of the Cherokee the corn is sometimes invoked as 'the Old Woman', and one of their myths relates how a hunter saw a fair woman issue from a single green stalk of corn. The Iroquois believe the Spirit of the Corn, the Spirit of Beans, and the Spirit of Squashes to be three sisters clad in the leaves of their respective plants, very fond of each other, and delighting to dwell together. This divine trinity is known by the name of *De-o-ha'-ko*, which means 'Our Life' or 'Our Supporters'. The three persons of the trinity have no individual names, and are never mentioned separately except by means of description. The Indians have a legend that of old the corn was easily cultivated, yielded abundantly, and had a grain exceedingly rich in oil, till the Evil One, envious of this good gift of the Great Spirit to man, went forth into the fields and blighted them. And still, when the wind rustles in the corn, the pious Indian fancies he hears the Spirit of the Corn bemoaning her blighted fruitfulness. The Huichol Indians of Mexico imagine maize to be a little girl, who may sometimes be heard weeping in the fields; so afraid is she of the wild beasts that eat the corn.

Believing the rice to be animated by a soul like that of a man, the Indonesians naturally treat it with the deference and the consideration which they shew to their fellows. Thus they behave towards the rice in bloom as they behave towards a pregnant woman; they abstain from firing guns or making loud noises in the field, lest they should so frighten the soul of the rice that it would miscarry and bear no grain; and for the same reason they will not talk of corpses or demons in the rice-fields. Moreover, they feed the blooming rice with foods of various kinds which are believed to be wholesome for women with child; but when the rice-ears are just beginning to form, they are looked upon as infants, and women go through the fields feeding them with rice-pap as if they were human babes. In such natural and obvious comparisons of the breeding plant to a breeding woman, and of the young grain to a young child, is to be sought the origin of the kindred Greek conception of the Corn-mother and the Corn-daughter, Demeter and Persephone, and we need not go further afield to search for it in a primitive division of labour between the sexes. But if the timorous feminine soul of the rice can be frightened into a miscarriage even by loud noises, it is easy to imagine what her feelings must be at harvest, when people are under the sad necessity of cutting down the rice with the

The rites of the agricultural year

North American Indians dance, feast and sacrifice for the good of the crops. De Bry, *America*, 1590, Bodleian Library, Oxford

knife. At so critical a season every precaution must be used to render the necessary surgical operation of reaping as inconspicuous and as painless as possible. For that reason, as we have seen, the reaping of the seed-rice is done with knives of a peculiar pattern, such that the blades are hidden in the reapers' hands and do not frighten the rice-spirit till the very last moment, when her head is swept off almost before she is aware; and from a like delicate motive the reapers at work in the fields employ a special form of speech, which the rice-spirit cannot be expected to understand, so that she has no warning or inkling of what is going forward till the heads of rice are safely deposited in the basket.

The European custom of representing the corn-spirit in the double form of bride and bridegroom has its parallel in a ceremony observed at the rice-harvest in Java. Before the reapers begin to cut the rice, the priest or sorcerer picks out a number of ears of rice, which are tied together, smeared with ointment, and adorned with flowers. Thus decked out, the ears are called the *padi-pĕngantèn*, that is, the Rice-bride and the Rice-bridegroom; their wedding feast is celebrated, and the cutting of the rice begins immediately afterwards. Later on, when the rice is being got in, a bridal chamber is partitioned off in the barn, and furnished with a new mat, a lamp, and all kinds of toilet articles. Sheaves of rice, to represent the wedding guests, are placed beside the Rice-bride and the Rice-bridegroom. Not till this has been done may the whole harvest be housed in the barn. And for the first forty days after the rice has been housed, no one may enter the barn, for fear of disturbing the newly-wedded pair.

Thus the theory which recognises in the European Corn-mother, Corn-maiden, and so forth, the embodiment in vegetable form of the animating spirit of the crops is amply confirmed by the evidence of peoples in other parts of the world, who, because they have lagged behind the European races in mental development, retain for that very reason a keener sense of the original motives for observing those rustic rites which among ourselves have sunk to the level of meaningless survivals. Now in the parallels which have been hitherto adduced from the customs of peoples outside Europe the spirit of the crops appears only in vegetable form. It remains, therefore, to show that other races besides our European peasantry have conceived the spirit of the crops as incorporate in or represented by living men and women. This topic, I may remind the reader, is germane to the theme of this book; for the more instances we discover of human beings representing in themselves the life or animating spirit of plants, the less difficulty will be felt at classing amongst them the King of the Wood at Nemi.

The Mandans and Minnetarees of North America used to hold a festival in spring which they called the corn-medicine festival of the women. They thought that a certain Old Woman Who Never Dies made the crops to grow, and that, living somewhere in the south, she sent the migratory waterfowl in spring as her tokens and representatives. Each sort of bird represented a special kind of crop cultivated by the Indians: the wild goose stood for the maize, the wild swan for the gourds, and the wild duck for the beans. So when the feathered messengers of the Old Woman began to arrive in spring the Indians celebrated the corn-medicine festival of the women. Scaffolds were set up, on which the people hung dried meat and other things by way of offerings to the Old Woman; and on a certain day the old women of the tribe, as representatives of the Old Woman Who Never Dies, assembled at the scaffolds each bearing in her hand an ear of maize fastened to a stick. They first planted these sticks in the ground, then danced round the scaffolds, and finally took up the sticks again in their arms. Meanwhile old men beat drums and shook rattles as a musical accompaniment to the performance of the old women. Further, young women came and put dried flesh into the mouths of the old women, for which they received in return a grain of the consecrated maize to eat. Three or four grains of the holy corn were also placed in the dishes of the young women, to be afterwards carefully mixed with the seed-corn, which they were supposed to fertilise. The dried flesh hung on the scaffold belonged to the old women, because they represented the Old Woman Who Never Dies. A similar corn-medicine festival was held in autumn for the purpose of attracting the herds of buffaloes and securing a supply of meat. At that time every woman carried in her arms an up-rooted plant of maize. They gave the name of the Old Woman Who Never Dies both to the maize and to those birds which they regarded as symbols of the fruits of the earth, and they prayed to them in autumn saying, 'Mother, have pity on us! send us not the bitter cold too soon, lest we have not meat enough! let not all the game depart, that we may have something for the winter!' In autumn, when the birds were flying south, the Indians thought that they were going home to the Old Woman and taking to her the offerings that had been hung up on the scaffolds, especially the dried meat, which she ate. Here then we have the spirit or divinity of the corn conceived as an Old Woman and represented in bodily form by old women, who in their capacity of representatives receive some at least of the offerings which are intended for her.

Compared with personages like the Corn-mother and maiden of early modern Europe, the Demeter and Persephone of Greece are late products of religious growth. Yet as members of the Aryan family the Greeks must at one time or another have observed harvest customs like those which are still practised by Celts, Teutons, and Slavs, and which, far beyond the limits of the Aryan world, have been practised by the Indians of Peru, the Dyaks of Borneo, and many other natives of the East Indies – a sufficient proof that the ideas on which these customs rest are not confined to any one race, but naturally suggest themselves to all untutored peoples engaged in agriculture. It is probable, therefore, that Demeter and Persephone, those stately and beautiful figures of Greek mythology, grew out of the same simple beliefs and practices which still prevail among our modern peasantry, and that they were represented by rude dolls made out of the yellow sheaves on many a harvest-field long before their breathing images were wrought in bronze and marble by the master hands of Phidias and Praxiteles. A reminiscence of that olden time – a scent, so to say, of the harvest-field – lingered to the last in the title of the Maiden (*Kore*) by which Persephone was commonly known. Thus if the prototype of Demeter is the Corn-mother of Germany, the prototype of Persephone is the Harvest-maiden, which, autumn after autumn, is still made from the last sheaf on the Braes of Balquhidder. Indeed, if we knew more about the peasant-farmers of ancient Greece, we should probably find that even in classical times they continued annually to fashion their Corn-mothers (Demeters) and Maidens (Persephones) out of the ripe corn on the harvest-fields. But unfortunately the Demeter and Persephone whom we know were the denizens of towns, the majestic inhabitants of lordly temples; it was for such divinities alone that the refined writers of antiquity had eyes; the uncouth rites performed by rustics amongst the corn were beneath their notice. Even if they noticed them, they probably never dreamed of any connexion between the puppet of corn-stalks on the sunny stubble-field and the marble divinity in the shady coolness of the temple. Still the writings even of these town-bred and cultured persons afford us an occasional glimpse of a Demeter as rude as the rudest that a remote German village can shew.

Thus the story that Iasion begat a child Plutus ('wealth', 'abundance') by Demeter on a thrice-ploughed field, may be compared with the West Prussian custom of the mock birth of a child on the harvest-field. In this Prussian custom the pretended mother represents the Corn-mother (*Žytniamatka*), that is, the ripe grain; the pretended child represents the Corn-baby, that is, this year's corn, and the whole ceremony is a charm to ensure a crop next year. The custom and the legend alike point to an older practice of performing, among the sprouting crops in spring or the stubble in autumn, one of those real or mimic acts of procreation by which, as we have seen, primitive man often seeks to infuse his own vigorous life into the languid or decaying energies of nature.

The Greek Demeter would then be the ripe crop of this year; Persephone would be the seed-corn taken from it and sown in autumn, to reappear in spring. The descent of Persephone into the lower world would thus be a mythical expression for the sowing of the seed; her reappearance in spring would signify the sprouting of the young corn. In this way the Persephone of one year becomes the Demeter of the next, and this may very well have been the original form of the myth.

Persephone, the seed corn
ABOVE. Greek myth associated the pomegranate with fertility, because it had so many seeds. When Pluto snatched Persephone away to the underworld, he gave her the seed of the pomegranate to eat, thus ensuring that she would return to him every year, just as the seed is sown in the earth before the plant can grow above ground. *Botanical Magazine*, XLIII, 1816. Courtesy of the Sherardian Professor of Botany, University of Oxford
RIGHT. Persephone, the corn-maiden, rises from the ground holding three ears of corn. Greek coin from Lampsacus, British Museum, London

3. Lityerses

In the preceding pages an attempt has been made to shew that in the Corn-mother and Harvest-maiden of Northern Europe we have the prototypes of Demeter and Persephone. But an essential feature is still wanting to complete the resemblance. A leading incident in the Greek myth is the death and resurrection of Persephone; it is this incident which, coupled with the nature of the goddess as a deity of vegetation, links the myth with the cults of Adonis; and it is in virtue of this incident that the myth finds a place in our discussion of the Dying God. It remains, therefore, to see whether the conception of the annual death and resurrection of a god, which figures so prominently in these great Greek and Oriental worships, has not also its origins or its analogy in the rustic rites observed by reapers and vine-dressers amongst the corn-shocks and the vines.

Our general ignorance of the popular superstitions and customs of the ancients has already been confessed. But the obscurity which thus hangs over the first beginnings of ancient religion is fortunately dissipated to some extent in the present case. The worship of Adonis had its seat, as we have seen, in Syria; where certain harvest and vintage customs are known to have been observed, the resemblance of which to the national rites of Greece struck the ancients themselves, and, compared with the harvest customs of modern peasants and barbarians, seems to throw some light on the origin of the rites in question.

Similar customs were observed in Egypt. We have it on the authority of Diodorus, that in ancient Egypt the reapers were wont to lament over the first sheaf cut, invoking Isis as the goddess to whom they owed the discovery of corn. To the plaintive song or cry sung or uttered by Egyptian reapers the Greeks gave the name of Maneros, and explained the name by a story that Maneros, the only son of the first Egyptian king, invented agriculture, and, dying an untimely death, was thus lamented by the people. It appears, however, that the name Maneros is due to a misunderstanding of the formula *mââ-ne-hra*, 'Come to the house', which has been discovered in various Egyptian writings, for example in the dirge of Isis in the Book of the Dead. Hence we may suppose that the cry *mââ-ne-hra* was chanted by the reapers over the cut corn as a dirge for the death of the corn-spirit (Isis or Osiris) and a prayer for its return. As the cry was raised over the first ears reaped, it would seem that the corn-spirit was believed by the Egyptians to be present in the first corn cut and to die under the sickle. In parts of Russia the first sheaf is treated much in the same way that the last sheaf is treated elsewhere. It is reaped by the mistress herself, taken home and set in the place of honour near the holy pictures; afterwards it is threshed separately, and some of its grain is mixed with the next year's seed-corn.

In Phoenicia and Western Asia a plaintive song, like that chanted by the Egyptian corn-reapers, was sung at the vintage and probably (to judge by analogy) also at harvest. This Phoenician song was called by the Greeks Linus or Ailinus and explained, like Maneros, as a lament for the death of a youth named Linus. Like Maneros, the name Linus or Ailinus appears to have originated in a verbal misunderstanding, and to be nothing more than the cry *ai lanu*, that is 'Woe to us', which the Phoenicians probably uttered in mourning for Adonis; at least Sappho seems to have regarded Adonis and Linus as equivalent.

In Phrygia the song, sung by harvesters both at reaping and at threshing, was called Lityerses. According to one story, Lityerses was a bastard son of Midas, King of Phrygia, and dwelt at Celaenae. He used to reap the corn, and had an enormous appetite. When a stranger happened to enter the corn-field or to pass by it, Lityerses gave him plenty to eat and drink, then took him to the corn-fields on the banks of the Maeander and compelled him to reap along with him. Lastly, it was his custom to wrap the stranger in a sheaf, cut off his head with a sickle, and carry away his body, swathed in the corn stalks. But at last Hercules undertook to reap with him, cut off his head with the sickle, and threw his body into the river. As Hercules is reported to have slain Lityerses in the same way that Lityerses slew others we may infer that Lityerses used to throw the bodies of his victims into the river. According to another version of the story, Lityerses, a son of Midas, was wont to challenge people to a reaping match with him, and if he vanquished them he used to thrash them; but one day he met with a stronger reaper, who slew him.

There are some grounds for supposing that in these stories of Lityerses we have the description of a Phrygian harvest custom in accordance with which certain persons, especially strangers passing the harvest field, were regularly regarded as embodiments of the corn-spirit, and as such were seized by the reapers, wrapt in sheaves, and beheaded, their bodies, bound up in the corn-stalks, being afterwards thrown into water as a rain-charm. The grounds for this supposition are, first, the resemblance of the Lityerses story to the harvest customs of European peasantry, and, second, the frequency of human sacrifices offered by savage races to promote the fertility of the fields. We will examine these grounds successively, beginning with the former.

In comparing the story with the harvest customs of Europe, three points deserve special attention, namely: I. the reaping match and the binding of persons in the sheaves; II. the killing of the corn-spirit or his representatives; III. the treatment of visitors to the harvest field or of strangers passing it.

In regard to the first head, we have seen that in modern Europe the person who cuts or binds or threshes the last sheaf is often exposed to rough treatment at the hands of his fellow-labourers. The person who is last at reaping, binding, or threshing, is regarded as the representative of the corn-spirit, and this idea is more fully expressed by binding him or her in corn-stalks. At Kloxin, near Stettin, the harvesters call out to the woman who binds the last sheaf, 'You have the Old Man, and must keep him'. The Old Man is a great bundle of corn decked with flowers and ribbons, and fashioned into a rude semblance of the human form. It is fastened on a rake or strapped on a horse, and brought with music to the village. As late as the first half of the nineteenth century the custom was to tie up the woman herself in pease-straw, and bring her with music to the farmhouse, where the harvesters danced with her till the pease-straw fell off.

Passing to the second point of comparison between the Lityerses story and European customs, we have now to see that in the latter the corn-spirit is often believed to be killed at reaping or threshing. In the Romsdal and other parts of Norway, when the haymaking is over, the people say that 'the Old Hay-man has been killed'. In some parts of Bavaria the man who gives the last stroke at threshing is said to have killed the Corn-man, the Oats-man, or the Wheat-man, according to the crop. In Carinthia, the thresher who gave the last stroke, and the person who untied the last sheaf on the threshing-floor, are bound hand and foot with straw bands, and crowns of straw are placed on their heads. Then they are tied, face to face, on a sledge, dragged through the village, and flung into a brook. The custom of throwing the representative of the corn-spirit into a stream, like that of drenching him with water, is as usual, a rain-charm.

Thus far the representatives of the corn-spirit have generally been the man or woman who cuts, binds, or threshes the last corn. We now come to the cases in which the corn-spirit is represented either by a stranger passing the harvest-field (as in the Lityerses tale), or by a visitor entering it for the first time. All over Germany it is customary for the reapers or threshers to lay hold of passing strangers and bind them with a rope made of corn-stalks, till they pay a forfeit; and when the farmer himself or one of his guests enters the field or the threshing-floor for the first time, he is treated in the same way. Sometimes the rope is only tied round his arm or his feet or his neck. But sometimes he is regularly swathed in corn. At Solör in Norway, whoever enters the field, be he the master or a stranger, is tied up in a sheaf and must pay a ransom. In the neighbourhood of Soest, when the farmer visits the flax-pullers for the first time, he is completely enveloped in flax. Passers-by are also surrounded by the women, tied up in flax, and compelled to stand brandy.

Thus, like the ancient Lityerses, modern European reapers have been wont to lay hold of a passing stranger and tie him up in a sheaf. It is not to be expected that they should complete the parallel by cutting off his head; but if they do not take such a strong step, their language and gestures are at least indicative of a desire to do so. For instance, in Mecklenburg on the first day of reaping, if the master or mistress or a stranger enters the field, or merely passes by it, all the mowers face towards him and sharpen their scythes, clashing their whet-stones against them in unison, as if they were making ready to mow. Then the woman who leads the mowers steps up

to him and ties a band round his left arm. He must ransom himself by payment of a forfeit. In customs such as these, whoever passes the harvest-field is regarded as a personification of the corn, in other words, as the corn-spirit; and a show is made of treating him like the corn by mowing, binding, and threshing him.

In other harvest-customs of modern Europe it is the person who cuts, binds, or threshes the last corn who is treated as an embodiment of the corn-spirit by being wrapt up in sheaves, killed in mimicry by agricultural implements, and thrown into the water. These coincidences with the Lityerses story seem to prove that the latter is a genuine description of an old Phrygian harvest-custom. But since in the modern parallels the killing of the personal representative of the corn-spirit is necessarily omitted or at most enacted only in mimicry, it is desirable to shew that in rude society human beings have been commonly killed as an agricultural ceremony to promote the fertility of the fields.

A particular account has been preserved of the sacrifice of a Sioux girl by the Pawnees in April 1837 or 1838. The girl was fourteen or fifteen years old and had been kept for six months and well treated. Two days before the sacrifice she was led from wigwam to wigwam accompanied by the whole council of chiefs and warriors. At each lodge she received a small billet of wood and a little paint, which she handed to the warrior next to her. In this way she called at every wigwam, receiving at each the same present of wood and paint. On the twenty-second of April she was taken out to be sacrificed, attended by the warriors, each of whom carried two pieces of wood which he had received from her hands. Her body having been painted half red and half black, she was attached to a sort of gibbet and roasted for some time over a slow fire, then shot to death with arrows. The chief sacrificer next tore out her heart and devoured it. While her flesh was still warm it was cut in small pieces from the bones, put in little baskets, and taken to a neighbouring corn-field. There the head chief took a piece of the flesh from a basket and squeezed a drop of blood upon the newly-deposited grains of corn. His example was followed by the rest, till all the seed had been sprinkled with the blood; it was then covered up with earth. According to one account the body of the victim was reduced to a kind of paste, which was rubbed or sprinkled not only on the maize but also on the potatoes, the beans, and other seeds to fertilise them. By this sacrifice they hoped to obtain good crops. Analogous sacrifices were made in most parts of the world.

But the best known case of human sacrifices, systematically offered to ensure good crops, is supplied by the Khonds or Kandhs, a Dravidian race in Bengal. Our knowledge of them is de-rived from the accounts written by British officers who, about the middle of the nine-teenth century, were engaged in putting them down. The sacrifices were offered to the Earth Goddess, Tari Pennu or Bera Pennu, and were believed to ensure good crops and immunity from all disease and accidents. In particular, they were considered necessary in the cultivation of turmeric, the Khonds arguing that the turmeric could not have a deep red colour without the shedding of blood. The victim or Meriah, as he was called, was acceptable to the goddess only if he had been purchased, or had been born a victim – that is, the son of a victim father, or had been devoted as a child by his father or guardian. Khonds in distress often sold their children for victims, 'considering the beatification of their souls certain, and their death, for the benefit of mankind, the most honourable possible'. A man of the Panua tribe was once seen to load a Khond with curses, and finally to spit in his face, be-cause the Khond had sold for a victim his own child, whom the Panua had wished to marry. A party of Khonds, who saw this, immediately pressed forward to comfort the seller of his child,

saying, 'Your child has died that all the world may live, and the Earth Goddess herself will wipe that spittle from your face.' The victims were often kept for years before they were sacri-ficed. Being regarded as consecrated beings, they were treated with extreme affection, mingled with deference, and were welcomed wherever they went. A Meriah youth, on attaining maturity, was generally given a wife, who was herself usually a Meriah or victim; and with her he received a portion of land and farm-stock. Their offspring were also victims. Human sacri-fices were offered to the Earth Goddess by tribes, branches of tribes, or villages, both at periodical festivals and on extraordinary occasions. The periodical sacrifices were generally so arranged by tribes and divisions of tribes that each head of a family was enabled, at least once a year, to procure a shred of the victim's flesh for his fields, generally about the time when his chief crop was laid down.

The flesh of the victim was believed to be endowed with a magical or physical power of fertilising the land. The same intrinsic power was ascribed to the blood and tears of the Meriah, his blood causing the redness of the turmeric and his tears producing rain; for it can hardly be doubted that, originally at least, the tears were supposed to bring down the rain, not merely to prognosticate it. Furthermore, the Meriah seems to have been regarded as divine. As such, he may originally have represented the Earth Goddess or, perhaps, a deity of vegetation; though in later times he came to be regarded rather as a victim offered to a deity than as himself an in-carnate god. This later view of the Meriah as a victim rather than a divinity may perhaps have received undue emphasis from the European writers who have described the Khond religion. Habituated to the later idea of sacrifice as an offering made to a god for the purpose of con-ciliating his favour, European observers are apt to interpret all religious slaughter in this sense, and to suppose that wherever such slaughter takes place, there must necessarily be a deity to whom the carnage is believed by the slayers to be acceptable. Thus their preconceived ideas may unconsciously colour and warp their descriptions of savage rites.

One more point in these savage customs deserves to be noted. The Pawnee chief devoured the heart of the Sioux girl. If, as we suppose, victims of this type were regarded as divine, it follows that in eating their flesh the worshippers believed themselves to be partaking of the body of their god.

The barbarous rites just described offer analogies to the harvest customs of Europe. Thus the fertilising virtue ascribed to the corn-spirit is shewn equally in the savage custom of mixing the victim's blood or ashes with the seed-corn and the European custom of mixing the grain from the last sheaf with the young corn in spring. The identification of the person with the corn appears in the savage custom of killing him and the European custom of pretending to do so. As regards the Lityerses story, we may conclude from the analogies it shows to European harvest customs that in Europe as in Phrygia the representative of the corn-spirit was annually killed upon the harvest-field. Grounds have been already shewn for believing that similarly in Europe the representative of the tree-spirit was annually slain. The proofs of these two remarkable and closely analogous customs are entirely independent of each other. Their coincidence seems to furnish fresh presumption in favour of both.

To the question, How was the representative of the corn-spirit chosen? one answer has been already given. Both the Lityerses story and European folk-custom shew that passing strangers were regarded as manifestations of the corn-spirit escaping from the cut or threshed corn, and as such were seized and slain. But this is not the only answer which the evidence suggests. According to the Phrygian legend the victims of Lityerses were not simply passing strangers, but persons whom he had vanquished in a reaping contest and afterwards wrapt up in corn-sheaves and beheaded. This suggests that the representative of the corn-spirit may have been selected by means of a competition on the harvest-field, in which the vanquished competitor was compelled to accept the fatal honour. The supposition is countenanced by European harvest-customs. In Europe there is sometimes a contest amongst the reapers to avoid being last, and the person who is vanquished in this competition, that is, who cuts the last corn, is often roughly handled. It is true that no pretence is made of killing him; but on the other hand a pretence is often made of killing the man who gives the last stroke at threshing, that is, who is vanquished in the threshing contest.

Thus the person who was killed on the harvest-field as the representative of the corn-spirit may have been either a passing stranger or the harvester who was last at reaping, binding, or threshing. But there is a third possibility, to which ancient legend and modern folk-custom alike point. Lityerses not only put strangers to death; he was himself slain, and apparently in the same way as he had slain others, namely, by being wrapt in a corn-sheaf, beheaded, and cast into the river; and it is implied that this happened to Lityerses on his own land. Similarly in modern harvest-customs the pretence of killing appears to be carried out quite as often on the person of the master (farmer or squire) as on that of strangers. Now when we remember that Lityerses was said to have been a son of the King of Phrygia, and that in one account he is himself called a king, and when we combine with this the tradition that he was put to death, apparently as a representative of the corn-spirit, we are led to conjecture that we have here another trace of the custom of annually slaying one of those divine or priestly kings who are known to have held ghostly sway in many parts of Western Asia and particularly in Phrygia. The custom appears, as we have seen, to have been so far modified in places that the king's son was slain in the king's stead. Of the custom thus modified the story of Lityerses would be, in one version at least, a reminiscence.

The Phoenician Linus song was sung at the vintage, at least in the west of Asia Minor, as we learn from Homer. The Linus song was probably sung also by Phoenician reapers, for Herodotus compares it to the Maneros song, which, as we have seen, was a lament raised by Egyptian reapers over the cut corn. Further, Linus was identified with Adonis, and Adonis has some claims to be regarded as especially a corn-deity. Thus the Linus lament, as sung at harvest, would be identical with the Adonis lament; each would

be the lamentation raised by reapers over the dead spirit of the corn. But whereas Adonis grew into a stately figure of mythology, adored and mourned in splendid cities far beyond the limits of his Phoenician home, Linus appears to have remained a simple ditty sung by reapers and vintagers among the corn-sheaves and the vines. The analogy of Lityerses and of folk-custom, both European and savage, suggests that in Phoenicia the slain corn-spirit – the dead Adonis – may formerly have been represented by a human victim; and this suggestion is possibly supported by the Harran legend that Tammuz (Adonis) was slain by his cruel lord, who ground his bones in a mill and scattered them to the wind.

There is some evidence that in Egypt the slain corn-spirit – the dead Osiris – was represented

Busiris
Hercules kills King Busiris over the sacrificial altar on which Busiris had been accustomed to slay strangers as representatives of the corn-spirit. Greek myth presented its greatest hero as the enemy of many similar ancient customs. Greek vase, Ashmolean Museum, Oxford

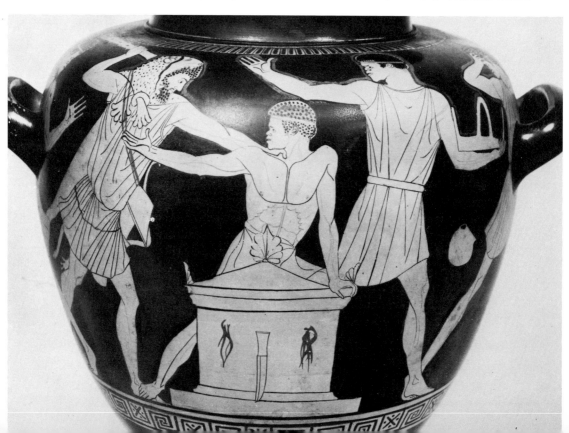

by a human victim, whom the reapers slew on the harvest-field, mourning his death in a dirge, to which the Greeks, through a verbal misunderstanding, gave the name of Maneros. For the legend of Busiris seems to preserve a reminiscence of human sacrifices once offered by the Egyptians in connexion with the worship of Osiris. Busiris was said to have been an Egyptian king who sacrificed all strangers on the altar of Zeus. The origin of the custom was traced to a dearth which afflicted the land of Egypt for nine years. A Cyprian seer informed Busiris that the dearth would cease if a man were annually sacrificed to Zeus. So Busiris instituted the sacrifice. But when Hercules came to Egypt, and was being dragged to the altar to be sacrificed, he burst his bonds and slew Busiris and his son. Here then is a legend that in Egypt a human victim was annually sacrificed to prevent the failure of the crops, and a belief is implied that an omission of the sacrifice would have entailed a recurrence of that infertility which it was the object of the sacrifice to prevent. The name Busiris was in reality the name of a city, *pe-Asar*, 'the house of Osiris', the city being so called because it contained the grave of Osiris. Indeed some high modern authorities believe that Busiris was the original home of Osiris, from which his worship spread to other parts of Egypt. The human sacrifices were said to have been offered at his grave, and the victims were red-haired men, whose ashes were scattered abroad by means of winnowing-fans.

The Egyptian tradition of Busiris admits of a consistent and fairly probable explanation. Osiris, the corn-spirit, was annually represented at harvest by a stranger, whose red hair made him a suitable representative of the ripe corn. This man, in his representative character, was slain on the harvest-field, and mourned by the reapers, who prayed at the same time that the corn-spirit might revive and return (*mââ-ne-rha*, Maneros) with renewed vigour in the following year. Finally, the victim, or some part of him, was burned, and the ashes scattered by winnowing-fans over the fields to fertilise them. Here the choice of the victim on the ground of his resemblance to the corn which he was to represent agrees with the Mexican customs already described.

Again, the scattering of the Egyptian victim's ashes over the fields resembles the Khond custom, and the use of winnowing-fans for the purpose is another hint of his identification with the corn. The story that the fragments of Osiris's body were scattered up and down the land, and buried by Isis on the spots where they lay, may very well be a reminiscence of a custom, like that observed by the Khonds, of dividing the human victim in pieces and burying the pieces, often at intervals of many miles from each other, in the fields. However, it is possible that the story of the dismemberment of Osiris, like the similar story told of Tammuz, may have been simply a mythical expression for the scattering of the seed.

Thus, if I am right, the key to the mysteries of Osiris is furnished by the melancholy cry of the Egyptian reapers, which down to Roman times could be heard year after year sounding across the fields, announcing the death of the corn-spirit, the rustic prototype of Osiris. Similar cries, as we have seen, were also heard on all the harvest-fields of Western Asia. By the ancients they are spoken of as songs; but to judge from the analysis of the names Linus and Maneros, they probably consisted only of a few words uttered in a prolonged musical note which could be heard for a great distance. Down to recent times, reapers in Devonshire and Pembrokeshire used to utter similar cries during the harvest, which were accompanied by rites analogous to those of Osiris. An observer commented that this was 'the people making their games, as they always do, to the spirit of the harvest'.

4. Eating the God

The Sacrament of First-Fruits

We have now seen that the corn-spirit can be represented in human form, and that he can be killed in the person of his representative and eaten sacramentally. To find examples of actually killing the human representative of the corn-spirit we had naturally to go to savage races; but the harvest-suppers of our European peasants have furnished unmistakable examples of the sacramental eating of animals as representatives of the corn-spirit. But further, as might have been anticipated, the new corn is itself eaten sacramentally, that is, as the body of the corn-spirit. In Wermland, Sweden, the farmer's wife uses the grain of the last sheaf to bake a loaf in the shape of a little girl; this loaf is divided amongst the whole household and eaten by them. Here the loaf represents the corn-spirit conceived as a maiden; just as in Scotland the corn-spirit is similarly conceived and represented by the last sheaf made up in the form of a woman and bearing the name of the Maiden. As usual, the corn-spirit is believed to reside in the last sheaf; and to eat a loaf made from the last sheaf is, therefore, to eat the corn-spirit itself.

Here the corn-spirit is represented and eaten in human shape. In other cases, though the new corn is not baked in loaves of human shape, still the solemn ceremonies with which it is eaten suffice to indicate that it is partaken of sacramentally, that is, as the body of the corn-spirit. For example, the following ceremonies used to be observed by Lithuanian peasants at eating the new corn. About the time of the autumn sowing, when all the corn had been got in and the threshing had begun, each farmer held a festival called Sabarios, that is, 'the mixing or throwing together'. He took nine good handfuls of each kind of crop — wheat, barley, oats, flax, beans, lentils, and the rest; and each handful he divided into three parts. The twenty-seven portions of each grain were then thrown on a heap and all mixed up together. The grain used had to be that which was first threshed and winnowed and which had been set aside and kept for this purpose. A part of the grain thus mixed was employed to bake little loaves, one for each of the household; the rest was mixed with more barley or oats and made into beer. The first beer brewed from this mixture was for the drinking of the farmer, his wife, and children; the second brew was for the servants. The beer being ready, the farmer chose an evening when no stranger was expected. Then he knelt down before the barrel of beer, drew a jugful of the liquor and poured it on the bung of the barrel, saying, 'O fruitful earth, make rye and barley and all kinds of corn to flourish.' Next he took the jug to the parlour, where his wife and children awaited him. On the floor of the parlour lay bound a black or white or speckled (not a red) cock and a hen of the same colour and of the same brood, which must have been hatched within the year. Then the farmer knelt down, with the jug in his hand, and thanked God for the harvest and prayed for a good crop next year. Next all lifted up their hands and said, 'O God, and thou, O earth, we give you this cock and hen as a free-will offering.' With that the farmer killed the fowls with the blows of a wooden spoon, for he might not cut their heads off. After the first prayer and after killing each of the birds he poured out a third of the beer. Then his wife boiled the fowls in a new pot which had never been used before. After that, a bushel was set, bottom upwards, on the floor, and on it were placed the little loaves mentioned above and the boiled fowls. Next the new beer was fetched, together with a ladle and three mugs, none of which was used except on this occasion. When the farmer had ladled the beer into the mugs, the family knelt down round the bushel. The father then uttered a prayer and drank off the three mugs of beer. The rest followed his example. Then the loaves and the flesh of the fowls were eaten, after which the beer went round again, till every one had emptied each of the three mugs nine times. None of the food should remain over; but if anything did happen to be left, it was consumed next morning with the same ceremonies. The bones were given to the dog to eat; if he did not eat them all up, the remains were buried under the dung in the cattle-stall. This ceremony was observed at the beginning of December. On the day on which it took place no bad word might be spoken. Such was the custom about two hundred years or more ago.

At the close of the rice harvest in the East Indian island of Buru, each clan (*fenna*) meets at a common sacramental meal, to which every member of the clan is bound to contribute a little of the new rice. This meal is called 'eating the soul of the rice', a name which clearly indicates the sacramental character of the repast. Some of the rice is also set apart and offered to the spirits. Shortly before the rice-harvest in Bolang Mongondo, another district of Celebes, an offering is made of a small pig or fowl. Then the priest plucks a little rice, first on his own field and next on those of his neighbours. All the rice thus plucked by him he dries along with his own, and then gives it back to the respective owners, who have it ground and boiled. When it is boiled the women take it back, with an egg, to the priest, who offers the egg in sacrifice and returns the rice to the women. Of this rice every member of the family, down to the youngest child, must partake. After this ceremony every one is free to get in his rice.

The Bororo Indians of Brazil think that it would be certain death to eat the new maize before it has been blessed by the medicine-man. The ceremony of blessing it is as follows. The half-ripe husk is washed and placed before the medicine-man, who by dancing and singing for several hours, and by incessant smoking, works himself up into a state of ecstasy, whereupon he bites into the husk, trembling in every limb and uttering shrieks from time to time. A similar ceremony is performed whenever a large animal or a large fish is killed. The Bororo are firmly persuaded that were any man to touch unconsecrated maize or meat, before the ceremony had been completed, he and his whole tribe would perish.

Even tribes which do not till the ground sometimes observe analogous ceremonies when they gather the first wild fruits or dig the first roots of the season. Thus among the Salish and Tinneh Indians of North-West America, 'before the young people eat the first berries or roots of the season, they always addressed the fruit or plant, and begged for its favour and aid. In some tribes regular First-fruit ceremonies were annually held at the time of picking the wild fruit or gathering the roots, and also among the salmon-eating tribes when the run of the "sockeye" salmon began. These ceremonies were not so much thanksgivings, as performances to ensure a plentiful crop or supply of the particular object desired, for if they were not properly and reverently carried out there was danger of giving offence to the "spirits" of the objects, and being deprived of them.'

These customs are instructive, because they clearly indicate the motive, or at least one of the motives, which underlies the ceremonies observed at eating the first fruits of the season. That motive in the case of these Indians is simply a belief that the plant itself is animated by a con-

The spirit of vegetation represented by an animal
At the annual rite of meeting the spring in China, an
effigy of a buffalo was brought to the temple and stoned.
The broken pieces were kept as safeguards of good luck
during the coming year. G.N. Wright, *China, Its Scenery,
Architecture, and Social Habits*, 1843, Bodleian Library,
Oxford

scious and more or less powerful spirit, who
must be propitiated before the people can safely
partake of the fruits or roots which are supposed
to be part of his body. Now if this is true of
wild fruits and roots, we may infer with some
probability that it is also true of cultivated fruits
and roots, such as yams, and in particular that it
holds good of the cereals, such as wheat, barley,
oats, rice, and maize. In all cases it seems reasonable to infer that the scruples which savages
manifest at eating the first fruits of any crop, and
the ceremonies which they observe before they
overcome their scruples, are due at least in large

measure to a notion that the plant or tree is
animated by a spirit or even a deity, whose
leave must be obtained, or whose favour must
be sought before it is possible to partake with
safety of the new crop. This indeed is plainly
affirmed of the Aino: they call the millet 'the
divine cereal', 'the cereal deity', and they pray
to and worship him before they will eat of the
cakes made from the new millet. And even
where the indwelling divinity of the first fruits
is not expressly affirmed, it appears to be implied both by the solemn preparations made for
eating them and by the danger supposed to be

TOP. Mithras kills the bull from whose side the blood springs as ears of corn. Roman cult statue, 2nd century, British Museum, London
ABOVE. Chinese cast-iron offering pig, c.1700, sacrificed to the Taoist deities of rivers to ensure a good harvest. Hardinge Collection, Gulbenkian Museum of Oriental Art, Durham

spirits comes now to be thought a sufficient preparation for eating the new corn; the higher powers having received their share, man is free to enjoy the rest. This mode of viewing the new fruits implies that they are regarded no longer as themselves instinct with divine life, but merely as a gift bestowed by the gods upon man, who is bound to express his gratitude and homage to his divine benefactors by returning to them a portion of their bounty.

Eating the God

The custom of eating bread sacramentally as the body of a god was practised by the Aztecs before the discovery and conquest of Mexico by the Spaniards. Twice a year, in May and December, an image of the great Mexican god Huitzilopochtli or Vitzilipuztli was made of dough, then broken in pieces, and solemnly eaten by his worshippers. The May ceremony was described by the historian Acosta, from whom we learn that the ancient Mexicans, even before the arrival of Christian missionaries, were fully acquainted with the theological doctrine of transubstantiation and acted upon it in the solemn rites of their religion. They believed that by consecrating bread their priests could turn it into the very body of their god, so that all who thereupon partook of the consecrated bread entered into a mystic communion with the deity by receiving a portion of his divine substance into themselves. The doctrine of transubstantiation, or the magical conversion of bread into flesh, was also familiar to the Aryans of ancient India long before the spread and even the rise of Christianity. The Brahmans taught that the rice-cakes offered in sacrifice were substitutes for human beings, and that they were actually converted into the real bodies of men by the manipulation of the priest. We read that 'when it [the rice-cake] still consists of rice-meal, it is the hair. When he pours water on it, it becomes skin. When he mixes it, it becomes flesh: for then it becomes consistent;

incurred by persons who venture to partake of them without observing the prescribed ritual. In all such cases, accordingly, we may not improperly describe the eating of the new fruits as a sacrament or communion with a deity, or at all events with a powerful spirit.

In some of the festivals which we have examined, the sacrament of first-fruits is combined with a sacrifice or presentation of them to gods or spirits, and in course of time the sacrifice of first-fruits tends to throw the sacrament into the shade, if not to supersede it. The mere fact of offering the first-fruits to the gods or

and consistent also is the flesh. When it is baked, it becomes bone: for then it becomes somewhat hard; and hard is the bone. And when he is about to take it off [the fire] and sprinkles it with butter, he changes it into marrow. This is the completeness which they call the fivefold animal sacrifice.'

At the festival of the winter solstice in December the Aztecs killed their god Huitzilopochtli in effigy first and ate him afterwards. As a preparation for this solemn ceremony an image of the deity in the likeness of a man was fashioned out of seeds of various sorts, which were kneaded into a dough with the blood of children. The bones of the god were represented by pieces of acacia wood. This image was placed on the chief altar of the temple, and on the day of the festival the king offered incense to it. Early next day it was taken down and set on its feet in a great hall. Then a priest, who bore the name and acted the part of the god Quetzalcoatl, took a flint-tipped dart and hurled it into the breast of the dough-image, piercing it through and through. This was called 'killing the god Huitzilopochtli so that his body might be eaten'. One of the priests cut out the heart of the image and gave it to the king to eat. The rest of the image was divided into minute pieces, of which every man, great and small, down to the male child in the cradle, received one to eat. But no woman might taste a morsel. The ceremony was called *teoqualo*, that is, 'god is eaten'.

Many Manii at Aricia

We are now able to suggest an explanation of the proverb 'There are many Manii at Aricia.' Certain loaves made in the shape of men were called by the Romans *maniae*, and it appears that this kind of loaf was especially made at Aricia. Now, Mania, the name of one of these loaves, was also the name of the Mother or Grandmother of Ghosts, to whom woollen effigies of men and women were dedicated at the festival of the Compitalia. These effigies were hung at the doors of all the houses in Rome; one effigy was hung up for every free person and every slave. The reason was that on this day the ghosts of the dead were believed to be going about, and it was hoped that, either out of good nature or through simple inadvertence, they would carry off the effigies at the door instead of the living people in the house. According to tradition, these woollen figures were substitutes for a former custom of sacrificing human beings. Upon data so fragmentary and uncertain, it is impossible to build with confidence; but it seems worth suggesting that the loaves in human form, which appear to have been baked at Aricia, were sacramental bread, and that in the old days, when the divine King of the Wood was annually slain, loaves were made in his image, like the paste figures of the gods in Mexico, India, and Europe, and were eaten sacramentally by his worshippers.

I learn from a correspondent that a similar custom is still observed annually at Frascati, in the Alban Hills, not very far from Aricia. He writes: 'During Lent the bakers of Frascati sell gingerbread cakes in the shape of human figures with three long horns, peppercorns for eyes, and a red riband around the neck. These, I was told, represent the Devil and are eaten as a symbolic renunciation of him and all his works. The custom, however, might well be pre-Christian, and the explanation a later addition.'

Part 6. The Scapegoat

*Having considered the death of the King of the Wood
as the personification of vegetation, Frazer goes on to
enquire into another aspect of his death, that is, his
death as scapegoat. He finds a variety of practices
whereby people have thought to transfer evils from
themselves to some object, plant or animal, or even to
another human being who was then either killed, or
expelled from society. The transference of evil
operates by contagious magic, and the expulsion of
evil by imitative magic.*

*In ancient Rome, the annual ceremony of the
expulsion of evils was at the same time a fertility
rite, since evils that afflict crops were among those
expelled. This dual function enables Frazer to
compare the scapegoat's death with the human
victims sacrificed for the continuing strength of the
Aztec fertility gods. And so he returns to an earlier
theme, the killing of a human being who
impersonates a god; however, the aim of the killing is
now not only to benefit the crops but also to avert evil
influences.*

*If we apply this to the death of the King of the
Wood, we see that he was killed both as the
impersonation of vegetation, where, by imitation, his
death and the rule of his successor stand for the death
and revival of nature; and as scapegoat, lest by
contagion his feebleness or old age contaminate the
reproductive power of nature.*

In medieval Christianity the devil presented a constant
threat to the good order of human life, and this
circumstance called for regular exorcisms of him by men.
As the personification of all evils, his vile appearance is
intended to provoke men's revulsion, and his animal
features reflect the fact that scapegoats frequently took the
form of animals. Devil and attendants, MS Douce 134,
fol. 98R, Bodleian Library, Oxford

1. The Transference of Evil

In the preceding parts of this work we have traced the practice of killing a god among peoples in the agricultural stage of society; and I have attempted to explain the motives which led men to adopt so curious a custom. One aspect of the custom still remains to be noticed. The accumulated misfortunes and sins of the whole people are sometimes laid upon the dying god, who is supposed to bear them away for ever, leaving the people innocent and happy. The notion that we can transfer our guilt and sufferings to some other being who will bear them for us is familiar to the savage mind. It arises from a very obvious confusion between the physical and the mental, between the material and the immaterial. Because it is possible to shift a load of wood, stones, or what not, from our own back to the back of another, the savage fancies that it is equally possible to shift the burden of his pains and sorrows to another, who will suffer them in his stead. Upon this idea he acts, and the result is an endless number of very unamiable devices for palming off upon some one else the trouble which a man shrinks from bearing himself. In short, the principle of vicarious suffering is commonly understood and practised by races who stand on a low level of social and intellectual culture. In the following pages I shall illustrate the theory and the practice as they are found among savages in all their naked simplicity, undisguised by the refinements of metaphysics and the subtleties of theology.

The devices to which the cunning and selfish savage resorts for the sake of easing himself at the expense of his neighbour are manifold; only a few typical examples out of a multitude can be cited. At the outset it is to be observed that the evil of which a man seeks to rid himself need not be transferred to a person; it may equally well be transferred to an animal or a thing, though in the last case the thing is often only a vehicle to convey the trouble to the first person who touches it.

In the western district of the island of Timor, when men or women are making long and tiring journeys, they fan themselves with leafy branches, which they afterwards throw away on

The omnipresence of demons
A sick man with the devil come to claim his soul and his guardian angel. Medieval manuscript, Cod. Gall. 28, fol. 5v, Bayerische Staatsbibliothek, Munich

particular spots where their forefathers did the same before them. The fatigue which they felt is thus supposed to have passed into the leaves and to be left behind. Others use stones instead of leaves. But it is not mere bodily fatigue which the savage fancies he can rid himself of by the simple expedient of throwing a stick or a stone. Unable clearly to distinguish the immaterial from the material, the abstract from the concrete, he is assailed by vague terrors, he feels himself exposed to some ill-defined danger on the scene of any great crime or great misfortune. The place to him seems haunted ground. The thronging memories that crowd upon his mind, if they are not mistaken by him for goblins and phantoms, oppress his fancy with a leaden weight. His impulse is to flee from the dreadful spot, to shake off the burden that seems to cling to him like a nightmare. This, in his simple sensuous way, he thinks he can do by casting something at the horrid place and hurrying by. For will not the contagion of misfortune, the horror that clutched at his heart-strings, be diverted from himself into the thing? will it not gather up in itself all the evil influences that threatened him, and so leave him to pursue his journey in safety and peace? Some such train of thought, if these gropings and fumblings of a mind in darkness deserve the name of thought, seems to explain the custom, observed by way-

In a popular Japanese legend, a carpenter of magical powers created various remarkable contrivances to assist him in his tasks. Here the Bishmonten, a spirit he created, drives off a hostile demon. Rokujuen, *The Magical Carpenter of Japan*, 1965, Charles Tuttle Co., Tokyo

farers in many lands, of throwing sticks or stones on places where something horrible has happened or evil deeds have been done. When Sir Francis Younghusband was travelling across the great desert of Gobi his caravan descended, towards dusk on a June evening, into a long depression between the hills, which was notorious as a haunt of robbers. His guide, with a terror-stricken face, told how not long before nine men out of a single caravan had been murdered, and the rest left in a pitiable state to continue their journey on foot across the awful desert. A horseman, too, had just been seen riding towards the hills. 'We had accordingly to keep a sharp lookout, and when we reached the foot of the hills, halted, and, taking the loads off the camels, wrapped ourselves up in our sheepskins and watched through the long hours of the night. Day broke at last and then we silently advanced and entered the hills. Very weird and fantastic in their rugged outline were they, and here and there a cairn of stones marked where some caravan had been attacked, and as we passed these each man threw one more stone on the heap.'

The stones may be thought to keep off an angry and dangerous ghost who might haunt the place. But if this theory seems adequately to account for some cases of the custom with which we are concerned, it apparently fails to explain others. Thus in Syria it is a common practice with pious Moslems, when they first come in sight of a very sacred place, such as Hebron or the tomb of Moses, to make a little heap of stones or to add a stone to a heap which has been already made. Hence every here and there the traveller passes a whole series of such heaps by the side of the track. In Northern Africa the usage is similar. Cairns are commonly erected on spots from which the devout pilgrim first discerns the shrine of a saint afar off; hence they are generally to be seen on the top of passes. For example, in Morocco, at the point of the road from Casablanca to Azemmour, where you first

Throwing away evils

BELOW. Apacheta in the Andes, where each traveller discards his weariness by adding another stone to the heap by the wayside. Photo: C. N. Wallis

BOTTOM. 'Stoning the Great Devil': the ancient custom of throwing stones on a heap still survives as part of the Muslim pilgrimage to Mecca, at a site near the sacred city. The stones are thrown at a buttress of crude masonry. One story has it that the buttress symbolizes the person who guided the King of Ethiopia on his journey to destroy Mecca in the year of Muhammed's birth. Sir Richard Burton, *Pilgrimage to El-Medinah and Meccah*, 1855–6, Bodleian Library, Oxford

come in sight of the white city of the saint gleaming in the distance, there rises an enormous cairn of stones shaped like a pyramid several hundreds of feet high, and beyond it on both sides of the road there is a sort of avalanche of stones, either standing singly or arranged in little pyramids. Every pious Mohammedan whose eyes are gladdened by the blessed sight of the sacred town adds his stone to one of the piles or builds a little pile for himself. Customs such as these could be interpreted as a form of ceremonial purification, which among primitive peoples is commonly conceived as a sort of physical rather than moral purgation, a mode of sweeping or scouring away the morbid matter by which the polluted person is supposed to be infected.

Such customs seem to indicate the gradual transformation of an old magical ceremony into a religious rite with its characteristic features of prayer and sacrifice. Yet behind these later accretions, as we may perhaps regard them, it seems possible in many, if not in all, cases to discern the nucleus to which they have attached themselves, the original idea which they tend to conceal and in time to transmute. That idea is the transference of evil from man to a material substance which he can cast from him like an outworn garment.

Animals are often employed as a vehicle for carrying away or transferring the evil. Thus, among the Majhwar, a Dravidian race of South Mirzapur, if a man has died of a contagious disease, such as cholera, the village priest walks in front of the funeral procession with a chicken in his hands, which he lets loose in the direction of some other village as a scapegoat to carry the infection away. None but another very experienced priest would afterwards dare to touch or eat such a chicken.

Again, men sometimes play the part of scapegoat by diverting to themselves the evils that threaten others. An ancient Hindoo ritual describes how the pangs of thirst may be transferred from a sick man to another. The operator seats the pair on branches, back to back, the sufferer with his face to the east, and the whole man with his face to the west. Then he stirs some gruel in a vessel placed on the patient's head and hands the stir-about to the other man to drink. In this way he transfers the pangs of thirst from the thirsty soul to the other, who obligingly receives them in his stead. In 1590 a Scotch witch of the name of Agnes Sampson was convicted of curing a certain Robert Kers of a disease 'laid upon him by a westland warlock when he was at Dumfries, which sickness she took upon herself, and kept the same with great groaning and torment till the morn, at which time there was a great din heard in the house'. The noise was made by the witch in her efforts to shift the disease, by means of clothes, from herself to a cat or dog. Unfortunately the attempt partly miscarried. The disease missed the animal and hit Alexander Douglas of Dalkeith, who dwined and died of it, while the original patient, Robert Kers, was made whole.

In Travancore, when a rajah is near his end, they seek out a holy Brahman, who consents to take upon himself the sins of the dying man in consideration of the sum of ten thousand rupees. Thus prepared to immolate himself on the altar of duty as a vicarious sacrifice for sin, the saint is introduced into the chamber of death, and closely embraces the dying rajah, saying to him, 'O King, I undertake to bear all your sins and diseases. May your Highness live long and reign happily.' Having thus, with a noble devotion, taken to himself the sins of the sufferer, and likewise the rupees, he is sent away from the country and never more allowed to return. Closely akin to this is the old Welsh custom known as 'sin-eating'. According to Aubrey, 'In the County of Hereford was an old Custome at funeralls to hire poor people, who were to take upon them all the sinnes of the party deceased. One of them I remember lived in a cottage on Rosse high-way.

(He was a long, leane, ugly, lamentable poor raskal.) The manner was that when the corps was brought out of the house and layd on the Biere; a Loafe of bread was brought out, and delivered to the Sinne-eater over the corps, as also a Mazar-bowle of maple (Gossips bowle) full of beer, which he was to drinke up, and six-pence in money, in consideration whereof he took upon him (ipso facto) all the Sinnes of the Defunct, and freed him (or her) from walking after they were dead . . . This Custome (though rarely used in our dayes) yet by some people was observed even in the strictest time of ye Presby-terian government: as at Dynder, volens nolens the Parson of ye Parish, the kinred of a woman deceased there had this ceremonie punctually performed according to her Will.'

In Europe, the most common receptacle for sickness and trouble of all sorts is a tree. Often the patient knocks a wedge, a peg, or a nail into it, believing that he thus pegs or nails the sickness or pain into the wood. Thus a Bohemian cure for fever is to go to a tree and hammer a wedge into it with the words 'There, I knock you in, that you may come no more out to me.'

From the knocking the mischief into a tree or a log it is only a step to knocking it into a stone, a door-post, a wall, or such like. At the head of Glen Mor, near Port Charlotte, in Islay, there may be seen a large boulder, and it is said that whoever drives a nail into this stone will there-after be secure from attacks of toothache. Again, the great plague which devastated the ancient world in the reign of Marcus Antoninus is said to have originated in the curiosity and greed of some Roman soldiers, who, pillaging the city of Seleucia, came upon a narrow hole in a temple and incautiously enlarged the opening in the expectation of discovering treasure. But that which came forth from the hole was not treasure but the plague. It had been pent up in a secret chamber by the magic art of the Chaldeans; but now, released from its prison by the rash act of spoilers, it stalked abroad and spread death and destruction from the Euphrates to the Nile and the Atlantic.

The simple ceremony, in which to this day the superstition of European peasants sees a sovereign remedy for plague and fever and toothache, has come down to us from a remote antiquity; for it was solemnly performed from time to time by the highest magistrate at Rome, to stay the ravages of pestilence or retrieve disaster that threatened the foundations of the national life. In the fourth century before our era the city of Rome was desolated by a great plague which raged for three years, carrying off some of the highest dignitaries and a great multitude of common folk. The historian who records the calamity informs us that when a banquet had been offered to the gods in vain, and neither human counsels nor divine help availed to mitigate the violence of the disease, it was resolved for the first time in Roman his-tory to institute dramatical performances as an appropriate means of appeasing the wrath of the celestial powers. Accordingly actors were fetched from Etruria, who danced certain simple and decorous dances to the music of a flute. But even this novel spectacle failed to amuse or touch, to move to tears or laughter the sullen gods. The plague still raged, and at the very moment when the actors were playing their best in the circus beside the Tiber, the yellow river rose in angry flood and drove players and spectators, wading and splashing through the fast-deepening waters, away from the show. It was clear that the gods spurned plays as well as prayers and banquets; and in the general conster-nation it was felt that some more effectual measure should be taken to put an end to the scourge. Old men remembered that a plague had once been stayed by the knocking of a nail into a wall; and accordingly the Senate resolved that now in their extremity, when all other means had failed, a supreme magistrate should be

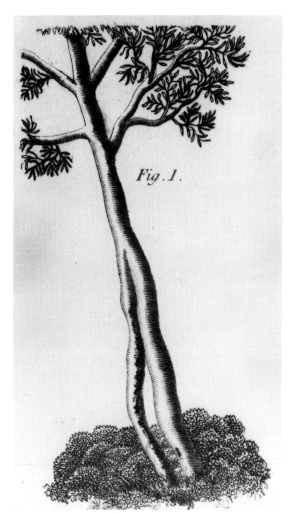

Nailing evils
With each nail sickness and pain have been transferred to this fetish in human form from Nganzi village, Kakonga, Africa. Pitt Rivers Museum, University of Oxford

The transference of evil to cleft objects
A child who was passed through the cleft of this ash tree was cured of a rupture. *Gentleman's Magazine*, 1802, Bodleian Library, Oxford

appointed for the sole purpose of performing this solemn ceremony. The appointment was made, the nail was knocked, and the plague ceased, sooner or later. What better proof could be given of the saving virtue of a nail?

We have considered the primitive principle of the transference of ills to another person, animal, or thing. A consideration of the means taken, in accordance with this principle, to rid individuals

of their troubles and distresses led us to believe that at Rome similar means had been adopted to free the whole community, at a single blow of the hammer, from diverse evils that afflicted it. I now propose to shew that such attempts to dismiss at once the accumulated sorrows of a people are by no means rare or exceptional, but that on the contrary they have been made in many lands, and that from being occasional they tend to become periodic and annual. The endeavour of primitive people to make a clean sweep of all their troubles generally takes the form of a grand hunting out and expulsion of devils or ghosts who, it is thought, are the cause of all afflictions. They think that if they can only shake off these their accursed tormentors, they will make a fresh start in life, happy and innocent; the tales of Eden and the old poetic golden age will come true again. The public attempts to expel the accumulated ills of a whole community may be divided into two classes, according as the expelled evils are immaterial and invisible or are embodied in a material vehicle or scapegoat. The former may be called the direct or immediate expulsion of evils; the latter the indirect or mediate expulsion, or the expulsion by scapegoat.

We will first consider the immediate expulsion of the evils of a whole community. Such expulsions can take place at any time of sickness or general distress, although from being occasional, they tend to become periodic. It comes to be thought desirable to have a general riddance of evil spirits at fixed times, usually once a year, so that the people may make a fresh start in life. In Christian Europe the old heathen custom of expelling the powers of evil at certain periods of the year has survived to modern times. Witches and wizards were thought to be particularly mischievous on the twelve days from Christmas to Twelfth Night, the Eve of St George, the Eve of May Day (Walpurgis Night), and Midsummer Eve. Special precautions had accordingly to be taken at these times.

Thus, in the long and spacious Piazza Navona at Rome, on the night before Epiphany a dense crowd assembles and diverts itself by raising a hideous uproar. Soon after supper troops of young folk and others march through the streets, preceded by puppets or pasteboard figures and all making the utmost possible din. They converge from different quarters on the Piazza Navona, there to unite in one prolonged and deafening outburst of clangorous discord. The favourite musical instruments employed in this cats' concert are penny trumpets, of which, together with tambourines, bells, and so forth, the shops take care to provide a large stock as a preparation for the pandemonium of the evening. The ceremony is supposed to be in honour of a certain mythical old hag called Befana, effigies of whom, made of rags, are put by women and children in the windows on Twelfth Night. Her name Befana is clearly a popular corruption of Epiphany, the ecclesiastical name of the festival; but viewed in connexion with the popular celebrations which we have examined she may be suspected to be of heathen rather than Christian origin. In fact we may conjecture that she was of old a witch, and that the noisy rite in the Piazza Navona is nothing but a relic of an annual expulsion of witches at this season.

In the Shetland Islands the Yule or Christmas holidays begin, or used to begin, seven days before Christmas and last till Antinmas, that is, the twenty-fourth day after Christmas. In the Shetland parlance these holidays are known as 'the Yules'. On the first night, called Tul-ya's e'en, seven days before Christmas, certain mischievous elves, whom the Shetlanders name Trows, 'received permission to leave their homes in the heart of the earth and dwell, if it so pleased them, among the dwellings of men'. Hence, on the last day of the holidays, the twenty-fourth day after Christmas, which in Shetland goes by the name of Up-helly-a', Uphellia, or Uphaliday, 'the doors were all opened, and a great deal of pantomimic chasing and driving and dispersing of unseen creatures took place. Many pious ejaculations were uttered, and iron was ostentatiously displayed, "for Trows can never abide the sight o' iron". The Bible was read and quoted. People moved about in groups or couples, never singly, and infants were carefully guarded as well as sained by vigilant and learned "wise women". Alas, the poor Trows! their time of frolic and liberty was ended, and on Twenty-fourth night they retired to their gloomy abodes beneath the sod, seldom finding opportunity to reappear again, and never with the same licence, until the Yules returned.'

We come now to the second class of expulsions, in which the evil influences are embodied in a visible form or are at least supposed to be loaded upon a material medium, which acts as a vehicle to draw them off from the people, village, or town. In Munzerabad, a district of Mysore in Southern India, when cholera or smallpox has broken out in a parish, the inhabitants assemble and conjure the demon of the disease into a wooden image, which they carry, generally at midnight, into the next parish. The inhabitants of that parish in like manner pass the image on to their neighbours, and thus the demon is expelled from one village after another, until he comes to the bank of a river into which he is finally thrown. Russian villagers seek to protect themselves against epidemics, whether of man or beast, by drawing a furrow with a plough right round the village. The plough is dragged by four widows and the ceremony is performed at night; all fires and lights must be extinguished while the plough is going the round. The people think that no unclean spirit can pass the furrow which has thus been traced.

The vehicle which conveys away the demons may be of various kinds. A common one is a little ship or boat. Thus, in the southern district of the island of Ceram, when a whole village suffers from sickness, a small ship is made and filled with rice, tobacco, eggs, and so forth, which have been contributed by all the people. A little sail is hoisted on the ship. When all is ready, a man calls out in a very loud voice, 'O all ye sicknesses, ye smallpoxes, agues, measles, etc., who have visited us so long and wasted us so sorely, but who now cease to plague us, we have

made ready this ship for you and we have furnished you with provender sufficient for the voyage. Ye shall have no lack of food nor of betel-leaves nor of areca nuts nor of tobacco. Depart, and sail away from us directly; never come near us again; but go to a land which is far from here. Let all the tides and winds waft you speedily thither, and so convey you thither that for the time to come we may live sound and well, and that we may never see the sun rise on you again.' Then ten or twelve men carry the vessel to the shore, and let it drift away with the land-breeze, feeling convinced that they are free from sickness for ever, or at least till the next time. If sickness attacks them again, they are sure it is not the same sickness, but a different one, which in due time they dismiss in the same manner. When the demon-laden bark is lost to sight, the bearers return to the village, whereupon a man cries out, 'The sicknesses are now gone, vanished, expelled, and sailed away.' At this all the people come running out of their houses, passing the word from one to the other with great joy, beating on gongs and on tinkling instruments.

Often the vehicle which carries away the collected demons or ills of a whole community is an animal or scapegoat, and occasionally the scapegoat is a man. For example, from time to time the gods used to warn the King of Uganda that his foes the Banyoro were working magic against him and his people to make them die of disease. To avert such a catastrophe the king would send a scapegoat to the frontier of Bunyoro, the land of the enemy. The scapegoat consisted of either a man and a boy or a woman and her child, chosen because of some mark or bodily defect, which the gods had noted and by which the victims were to be recognised. With the human victims were sent a cow, a goat, a fowl, and a dog; and a strong guard escorted them to the land which the god had indicated. There the limbs of the victims were broken and they were left to die a lingering death in the enemy's country, being too crippled to crawl back to Uganda. The disease or plague was thought to have been thus transferred to the victims and to have been conveyed back in their persons to the land from which it came. So, too, after a war the gods sometimes advised the king to send back a scapegoat in order to free the warriors from some evil that had attached itself to the army. One of the women slaves, a cow, a goat, a fowl, and a dog would be chosen from among the captives and sent back to the borders of the country whence they had come; there they were maimed and left to die. After that the army would be pronounced clean and allowed to return to the capital. In each case a bundle of herbs would be rubbed over the people and the cattle, and would then be tied to the victims, who would thus carry back the evil with them.

Similar mediate public expulsions of evil take place at regular intervals. Every year, at the beginning of the dry season, the Nicobar Islanders carry the model of a ship through their villages. The devils are chased out of the huts, and driven on board the little ship, which is then launched and suffered to sail away with the wind. The ceremony has been described by a catechist, who witnessed it at Car Nicobar in July 1897. For three days the people were busy preparing two very large floating cars, shaped like canoes, fitted with sails, and loaded with certain leaves, which possessed the valuable property of expelling devils. While the young people were thus engaged, the exorcists and the elders sat in a house singing songs by turns; but often they would come forth, pace the beach armed with rods, and forbid the devil to enter the village. The fourth day of the solemnity bore the name of *Intō-nga-Sīya*, which means 'Expelling the Devil by Sails'. In the evening all the villagers assembled, the women bringing baskets of ashes and bunches of devil-expelling leaves. These leaves were then distributed to everybody, old and young. When all was ready, a band of robust men, attended by a guard of exorcists, carried one of the cars down to the sea on the right side of the village graveyard, and set it floating in the water. As soon as they had returned, another band of men carried the other car to the beach and floated it similarly in the sea to the left of the graveyard. The demon-laden barks being now launched, the women threw ashes from the shore, and the whole crowd shouted, saying, 'Fly away, devil, fly away, never come again!' The wind and the tide being favourable, the canoes sailed quickly away; and that night all the people feasted together with great joy, because the devil had departed in the direction of Chowra. A similar expulsion of devils takes place once a year in other Nicobar villages; but the ceremonies are held at different times in different places. On the Day of Atonement, which was the tenth day of the seventh month, the Jewish high-priest laid both his hands on the head of a live goat, confessed over it all the iniquities of the children of Israel, and, having thereby transferred the sins of the people to the beast, sent it away into the wilderness.

The scapegoat upon whom the sins of the people are periodically laid, may also be a human being. In Siam it used to be the custom on one day of the year to single out a woman broken down by debauchery, and carry her on a litter through all the streets to the music of drums and hautboys. The mob insulted her and pelted her with dirt; and after having carried her through the whole city, they threw her on a dunghill or a hedge of thorns outside the ramparts, forbidding her ever to enter the walls again. They believed that the woman thus drew upon herself all the malign influences of the air and of evil spirits.

Human scapegoats, as we shall see presently, were well known in classical antiquity, and even in mediaeval Europe the custom seems not to have been wholly extinct. In the town of

The scapegoat as an animal
LEFT. Sacrifice of a pig beneath the cosmic tree, Nepal.
Photo: Nick Allen
TOP. Baiting the buffalo at the Sohrae festival of the
Santals, India. Photo: W.G. Archer
ABOVE. Charles V of Spain fighting a bull in the plaza of
Valladolid. Drawing by Goya, Museo del Prado, Madrid

Halberstadt, in Thüringen, there was a church said to have been founded by Charlemagne. In this church every year they chose a man, who was believed to be stained with heinous sins. On the first day of Lent he was brought to the church, dressed in mourning garb, with his head muffled up. At the close of the service he was turned out of the church. During the forty days of Lent he perambulated the city barefoot, neither entering the churches nor speaking to any one. The canons took it in turn to feed him. After midnight he was allowed to sleep in the streets. On the day before Good Friday, after the consecration of the holy oil, he was re-admitted to the church and absolved from his sins. The people gave him money. He was called Adam, and was now believed to be in a state of innocence.

Sometimes the scapegoat is a divine animal. The people of Malabar share the Hindoo reverence for the cow, to kill and eat which 'they esteem to be a crime as heinous as homicide or wilful murder'. Nevertheless the 'Bramans transfer the sins of the people into one or more Cows, which are then carry'd away, both the Cows and the Sins wherewith these Beasts are charged, to what place the Braman shall appoint'.

Lastly, the scapegoat may be a divine man. Thus, in November the Gonds of India worship Ghansyam Deo, the protector of the crops, and at the festival the god himself is said to descend on the head of one of the worshippers, who is suddenly seized with a kind of fit and,

after staggering about, rushes off into the jungle, where it is believed that, if left to himself, he would die mad. However, they bring him back, but he does not recover his senses for one or two days. The people think that one man is thus singled out as a scapegoat for the sins of the rest of the village. In the temple of the Moon the Albanians of the Eastern Caucasus kept a number of sacred slaves, of whom many were inspired and prophesied. When one of these men exhibited more than usual symptoms of inspiration or insanity, and wandered solitary up and down the woods, like the Gond in the jungle, the high priest had him bound with a sacred chain and maintained him in luxury for a year. At the end of the year he was anointed with unguents and led forth to be sacrificed. A man whose business it was to slay these human victims and to whom practice had given dexterity, advanced from the crowd and thrust a sacred spear into the victim's side, piercing his heart. From the manner in which the slain man fell, omens were drawn as to the welfare of the commonwealth. Then the body was carried to a certain spot where all the people stood upon it as a purificatory ceremony. This last circumstance clearly indicates that the sins of the people were transferred to the victim, just as the Jewish priest transferred the sins of the people to the scapegoat by laying his hands on the animal's head; and since the man was believed to be possessed by the divine spirit, we have here an undoubted example of a man-god slain to take away the sins and misfortunes of the people.

2. On Scapegoats

The foregoing survey of the custom of publicly expelling the accumulated evils of a village or town or country suggests a few general observations.

In the first place, it will not be disputed that what I have called the immediate and the mediate expulsions of evil are identical in intention; in other words, that whether the evils are conceived of as invisible or as embodied in a material form, is a circumstance entirely subordinate to the main object of the ceremony, which is simply to effect a total clearance of all the ills that have been infesting a people. If any link were wanting to connect the two kinds of expulsion, it would be furnished by such a practice as that of sending the evils away in a litter or a boat. For here, on the one hand, the evils are invisible and intangible; and, on the other hand, there is a visible and tangible vehicle to convey them away. And a scapegoat is nothing more than such a vehicle.

In the second place, when a general clearance of evils is resorted to periodically, the interval between the celebrations of the ceremony is commonly a year, and the time of year when the ceremony takes place usually coincides with some well-marked change of season, such as the beginning or end of winter in the arctic and temperate zones, and the beginning or end of the rainy season in the tropics. The increased mortality which such climatic changes are apt to produce, especially amongst ill-fed, ill-clothed, and ill-housed savages, is set down by primitive man to the agency of demons, who must accordingly be expelled. Hence, in the tropical regions of New Britain and Peru, the devils are or were driven out at the beginning of the rainy season;

hence, on the dreary coasts of Baffin Land, they are banished at the approach of the bitter arctic winter. When a tribe has taken to husbandry, the time for the general expulsion of devils is naturally made to agree with one of the great epochs of the agricultural year, as sowing, or harvest; but, as these epochs themselves naturally coincide with changes of season, it does not follow that the transition from the hunting or pastoral to the agricultural life involves any alteration in the time of celebrating this great annual rite. Some of the agricultural communities of India and the Hindoo Koosh hold their general clearance of demons at harvest, others at sowing-time. But, at whatever season of the year it is held, the general expulsion of devils commonly marks the beginning of the new year. For, before entering on a new year, people are anxious to rid themselves of the troubles that have harassed them in the past; hence it comes about that in so many communities the beginning of the new year is inaugurated with a solemn and public banishment of evil spirits.

In the third place, it is to be observed that the public and periodic expulsion of devils is commonly preceded or followed by a period of general license, during which the ordinary restraints of society are thrown aside, and all offences, short of the gravest, are allowed to pass unpunished. In Guinea and Tonquin the period of license precedes the public expulsion of demons; and suspension of the ordinary government in Lhasa previous to the expulsion of the scapegoat is perhaps a relic of a similar period of universal license. Amongst the Hos of India the period of license follows the expulsion of the devil. Amongst the Iroquois it hardly appears whether it preceded or followed the banishment of evils. In any case, the extraordinary relaxation of all ordinary rules of conduct on such occasions is doubtless to be explained by the general clearance of evils which precedes or follows it. On the one hand, when a general riddance of evil and absolution from all sin is in immediate prospect, men are encouraged to give the rein to their passions, trusting that the coming ceremony will wipe out the score which they are running up so fast. On the other hand, when the ceremony has just taken place, men's minds are freed from the oppressive sense, under which they generally labour, of an atmosphere surcharged with devils; and in the first revulsion of joy they overleap the limits commonly imposed by custom and morality. When the ceremony takes place at harvest-time, the elation of feeling which it excites is further stimulated by the state of physical wellbeing produced by an abundant supply of food.

Fourthly, the employment of a divine man or animal as a scapegoat is especially to be noted; indeed, we are here directly concerned with the custom of banishing evils only in so far as these evils are believed to be transferred to a god who is afterwards slain. It may be suspected that the custom of employing a divine man or animal as a public scapegoat is much more widely diffused than appears from the examples cited. For, as has already been pointed out, the custom of killing a god dates from so early a period of human history that in later ages, even when the custom continues to be practised, it is liable to be misinterpreted. The divine character of the animal or man is forgotten, and he comes to be regarded merely as an ordinary victim. This is especially likely to be the case when it is a divine man who is killed. For when a nation becomes civilised, if it does not drop human sacrifices altogether, it at least selects as victims only such wretches as would be put to death at any rate. Thus the

The annual expulsion of evils
Situa, the public expulsion of evils in September, in Inca Peru. 'In this month, the Incas used to have sicknesses expelled from the villages . . . by men armed as though to fight in a war. They wielded firebrands, saying, "Go away, sicknesses . . . from the people of this village, leave us alone."' Text and illustration from facsimile of Guaman Poma de Ayala, *Nueva Corónica* (c.1615), Institut d'Ethnologie, Paris

killing of a god may sometimes come to be confounded with the execution of a criminal.

If we ask why a dying god should be chosen to take upon himself and carry away the sins and sorrows of the people, it may be suggested that in the practice of using the divinity as a scapegoat we have a combination of two customs which were at one time distinct and independent. On the one hand we have seen that it has been customary to kill the human or animal god in order to save his divine life from being weakened by the inroads of age. On the other hand we have seen that it has been customary to have a general expulsion of evils and sins once a year. Now, if it occurred to people to combine these two customs, the result would be the employment of the dying god as a scapegoat. He was killed, not originally to take away sin, but to save the divine life from the degeneracy of old age; but, since he had to be killed at any rate, people may have thought that they might as well seize the opportunity to lay upon him the burden of their sufferings and sins, in order that he might bear it away with him to the unknown world beyond the grave.

The use of the divinity as a scapegoat clears up the ambiguity which, as we saw, appears to hang about the European folk-custom of 'carrying out Death'. Grounds have been shewn for believing that in this ceremony the so-called Death was originally the spirit of vegetation, who was annually slain in spring, in order that he might come to life again with all the vigour of youth. But, as I pointed out, there are certain features in the ceremony which are not explicable on this hypothesis alone. Such are the marks of joy with which the effigy of Death is carried out to be buried or burnt, and the fear and abhorrence of it manifested by the bearers. But these features become at once intelligible if we suppose that the Death was not merely the dying god of vegetation, but also a public scapegoat, upon whom were laid all the evils that had afflicted the people during the past year. Joy on such an occasion is natural and appropriate; and if the dying god appears to be the object of that fear and abhorrence which are properly due not to himself, but to the sins and misfortunes with which he is laden, this arises merely from the difficulty of distinguishing, or at least of marking the distinction, between the bearer and the burden.

When the burden is of a baleful character, the bearer of it will be feared and shunned just as much as if he were himself imbued with those dangerous properties of which, as it happens, he is only the vehicle. Similarly we have seen that disease-laden and sin-laden boats are dreaded and shunned by East Indian peoples. Again, the view that in these popular customs the Death is a scapegoat as well as a representative of the divine spirit of vegetation derives some support from the circumstance that its expulsion is always celebrated in spring and chiefly by Slavonic peoples. For the Slavonic year began in spring; and thus, in one of its aspects, the ceremony of 'Carrying out Death' would be an example of the widespread custom of expelling the accumulated evils of the old year before entering on a new one.

3. Human Scapegoats in Classical Antiquity

The Human Scapegoat in Ancient Rome

We are now prepared to notice the use of the human scapegoat in classical antiquity. Every year on the fourteenth of March a man clad in skins was led in procession through the streets of Rome, beaten with long white rods, and driven out of the city. He was called Mamurius Veturius, that is 'the old Mars', and as the ceremony took place on the day preceding the first full moon of the old Roman year (which began on the first of March), the skin-clad man must have represented the Mars of the past year, who was driven out at the beginning of a new one. Now Mars was originally not a god of war but of vegetation. For it was to Mars that the Roman husbandman prayed for the prosperity of his corn and his vines, his fruit-trees and his copses; it was to Mars that the priestly college of the Arval Brothers, whose business it was to sacrifice for the growth of the crops, addressed their petitions almost exclusively; and it was to Mars that a horse was sacrificed in October to secure an abundant harvest. Moreover, it was to Mars, under his title of 'Mars of the woods' (*Mars Silvanus*), that farmers offered sacrifice for the welfare of their cattle. In the Roman ceremony of expulsion the representative of the god appears to have been treated not only as a deity of vegetation but also as a scapegoat. His expulsion implies this; for there is no reason why the god of vegetation, as such, should be expelled the city. But it is otherwise if he is also a scapegoat; it then becomes necessary to drive him beyond the boundaries, that he may carry his sorrowful burden away to other lands. And, in fact, Mamurius Veturius appears to have been driven away to the land of the Oscans, the enemies of Rome.

The blows with which the 'old Mars' was expelled from the city seem to have been administered by the dancing priests of Mars, the Salii. Thus on the fourteenth day of March every year Rome witnessed the curious spectacle of the human incarnation of a god chased by the god's own priests with blows from the city. The rite becomes at least intelligible on the theory that the man so beaten and expelled stood for the outworn deity of vegetation, who had to be replaced by a fresh and vigorous young divinity at the beginning of a New Year. The dancing priests of the god derived their name of Salii from the leaps or dances which they were bound to execute as a solemn religious ceremony every year in the Comitium, the centre of Roman political life. Twice a year, in the spring month of March and the autumn month of October, they discharged this sacred duty; and as they did so they invoked Saturn, the Roman god of sowing. As the Romans sowed the corn both in spring and autumn, and as down to the present time in Europe superstitious rustics are wont to dance and leap high in spring for the purpose of making the crops grow high, we may conjecture that the leaps and dances performed by the Salii, the priests of the old Italian god of vegetation, were similarly supposed to quicken the growth of the corn by homoeopathic or imitative magic. Similarly, 'the natives of Aracan dance in order to render propitious the spirits whom they believe to preside over the sowing and over the harvest. There are definite times for doing it, and we may say that in their eyes it is, as it were, an act of religion.' Another people who dance diligently to obtain good crops are the Tarahumare Indians of Mexico. The two principal dances of these Indians, the *rutuburi* and the *yumari*, are supposed to have been taught them by the turkey and the deer respectively. They are danced by numbers of men and women, the two sexes keeping apart from each other in the dance, while the shaman sings and shakes his rattle. But 'a large gathering is not necessary in order to pray to the gods by dancing. Sometimes the family dances alone, the father teaching the boys. While doing agricultural work, the Indians often depute one man to dance *yumari* near the house, while the others attend to the work in the fields. It is a curious sight to see a lone man taking his devotional exercise to the tune of his rattle in front of an apparently deserted dwelling. The lonely worshipper is doing his share of the general work by bringing down the fructifying rain and by warding off disaster, while the rest of the family and their friends plant, hoe, weed, or harvest. In the evening, when they return from the field, they may join him for a little while; but often he goes on alone, dancing all night, and singing himself hoarse, and the Indians told me that this is the very hardest kind of work, and exhausting even to them. Solitary worship is also observed by men who go out hunting deer or squirrels for a communal feast. Every one of them dances *yumari* alone in front of his house for two hours to insure success on the hunt; and when putting corn to sprout for the making of *tesvino* the owner of the house dances for a while, that the corn may sprout well.' Another dance is thought to cause the grass and funguses to grow, and the deer and rabbits to multiply; and another is supposed to draw the clouds together from the north and south, so that they clash and descend in rain.

We have seen that in many parts of Germany, Austria, and France the peasants are still, or were till lately, accustomed to dance and leap high in order that the crops may grow tall. Such leaps and dances are sometimes performed by the sower immediately before or after he sows the seed; but often they are executed by the people on a fixed day of the year, which in some places is Twelfth Night (the sixth of January), or Candlemas (the second of February) or Walpurgis Night, that is, the Eve of May Day; but apparently the favourite season for these performances is the last day of the Carnival, namely Shrove Tuesday. In such cases the leaps and dances are performed by every man for his own behoof; he skips and jumps merely in order that his own corn, or flax, or hemp may spring up and thrive. But sometimes in modern Europe, as (if I am right) in ancient Rome, the duty of dancing for the crops was committed to bands or troops of men, who cut their capers for the benefit of the whole community.

Concerning these masquerades and processions, as they have been or still are celebrated in modern Europe, we may say in general that they appear to have been originally intended both to stimulate the growth of vegetation in spring and to expel the demoniac or other evil influences which were thought to have accumulated during the preceding winter or year; and that these two motives of stimulation and expulsion, blended and perhaps confused together, appear to explain the quaint costumes of the mummers, the multitudinous noises which they make, and the blows which they direct either at invisible foes or at the visible and tangible persons of their fellows. In the latter case the beating may be supposed to serve as a means of forcibly freeing the sufferers from the demons or other evil things that cling to them unseen.

To apply these conclusions to the Roman custom of expelling Mamurius Veturius or 'the Old Mars' every year in spring, we may say that they lend some support to the theory which sees in 'the Old Mars' the outworn deity of vegetation driven away to make room, either for a

Propitiation of evil powers and spirits of the dead
Spirits and supernatural powers are often ambivalent.
Their malevolence may need to be exorcized, but they
can also be propitiated by offerings to secure their
beneficence. Here an egg is offered to the goddess of
disease, Nepal. Photo: Nick Allen

Among the powers who must be respected are the spirits
of the dead, because they can still affect the living, for
good or ill. Porpa, a royal official, and his wife are shown
in the after life, receiving gifts of food from their living
children. Egyptian wooden box, *c*.2580 BC, Gulbenkian
Museum of Oriental Art, Durham

younger and more vigorous personification of
vernal life, or perhaps for the return of the same
deity refreshed and renovated by the treatment
to which he had been subjected. So far as 'the
Old Mars' was supposed to carry away with him
the accumulated weaknesses and other evils of
the past year, so far would he serve as a public
scapegoat, like the effigy in the Slavonic custom
of 'Carrying out Death', which appears not only
to represent the vegetation-spirit of the past year,
but also to act as a scapegoat, carrying away
with it a heavy load of suffering, misfortune,
and death.

The Human Scapegoat in Ancient Greece

The ancient Greeks were also familiar with the
use of a human scapegoat. In Plutarch's native
town of Chaeronea a ceremony of this kind was
performed by the chief magistrate at the Town
Hall, and by each householder at his own home.

It was called the 'expulsion of hunger'. A slave
was beaten with rods of the *agnus castus*, and
turned out of doors with the words, 'Out with
hunger, and in with wealth and health.' When
Plutarch held the office of chief magistrate of his
native town he performed this ceremony at the
Town Hall, and he has recorded the discussion to
which the custom afterwards gave rise.

But in civilized Greece the custom of the
scapegoat took darker forms than the innocent
rite over which the amiable and pious Plutarch
presided. Whenever Marseilles, one of the
busiest and most brilliant of Greek colonies,
was ravaged by a plague, a man of the poorer
classes used to offer himself as a scapegoat. For a
whole year he was maintained at the public
expense, being fed on choice and pure food. At
the expiry of the year he was dressed in sacred
garments, decked with holy branches, and led
through the whole city, while prayers were

The ambivalent power of the dead is expressed particularly clearly in a Japanese ritual. Once a year the spirits of the ancestors are welcomed and feasted, but on the following night, as shown here, are expelled with stones, lest their lingering presence cause harm. 18th-century engraving, Bodleian Library, Oxford

goat or vicarious sacrifice for the life of all the others; six days before his execution he was excommunicated, 'in order that he alone might bear the sins of all the people'.

As practised by the Greeks of Asia Minor in the sixth century before our era, the custom of the scapegoat was as follows. When a city suffered from plague, famine, or other public calamity, an ugly or deformed person was chosen to take upon himself all the evils which afflicted the community. He was brought to a suitable place, where dried figs, a barley loaf, and cheese were put into his hand. These he ate. Then he was beaten seven times upon his genital organs with squills and branches of the wild fig and other wild trees, while the flutes played a particular tune. Afterwards he was burned on a pyre built of the wood of forest trees; and his ashes were cast into the sea. A similar custom appears to have been annually celebrated by the Asiatic Greeks at the harvest festival of the Thargelia.

In the ritual just described the scourging of the victim with squills, branches of the wild fig, and so forth, cannot have been intended to aggravate his sufferings, otherwise any stick would have been good enough to beat him with. The ancients attributed to squills a magical power of averting evil influences, and accordingly they hung them up at the doors of their houses and made use of them in purificatory rites.

Thus the object of beating the human scapegoat on the genital organs with squills and so on, must have been to release his reproductive energies from any restraint or spell under which they might be laid by demoniacal or other malignant agency; and as the Thargelia at which he was annually sacrificed was an early harvest festival celebrated in May, we must recognize in him a representative of the creative and fertilizing god of vegetation. The representative of the god was annually slain for the purpose I have indicated, that of maintaining the divine

uttered that all the evils of the people might fall on his head. He was then cast out of the city or stoned to death by the people outside the walls. The Athenians regularly maintained a number of degraded and useless beings at the public expense; and when any calamity, such as plague, drought, or famine, befell the city, they sacrificed two of these outcasts as scapegoats. One of the victims was sacrificed for the men and the other for the women. They were led about the city and then sacrificed, apparently by being stoned to death outside the city. But such sacrifices were not confined to extraordinary occasions of public calamity; it appears that every year, at the festival of the Thargelia in May, two victims, one for the men and one for the women, were led out of Athens and stoned to death. The city of Abdera in Thrace was publicly purified once a year, and one of the burghers, set apart for the purpose, was stoned to death as a scape-

life in perpetual vigour, untainted by the weakness of age: and before he was put to death it was not unnatural to stimulate his reproductive powers in order that these might be transmitted in full activity to his successor, the new god or new embodiment of the old god, who was doubtless supposed immediately to take the place of the one slain. Similar reasoning would lead to a similar treatment of the scapegoat on special occasions, such as drought or famine.

Hence, the beating inflicted on the human victims at the Greek Thargelia is most naturally explained as a charm to increase the reproductive energies of the men or women either by communicating to them the fruitfulness of the plants and branches, or by ridding them of maleficent influences; and this interpretation is confirmed by the observation that the two victims represented the two sexes, one of them standing for the men in general and the other for the women. The season of the year when the ceremony was performed, namely the time of the corn harvest, tallies well with the theory that the rite had an agricultural significance.

If these considerations are just, we must apparently conclude that while the human victims at the Thargelia certainly appear in later classical times to have figured chiefly as public scapegoats, who carried away with them the sins, misfortunes, and sorrows of the whole people, at an earlier time they may have been looked on as embodiments of vegetation, perhaps of the corn but particularly of the fig-trees; and that the beating which they received and the death which they died were intended primarily to brace and refresh the powers of vegetation then beginning to droop and languish under the torrid heat of the Greek summer.

The view here taken of the Greek scapegoat, if it is correct, obviates an objection which might otherwise be brought against the main argument of this book. To the theory that the priest of Aricia was slain as a representative of the spirit of the grove, it might have been objected that such a custom has no analogy in classical antiquity. But reasons have now been given for believing that the human being periodically and occasionally slain by the Asiatic Greeks was regularly treated as an embodiment of a divinity of vegetation. Probably the persons whom the Athenians kept to be sacrificed were similarly treated as divine. That they were social outcasts did not matter. In the primitive view a man is not chosen to be the mouth-piece or embodiment of a god on account of his high moral qualities or social rank. The divine afflatus descends equally on the good and the bad, the lofty and the lowly. If then the civilized Greeks of Asia and Athens habitually sacrificed men whom they regarded as incarnate gods, there can be no inherent improbability in the supposition that at the dawn of history a similar custom was observed by the semi-barbarous Latins in the Arician Grove.

4. Killing the God in Mexico

By no people does the custom of sacrificing the human representative of a god appear to have been observed so commonly and with so much solemnity as by the Aztecs of ancient Mexico. With the ritual of these remarkable sacrifices we are well acquainted, for it has been fully described by the Spaniards who conquered Mexico in the sixteenth century, and whose curiosity was naturally excited by the discovery in this distant region of a barbarous and cruel religion which presented many curious points of analogy to the doctrine and ritual of their own church. 'They took a captive', says the Jesuit Acosta, 'such as they thought good; and afore they did sacrifice him unto their idols, they gave him the name of the idol, to whom he should be sacrificed, and apparelled him with the same ornaments like their idol, saying, that he did represent the same idol. And during the time that this representation lasted, which was for a year in some feasts, in others six months, and in others less, they reverenced and worshipped him in the same manner as the proper idol; and in the meantime he did eat, drink, and was merry. When he went through the streets, the people came forth to worship him, and every one brought him an alms, with children and sick folks, that he might cure them, and bless them,

Human sacrifice
The Aztec victim in the clothes of the god makes music and dances before being sacrificed and dismembered. Kingsborough, *Antiquities of Mexico*, 1830–48, Bodleian Library, Oxford

Victims of human sacrifice have been found in the swamps of northern Germany and Scandinavia. The Tollund man was thrown into a swamp with a noose around his neck about two thousand years ago. Silkeborg Museum, Denmark

suffering him to do all things at his pleasure, only he was accompanied with ten or twelve men lest he should fly. And he (to the end he might be reverenced as he passed) sometimes sounded upon a small flute, that the people might prepare to worship him. The feast being come, and he grown fat, they killed him, opened him, and ate him, making a solemn sacrifice of him.'

This general description of the custom may now be illustrated by particular examples. Thus at the festival called Toxcatl, the greatest festival of the Mexican year, a young man was annually sacrificed in the character of Tezcatlipoca, 'the god of gods', after having been maintained and worshipped as that great deity in person for a whole year. According to the old Franciscan monk Sahagun, our best authority on the Aztec religion, the sacrifice of the human god fell at Easter or a few days later, so that, if he is right, it would correspond in date as well as in character to the Christian festival of the death and resurrection of the Redeemer. More exactly he tells us that the sacrifice took place on the first day of the fifth Aztec month, which according to him began on the twenty-third or twenty-seventh day of April. However, according to other Spanish authorities of the sixteenth century the festival lasted from the ninth to the nineteenth day of May, and the sacrifice of the human victim in the character of the god was performed on the last of these days. Whatever the exact date of the celebration may have been, we are told that the 'feast was not made to any other end, but to demand rain, in the same manner that we solemnize the Rogations; and this feast was always in May, which is the time that they have most need of rain in those countries.'

At this festival the great god died in the person of one human representative and came to life again in the person of another, who was destined to enjoy the fatal honour of divinity for a year and to perish, like all his predecessors, at the end of it. The young man singled out for this high dignity was carefully chosen from among the captives on the ground of his personal beauty. He had to be of unblemished body, slim as a reed and straight as a pillar, neither too tall nor too short. If through high living he grew too fat, he was obliged to reduce himself by drinking salt water. And in order that he might behave in his lofty station with becoming grace and dignity he was carefully trained to comport himself like a gentleman of the first quality, to speak correctly and elegantly, to play the flute, to smoke cigars and to snuff at flowers with a dandified air. He was honourably lodged in the temple where the nobles waited on him and paid him homage, bringing him meat and serving him like a prince. The king himself saw to it that he was apparelled in gorgeous attire, 'for already he esteemed him as a god'. Eagle down was gummed to his head and white cock's feathers were stuck in his hair, which drooped to his girdle. A wreath of flowers like roasted maize crowned his brows, and a garland of the same flowers passed over his shoulders and under his arm-pits. Golden ornaments hung from his nose, golden armlets adorned his arms, golden bells jingled on his legs at every step he took; earrings of turquoise dangled from his ears, bracelets of turquoise bedecked his wrists; necklaces of shells encircled his neck and depended on his breast; he wore a mantle of network, and round his middle a rich waist-cloth. When this bejewelled exquisite lounged through the streets playing on his flute, puffing at a cigar, and smelling at a nosegay, the people whom he met threw themselves on the earth before him and prayed to him with sighs and tears, taking up the dust in their hands and putting it in their mouths in token of the deepest humiliation and subjection. Women came forth with children in their arms and presented them to him, saluting him as a god. For 'he passed for our Lord God; the people acknowledged him as the Lord'. All who thus worshipped him on his passage he saluted gravely and courteously. Lest he should flee, he was everywhere attended by a guard of eight pages in the royal livery, four of them with shaven crowns like the palace-slaves, and four of them with the flowing locks of warriors; and if he contrived to escape, the captain of the guard had to take his place as the representative of the god and to die in his stead. Twenty days before he was to die, his costume was changed, and four damsels, delicately nurtured and bearing the names of four goddesses – the Goddess of Flowers, the Goddess of the Young Maize, the Goddess 'Our Mother among the Water', and the Goddess of Salt – were given him to be his brides, and with them he consorted. During the last five days divine honours were showered on the destined victim. The king remained in his palace while the whole court went after the human god. Solemn banquets and dances followed each other in regular succession and at appointed places. On the last day the young man, attended by his wives and pages, embarked in a canoe covered with a royal canopy and was ferried across the lake to a spot where a little hill rose from the edge of the water. It was called the Mountain of Parting, because here his wives bade him a last farewell. Then, accompanied only by his pages, he repaired to a small and lonely temple by the wayside. Like the Mexican temples in general, it was built in the form of a pyramid; and as the young man ascended the stairs he broke at every step one of the flutes on which he had played in the days of his glory. On reaching the summit he was seized and held down by the priests on his back upon a block of stone, while one of them cut open his breast, thrust his hand into the wound, and wrenching out his heart held it up in sacrifice to the sun. The body of the dead god was not, like the bodies of common victims, sent rolling down the steps of the temple, but was carried down to the foot, where the head was cut off and spitted on a pike. Such was the regular end of the man who personated the greatest god of the Mexican pantheon.

But he was not the only man who played the part of a god and was sacrificed as such. Several other divinities were worshipped in this fashion. Among them was the Maize Goddess Chicomecohuatl. At the festival in her honour the identification between divinity and victim appears to have been complete. The golden maize cobs which the girl who was to be sacrificed wore round her neck, the artificial maize cobs which she carried in her hands, the green feather which was stuck in her hair in imitation (we are told) of a green ear of maize, all set her forth as a personification of the corn-spirit; and we are expressly informed that she was specially chosen as a young girl to represent the young maize, which at the time of the festival had not yet fully ripened. Further, her identification with the corn and the corn-goddess was clearly announced by making her stand on the heaps of maize and there receive the homage and blood-offerings of the whole people, who thereby returned her thanks for the benefits which in her character of a divinity she was supposed to have conferred upon them. Once more, the practice of beheading her on a heap of corn and seeds and sprinkling her blood, not only on the image of the Maize Goddess, but on the piles of maize, peppers, pumpkins, seeds, and vegetables, can seemingly have had no other object but to quicken and strengthen the crops of corn and the fruits of the earth in general by infusing into their representatives the blood of the Corn Goddess herself. The analogy of this Mexican sacrifice, the meaning of which appears to be indisputable, may be allowed to strengthen the interpretation which I have given of other human sacrifices offered for the crops. If the Mexican girl, whose blood was sprinkled on the maize, indeed personated the Maize Goddess, it becomes more than ever probable that the girl whose blood the Pawnees similarly sprinkled on

The flayed god of Mexico
Xipe Totec was one of several Mexican divinities whose human impersonators could also be his victims. Stone mask of the Aztec Xipe Totec; the inside of the mask (right) shows the god wearing the skin of one of his victims. British Museum, London

the seed corn personated in like manner the female Spirit of the Corn; and so with the other human beings whom other races have slaughtered for the sake of promoting the growth of the crops.

Lastly, the concluding act of the sacred drama, in which the body of the dead Maize Goddess was flayed and her skin worn, together with all her sacred insignia, by a man who danced before the people in this grim attire, seems to be best explained on the hypothesis that it was intended to ensure that the divine death should be immediately followed by the divine resurrection. If that was so, we may infer with some degree of probability that the practice of killing a human representative of a deity has commonly, perhaps always, been regarded merely as a means of perpetuating the divine energies in the fulness of youthful vigour, untainted by the weakness and frailty of age, from which they must have suffered if the deity had been allowed to die a natural death.

The rites described in the preceding pages suf-fice to prove that human sacrifices of the sort I suppose to have prevailed at Aricia were, as a matter of fact, systematically offered on a large scale by a people whose level of culture was probably not inferior, if indeed it was not distinctly superior, to that occupied by the Italian races at the early period to which the origin of the Arician priesthood must be referred. The positive and indubitable evidence of the prevalence of such sacrifices in one part of the world may reasonably be allowed to strengthen the probability of their prevalence in places for which the evidence is less full and trustworthy. Taken all together, the facts which we have passed in review seem to shew that the custom of killing men whom their worshippers regard as divine has prevailed in many parts of the world. But to clinch the argument, it is clearly desirable to prove that the custom of putting to death a human representative of a god was known and practised in ancient Italy elsewhere than in the Arician Grove. This proof I now propose to adduce.

5. The Saturnalia and Kindred Festivals

The Roman Saturnalia

In an earlier part of this book we saw that many peoples have been used to observe an annual period of license, when the customary restraints of law and morality are thrown aside, when the whole population give themselves up to extravagant mirth and jollity, and when the darker passions find a vent which would never be allowed them in the more staid and sober course of ordinary life. Such outbursts of the pent-up forces of human nature, too often degenerating into wild orgies of lust and crime, occur most commonly at the end of the year, and are frequently associated, as I have had occasion to point out, with one or other of the agricultural seasons, especially with the time of sowing or of harvest. Now, of all these periods of license the one which is best known and which in modern languages has given its name to the rest, is the Saturnalia. This famous festival fell in December, the last month of the Roman year, and was popularly supposed to commemorate the merry reign of Saturn, the god of sowing and of husbandry, who lived on earth long ago as a righteous and beneficent king of Italy, drew the rude and scattered dwellers on the mountains together, taught them to till the ground, gave them laws, and ruled in peace. His reign was the fabled Golden Age: the earth brought forth abundantly: no sound of war or discord troubled the happy world: no baleful love of lucre worked like poison in the blood of the industrious and contented peasantry. Slavery and private property were alike unknown: all men had all things in common. At last the good god, the kindly king, vanished suddenly; but his memory was cherished to distant ages, shrines were reared

in his honour, and many hills and high places in Italy bore his name. Yet the bright tradition of his reign was crossed by a dark shadow: his altars are said to have been stained with the blood of human victims, for whom a more merciful age afterwards substituted effigies. Of this gloomy side of the god's religion there is little or no trace in the descriptions which ancient writers have left us of the Saturnalia. Feasting and revelry and all the mad pursuit of pleasure are the features that seem to have especially marked this carnival of antiquity, as it went on for seven days in the streets and public squares and houses of ancient Rome from the seventeenth to the twenty-third of December.

But no feature of the festival is more remarkable, nothing in it seems to have struck the ancients themselves more than the license granted to slaves at this time. The distinction between the free and the servile classes was temporarily abolished. The slave might rail at his master, intoxicate himself like his betters, sit down at table with them, and not even a word of reproof would be administered to him for conduct which at any other season might have been punished with stripes, imprisonment, or death. Nay, more, masters actually changed places with their slaves and waited on them at table; and not till the serf had done eating and drinking was the board cleared and dinner set for his master.

Now, when we remember that the liberty allowed to slaves at this festive season was supposed to be an imitation of the state of society in Saturn's time, and that in general the Saturnalia passed for nothing more or less than a temporary revival or restoration of the reign of that merry monarch, we are tempted to surmise that the mock king who presided over the revels may have originally represented Saturn himself. The conjecture is strongly confirmed, if not established, by a very curious and interesting account of the way in which the Saturnalia was celebrated by the Roman soldiers stationed on the Danube in the reign of Maximian and Diocletian. The account is preserved in a narrative of the martyrdom of St Dasius. According to this and other narratives, of which the longest is probably based on official documents, the Roman soldiers at Durostorum in Lower Moesia celebrated the Saturnalia year by year in the following manner. Thirty days before the festival they chose by lot from amongst themselves a young and handsome man, who was then clothed in royal attire to resemble Saturn. Thus arrayed and attended by a multitude of soldiers he went about in public with full license to indulge his passions and to taste of every pleasure, however base and shameful. But if his reign was merry, it was short and ended tragically; for when the thirty days were up and the festival of Saturn had come, he cut his own throat on the altar of the god whom he personated. In the year 303 AD the lot fell upon the Christian soldier Dasius, but he refused to play the part of the heathen god and soil his last days by debauchery. The threats and arguments of his commanding officer Bassus failed to shake his constancy, and accordingly he was beheaded, as the Christian martyrologist records with minute accuracy, at Durostorum by the soldier John on Friday the twentieth day of November, being the twenty-fourth day of the moon, at the fourth hour.

This account sets in a new and lurid light the office of the King of the Saturnalia, the ancient Lord of Misrule, who presided over the winter revels at Rome in the time of Horace and of Tacitus. It seems to prove that his business had not always been that of a mere harlequin or merry-andrew whose only care was that the revelry should run high and the fun grow fast and furious. The martyrologist's account of the Saturnalia agrees so closely with the accounts of similar rites elsewhere, which could not possibly have been known to him, that the substantial accuracy of his description may be regarded as established; and further, since the custom of putting a mock king to death as a representative of a god cannot have grown out of a practice of appointing him to preside over a holiday revel, whereas the reverse may very well have happened, we are justified in assuming that in an earlier and more barbarous age it was the universal practice in ancient Italy, wherever the worship of Saturn prevailed, to choose a man who played the part and enjoyed all the traditionary privileges of Saturn for a season, and then died, whether by his own or another's hand, whether by the knife or the fire or on the gallows-tree, in the character of the good god who gave his life for the world.

The resemblance between the Saturnalia of ancient and the Carnival of modern Italy has often been remarked; but in the light of all the facts that have come before us, we may well ask whether the resemblance does not amount to identity. In Italy, Spain, and France, that is, in the countries where the influence of Rome has been deepest and most lasting, a conspicuous feature of the Carnival is a burlesque figure personifying the festive season, which after a short career of glory and dissipation is publicly shot, burnt, or otherwise destroyed, to the feigned grief or genuine delight of the populace. If the view here suggested of the Carnival is correct, this grotesque personage is no other than a direct successor of the old King of the Saturnalia, the master of the revels, the real man who personated Saturn and, when the revels were over, suffered a real death in his assumed character. The King of the Bean on Twelfth Night and the mediaeval Bishop of Fools, Abbot

Ancient rites survive in modern customs
The Horn dance at Abbots Bromley, Staffordshire, was
photographed in 1906 by Sir Benjamin Stone, who
thought that it commemorated the Forest Charter of
Henry III, which mitigated penalties imposed on poachers
in the royal forests. But Frazer would see in this dance the
survival of a much more ancient ritual, such as may be
represented on the Gundestrup cauldron of the 1st
millennium BC.
TOP. Horn dance, Abbots Bromley. *Sir Benjamin Stone's
Pictures*, 1906, Balfour Library, Pitt Rivers Museum,
University of Oxford
ABOVE. Panel from the Gundestrup cauldron, 1st
millennium BC, Nationalmuseet, Copenhagen

of Unreason, or Lord of Misrule are figures of
the same sort and may perhaps have had a similar
origin. We will consider them in the following
section.

The King of the Bean and the Festival of Fools

The custom of electing by lot a King and often
also a Queen of the Bean on Twelfth Night
(Epiphany, the sixth of January) or on the eve of
that festival used to prevail in France, Belgium,
Germany, and England, and it is still kept up in
some parts of France. It may be traced back to
the first half of the sixteenth century at least,
and no doubt dates from a very much more
remote antiquity. At the French court the Kings
themselves did not disdain to countenance the
mock royalty, and Louis XIV even supported
with courtly grace the shadowy dignity in his
own person. Every family as a rule elected its
own King. On the eve of the festival a great
cake was baked with a bean in it; the cake was
divided in portions, one for each member of the
family, together with one for God, one for the
Virgin, and sometimes one also for the poor.
The person who obtained the portion containing
the bean was proclaimed King of the Bean.
Where a Queen of the Bean was elected as well
as a King, a second bean was sometimes baked
in the cake for the Queen. Immediately on his
election the King of the Bean was enthroned,
saluted by all, and thrice lifted up, while he
made crosses with chalk on the beams and
rafters of the ceiling. Great virtue was attributed to these white crosses. They were supposed
to protect the house for the whole year against

> all injuryes and harmes
> Of cursed devils, sprites, and bugges, of conjurings and
> charmes.

Then feasting and revelry began and were kept
up merrily without respect of persons. Every
time the King or Queen drank, the whole com-

pany was expected to cry, 'The King drinks!' or 'The Queen drinks!' Any person who failed to join in the cry was punished by having his face blackened with soot or a burned cork or smeared with the wine lees. In parts of the Ardennes the custom was to fasten great horns of paper in the hair of the delinquent and to put a huge pair of spectacles on his nose; and he had to wear these badges of infamy till the end of the festival.

So far, apart from the crosses chalked up to ban hob-goblins, witches, and bugs, the King and Queen of the Bean might seem to be merely playful personages appointed at a season of festivity to lead the revels. However, a more serious significance was sometimes attached to the office and to the ceremonies of Twelfth Day in general. Thus in Lorraine the height of the hemp crop in the coming year was prognosticated from the height of the King and Queen; if the King was the taller of the two, it was supposed that the male hemp would be higher than the female, but that the contrary would happen if the Queen were taller than the King. Again, in the Vosges Mountains, on the borders of Franche-Comté, it is customary on Twelfth Day for people to dance on the roofs in order to make the hemp grow tall. Further, in many places the beans used in the cake were carried to the church to be blessed by the clergy, and people drew omens from the cake as to the good or ill that would befall them throughout the year.

In Franche-Comté, particularly in the Montagne du Doubs, it is still the custom on the Eve of Twelfth Night (the fifth of January) to light bonfires, which appear to have, in the popular mind, some reference to the crops. The whole population takes part in the festivity. In the afternoon the young folk draw a cart about the street collecting fuel. Some people contribute faggots, others bundles of straw or of dry hemp stalks. Towards evening the whole of the fuel thus collected is piled up a little way from the houses and set on fire. While it blazes, the people dance round it, crying, 'Good year, come back! Bread and wine, come back!' According to one Herefordshire informant, 'on Twelfth Day they make twelve fires of straw and one large one to burn the old witch; they sing, drink, and dance round it; without this festival they think they should have no crop'. This explanation of the large fire on Twelfth Day is remarkable and may supply the key to the whole custom of kindling fires on the fields or in the orchards on that day. We have seen that witches and fiends of various sorts are believed to be let loose during the Twelve Days and that in some places they are formally driven away on Twelfth Night. It may well be that the fires lighted on that day were everywhere primarily intended to burn the witches and other maleficent beings swarming invisible in the mischief-laden air, and that the benefit supposed to be conferred by the fires on the crops was not so much the positive one of quickening the growth of vegetation by genial warmth as the negative one of destroying the baleful influences which would otherwise blast the fruits of the earth and of the trees.

In this English custom observed on Twelfth Night the twelve fires probably refer either to the twelve days from Christmas to Epiphany or to the twelve months of the year. In favour of this view it may be said that according to a popular opinion, which has been reported in England and is widely diffused in Germany, the German provinces of Austria, France and Scotland, the weather of the twelve days in question determines the weather of the twelve following

Sacred stones: from magic to religion
The pilgrimage to the Kaaba at Mecca is one of the principal ways in which a Muslim gives expression to his faith in Allah – but originally the Kaaba was merely one of many sacred stones that guaranteed fortune and prosperity to the tribes of pre-Islamic Arabia.
OPPOSITE. The Kaaba in the Great Mosque, Mecca. Daily Telegraph Colour Library. Photo: Abuhander

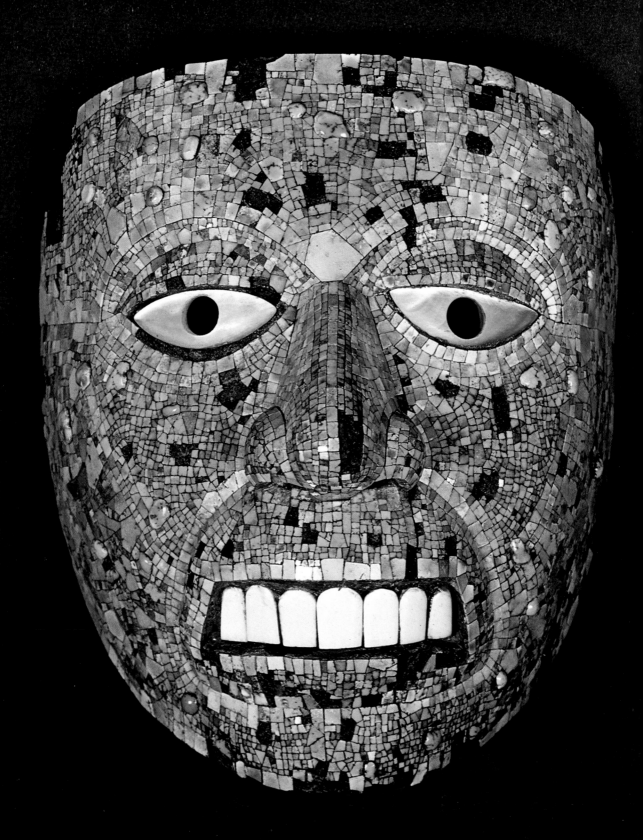

months, so that from the weather on each of these days it is possible to predict the weather of the corresponding month in the ensuing year.

Thus in the popular mind the twelve days from Christmas to Epiphany are conceived as a miniature of the whole year, the character of each particular day answering to the character of a particular month. The conception appears to be pre-Christian for it meets us again among the Aryans of the Vedic age in India. They, too, appear to have invested twelve days in mid-winter with a sacred character as a time when the three Ribhus or genii of the seasons rested from their labours in the home of the sun-god; and these twelve rest-days they called 'an image or copy of the year'.

It is possible that the twelve days from Christmas to Epiphany were an ancient intercalary period inserted for the purpose of equating the lunar to the solar year. On this basis we can better understand the curious superstitions that have clustered round them and the quaint customs that have been annually observed during their continuance. To the primitive mind it might well seem that an intercalary period stands outside of the regular order of things, forming part neither of the lunar nor of the solar system; it is an excrescence, an eddy which interrupts the even flow of months and years. Hence it may be inferred that the ordinary rules of conduct do not apply to such extraordinary periods, and that accordingly men may do in them what they would never dream of doing at other times. Thus intercalary days tend to degenerate into

Killing the god in Mexico
OPPOSITE. This 15th-century mosaic mask of turquoise with eyes of pearl shell and teeth of white shell probably represents Quetzalcoatl, the great Mexican god of light and wisdom. Like other Aztec gods, he was impersonated by human beings who were afterwards sacrificed to him. At the death of a king, masks such as this one were placed over the face of the image of the god, and also on the dead king before burial. British Museum, London

seasons of unbridled license; they form an inter-regnum during which the customary restraints of law and morality are suspended and the ordinary rulers abdicate their authority in favour of a temporary regent, a sort of puppet king, who bears a more or less indefinite, capricious, and precarious sway over a community given up for a time to riot, turbulence, and disorder. If that is so – though it must be confessed that the view here suggested is to a great extent conjectural – we may perhaps detect the last surviving representatives of such puppet kings in the King of the Bean and other grotesque figures of the same sort who used to parade with the mimic pomp of sovereignty on one or other of the twelve days between Christmas and Epiphany.

Saturnalia in Western Asia

When we pass from Europe to western Asia, from ancient Rome to ancient Babylon and the regions where Babylonian influence penetrated, we are still met with festivals which bear the closest resemblance to the oldest form of the Italian Saturnalia. The reader may remember the festival of the Sacaea, on which I had occasion to touch in an earlier part of this work. It was held at Babylon during five days of the month Lous, beginning with the sixteenth day of the month. During its continuance, just as at the Saturnalia, masters and servants changed places, the servants issuing orders and the masters obeying them; and in each house one of the servants, dressed as a king and bearing the title of Zoganes, bore rule over the household. Further, just as at the Saturnalia in its original form a man was dressed as King Saturn in royal robes, allowed to indulge his passions and caprices to the full, and then put to death, so at the Sacaea a condemned prisoner, who probably also bore for the time being the title of Zoganes, was arrayed in the king's attire and suffered to play the despot, to use the king's concubines, and to give himself up to feasting and debauchery without restraint, only however in the end to be stript of his borrowed finery, scourged, and hanged or crucified.

Now the Sacaean festival, described by the Babylonian priest Berosus in the first book of his history of Babylon, has been plausibly identified with the great Babylonian festival of the New Year called Zakmuk, Zagmuk, Zakmuku, or Zagmuku, which has become known to us in recent times through inscriptions. The New Year festival, which occupied at least the first eleven days of Nisan, probably included the spring equinox. It was held in honour of Marduk or Merodach, the chief god of Babylon, whose great temple of Esagila in the city formed the religious centre of the solemnity. For here, in a splendid chamber of the vast edifice, all the gods were believed to assemble at this season under the presidency of Marduk for the purpose of determining the fates for the new year, especially the fate of the king's life. On this occasion the king of Babylon was bound annually to renew his regal power by grasping the hands of the image of Marduk in his temple, as if to signify that he received the kingdom directly from the deity and was unable without the divine assistance and authority to retain it for more than a year. Another notable feature of the Babylonian festival of the New Year appears to have been a ceremonial marriage of the god Marduk; for in a hymn relating to the solemnity it is said of the deity that 'he hastened to his bridal'. The festival was of hoar antiquity, for it was known to Gudea, an old-king of Southern Babylonia who flourished between two and three thousand years before the beginning of our era, and it is mentioned in an early account of the Great Flood. At a much later period it is repeatedly referred to by King Nebuchadnezzar and his successors.

Unfortunately the notices of this Babylonian festival of the New Year which have come down to us deal chiefly with its mythical aspect and throw little light on the mode of its celebration. Hence its identity with the Sacaea must remain for the present a more or less probable hypothesis. In favour of the hypothesis may be alleged the very significant statement that the fate of the king's life was supposed to be determined by the gods, under the presidency of Marduk, at the Zakmuk or New Year's festival. When we remember that the central feature of the Sacaea appears to have been the saving of the king's life for another year by the vicarious sacrifice of a criminal on the cross or the gallows, we can understand that the season was a critical one for the king, and that it may well have been regarded as determining his fate for the ensuing twelve months. The annual ceremony of renewing the king's power by contact with the god's image, which formed a leading feature of the Zakmuk festival, would be very appropriately performed immediately after the execution or sacrifice of the temporary king who died in the room of the real monarch.

Another argument in favour of the identity of the two festivals is furnished by the connexion which has been traced between both of them and the Jewish feast of Purim. There are good grounds for believing that Purim was unknown to the Jews until after the exile, and that they learned to observe it during their captivity in the East. The feast of Purim was and is held on the fourteenth and fifteenth days of Adar, the last month of the Jewish year, which corresponds roughly to March. Thus the date agrees nearly, though not exactly, with the date of the Babylonian Zakmuk, which fell a fortnight later in the early days of the following month Nisan. When to this we add the joyous, nay, extravagant festivity which has always been characteristic of Purim, and is entirely in keeping with a New Year celebration, we may perhaps be thought to have made out a fairly probable case for holding that the Jewish feast is derived from the Babylonian New Year festival of Zakmuk. If the links which bind Purim to

Zakmuk are reasonably strong, the chain of evidence which connects the Jewish festival with the Sacaea is much stronger. The two days of the festival, according to the author of the book of Esther, were to be kept for ever as 'days of feasting and gladness, and of sending portions one to another, and gifts to the poor'. And this joyous character the festival seems always to have retained. Indeed Purim has been described as the Jewish Bacchanalia, and we are told that at this season everything is lawful which can contribute to the mirth and gaiety of the festival. Writers of the seventeenth century assert that during the two days, and especially on the evening of the second day, the Jews did nothing but feast and drink to repletion, play, dance, sing, and make merry; in particular they disguised themselves, men and women exchanging clothes, and thus attired ran about like mad, in open defiance of the Mosaic law, which expressly forbids men to dress as women and women as men.

When we examine the narrative which professes to account for the institution of Purim, we discover in it not only the strongest traces of Babylonian origin, but also certain singular analogies to those very features of the Sacaean festival with which we are here more immediately concerned. The book of Esther turns upon the fortunes of two men, the vizier Haman and the despised Jew Mordecai, at the court of a Persian king. Mordecai, we are told, had given mortal offence to the vizier, who accordingly prepares a tall gallows on which he hopes to see his enemy hanged, while he himself expects to receive the highest mark of the king's favour by being allowed to wear the royal crown and the royal robes, and thus attired to parade the streets mounted on the king's own horse and attended by one of the noblest princes, who should proclaim to the multitude his temporary exaltation and glory. But the artful intrigues of the wicked vizier miscarried and resulted in precisely the opposite of what he had hoped and expected; for the royal honours which he had looked for fell to his rival Mordecai, and he himself was hanged on the gallows which he had made ready for his foe. In this story we seem to detect a reminiscence, more or less confused, of the Zoganes of the Sacaea, in other words, of the custom of investing a private man with the insignia of royalty for a few days and then putting him to death on the gallows or the cross. It is true that in the narrative the part of the Zoganes is divided between two actors, one of whom hopes to play the king but is hanged instead, while the other acts the royal part and escapes the gallows to which he was destined by his enemy. But this bisection, so to say, of the Zoganes may have been deliberately invented by the Jewish author of the book of Esther for the sake of setting the origin of Purim, which it was his purpose to explain, in a light that should reflect glory on his own nation. Or, perhaps more probably, it points back to a custom of appointing two mock kings at the Sacaea, one of whom was put to death at the end of the festival, while the other was allowed to go free, at least for a time. We shall be the more inclined to adopt the latter hypothesis when we observe that corresponding to the two rival aspirants to the temporary kingship there appear in the Jewish narrative two rival queens, Vashti and Esther, one of whom succeeds to the high estate from which the other has fallen. Further, it is to be noted that Mordecai, the successful candidate for the mock kingship, and Esther, the successful candidate for the queenship, are linked together by close ties both of interest and blood, the two being said to be cousins. This suggests that in the original story or the original custom there may have figured two pairs of kings and queens, of whom one pair is represented in the Jewish narrative by Mordecai and Esther and the other by Haman and Vashti.

Some confirmation of this view is furnished

by the names of two out of the four personages. It seems to be now generally recognized by Biblical scholars that the name Mordecai, which has no meaning in Hebrew, is nothing but a slightly altered form of Marduk or Merodach, the name of the chief god of Babylon, whose great festival was the Zakmuk; and further, it is generally admitted that Esther in like manner is equivalent to Ishtar, the great Babylonian goddess whom the Greeks called Astarte, and who is more familiar to English readers as Ashtaroth.

If we are right in tracing the origin of Purim to the Babylonian Sacaea and in finding the counterpart of the Zoganes in Haman and Mordecai, it would appear that the Zoganes during his five days of office personated not merely a king but a god, whether that god was the Babylonian Marduk or some other deity not yet identified. The union of the divine and royal characters in a single person is so common that we need not be surprised at meeting with it in ancient Babylon. And the view that the mock king of the Sacaea died as a god on the cross or the gallows is no novelty. The acute and learned Movers long ago observed that 'we should be overlooking the religious significance of oriental festivals and the connexion of the Sacaea with the worship of Anaitis, if we were to treat as a mere jest the custom of disguising a slave as a king. We may take it for certain that with the royal dignity the king of the Sacaea assumed also the character of an oriental ruler as representative of the divinity, and that when he took his pleasure among the women of the king's harem, he played the part of Sandan or Sardanapalus himself. For according to ancient oriental ideas the use of the king's concubines constituted a claim to the throne, and we know from Dio that the five-days' king received full power over the harem.'

Also, we may incline to view with favour Movers's further conjecture, that a female slave may have been appointed to play the divine queen to the part of the divine king supported by the Zoganes, and that reminiscences of such a queen have survived in the myth or legend of Semiramis. According to tradition, Semiramis was a fair courtesan beloved by the king of Assyria, who took her to wife. She won the king's heart so far that she persuaded him to yield up to her the kingdom for five days, and having assumed the sceptre and the royal robes she made a great banquet on the first day, but on the second day she shut up her husband in prison or put him to death and thenceforward reigned alone. Further, it has been shown that the worship of the Persian goddess Anaitis is not only modelled on Astarte worship in general, but corresponds to that particular type of it which was specially associated with the name of Semiramis. The identity of Anaitis and the mythical Semiramis is clearly proved by the circumstance that the great sanctuary of Anaitis at Zela in Pontus was actually built upon a mound of Semiramis; probably the old worship of the Semitic goddess always continued there even after her Semitic name of Semiramis or Astarte had been changed to the Persian name of Anaitis, perhaps in obedience to a decree of the Persian king Artaxerxes II, who first spread the worshop of Anaitis in the west of Asia. It is highly significant, not only that the Sacaean festival was annually held at this ancient seat of the worship of Semiramis or Astarte; but further, that the whole city of Zela was formerly inhabited by sacred slaves and harlots, ruled over by a supreme pontiff, who administered it as a sanctuary rather than as a city. Formerly, we may suppose, this priestly king himself died a violent death at the Sacaea in the character of the divine lover of Semiramis, while the part of the goddess was played by one of the sacred prostitutes. The probability of this is greatly strengthened by the existence of the so-called mound of Semiramis under the sanctuary. For the mounds of Semiramis, which were pointed out all over western

Asia, were said to have been the graves of her lovers whom she buried alive. The tradition ran that the great and lustful queen Semiramis, fearing to contract a lawful marriage lest her husband should deprive her of power, admitted to her bed the handsomest of her soldiers, only, however, to destroy them all afterwards. Now this tradition is one of the surest indications of the identity of the mythical Semiramis with the Babylonian goddess Ishtar or Astarte. For the famous Babylonian epic which recounts the deeds of the hero Gilgamesh tells how, when he clothed himself in royal robes and put his crown on his head, the goddess Ishtar was smitten with love of him and wooed him to be her mate. But Gilgamesh rejected her insidious advances, for he knew the sad fate that had overtaken all her lovers, and he reproached the cruel goddess, saying:

Tammuz, the lover of thy youth,
Thou causest to weep every year.
The bright-coloured *allallu* bird thou didst love.
Thou didst crush him and break his pinions.
In the woods he stands and laments, 'O my pinions!'
Thou didst love the lion of perfect strength,
Seven and seven times thou didst dig pit-falls for him.
Thou didst love the horse that joyed in the fray,
With whip and spur and lash thou didst urge him on.
Thou didst force him on for seven double hours,
Thou didst force him on when wearied and thirsty;
His mother the goddess Silili thou madest weep.
Thou didst also love a shepherd of the flock,
Who continually poured out for thee the libation,
And daily slaughtered kids for thee;
But thou didst smite him, and didst change him into a
    wolf,
So that his own sheep-boys hunted him,
And his own hounds tore him to pieces.

The hero also tells the miserable end of a gardener in the service of the goddess's father. The hapless swain had once been honoured with the love of the goddess, but when she tired of him she changed him into a cripple so that he could not rise from his bed. Therefore Gilgamesh fears to share the fate of all her former lovers and spurns her proffered favours. But it is not merely that the myth of Ishtar thus tallies with the legend of Semiramis; the worship of the goddess was marked by a profligacy which has found its echo in the loose character ascribed by tradition to the queen. Inscriptions, which confirm and supplement the evidence of Herodotus, inform us that Ishtar was served by harlots of three different classes all dedicated to her worship. Indeed, there is reason to think that these women personated the goddess herself, since one of the names given to them is applied also to her.

Thus we can hardly doubt that the mythical Semiramis is substantially a form of Ishtar or Astarte, the great Semitic goddess of love and fertility; and if this is so, we may assume with at least a fair degree of probability that the high pontiff of Zela or his deputy, who played the king of the Sacaea at the sanctuary of Semiramis, perished as one of the unhappy lovers of the goddess, perhaps as Tammuz, whom she caused 'to weep every year'. When he had run his brief meteoric career of pleasure and glory, his bones would be laid in the great mound which covered the mouldering remains of many mortal gods, his predecessors, whom the goddess had honoured with her fatal love.

Here then at the great sanctuary of the goddess in Zela it appears that her myth was regularly translated into action; the story of her love and the death of her divine lover was performed year by year as a sort of mystery-play by men and women who lived for a season and sometimes died in the character of the visionary beings whom they personated. The intention of these sacred dramas, we may be sure, was neither to amuse nor to instruct an idle audience, and as little were they designed to gratify the actors, to whose baser passions they gave the reins for a time. They were solemn rites which mimicked the doings of divine beings, because man fancied that by such mimicry he was able to arrogate to himself the divine functions and to exercise them for the good of his fellows. The operations of nature, to his thinking, were carried on by mythical personages very like himself; and if he could only assimilate himself to them completely he would be able to wield all their powers. This is probably the original motive of most religious dramas or mysteries among rude peoples. The dramas are played, the mysteries are performed, not to teach the spectators the doctrines of their creed, still less to entertain them, but for the purpose of bringing about those natural effects which they represent in mythical disguise; in a word, they are magical ceremonies and their mode of operation is mimicry or sympathy. We shall probably not err in assuming that many myths, which we now know only as myths, had once their counterpart in magic; in other words, that they used to be acted as a means of producing in fact the events which they describe in figurative language. Ceremonies often die out while myths survive, and thus we are left to infer the dead ceremony from the living myth. If myths are, in a sense, the reflections or shadows of men cast upon the clouds, we may say that these reflections continue to be visible in the sky and to inform us of the doings of the men who cast them, long after the men themselves are not only beyond our range of vision but sunk beneath the horizon.

The conclusions which we have reached in regard to the legend of Semiramis and her lovers probably holds good of all the similar tales that were current in antiquity throughout the East; in particular, it may be assumed to apply to the myths of Aphrodite and Adonis in Syria, and of Isis and Osiris in Egypt. If we could trace these stories back to their origin, we might find that in every case a human couple acted year by year the parts of the loving goddess and the dying god. The license accorded to the man who played the dying god at the Sacaea speaks strongly in favour of the hypothesis that before

the incarnate deity was put to a public death he was in all cases allowed, or rather required, to enjoy the embraces of a woman who played the goddess of love. The reason for such an enforced union of the human god and goddess is not hard to divine. If primitive man believes that the growth of the crops can be stimulated by the intercourse of common men and women, what showers of blessings will he not anticipate from the commerce of a pair whom his fancy invests with all the dignity and powers of deities of fertility?

If the Jewish festival of Purim was, as I have attempted to shew, directly descended either from the Sacaea or from some other Semitic festival, of which the central feature was the sacrifice of a man in the character of a god, we should expect to find traces of human sacrifice lingering about it in one or other of those mitigated forms to which I have just referred. This expectation is fully borne out by the facts. For from an early time it has been customary with the Jews at the feast of Purim to burn or otherwise destroy effigies of Haman. The practice was well known under the Roman empire, for in the year 408 AD the emperors Honorius and Theodosius issued a decree commanding the governors of the provinces to take care that the Jews should not burn effigies of Haman on a cross at one of their festivals. We learn from the decree that the custom gave great offence to the Christians, who regarded it as a blasphemous parody of the central mystery of their own religion, little suspecting that it was nothing but a continuation, in a milder form, of a rite that had probably been celebrated in the East long ages before the birth of Christ. Apparently the custom long survived the publication of the edict, for in a form of abjuration which the Greek church imposed on Jewish converts and which seems to date from the tenth century, the renegade is made to speak as follows: 'I curse also those who celebrate the festival of the so-called

Mordecai on the first Sabbath [Saturday] of the Christian fast, and who nail Haman forsooth to the tree, attaching to it the symbol of the cross and burning him along with it, while they heap all sorts of imprecations and curses on the Christians.'

At the Sacaea, then, a man who personated a god or hero of the type of Tammuz or Adonis, enjoyed the favours of a woman, probably a sacred harlot, who represented the great Semitic goddess Ishtar or Astarte; and after he had thus done his part towards securing, by means of sympathetic magic, the revival of plant life in spring, he was put to death. We may suppose that the death of this divine man was mourned over by his worshippers, and especially by women, in much the same fashion as the women of Jerusalem wept for Tammuz at the gate of the temple, and as Syrian damsels mourned the dead Adonis, while the river ran red with his blood. Such rites appear, in fact, to have been common all over western Asia; the particular name of the dying god varied in different places, but in substance the ritual was the same. Fundamentally, the custom was a religious or rather magical ceremony intended to ensure the revival and reproduction of life in spring.

Now, if this interpretation of the Sacaea is correct, it is obvious that one important feature of the ceremony is wanting in the brief notices of the festival that have come down to us. The death of the man-god at the festival is recorded, but nothing is said of his resurrection. Yet if he really personated a being of the Adonis or Attis type, we may feel pretty sure that his dramatic death was followed at a shorter or longer interval by his dramatic revival, just as at the festivals of Attis and Adonis the resurrection of the dead god quickly succeeded to his mimic death. Here, however, a difficulty presents itself. At the Sacaea the man-god died a real, not a mere mimic death; and in ordinary life the resurrection even of a man-god is at least not an every-day occurrence. What was to be done? The man, or rather the god, was undoubtedly dead. How was he to come to life again? Obviously the best, if not the only way, was to set another and living man to support the character of the reviving god, and we may conjecture that this was done. We may suppose that the insignia of royalty which had adorned the dead man were transferred to his successor, who, arrayed in them, would be presented to his rejoicing worshippers as their god come to life again; and by his side would probably be displayed a woman in the character of his divine consort, the goddess Ishtar or Astarte. In favour of this hypothesis it may be observed that it at once furnishes a clear and intelligible explanation of a remarkable feature in the book of Esther which has not yet, so far as I am aware, been adequately elucidated; I mean that apparent duplication of the principal characters to which I have already directed the reader's attention. If I am right, Haman represents the temporary king or mortal god who was put to death at the Sacaea; and his rival Mordecai represents the other temporary king who, on the death of his predecessor, was invested with his royal insignia, and exhibited to the people as the god come to life again. Similarly Vashti, the deposed queen in the narrative, corresponds to the woman who played the part of queen and goddess to the first mock king, the Haman; and her successful rival, Esther or Ishtar, answers to the woman who figured as the divine consort of the second mock king, the Mordecai or Marduk. We have seen that the mock king of the Sacaea did actually possess the right of using the real king's concubines. In the parallel ritual of Adonis the marriage of the goddess with her ill-fated lover was publicly celebrated the day before his mimic death. A clear reminiscence of the time when the relation between Esther and Mordecai was conceived as much more intimate than mere cousinship appears to be preserved in some of the Jewish plays acted at Purim, in which Mordecai appears as the lover of Esther; and this significant indication is confirmed by the teaching of the rabbis that King Ahasuerus never really knew Esther, but that a phantom in her likeness lay with him while the real Esther sat on the lap of Mordecai.

We are now in a position finally to unmask the leading personages in the book of Esther. I have attempted to shew that Haman and Vashti are little more than doubles of Mordecai and Esther, who in turn conceal under a thin disguise the features of Marduk and Ishtar, the great god and goddess of Babylon. But why, the reader may ask, should the divine pair be thus duplicated and the two pairs set in opposition to each other? The answer is suggested by the popular European celebrations of spring. If my interpretation of these customs is right, the contrast between the summer and winter, or between the life and death, which figure in effigy or in the persons of living representatives at the spring ceremonies of our peasantry, is fundamentally a contrast between the dying or dead vegetation of the old and the sprouting vegetation of the

Ritual contests
Contemporary rituals enshrine more ancient contests between protagonists representing the declining energies of the old year, and the youthful vigour of the new. BELOW. Christmas contest in Santo Tomas, Peru. Photo: C.N. Wallis

new year – a contrast which would lose nothing of its point when, as in ancient Rome and Babylon and Persia, the beginning of spring was also the beginning of the new year. In these and in all the ceremonies we have been examining the antagonism is not between powers of a different order, but between the same power viewed in different aspects as old and young; it is, in short, nothing but the eternal and pathetic contrast between youth and age. And as the power or spirit of vegetation is represented in religious ritual and popular custom by a human

Football match, Arsenal v. Stoke, 1971. Photo: Syndication International Ltd, London

pair, whether they be called Ishtar and Tammuz, or Venus and Adonis, or the Queen and King of May, so we may expect to find the old decrepit spirit of the past year personated by one pair, and the fresh young spirit of the new year by another. This, if my hypothesis is right, is the ultimate explanation of the struggle between Haman and Vashti on the one side, and their doubles Mordecai and Esther on the other. In the last analysis both pairs stood for the powers that make for the fertility of plants and perhaps also of animals; but the one pair embodied the failing energies of the past, and the other the vigorous and growing energies of the coming year. Both powers, on my hypothesis, were personified not merely in myth, but in custom; for year by year a human couple undertook to quicken the life of nature by a union in which, as in a microcosm, the lives of tree and plant, of herb and flower, of bird and beast were supposed in some mystic fashion to be summed up. Originally, we may conjecture, such couples exercised their functions for a whole year, on the conclusion of which the male partner – the divine king – was put to death; but in historical times it seems that, as a rule, the human god – the Saturn, Zoganes, Tammuz, or whatever he was called – enjoyed his divine privileges, and discharged his divine duties only for a short part of the year. This curtailment of his reign on earth was probably introduced at the time when the old hereditary divinities or deified kings contrived to shift the most painful part of their duties to a substitute, whether that substitute was a son or a slave or a malefactor. Having to die as a king, it was necessary that the substitute should also live as a king for a season; but the real monarch would naturally restrict within the narrowest limits both of time and of power a reign which, so long as it lasted, necessarily encroached upon and indeed superseded his own. What became of the divine king's female partner, the human goddess who shared his bed and transmitted his beneficent energies to the rest of nature, we cannot say. So far as I am aware, there is little or no evidence that she like him suffered death when her primary function was discharged. The nature of maternity suggests an obvious reason for sparing her a little longer, till that mysterious law, which links together woman's life with the changing aspects of the nightly sky, had been fulfilled by the birth of an infant god, who should in his turn, reared perhaps by her tender care, grow up to live and die for the world.

Conclusion

We may now sum up the general results of the enquiry which we have pursued in the present chapter. We have found evidence that festivals of the type of the Saturnalia, characterized by an inversion of social ranks and the sacrifice of a man in the character of a god, were at one time held in the ancient world from Italy to Babylon. Such festivals seem to date from an early age in the history of agriculture, when people lived in small communities, each presided over by a sacred or divine king, whose primary duty was to secure the orderly succession of the seasons, the fertility of the earth, and the fecundity both of cattle and of women. Associated with him was his wife or other female consort, with whom he performed some of the necessary ceremonies, and who therefore shared his divine character. Originally his term of office appears to have been limited to a year, on the conclusion of which he was put to death; but in time he contrived by force or craft to extend his reign and sometimes to procure a substitute, who after a short and more or less nominal tenure of the crown was slain in his stead. At first the substitute for the divine father was probably the divine son, but afterwards this rule was no longer insisted on, and still later the growth of a humane feeling demanded that the victim should always be a condemned criminal. In this advanced stage of degeneration it is no wonder if the light of divinity suffered eclipse, and many should fail to detect the god in the malefactor. Yet the downward career of fallen deity does not stop here; even a criminal comes to be thought too good to personate a god on the gallows or in the fire; and then there is nothing left but to make up a more or less grotesque effigy, and so to hang, burn, or otherwise destroy the god in the person of this sorry representative.

If there is any truth in the analysis of the Saturnalia and kindred festivals which I have now brought to a close, it seems to point to a remarkable homogeneity of civilization throughout southern Europe and western Asia in prehistoric times. How far such homogeneity of civilization may be taken as evidence of homogeneity of race is a question for the ethnologist; it does not concern us here. But without discussing it, I may remind the reader that in the far east of Asia we have met with temporary kings whose magical functions and intimate relation to agriculture stand out in the clearest light; while India furnishes examples of kings who have regularly been obliged to sacrifice themselves at the end of a term of years. All these things appear to hang together; all of them may, perhaps, be regarded as the shattered remnants of a uniform zone of religion and society which at a remote era belted the Old World from the Mediterranean to the Pacific. Whether that was so or not, I may at least claim to have made it probable that if the King of the Wood at Aricia lived and died as an incarnation of a sylvan deity, the functions he thus discharged were by no means singular, and that for the nearest parallel to them we need not go beyond the bounds of Italy, where the divine king Saturn – the god of the sown and sprouting seed – was annually slain in the person of a human representative at his ancient festival.

Part 7. Balder the Beautiful

One last issue remains to be explained: why did the prospective priest of Nemi have to break a branch from the sacred tree of the grove before killing his predecessor?

In Taboo and the Perils of the Soul, *Frazer discussed possible absences of the soul from the body when they are viewed as a danger to the life of the individual concerned. However, the soul may also be absent for safe-keeping. Thus, the soul of the Norse god Balder was kept in the mistletoe, which therefore was the only thing that could kill him. We already know the King of the Wood to be the impersonation of the oak god Jupiter, and Frazer now suggests that the branch his successor had to pick before killing him was a mistletoe that grew on the sacred oak in the grove and contained his soul.*

At this point Frazer adds two further taboos to those affecting kings and priests – they may not touch the earth, nor may they see the sun, lest their sacred charge be spilled. Thus we have an analogy between the King of the Wood, whose life was ruled by these taboos, and the mistletoe, suspended as it is between heaven and earth.

Balder's remains were laid on a ship that was then set on fire and launched at sea. This burning of the god leads Frazer to a consideration of fire-festivals, and he shows that originally human beings or animals were sometimes burned in the fires, in order to protect crops and animals from ills that might befall them. In other words such fires were a manner of expelling evils. Thus we return by another route – Balder's burial and the fire-festivals – to one of the principal themes of The Golden Bough, *that is, to magical rites for the prosperity of the crops, one of which was the killing of the King of the Wood at Nemi.*

In myths the world over, the lives of gods, plants and men form a continuous chain of mutual interdependence. In the myth of Balder, the life of the god depends on the mistletoe. Conversely, plants may depend for their life on the intervention of the gods. This 20th-century Navaho sand painting depicts a mythical scene in which the supernatural Rainboy and Raingirl walk around a lake from which spring the four sacred plants of the Navajo. The growth of these plants depends on the sun and rain, which only Rainboy and Raingirl can bring, thereby ensuring the life of both plants and men. Wheelwright Museum, Santa Fe, USA

1. Between Heaven and Earth

Not to Touch the Earth, not to See the Sun
We have travelled far since we turned our backs on Nemi and set forth in quest of the secret of the Golden Bough. We now enter on the last stage of our long journey. The reader who has had the patience to follow the enquiry thus far may remember that at the outset two questions were proposed for answer: Why had the priest of Aricia to slay his predecessor? And why, before doing so, had he to pluck the Golden Bough? Of these two questions the first has now been answered. The priest of Aricia, if I am right, was one of those sacred kings or human divinities on whose life the welfare of the community and even the course of nature in general are believed to be intimately dependent. It does not appear that the subjects or worshippers of such a spiritual potentate form to themselves any very clear notion of the exact relationship in which they stand to him; probably their ideas on the point are vague and fluctuating, and we should err if we attempted to define the relationship with logical precision. All that the people know, or rather imagine, is that somehow they themselves, their cattle, and their crops are mysteriously bound up with their divine king, so that according as he is well or ill the community is healthy or sickly, the flocks and herds thrive or languish with disease, and the fields yield an abundant or a scanty harvest. The worst evil which they can conceive of is the natural death of their ruler, whether he succumb to sickness or old age, for in the opinion of his followers such a death would entail the most disastrous consequences on themselves and their possessions; fatal epidemics would sweep away man and beast, the earth would refuse her in-

crease, nay the very frame of nature itself might be dissolved. To guard against these catastrophes it is necessary to put the king to death while he is still in the full bloom of his divine manhood, in order that his sacred life, transmitted in unabated force to his successor, may renew its youth, and thus by successive transmissions through a perpetual line of vigorous

Divine and royal persons
Divine and royal persons are raised off the ground and sheltered from the sun lest their sacred charge be spilled.
OPPOSITE. Our Lady of the Immaculate Conception at the Wititi festival, 8th December, in the Peruvian highlands. Photo: C.N. Wallis
BELOW. Chieftain and his wife from Sierra Leone. Pitt Rivers Museum, University of Oxford. Photo: Rattray

incarnations may remain eternally fresh and young, a pledge and security that men and animals shall in like manner renew their youth by a perpetual succession of generations, and that seedtime and harvest, and summer and winter, and rain and sunshine shall never fail. That, if my conjecture is right, was why the priest of Aricia, the King of the Wood at Nemi, had regularly to perish by the sword of his successor.

But we have still to ask, What was the Golden Bough? and why had each candidate for the Arician priesthood to pluck it before he could slay the priest? These questions I will now try to answer.

It will be well to begin by noticing two of those rules or taboos by which, as we have seen, the life of divine kings or priests is regulated. The first of the rules to which I desire to call the reader's attention is that the divine personage may not touch the ground with his foot. This rule was observed by the supreme pontiff of the Zapotecs in Mexico; he profaned his sanctity if he so much as touched the ground with his foot. Montezuma, emperor of Mexico, never set foot on the ground; he was always carried on the shoulders of noblemen, and if he lighted anywhere they laid rich tapestry for him to walk upon. For the Mikado of Japan to touch the ground with his foot was a shameful degradation; indeed, in the sixteenth century, it was enough to deprive him of his office. Outside his palace he was carried on men's shoulders: within it he walked on exquisitely wrought mats.

Apparently holiness, magical virtue, taboo, or whatever we may call that mysterious quality which is supposed to pervade sacred or tabooed persons, is conceived by the primitive philosopher as a physical substance or fluid, with which the sacred man is charged just as a Leyden jar is charged with electricity; and exactly as the electricity in the jar can be discharged by contact with a good conductor, so the holiness or

magical virtue in the man can be discharged and drained away by contact with the earth, which on this theory serves as an excellent conductor for the magical fluid. Hence in order to preserve the charge from running to waste, the sacred or tabooed personage must be carefully prevented from touching the ground; in electrical language he must be insulated, if he is not to be emptied of the precious substance or fluid with which he, as a vial, is filled to the brim. And in many cases apparently the insulation of the tabooed person is recommended as a precaution not merely for his own sake but for the sake of others; for since the virtue of holiness or taboo is, so to say, a powerful explosive which the smallest touch may detonate, it is necessary in the interest of the general safety to keep it within narrow bounds, lest breaking out it should blast, blight, and destroy whatever it comes into contact with.

But things as well as persons are often charged with the mysterious quality of holiness or taboo; hence it frequently becomes necessary for similar reasons to guard them also from coming into contact with the ground, lest they should in like manner be drained of their valuable properties and be reduced to mere commonplace material objects, empty husks from which the good grain has been eliminated. Thus, for example, the most sacred object of the Arunta tribe in Central Australia is, or rather used to be, a pole about twenty feet high, which is completely smeared with human blood, crowned with an imitation of a human head, and set up on the ground where the final initiatory ceremonies of young men are performed. A young gum-tree is chosen to form the pole, and it must be cut down and transported in such a way that it does not touch the earth till it is erected in its place on the holy ground. Apparently the pole represents some famous ancestor of the olden time.

Sometimes magical implements and remedies are supposed to lose their virtue by contact with

the ground, the volatile essence with which they are impregnated being no doubt drained off into the earth. Thus in the Boulia district of Queensland the magical bone, which the native sorcerer points at his victim as a means of killing him, is never by any chance allowed to touch the earth. The wives of rajahs in Macassar, a district of southern Celebes, pride themselves on their luxuriant tresses and are at great pains to oil and preserve them. Should the hair begin to grow thin, the lady resorts to many devices to stay the ravages of time; among other things she applies to her locks a fat extracted from crocodiles and venomous snakes. The unguent is believed to be very efficacious, but during its application the woman's feet may not come into contact with the ground, or all the benefit of the nostrum would be lost.

The second rule to be here noted is that the sun may not shine upon the divine person. This rule was observed both by the Mikado and by the pontiff of the Zapotecs. The latter 'was looked upon as a god whom the earth was not worthy to hold, nor the sun to shine upon'. The Japanese would not allow that the Mikado should expose his sacred person to the open air, and the sun was not thought worthy to shine on his head. The Indians of Granada, in South America, 'kept those who were to be rulers or commanders, whether men or women, locked up for several years when they were children, some of them seven years, and this so close that they were not to see the sun, for if they should happen to see it they forfeited their lordship, eating certain sorts

Taboos of holiness are paralleled by taboos of pollution
TOP. At a Malay wedding the bridal couple are prince and princess for a day. They sit in mock royal state, raised from the ground and sheltered from the sun.
LEFT. In a Malay burial procession neither sun nor earth are contaminated by contact with the corpse. Photos: William D. Wilder

of food appointed; and those who were their keepers at certain times went into their retreat or prison and scourged them severely'. So, too, the heir to the kingdom of Sogamoso, before succeeding to the crown, had to fast for seven years in the temple, being shut up in the dark and not allowed to see the sun or light. The prince who was to become Inca of Peru had to fast for a month without seeing light.

Acarnanian peasants tell of a handsome prince called Sunless, who would die if he saw the sun. So he lived in an underground palace on the site of the ancient Oeniadae, but at night he came forth and crossed the river to visit a famous enchantress who dwelt in a castle on the further bank. She was loth to part with him every night long before the sun was up, and as he turned a deaf ear to all her entreaties to linger, she hit upon the device of cutting the throats of all the cocks in the neighbourhood. So the prince, whose ear had learned to expect the shrill clarion of the birds as the signal of the growing light, tarried too long, and hardly had he reached the ford when the sun rose over the Aetolian mountains, and its fatal beams fell on him before he could regain his dark abode.

The Seclusion of Girls at Puberty

Now it is remarkable that the foregoing two rules – not to touch the ground and not to see the sun – are observed either separately or conjointly by girls at puberty in many parts of the world. Thus amongst the negroes of Loango girls at puberty are confined in separate huts, and they may not touch the ground with any part of their bare body. Among the Zulus and kindred tribes of South Africa, when the first signs of puberty shew themselves 'while a girl is walking, gathering wood, or working in the field, she runs to the river and hides herself among the reeds for the day, so as not to be seen by men. She covers her head carefully with her blanket that the sun may not shine on it and shrivel her

up into a withered skeleton, as would result from exposure to the sun's beams. After dark she returns to her home and is secluded' in a hut for some time. During her seclusion, which lasts for about a fortnight, neither she nor the girls who wait upon her may drink any milk, lest the cattle should die. And should she be overtaken by the first flow while she is in the fields, she must, after hiding in the bush, scrupulously avoid all pathways in returning home.

When symptoms of puberty appeared on a girl for the first time, the Guaranis of Southern Brazil, on the borders of Paraguay, used to sew her up in her hammock, leaving only a small opening in it to allow her to breathe. In this condition, wrapt up and shrouded like a corpse, she was kept for two or three days or so long as the symptoms lasted, and during this time she had to observe a most rigorous fast. After that she was entrusted to a matron, who cut the girl's hair and enjoined her to abstain most strictly from eating flesh of any kind until her hair should be grown long enough to hide her ears. Meanwhile the diviners drew omens of her future character from the various birds or animals that flew past or crossed her path. If they saw a parrot, they would say she was a chatterbox; if an owl, she was lazy and useless for domestic labours, and so on.

In Cambodia a girl at puberty is put to bed under a mosquito curtain, where she should stay

Need-fires and disaster
The custom of lighting fires at times of extreme need (hence the expression need-fire) is recorded in most parts of Europe from the early Middle Ages. Their purpose was to avert whatever form of evil had stricken the community. It was a last resort, a final effort of self-help. OPPOSITE. In Bruegel's painting *The Triumph of Death*, the last resort has failed. Death unhindered devours all, and the need-fires, their smoke blackening the sky, merely heighten the calamity, and the defeat of human resources. Museo del Prado, Madrid

a hundred days. Usually, however, four, five, ten, or twenty days are thought enough; and even this, in a hot climate and under the close meshes of the curtain, is sufficiently trying. According to another account, a Cambodian maiden at puberty is said to 'enter into the shade'. During her retirement, which, according to the rank and position of her family, may last any time from a few days to several years, she has to observe a number of rules, such as not to be seen by a strange man, not to eat flesh or fish, and so on. She goes nowhere, not even to the pagoda. But this state of seclusion is discontinued during eclipses; at such times she goes forth and pays her devotions to the monster who is supposed to cause eclipses by catching the heavenly bodies between his teeth. This permission to break her rule of retirement and appear abroad during an eclipse seems to shew how literally the injunction is interpreted which forbids maidens entering on womanhood to look upon the sun.

According to the Talmud, if a woman at the beginning of her period passes between two men, she thereby kills one of them; if she passes between them towards the end of her period, she only causes them to quarrel violently. Maimonides tells us that down to his time it was a common custom in the East to keep women at their periods in a separate house and to burn everything on which they had trodden; a man

The tree of life

OPPOSITE. Christ on the cross amid vine scrolls in the apse of San Clemente, Rome. Photo: Scala

Faithful cross among all others
one and only holy tree;
none in foliage, none in blossom,
none in fruit thy peer may be.
Venantius Fortunatus

who spoke with such a woman or who was merely exposed to the same wind that blew over her, became thereby unclean. The beliefs and superstitions of this sort that prevail among the western tribes of the great Déné or Tinneh stock, to which the Chippeways belong, have been well described by an experienced missionary. Prominent among the ceremonial rites of these Indians, he says, 'are the observances peculiar to the fair sex, and many of them are remarkably analogous to those practised by the Hebrew women, so much so that, were it not savouring of profanity, the ordinances of the Déné ritual code might be termed a new edition "revised and considerably augmented" of the Mosaic ceremonial law'.

The philosophic student of human nature will observe, or learn, without surprise that ideas thus deeply ingrained in the savage mind reappear at a more advanced stage of society in those elaborate codes which have been drawn up for the guidance of certain peoples by lawgivers who claim to have derived the rules they inculcate from the direct inspiration of the deity. However we may explain it, the resemblance which exists between the earliest official utterances of the deity and the ideas of savages is unquestionably close and remarkable; whether it be, as some suppose, that God communed face to face with man in those early days, or, as others maintain, that man mistook his wild and wandering thoughts for a revelation from heaven. Be that as it may, certain it is that the natural uncleanness of woman at her monthly periods is a conception which has occurred, or been revealed, with singular unanimity to several ancient legislators among whom are the Hindoo lawgiver Manu, Zoroaster and Moses.

Thus the object of secluding women at menstruation is to neutralize the dangerous influences which are supposed to emanate from them at such times. That the danger is believed to be especially great at the first menstruation appears

The seclusion of girls at puberty
The seclusion of girls at puberty has in some societies taken unusual forms. Among the Tunabo of Columbia, girls are required to cover their heads with an extraordinary leaf mask, which formerly was worn for three years. The picture shows a secluded girl participating in a ritual before she finally removes her mask. Photo: Ann Osborn

from the unusual precautions taken to isolate girls at this crisis. Two of these precautions have been illustrated above, namely, the rules that the girl may not touch the ground nor see the sun. The general effect of these rules is to keep her suspended, so to say, between heaven and earth. She is rendered harmless by being, in electrical language, insulated. But the precautions thus taken to isolate or insulate the girl are dictated by a regard for her own safety as well as for the safety of others. For it is thought that she herself would suffer if she were to neglect the prescribed regimen.

The same explanation applies to the observance of the same rules by divine kings and priests. The uncleanness, as it is called, of girls at puberty and the sanctity of holy men do not, to the primitive mind, differ materially from each other. They are only different manifestations of the same mysterious energy which, like energy in general, is in itself neither good nor bad, but becomes beneficent or maleficent according to its application. Accordingly, if, like girls at puberty, divine personages may neither touch the ground nor see the sun, the reason is, on the one hand, a fear lest their divinity might, at contact with earth or heaven, discharge itself with fatal violence on either; and, on the other hand, an apprehension that the divine being, thus drained of his ethereal virtue, might thereby be incapacitated for the future performance of those magical functions, upon the proper discharge of which the safety of the people and even of the world is believed to hang. Thus the rules in question fall under the head of the taboos which we examined in the second part of this work; they are intended to preserve the life of the divine person and with it the life of his subjects and worshippers. Nowhere, it is thought, can his precious yet dangerous life be at once so safe and so harmless as when it is neither in heaven nor in earth, but, as far as possible, suspended between the two.

2. The Myth of Balder

A deity whose life might in a sense be said to be neither in heaven nor on earth but between the two, was the Norse Balder, the good and beautiful god, the son of the great god Odin, and himself the wisest, mildest, best beloved of all the immortals. The story of his death, as it is told in the younger or prose *Edda*, runs thus. Once on a time Balder dreamed heavy dreams which seemed to forebode his death. Thereupon the gods held a council and resolved to make him secure against every danger. So the goddess Frigg took an oath from fire and water, iron and all metals, stones and earth, from trees, sicknesses and poisons, and from all four-footed beasts, birds, and creeping things, that they would not hurt Balder. When this was done Balder was deemed invulnerable; so the gods amused themselves by setting him in their midst, while some shot at him, others hewed at him and others threw stones at him. But whatever they did, nothing could hurt him; and at this they were all glad. Only Loki, the mischief-maker, was displeased, and he went in the guise of an old woman to Frigg, who told him that the weapons of the gods could not wound Balder, since she had made them all swear not to hurt him. Then Loki asked, 'Have all things sworn to spare Balder?' She answered, 'East of Walhalla grows a plant called mistletoe; it seemed to me too young to swear.' So Loki went and pulled the mistletoe and took it to the assembly of the gods. There he found the blind god Hother standing at the outside of the circle. Loki asked him, 'Why do you not shoot at Balder?' Hother answered, 'Because I do not see where he stands; besides I have no weapon.' Then said Loki, 'Do like the rest and shew Balder honour, as they all

do. I will shew you where he stands, and do you shoot at him with this twig.' Hother took the mistletoe and threw it at Balder, as Loki directed him. The mistletoe struck Balder and pierced him through and through, and he fell down dead. And that was the greatest misfortune that ever befell gods and men. For a while the gods stood speechless, then they lifted up their voices and wept bitterly. They took Balder's body and brought it to the sea-shore. There stood Balder's ship; it was called Ringhorn, and was the hugest of all ships. The gods wished to launch the ship and to burn Balder's body on it, but the ship would not stir. So they sent for a giantess called Hyrrockin. She came riding on a wolf and gave the ship such a push that fire flashed from the rollers and all the earth shook. Then Balder's body was taken and placed on the funeral pile upon his ship. When his wife Nanna saw that, her heart burst for sorrow and she died. So she was laid on the funeral pile with her husband, and fire was put to it. Balder's horse, too, with all its trappings, was burned on the pile.

In the older or poetic *Edda* the tragic tale of Balder is hinted at rather than told at length. Among the visions which the Norse Sibyl sees and describes in the weird prophecy known as the *Voluspa* is one of the fatal mistletoe. 'I behold', says she, 'Fate looming for Balder, Woden's son, the bloody victim. There stands the Mistletoe, slender and delicate, blooming high above the ground. Out of this shoot, so slender to look on, there shall grow a harmful fateful shaft. Hod shall shoot it, but Frigga in Fen-hall shall weep over the woe of Wal-hall.' Yet looking far into the future the Sibyl sees a brighter vision of a new heaven and a new

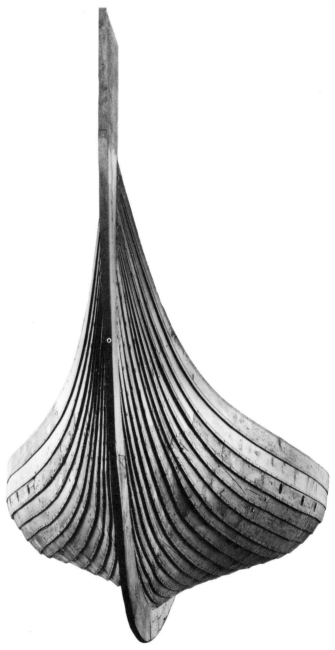

Balder's ship burial: the reality behind the myth

Different types of evidence can be collated to show that myths often reflect actual practices. Thus, both Balder, according to the *Edda* – an old Norse epic – and the old King of the Geats, according to the Anglo-Saxon epic *Beowulf*, were after their death laid on a ship, which was then set alight and launched on the sea. Burials of this kind were actually performed, although the only ships that survived were those hidden under mounds, for instance at Sutton Hoo, 7th century, and at Gokstad, Norway, 9th century.

LEFT. The hulk of the ship excavated at Sutton Hoo may be clearly distinguished in the ground. The burial chamber was in the centre of the ship. British Museum, London

ABOVE. Reconstruction of the Gokstad ship, in which a Norwegian prince was buried. Copyright University Museum of National Antiquities, Oslo, Norway

earth, where the fields unsown shall yield their increase and all sorrows shall be healed; then Balder will come back to dwell in Odin's mansions of bliss, in a hall brighter than the sun, shingled with gold, where the righteous shall live in joy for ever more.

Writing about the end of the twelfth century, the old Danish historian Saxo Grammaticus tells the story of Balder in a form which professes to be historical. According to him, Balder and Hother were rival suitors for the hand of Nanna, daughter of Gewar, King of Norway. Now Balder was a demigod and common steel could not wound his sacred body. The two rivals encountered each other in a terrific battle, and though Odin and Thor and the rest of the gods fought for Balder, yet was he defeated and fled away, and Hother married the princess. Nevertheless Balder took heart of grace and again met Hother in a stricken field. But he fared even worse than before; for Hother dealt him a deadly wound with a magic sword, which he had received from Miming, the satyr of the woods; and after lingering three days in pain Balder died of his hurt and was buried with royal honours in a barrow.

Whether he was a real or merely a mythical personage, Balder was worshipped in Norway. On one of the bays of the beautiful Sogne Fiord, which penetrates far into the depths of the solemn Norwegian mountains, with their sombre pine-forests and their lofty cascades dissolving into spray before they reach the dark water of the fiord far below, Balder had a great sanctuary. It was called Balder's Grove. A palisade enclosed the hallowed ground, and within it stood a spacious temple with the images of many gods, but none of them was worshipped with such devotion as Balder. So great was the awe with which the heathen regarded the place that no man might harm another there, nor steal his cattle, nor defile himself with women. But women cared for the images of the gods in the temple; they warmed them at the fire, anointed them with oil, and dried them with cloths.

Whatever may be thought of an historical kernel underlying a mythical husk in the legend of Balder, the details of the story suggest that it belongs to that class of myths which have been dramatized in ritual, or, to put it otherwise, which have been performed as magical ceremonies for the sake of producing those natural effects which they describe in figurative language. A myth is never so graphic and precise in its details as when it is, so to speak, the book of the words which are spoken and acted by the performers of the sacred rite. That the Norse story of Balder was a myth of this sort will become probable if we can prove that ceremonies resembling the incidents in the tale have been performed by Norsemen and other European peoples. Now the main incidents in the tale are two – first, the pulling of the mistletoe, and second, the death and burning of the god; and both of them may perhaps be found to have had their counterparts in yearly rites observed, whether separately or conjointly, by people in various parts of Europe. These rites will be described and discussed in the following chapters. We shall begin with the annual festivals of fire and shall reserve the pulling of the mistletoe for consideration later on.

3. The Fire-Festivals of Europe

All over Europe the peasants have been accustomed from time immemorial to kindle bonfires on certain days of the year, and to dance round or leap over them. Customs of this kind can be traced back on historical evidence to the Middle Ages, and their analogy to similar customs observed in antiquity goes with strong internal evidence to prove that their origin must be sought in a period long prior to the spread of Christianity. Indeed the earliest proof of their observance in Northern Europe is furnished by the attempts made by Christian synods in the eighth century to put them down as heathenish rites. Not uncommonly effigies are burned in these fires, or a pretence is made of burning a living person in them; and there are grounds for believing that anciently human beings were actually burned on these occasions. A general survey of the customs in question will bring out the traces of human sacrifice, and will serve at the same time to throw light on their meaning.

The seasons of the year when these bonfires are most commonly lit are spring and midsummer; but in some places they are kindled also at the end of autumn or during the course of the winter, particularly on Hallowe'en (the thirty-first of October), Christmas Day, and the Eve of Twelfth Day. We shall consider them in the

Paganism and Christianity in the high Andes
Both pagan and Christian elements mingle in the spring festivals of the high Andes. When the animals are giving birth and rain is desired for the pasture, offerings to the gods are burned in sacred fires.
LEFT. As the fire burns, a young llama is ceremonially wreathed with flowers and sprinkled with chicha (maize beer).
RIGHT. The offerings to the gods include chicha, sugarcane spirit (in a red-wine bottle), maize, animal fat and coca leaves (in the bag).

order in which they occur in the calendar year. The earliest of them is the winter festival of the Eve of Twelfth Day (the fifth of January); but as it has been already described in an earlier part of this work we shall pass it over here and begin with the fire-festivals of spring, which usually fall on the first Sunday of Lent (*Quadragesima* or *Invocavit*), Easter Eve, and May Day. The custom of kindling bonfires on the first Sunday in Lent has prevailed in Belgium, the north of France, and many parts of Germany.

It seems hardly possible to separate from these bonfires, kindled on the first Sunday in Lent, the fires in which, about the same season, the effigy called Death is burned as part of the ceremony of 'carrying out Death'. We have seen that at Spachendorf, in Austrian Silesia, on the morning of Rupert's Day (Shrove Tuesday?), a straw-man, dressed in a fur coat and a fur cap, is laid in a hole outside the village and there burned, and that while it is blazing every one seeks to snatch a fragment of it, which he fastens to a branch of the highest tree in his garden or buries in his field, believing that this will make the crops to grow better. The ceremony is known as the 'burying of Death'. Even when the straw-man is not designated as Death, the meaning of the observance is probably the same; for the name Death, as I have tried to shew, does not express the original intention of the ceremony. At Cobern in the Eifel Mountains the lads make up a straw-man on Shrove Tuesday. The effigy is formally tried and accused of having perpetrated all the thefts that have been committed in the neighbourhood throughout the year. Being condemned to death, the straw-man is led through the village, shot, and burned upon a pyre. They dance round the blazing pile, and the last bride must leap over it.

Another occasion, on which these fire-

Libations of chicha are cast to the gods.

For good measure, a cross, sign of the Christian god, is decked with flowers to restore its protective powers for the coming year. Photos: C.N. Wallis

festivals are held is Easter Eve, the Saturday before Easter Sunday. On that day it has been customary in Catholic countries to extinguish all the lights in the churches, and then to make a new fire, sometimes with flint and steel, sometimes with a burning-glass. In parts of Germany a bonfire is lit from this new fire, and some of the sticks are kept to protect houses from lightning and fields from blight and hail. Sometimes an effigy called Judas is burnt in the bonfire.

Usages of this kind are not confined to the Latin church, but are common in the Greek church also. At Athens the new fire is kindled in the cathedral at midnight on Holy Saturday. A dense crowd with unlit candles in their hands fills the square in front of the cathedral; the king, the archbishop, and the highest dignitaries of the church, arrayed in their gorgeous robes, occupy a platform; and at the exact moment of the resurrection the bells ring out, and the whole square bursts as by magic into a blaze of light. Theoretically all the candles are lit from the sacred new fire in the cathedral, but practically it may be suspected that the matches which bear the name of Lucifer have some share in the sudden illumination. Effigies of Judas used to be burned at Athens on Easter Saturday, but the custom has been forbidden by the Government. However, firing goes on more or less continuously all over the city both on Easter Saturday and Easter Sunday, and the cartridges used on this occasion are not always blank. The shots are aimed at Judas, but sometimes they miss him and hit other people. Outside of Athens the practice of burning Judas in effigy still survives in some places. For example, in Cos a straw image of the traitor is made on Easter Day, and after being hung up and shot at it is burned. A similar custom appears to prevail at Thebes; it used to be observed by the Macedonian peasantry, and it is still kept up at Therapia, a fashionable summer resort of Constantinople.

Kindling the new fire
The Patriarch of Jerusalem emerges from the Church of the Holy Sepulchre, built over Christ's tomb, with the new fire of Easter Night. Photo: Christina Gascoigne

In spite of the thin cloak of Christianity thrown over these customs by representing the new fire as an emblem of Christ and the figure burned in it as an effigy of Judas, we can hardly doubt that both practices are of pagan origin. Neither of them has the authority of Christ or of his disciples; but both of them have abundant analogies in popular custom and superstition.

In the central Highlands of Scotland, in Wales and Ireland bonfires, known as the Beltane fires, were formerly kindled with great ceremony on the first of May, and the traces of human sacrifices at them were particularly clear and unequivocal. The custom of lighting the bonfires lasted in various places far into the eighteenth century, and the descriptions of the ceremony by writers of that period present such a curious and interesting picture of ancient heathendom surviving in our own country that I will reproduce one account in the words of its author,

John Ramsay, laird of Ochtertyre, near Crieff, the patron of Burns and the friend of Sir Walter Scott. Ramsay says: 'But the most considerable of the Druidical festivals is that of Beltane, or May-day, which was lately observed in some parts of the Highlands with extraordinary ceremonies. Of later years it is chiefly attended to by young people, persons advanced in years considering it as inconsistent with their gravity to give it any countenance. Yet a number of circumstances relative to it may be collected from tradition, or the conversation of very old people, who witnessed this feast in their youth, when the ancient rites were better observed.

'This festival is called in Gaelic *Beal-tene* – i.e., the fire of Bel. . . . Like the other public worship of the Druids, the Beltane feast seems to have been performed on hills or eminences. They thought it degrading to him whose temple is the universe, to suppose that he would dwell in any house made with hands. Their sacrifices were therefore offered in the open air, frequently upon the tops of hills, where they were presented with the grandest views of nature, and were nearest the seat of warmth and order. And, according to tradition, such was the manner of celebrating this festival in the Highlands within the last hundred years. But since the decline of superstition, it has been celebrated by the people of each hamlet on some hill or rising ground around which their cattle were pasturing. Thither the young folks repaired in the morning, and cut a trench, on the summit of which a seat of turf was formed for the company. And in the middle a pile of wood or other fuel was placed, which of old they kindled with *tein-eigin* – i.e., forced-fire or *need-fire*. Although, for many years past, they have been contented with common fire, yet we shall now describe the process, because it will hereafter appear that recourse is still had to the *tein-eigin* upon extraordinary emergencies.

'The night before, all the fires in the country were carefully extinguished, and next morning the materials for exciting this sacred fire were prepared. The most primitive method seems to be that which was used in the islands of Skye, Mull, and Tiree. A well-seasoned plank of oak was procured, in the midst of which a hole was bored. A wimble of the same timber was then applied, the end of which they fitted to the hole. But in some parts of the mainland the machinery was different. They used a frame of green wood, of a square form, in the centre of which was an axle-tree. In some places three times three persons, in others three times nine, were required for turning round by turns the axle-tree or wimble. If any of them had been guilty of murder, adultery, theft, or other atrocious crime, it was imagined either that the fire would not kindle, or that it would be devoid of its usual virtue. So soon as any sparks were emitted by means of the violent friction, they applied a species of agaric which grows on old birch-trees, and is very combustible. This fire had the appearance of being immediately derived from heaven, and manifold were the virtues ascribed to it. They esteemed it a preservative against witchcraft, and a sovereign remedy against malignant diseases, both in the human species and in cattle; and by it the strongest poisons were supposed to have their nature changed.

'After kindling the bonfire with the *tein-eigin* the company prepared their victuals. And as soon as they had finished their meal, they amused themselves a while in singing and dancing round the fire. Towards the close of the entertainment, the person who officiated as master of the feast produced a large cake baked with eggs and scalloped round the edge, called *am bonnach beal-tine* – i.e., the Beltane cake. It was divided into a number of pieces, and distributed in great form to the company. There was one particular piece which whoever got was called *cailleach beal-tine* – i.e., the Beltane *carline*, a term of great reproach. Upon his being known, part of the company laid hold of him and made a show of putting him into the fire; but the majority interposing, he was rescued. And in some places they laid him flat on the ground, making as if they would quarter him. Afterwards, he was pelted with egg-shells, and retained the odious appellation during the whole year. And while the feast was fresh in people's memory, they affected to speak of the *cailleach beal-tine* as dead.'

But the season at which these fire-festivals have been mostly generally held all over Europe is the summer solstice, that is Midsummer Eve (the twenty-third of June) or Midsummer Day (the twenty-fourth of June). A faint tinge of Christianity has been given to them by naming Midsummer Day after St John the Baptist, but we cannot doubt that the celebration dates from a time long before the beginning of our era. The summer solstice, or Midsummer Day, is the great turning-point in the sun's career, when, after climbing higher and higher day by day in the sky, the luminary stops and thenceforth retraces his steps down the heavenly road. Such a moment could not but be regarded with anxiety by primitive man. Midsummer fires have prevailed all over this quarter of the globe, from Ireland on the west to Russia on the east, and from Norway and Sweden on the north to Spain and Greece on the south. According to a mediaeval writer, the three great features of the midsummer celebration were the bonfires, the procession with torches round the fields, and the custom of rolling a wheel. He tells us that boys burned bones and filth of various kinds to make a foul smoke, and that the smoke drove away certain noxious dragons which at this time, excited by the summer heat, copulated in the air and poisoned the wells and rivers by dropping their seed into them; and he explains the custom of trundling a wheel to mean that the sun, having now reached the highest point in the ecliptic, begins thenceforward to descend.

Though the pagan origin of the custom may be regarded as certain, the Catholic Church threw a Christian cloak over it by boldly declaring that the bonfires were lit in token of the general rejoicing at the birth of the Baptist, who opportunely came into the world at the solstice of summer, just as his greater successor did at the solstice of winter; so that the whole year might be said to revolve on the golden hinges of these two great birthdays.

The custom of kindling bonfires on Midsummer Day or on Midsummer Eve is widely spread among the Mohammedan peoples of North Africa, particularly in Morocco and Algeria; it is common both to the Berbers and to many of the Arabs or Arabic-speaking tribes. In these countries Midsummer Day (the twenty-fourth of June, Old Style) is called *l 'ánsăra*. The fires are lit in the courtyards, at cross-roads, in the fields, and sometimes on the threshing-floors. Plants which in burning give out a thick smoke and an aromatic smell are much sought after for fuel on these occasions; among the plants used for the purpose are giant-fennel, thyme, rue, chervil-seed, camomile, geranium, and penny-royal. People expose themselves, and especially their children, to the smoke, and drive it towards the orchards and the crops. Also they leap across the fires; in some places everybody ought to repeat the leap seven times. Moreover they take burning brands from the fires and carry them through the houses in order to fumigate them. They pass things through the fire, and bring the sick into contact with it, while they utter prayers for their recovery. The ashes of the bonfires are also reputed to possess beneficial properties; hence in some places people rub their hair or their bodies with them.

The celebration of a midsummer festival by Mohammedan peoples is particularly remarkable, because the Mohammedan calendar, being purely lunar and uncorrected by intercalation, necessarily takes no note of festivals which

Wheels and the sun
Symbols and reality of the midsummer fire-festivals are
combined in this prehistoric ceremonial chariot from
Trundholm, Denmark. Nationalmuseet, Copenhagen

occupy fixed points in the solar year; all strictly
Mohammedan feasts, being pinned to the
moon, slide gradually with that luminary
through the whole period of the earth's revolution about the sun. This fact of itself shows
that among the Mohammedan peoples of
Northern Africa, as among the Christian
peoples of Europe, the midsummer festival is
quite independent of the religion which the
people publicly profess, and is a relic of a far
older paganism.

Among the heathen forefathers of the European peoples the most popular and widespread
fire-festival of the year was the great celebration of Midsummer Eve or Midsummer Day, to
which corresponded the fire-festival of mid-
winter. Among the Celtic peoples who inhabit
the Land's End of Europe, on the other hand,
the principal fire-festivals were those of May
Day or Beltane, and of Hallowe'en. These two
dates mark the times when the herdsman drives
his cattle to pasture and when, at the approach
of winter, he brings them home again to the
stall. The Celtic bisection of the year into two

halves at the beginning of May and the beginning of November thus dates from a time when
the Celts were mainly a pastoral people, dependent for their subsistence on their herds, and
when accordingly the great epochs of the year
for them were the days on which the cattle went
forth from the homestead in early summer and
returned to it again in early winter. Even in
Central Europe, remote from the region now
occupied by the Celts, a similar bisection of the
year may be clearly traced in the great popularity, on the one hand, of May Day and its Eve
(Walpurgis Night), and, on the other hand, of
the Feast of All Souls at the beginning of
November, which under a thin Christian cloak
conceals an ancient pagan festival of the dead.
Hence we may conjecture that everywhere
throughout Europe the celestial division of the
year according to the solstices was preceded by
what we may call a terrestrial division of the
year according to the beginning of summer and
the beginning of winter.

Be that as it may, the two great Celtic festivals
of May Day and the first of November or, to

be more accurate, the Eves of these two days, closely resemble each other in the manner of their celebration and in the superstitions associated with them, and alike, by the antique character impressed upon both, betray a remote and purely pagan origin. The festival of May Day or Beltane, as the Celts called it, which ushered in summer, has already been described; it remains to give some account of the corresponding festival of Hallowe'en, which announced the arrival of winter.

· Of the two feasts Hallowe'en was perhaps of old the more important; since the Celts would seem to have dated the beginning of the year from it rather than from Beltane. In the Isle of Man, one of the fortresses in which the Celtic language and lore longest held out against the siege of the Saxon invaders, the first of November, Old Style, has been regarded as New Year's Day down to recent times. Thus Manx mummers used to go round on Hallowe'en (Old Style), singing, in the Manx language, a sort of Hogmanay song which began 'Tonight is New Year's Night, *Hogunnaa*!' One of Sir John Rhys's Manx informants, an old man of sixty-seven, 'had been a farm servant from the age of sixteen till he was twenty-six to the same man, near Regaby, in the parish of Andreas, and he remembers his master and a near neighbour of his discussing the term New Year's Day as applied to the first of November, and explaining to the younger men that it had always been so in old times. In fact, it seemed to him natural enough, as all tenure of land ends at that time, and as all servant men begin their service then.'

Not only among the Celts but throughout Europe, Hallowe'en, the night which marks the transition from autumn to winter, seems to have been of old the time of year when the souls of the departed were supposed to revisit their old homes in order to warm themselves by the fire and to comfort themselves with the good

Hallowe'en
Late autumn is the season of fairies, witches and the dead. The ancient Celtic New Year was at this time, when fires served to protect humans from the nonhuman.

The fairies
TOP. Cassillis Downan, where, according to Burns' *Halloween*, the fairies assemble. Engraving from Burns, *Works*, II, 1888, Bodleian Library, Oxford
ABOVE. While the fairies are abroad, humans stay indoors around the fire. Broadsheet of *c*.1795, one of the earliest publications of Burns' *Halloween*, Bodleian Library, Oxford

cheer provided for them in the kitchen or the parlour by their affectionate kinsfolk. It was, perhaps, a natural thought that the approach of winter should drive the poor shivering hungry ghosts from the bare fields and the leafless woodlands to the shelter of the cottage with its familiar fireside.

But it is not only the souls of the departed who are supposed to be hovering unseen on the day 'when autumn to winter resigns the pale year'. Witches then speed on their errands of mischief, some sweeping through the air on besoms, others galloping along the roads on tabby-cats, which for that evening are turned into coal-black steeds. The fairies, too, are all let loose, and hobgoblins of every sort roam freely about.

In all Celtic countries Hallowe'en seems to have been the great season of the year for prying into the future; all kinds of divination were put in practice that night. We read that Dathi, a king of Ireland in the fifth century, happening to be at the Druids' Hill (*Cnoc-nandruad*) in the county of Sligo one Hallowe'en, ordered his druid to forecast for him the future from that day till the next Hallowe'en should come round. The druid passed the night on the top of the hill, and next morning made a prediction to the king which came true. In Wales Hallowe'en was the weirdest of all the *Teir Nos Ysbrydion*, or Three Spirit Nights, when the wind, 'blowing over the feet of the corpses', bore sighs to the houses of those who were to die within the year. People thought that if on that night they went out to a cross-road and listened to the wind, they would learn all the most important things that would befall them during the next twelve months.

The winter solstice, which the ancients erroneously assigned to the twenty-fifth of December, was celebrated in antiquity as the Birthday of the Sun, and festal lights or fires were kindled on this joyful occasion. Our

The witches
The witches abroad. Burns' *Tam o' Shanter* describes the contrast between a homely winter existence indoors and the more imponderable world outside.
TOP. Tam o' Shanter watches the witches dance in a derelict church.
ABOVE. When the witches noticed him he fled and was pursued, but only as far as the bridge of Doon, for no witch may pass a bridge that crosses running water. A witch grabbed the horse's tail and ripped it off before he galloped over the keystone of the bridge. Broadsheet of *c*.1795, Bodleian Library, Oxford

Christmas festival is nothing but a continuation under a Christian name of this old solar festivity; for the ecclesiastical authorities saw fit, about the end of the third or the beginning of the fourth century, arbitrarily to transfer the nativity of Christ from the sixth of January to the twenty-fifth of December, for the purpose of diverting to their Lord the worship which the heathen had hitherto paid on that day to the sun.

In modern Christendom the ancient fire-festival of the winter solstice appears to survive, or to have survived down to recent years, in the old custom of the Yule log, clog, or block, as it was variously called in England. The custom was widespread in Europe, but seems to have flourished especially in England, France, and among the South Slavs; at least the fullest accounts of the custom come from these quarters. The Yule log was the winter counterpart of the Midsummer bonfire, kindled within doors instead of in the open air on account of the cold and inclement weather of the season.

Among the Germans the custom of the Yule log is known to have been observed in the eleventh century; for in the year 1184 the parish priest of Ahlen, in Münsterland, spoke of 'bringing a tree to kindle the festal fire at the Lord's Nativity'. Down to about the middle of the nineteenth century the old rite was kept up in some parts of central Germany, as we learn from an account of it given by a contemporary writer. After mentioning the custom of feeding the cattle and shaking the fruit-trees on Christmas night, to make them bear fruit, he goes on as follows: 'Other customs pointing back to the far-off times of heathendom may still be met with among the old-fashioned peasants of the mountain regions. Such is in the valleys of the Sieg and Lahn the practice of laying a new log as a foundation of the hearth. A heavy block of oak-wood, generally a stump grubbed up from the ground, is fitted either into the floor of the hearth, or into a niche made for the purpose in the wall under the hook on which the kettle hangs. When the fire on the hearth glows, this block of wood glows too, but it is so placed that it is hardly reduced to ashes within a year. When the new foundation is laid, the remains of the old block are carefully taken out, ground to powder, and strewed over the fields during the Twelve Nights. This, so people fancied, promotes the fruitfulness of the year's crops.'

'In almost all the families of the Ardennes,' we are told, 'at the present day they never fail to put the Yule log on the fireplace, but formerly it was the object of a superstitious worship which is now obsolete. The charred remains of it, placed under the pillow or under the house, preserved the house from storms, and before it was burned the Virgin used to come and sit on it, invisible, swaddling the infant Jesus. At Nouzon, twenty years ago, the traditional log was brought into the kitchen on Christmas Eve, and the grandmother, with a sprig of box in her hand, sprinkled the log with holy water as soon as the clock struck the first stroke of midnight. As she did so she chanted,

When Christmas comes,
Every one should rejoice,
For it is a New Covenant.

Following the grandmother and joining in the song, the children and the rest of the family marched thrice round the log, which was as fine a log as could be got.'

It is remarkable how common the belief appears to have been that the remains of the Yule log, if kept throughout the year, had power to protect the house against fire and especially against lightning. As the Yule log was frequently of oak, it seems possible that this belief may be a relic of the old Aryan creed which associated the oak-tree with the god of thunder.

The fire-festivals hitherto described are all celebrated periodically at certain stated times of the year. But besides these regularly recurring celebrations the peasants in many parts of Europe have been wont from time immemorial to resort to a ritual of fire at irregular intervals in seasons of distress and calamity, above all when their cattle were attacked by epidemic disease. No account of the popular European fire-festivals would be complete without some notice of these remarkable rites, which have all the greater claim on our attention because they may perhaps be regarded as the source and origin of all the other fire-festivals; certainly they must date from a very remote antiquity. The general name by which they are known among the Teutonic peoples is need-fire.

The history of the need-fire can be traced back to the early Middle Ages; for in the reign of Pippin, King of the Franks, the practice of kindling need-fires was denounced as a heathen superstition by a synod of prelates and nobles held under the presidency of Boniface, Archbishop of Mainz. In Germany the need-fires would seem to have been popular down to the second half of the nineteenth century. Thus in the year 1598, when a fatal cattle-plague was raging at Neustadt, near Marburg, a wise man of the name of Joh. Köhler induced the authorities of the town to adopt the following remedy. A new waggon-wheel was taken and twirled round an axle, which had never been used before, until the friction elicited fire. With this fire a bonfire was next kindled between the gates of the town, and all the cattle were driven through the smoke and flames. Moreover, every householder had to rekindle the fire on his hearth by means of a light taken from the bon-fire. Strange to say, this salutary measure had no effect whatever in staying the cattle-plague, and seven years later the sapient Joh. Köhler himself was burnt as a witch. The farmers whose pigs and cows had derived no benefit from the need-fire, perhaps assisted as spectators at the burning, and, while they shook their heads, agreed among themselves that it served Joh. Köhler perfectly right. According to a writer who published his book about nine years afterwards, some of the Germans, especially in the Wassgaw mountains, confidently believed that a cattle-plague could be stayed by driving the animals through a need-fire which had been kindled by the violent friction of a pole on a quantity of dry oak wood; but it was a necessary condition of success that all fires in the village should previously be extinguished with water, and any householder who failed to put out his fire was heavily fined. Slavonic peoples hold the need-fire in high esteem. They call it 'living fire', and attribute to it a healing virtue. The ascription of medicinal power to fire kindled by the friction of wood is said to be especially characteristic of the Slavs who inhabit the Carpathian Mountains and the Balkan peninsula. In England the earliest notice of the need-fire seems to be contained in the Chronicle of Lanercost for the year 1268. The annalist tells with pious horror how, when an epidemic was raging in that year among the cattle, 'certain beastly men, monks in garb but not in mind, taught the idiots of their country to make fire by friction of wood and to set up an image of Priapus, whereby they thought to succour the animals'. In Scotland, need-fires were thought to be one of the most efficacious remedies against witchcraft.

4. The Interpretation of the Fire-Festivals

The foregoing survey of the popular fire-festivals of Europe suggests some general observations. In the first place we can hardly help being struck by the resemblance which the ceremonies bear to each other, at whatever time of the year and in whatever part of Europe they are celebrated. The custom of kindling great bonfires, leaping over them, and driving cattle through or round them would seem to have been practically universal throughout Europe, and the same may be said of the processions or races with blazing torches round fields, orchards, pastures, or cattle-stalls. Less widespread are the customs of hurling lighted discs into the air and trundling a burning wheel down hill; for to judge by the evidence which I have collected these modes of distributing the beneficial influence of the fire have been confined in the main to Central Europe. The ceremonial of the Yule log is distinguished from that of the other fire-festivals by the privacy and domesticity which characterize it; but this distinction may well be due simply to the rough weather of midwinter, which is apt not only to render a public assembly in the open air disagreeable, but also at any moment to defeat the object of the assembly by extinguishing the all-important fire under a downpour of rain or a fall of snow. Apart from these local or seasonal differences, the general resemblance between the fire-festivals at all times of the year and in all places is tolerably close. And as the ceremonies themselves resemble each other, so do the benefits which the people expect to reap from them. Whether applied in the form of bonfires blazing at fixed points, or of torches carried about from place to place, or of embers and ashes taken from the smouldering heap of fuel, the fire is believed to promote the growth of the crops and the welfare of man and beast, either positively by stimulating them, or negatively by averting the dangers and calamities which threaten them from such causes as thunder and lightning, conflagration, blight, mildew, vermin, sterility, disease, and not least of all witchcraft. Hence, when we remember the great hold which the dread of witchcraft has had on the popular European mind in all ages, we may suspect that the primary intention of all these fire-festivals was simply to destroy or at all events get rid of the witches, who were regarded as the causes of nearly all man's misfortunes.

This suspicion is confirmed when we examine the evils for which the bonfires and torches were supposed to provide a remedy. Foremost, perhaps, among these evils we may reckon the diseases of cattle; and of all the ills that witches are believed to work there is probably none which is so constantly insisted on as the harm they do to the herds, particularly by stealing the milk from the cows. Now it is significant that the need-fire, which may perhaps be regarded as the parent of the periodic fire-festivals, was kindled above all as a remedy for a murrain or other disease of cattle; and the circumstance suggests, what on general grounds seems probable, that the custom of kindling the need-fire goes back to a time when the ancestors of the European peoples subsisted chiefly on the products of their herds, and when agriculture as yet played a subordinate part in their lives. Witches and wolves are the two great foes still dreaded by the herdsman in many parts of Europe; and we need not wonder that he should resort to fire as a powerful means of banning them both.

Death, fires and fertility reflect the myth of Balder
TOP. The body of a king burned for the good of the
crops, a report from India by a 16th-century traveller. De
Bry, *India Orientalis*, 1605, Bodleian Library, Oxford
CENTRE. A possible survival of Balder's ship burial,
Garland Day at Abbotsbury, England, where until
recently garlands were taken out to sea and left. *Sir
Benjamin Stone's Pictures*, 1906, Bodleian Library, Oxford
ABOVE. A striking convergence of the themes of annual
fires and the burial of a Nordic king is found in the fire-
festival at Lerwick in the Shetland Isles, at the end of
January. Photo: The British Tourist Board

The bonfires are often supposed to protect the
fields against hail and the homestead against
thunder and lightning. Both are thought to be
caused by witches; hence the fire which bans the
witches necessarily serves at the same time as a
talisman against hail, thunder, and lightning.
Further, brands taken from the bonfires are commonly kept in the houses to guard them against
conflagration; and though this may perhaps be
done on the principle of homoeopathic magic,
one fire being thought to act as a preventive of
another, it is also possible that the intention may
be to keep witch-incendiaries at bay. Again,
people leap over the bonfires as a preventive of
colic, and look at the flames steadily in order to
preserve their eyes in good health; and both
colic and sore eyes are in Germany, and probably elsewhere, set down to the machinations of
witches. Once more, to leap over the Midsummer fires or to circumambulate them is thought
to prevent a person from feeling pains in his back
at reaping; and in Germany such pains are called
'witch-shots' and ascribed to witchcraft.

On the whole, then, the theory of the purificatory virtue of the ceremonial fires appears
to be in accordance with the evidence. But
Europe is not the only part of the world where
ceremonies of this sort have been performed; elsewhere the passage through the
flames or smoke or over the glowing embers
of a bonfire, which is the central feature of most
of the rites, has been employed as a cure or a
preventive of various ills. We have seen that
the midsummer ritual of fire in Morocco is
practically identical with that of our European
peasantry; and customs more or less similar have
been observed by many races in various parts of
the world. Thus we can now understand why
festivals of fire played so important a part in the
religion of our heathen forefathers; the observance of such festivals flowed directly from their
overmastering fear of witchcraft and from their
theory as to the best way of combatting that evil.

5. The Burning of Human Beings in the Fires

We have still to ask, What is the meaning of burning effigies in the fire at these festivals? After the preceding investigation the answer to the question seems obvious. As the fires are often alleged to be kindled for the purpose of burning the witches, and as the effigy burnt in them is sometimes called 'the Witch', we might naturally be disposed to conclude that all the effigies consumed in the flames on these occasions represent witches or warlocks and that the custom of burning them is merely a substitute for burning the wicked men and women themselves, since on the principle of homoeopathic or imitative magic you practically destroy the witch herself in destroying her effigy. On the whole this explanation of the burning of straw figures in human shape at the festivals appears to be the most probable.

At the same time, the effigies can hardly be separated from the effigies of Death which are burned or otherwise destroyed in spring; and grounds have been already given for regarding the so-called effigies of Death as really representatives of the tree-spirit or spirit of vegetation. Are the other effigies, which are burned in the spring and midsummer bonfires, susceptible of the same explanation? It would seem so. For just as the fragments of the so-called Death are stuck in the fields to make the crops grow, so the charred embers of the figure burned in the spring bonfires are sometimes laid on the fields in the belief that they will keep vermin from the crop.

Yet in the popular customs connected with the fire-festivals of Europe there are certain features which appear to point to a former practice of human sacrifice. We have seen reasons for believing that in Europe living persons have often acted as representatives of the tree-spirit and corn-spirit and have suffered death as such. There is no reason, therefore, why they should not have been burned, if any special advantages were likely to be attained by putting them to death in that way. The consideration of human suffering is not one which enters into the calculations of primitive man. Now, in the fire-festivals which we are discussing, the pretence of burning people is sometimes carried so far that it seems reasonable to regard it as a mitigated survival of an older custom of actually burning them. Thus in Jumièges in Normandy the man clad all in green, who bore the title of the Green Wolf, was pursued by his comrades, and when they caught him they feigned to fling him upon the mid-summer bonfire.

Of human sacrifices offered on these occasions the most unequivocal traces are those which, about a hundred years ago, still lingered at the Beltane fires in the Highlands of Scotland, that is, among a Celtic people who, situated in a remote corner of Europe and almost completely isolated from foreign influence, had till then conserved their old heathenism better perhaps than any other people in the west of Europe. It is significant, therefore, that human sacrifices by fire are known, on unquestionable evidence, to have been systematically practised by the Celts. The earliest description of these sacrifices has been bequeathed to us by Julius Caesar. The following seem to have been the main outlines of the custom. Condemned criminals were reserved by the Celts in order to be sacrificed to the gods at a great festival which took place once in every five years. The more there were of such

The burning of the effigies in fires to avert evil influences
Guy Fawkes Night in Lewes, Sussex, in 1976. Effigies of Pope Paul V and Guy Fawkes are carried in procession before being burned. This contemporary commemoration of the Gunpowder Plot retains an accurate memory of the kind of evil that was to be averted. Photo: Homer Sykes, © *Once a Year*

victims, the greater was believed to be the fertility of the land. If there were not enough criminals to furnish victims, captives taken in war were immolated to supply the deficiency. When the time came the victims were sacrificed by the Druids or priests. Some they shot down with arrows, some they impaled, and some they burned alive in the following manner. Colossal images of wicker-work or of wood and grass were constructed; these were filled with live men, cattle, and animals of other kinds; fire was then applied to the images, and they were burned with their living contents.

Such were the great festivals held once every five years. But besides these quinquennial festivals, celebrated on so grand a scale, and with, apparently, so large an expenditure of human life, it seems reasonable to suppose that festivals of the same sort, only on a lesser scale, were held annually, and that from these annual festivals are lineally descended some at least of the fire-festivals which, with their traces of human sacri-fices, are still celebrated year by year in many parts of Europe. The gigantic images con-structed of osiers or covered with grass in which the Druids enclosed their victims remind us of the leafy framework in which the human repre-sentative of the tree-spirit is still so often encased. Hence, seeing that the fertility of the land was apparently supposed to depend upon the due performance of these sacrifices, we may inter-pret the Celtic victims, cased in osiers and grass, as representatives of the tree-spirit or spirit of vegetation.

These wicker giants of the Druids seem to have had till lately their representatives at the spring and mid-summer festivals of modern Europe. At Douay, for example, down to the early part of the nineteenth century, a pro-cession took place annually on the Sunday near-est to the seventh of July. The great feature of the procession was a colossal figure, some twenty or thirty feet high, made of osiers, and called 'the giant', which was moved through the streets by means of rollers and ropes worked by men who were enclosed within the effigy. The wooden head of the giant is said to have been carved and painted by Rubens. The figure was armed as a knight with lance and sword, helmet and shield. Behind him marched his wife and his three children, all constructed of osiers on the same principle, but on a smaller scale.

It appears that the sacrificial rites of the Celts of ancient Gaul can be traced in the popular festivals of modern Europe. Naturally it is in France, or rather in the wider area comprised within the limits of ancient Gaul, that these rites have left the clearest traces in the customs of burning giants of wicker-work and animals enclosed in wicker-work or baskets. These customs, it will have been remarked, are generally observed at or about midsummer. From this we may infer that the original rites of which these are the degenerate successors were solemnized at midsummer. This inference harmonizes with the conclusion suggested by a general survey of European folk-custom, that the midsummer festival must on the whole have been the most widely diffused and the most solemn of all the yearly festivals celebrated by the primitive Aryans in Europe. At the same time we must bear in mind that among the British Celts the chief fire-festivals of the year appear certainly to have been those of Beltane (May Day) and Hallowe'en (the last day of October); and this suggests a doubt whether the Celts of Gaul also may not have celebrated their principal rites of fire, including their burnt sacrifices of men and animals, at the beginning of May or the beginning of November rather than at Midsummer.

We have still to ask, What is the meaning of such sacrifices? Why were men and animals burnt to death at these festivals? If we are right in interpreting the modern European fire-festivals as attempts to break the power of witchcraft by burning or banning the witches and warlocks, it seems to follow that we must ex-plain the human sacrifices of the Celts in the same manner; that is, we must suppose that the men whom the Druids burnt in wicker-work images were condemned to death on the ground that they were witches or wizards, and that the mode of execution by fire was chosen because burning alive is deemed the surest mode of getting rid of these noxious and dangerous beings. The same explanation would apply to the cattle and wild animals of many kinds which the Celts burned along with the men. One advantage of explaining the ancient Celtic sacrifices in this way is that it introduces, as it were, a harmony and consistency into the treatment which Europe has meted out to witches from the earliest times down to about two centuries ago, when the growing influence of rationalism discredited the belief in witchcraft and put a stop to the custom of burning witches. On this view the Christian Church in its dealings with the black art merely carried out the traditional policy of Druidism, and it might be a nice question to decide which of the two, in pursuance of that policy, exterminated the larger number of innocent men and women. Be that as it may, we can now perhaps understand why the Druids believed that the more persons they sentenced to death, the greater would be the fertility of the land. To a modern reader the connexion at first sight may not be obvious between the activity of the hangman and the productivity of the earth. But a little reflection may satisfy him that when the criminals who perish at the stake or on the gallows are witches, whose delight it is to blight the crops of the farmer or to lay them low under storms of hail, the execution of these wretches is really calculated to ensure an abundant harvest by removing one of the principal causes which paralyze the efforts and blast the hopes of the husbandman.

6. The Magic Flowers of Midsummer Eve

A feature of the great midsummer festival remains to be considered, which may perhaps help to clear up the doubt as to the meaning of the fire-ceremonies and their relation to Druidism. For in France and England, the countries where the sway of the Druids is known to have been most firmly established, Midsummer Eve is still the time for culling certain magic plants, whose evanescent virtue can be secured at this mystic season alone. Indeed all over Europe antique fancies of the same sort have lingered about Midsummer Eve, imparting to it a fragrance of the past, like withered rose leaves that, found by chance in the pages of an old volume, still smell of departed summers. Thus in Saintonge and Aunis, two of the ancient provinces of Western France, we read that 'of all the festivals for which the merry bells ring out there is not one which has given rise to a greater number of superstitious practices than the festival of St John the Baptist. The Eve of St John was the day of all days for gathering the wonderful herbs by means of which you could combat fever, cure a host of diseases, and guard yourself against sorcerers and their spells. But in order to attain these results two conditions had to be observed; first, you must be fasting when you gathered the herbs, and second, you must cull them before the sun rose. If these conditions were not fulfilled, the plants had no special virtue.' Indeed so widespread in France used to be the faith in the magic virtue of herbs culled on that day that there is a French proverb 'to employ all the herbs of St John in an affair', meaning 'to leave no stone unturned'.

The Germans of West Bohemia collect simples on St John's Night, because they believe the healing virtue of the plants to be especially powerful at that time. The theory and practice of the Huzuls in the Carpathian Mountains are similar; they imagine that the plants gathered on that night are not only medicinal but possess the power of restraining the witches; some say that the herbs should be plucked in twelve gardens or meadows. Among the simples which the Czechs and Moravians of Silesia cull at this season are dandelions, ribwort, and the bloom of the lime-tree. The Esthonians of the island of Oesel gather St John's herbs (*Jani rohhud*) on St John's Day, tie them up in bunches, and hang them up about the houses to prevent evil spirits from entering. A subsidiary use of the plants is to cure diseases; gathered at that time they have a greater medical value than if they were collected at any other season. Everybody does not choose exactly the same sorts of plants; some gather more and some less, but in the collection St John's wort (*Jani rohhi, Hypericum perforatum*) should never be wanting.

In Bulgaria St John's Day is the special season for culling simples. On this day, too, Bulgarian girls gather nosegays of a certain white flower, throw them into a vessel of water, and place the vessel under a rose-tree in bloom. Here it remains all night. Next morning they set it in the courtyard and dance singing round it. An old woman then takes the flowers out of the vessel, and the girls wash themselves with the water, praying that God would grant them health throughout the year. After that the old woman restores her nosegay to each girl and promises her a rich husband.

Nor is the superstition confined to Europe and to people of European descent. In Morocco also the Mohammedans are of opinion that certain plants, such as penny-royal, marjoram, and the oleander, acquire a special magic virtue (*baraka*) when they are gathered shortly before midsummer. Hence the people collect these plants at this season and preserve them for magical or medical purposes. Indeed such marvellous powers do these Arabs attribute to plants at this mystic season that a barren woman will walk naked about a vegetable garden on Midsummer Night in the hope of conceiving a child through the fertilizing influence of the vegetables.

Of the flowers which it has been customary to gather for purposes of magic or divination at midsummer none perhaps is so widely popular as St John's wort (*Hypericum perforatum*). The reason for associating this particular plant with the great summer festival is perhaps not far to seek, for the flower blooms about Midsummer Day, and with its bright yellow petals and masses of golden stamens it might well pass for a tiny copy on earth of the great sun which reaches its culminating point in heaven at this season.

Yet another plant whose root has been thought to yield the blood of St John is the mouse-ear hawkweed (*Hieracium pilosella*), which grows very commonly in dry exposed places, such as gravelly banks, sunny lawns, and the tops of park walls. More commonly in Germany the name of St John's flowers (*Johannisblumen*) appears to be given to the mountain arnica. In Voigtland the mountain arnica if plucked on St John's Eve and stuck in the fields, laid under the roof, or hung on the wall, is believed to protect house and fields from lightning and hail.

Another plant which possesses wondrous virtues, if only it be gathered on the Eve or the Day of St John, is mugwort (*Artemisia vulgaris*). Hence in France it goes by the name of the herb of St John. The custom of wearing girdles of mugwort on the Eve or Day of St John has caused the plant to be popularly known in Ger-

many and Bohemia as St John's girdle. In Bohemia such girdles are believed to protect the wearer for the whole year against ghosts, magic, misfortune, and sickness. Another plant which popular superstition has often associated with the summer solstice is vervain. In some parts of Spain people gather vervain after sunset on Midsummer Eve, and wash their faces next morning in the water in which the plants have been allowed to steep overnight. In Belgium vervain is gathered on St John's Day and worn as a safeguard against rupture.

At Kirchvers, in Hesse, people run out to the fields at noon on Midsummer Day to gather camomile; for the flowers, plucked at the moment when the sun is at the highest point of his course, are supposed to possess the medicinal qualities of the plant in the highest degree. In heathen times the camomile flower, with its healing qualities, its yellow calix and white stamens, is said to have been sacred to the kindly and shining Balder and to have borne his name, being called *Balders-brâ*, that is, Balder's eye-lashes.

More famous, however, than these are the

The magic flowers of midsummer
Some plants have genuine medicinal qualities, although the connection between cause and effect may be unknown. To be fully beneficial, the magic flowers of midsummer had to be gathered on Midsummer's Eve or Midsummer's Day, which, in the Church's calendar, is the day of St John.
TOP LEFT. Mugwort (*Artemisia vulgaris*), known as the herb of St John in France, guarded the corn from mice, and if worn in the belt prevented backache during the harvest. *Flora Danica*, 1799
TOP RIGHT. Hawkweed (*Hieracium pilosella*). The reddish juice of the roots was called the blood of St John in Germany, and was preserved in quills for good luck. If smeared on the clothes it would prosper dealings at the market held on St John's Day. *Flora Danica*, 1799
BOTTOM LEFT. St John's wort (*Hypericum perforatum*) cured sickness, and if hung up in the house protected it from lightning and evil spirits. *Flora Danica*, 1792
BOTTOM RIGHT. Marjoram (*Oreganum vulgare*). Crosses of Marjoram and St John's wort were a protection against witches on Walpurgis Night (1st May). *Flora Danica*, 1818

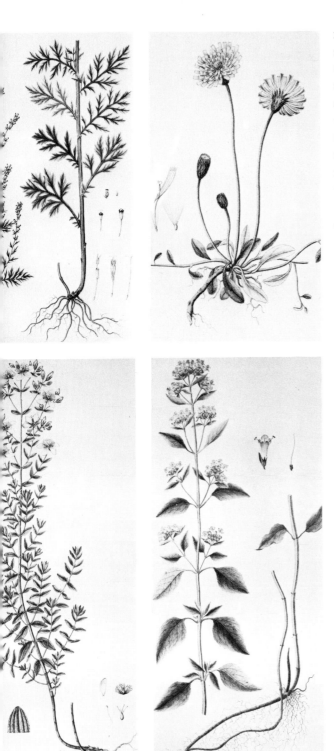

marvellous properties which popular superstition in many parts of Europe has attributed
to the fern at this season. At midnight on Midsummer Eve the plant is supposed to bloom and
soon afterwards to seed; and whoever catches
the bloom or the seed is thereby endowed with
supernatural knowledge and miraculous powers;
above all, he knows where treasures lie hidden
in the ground, and he can render himself invisible at will by putting the seed in his shoe.
But great precautions must be observed in procuring the wondrous bloom or seed, which else
quickly vanishes like dew on sand or mist in the
air. The seeker must neither touch it with his
hand nor let it touch the ground; he spreads a
white cloth under the plant, and the blossom or
the seed falls into it. Beliefs of this sort concerning fern-seed have prevailed, with trifling variations of detail, in England, France, Germany,
Austria, Italy, and Russia. Once more, people
have fancied that if they cut a branch of hazel
on Midsummer Eve it would serve them as a
divining rod to discover treasures and water.
This belief has existed in Moravia, Mecklenburg,
and apparently in Scotland as well as in Sweden.

I would suggest that the flowers, like the fires
of midsummer, are thought to transfer to mankind some effulgence of the sun's light and heat
which invests them for a time with powers above
the ordinary for the healing of diseases and the
unmasking and baffling of all the evil things that
threaten the life of man.

This consideration brings us back to the view
that while the purely destructive aspect of fire is
generally the most prominent and apparently the
most important at these festivals, we must not
overlook the additional force which by virtue
of homoeopathic or imitative magic the bonfires may be supposed both to derive from and
to impart to the sun, especially at the moment of
the summer solstice when his strength is greatest
and begins to decline, and when he can at once
give and receive help to the greatest advantage.

7. Balder and the Mistletoe

The reader may remember that the preceding account of the popular fire-festivals of Europe was suggested by the myth of the Norse god Balder, who is said to have been slain by a branch of mistletoe and burnt in a great fire. We have now to enquire how far the customs which have been passed in review help to shed light on the myth. In this enquiry it may be convenient to begin with the mistletoe, the instrument of Balder's death.

From time immemorial the mistletoe has been the object of superstitious veneration in Europe. It was worshipped by the Druids, as we learn from a famous passage of Pliny. After enumerating the different kinds of mistletoe, he proceeds: 'In treating of this subject, the admiration in which the mistletoe is held throughout Gaul ought not to pass unnoticed. The Druids, for so they call their wizards, esteem nothing more sacred than the mistletoe and the tree on which it grows, provided only that the tree is an oak. But apart from this they choose oak-woods for their sacred groves and perform no sacred rites without oak-leaves; so that the very name of Druids may be regarded as a Greek appellation derived from their worship of the oak. For they believe that whatever grows on these trees is sent from heaven, and is a sign that the tree has been chosen by the god himself. The mistletoe is very rarely to be met with; but when it is found, they gather it with solemn ceremony. This they do above all on the sixth day of the moon, from whence they date the beginnings of their months, of their years, and of their thirty years' cycle, because by the sixth day the moon has plenty of vigour and has not run half its course. After due preparations have been made for a sacrifice and a feast under the tree, they hail it as the universal healer and bring to the spot two white bulls, whose horns have never been bound before. A priest clad in a white robe climbs the tree and with a golden sickle cuts the mistletoe, which is caught in a white cloth. Then they sacrifice the victims, praying that God may make his own gift to prosper with those upon whom he has bestowed it. They believe that a potion prepared from mistletoe will make barren animals to bring forth, and that the plant is a remedy against all poison. So much of men's religion is commonly concerned with trifles.'

In another passage Pliny tells us that in medicine the mistletoe which grows on an oak was esteemed the most efficacious, and that its efficacy was by some superstitious people supposed to be increased if the plant was gathered on the first day of the moon without the use of iron, and if when gathered it was not allowed to touch the earth; oak-mistletoe thus obtained was deemed a cure for epilepsy; carried about by women it assisted them to conceive; and it healed ulcers most effectually, if only the sufferer chewed a piece of the plant and laid another piece on the sore. Yet, again, he says that mistletoe was supposed, like vinegar and an egg, to be an excellent means of extinguishing a fire.

If in these latter passages Pliny refers, as he apparently does, to the beliefs current among his contemporaries in Italy, it will follow that the Druids and the Italians were to some extent agreed as to the valuable properties possessed by mistletoe which grows on an oak; both of them deemed it an effectual remedy for a number of ailments, and both of them ascribed to it a quickening virtue, the Druids believing that a

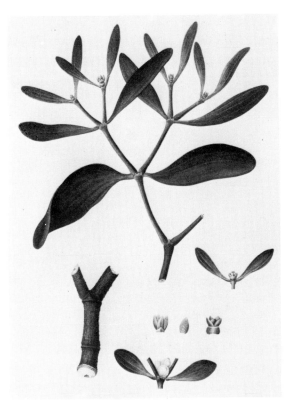

Suspended between heaven and earth
The mistletoe, seat of Balder's soul, was the only thing
that could kill him. *Flora Danica*, 1799

the opinion of modern European peasants, and even of the learned, has to some extent agreed with that of the ancients. The Druids appear to have called the plant, or perhaps the oak on which it grew, the 'all-healer'; and 'all-healer' is said to be still a name of the mistletoe in the modern Celtic speech of Brittany, Wales, Ireland, and Scotland. On St John's morning (Midsummer morning) peasants of Piedmont and Lombardy go out to search the oak-leaves for the 'oil of St John', which is supposed to heal all wounds made with cutting instruments. Originally, perhaps, the 'oil of St John' was simply the mistletoe, or a decoction made from it.

Again, mistletoe is said to open all locks. However, in the Tyrol it can only exert this power 'under certain circumstances', which are not specified. But perhaps the most precious of all the virtues of mistletoe is that it affords efficient protection against sorcery and witchcraft. That, no doubt, is the reason why in Austria a twig of mistletoe is laid on the threshold as a preventive of nightmare; and it may be the reason why in the north of England they say that if you wish your dairy to thrive you should give your bunch of mistletoe to the first cow that calves after New Year's Day, for it is well known that nothing is so fatal to milk and butter as witchcraft.

With regard to the time when the mistletoe should be gathered opinions have varied. The Druids gathered it above all on the sixth day of the moon, the ancient Italians apparently on the first day of the moon. In modern times some have preferred the full moon of March and others the waning moon of winter when the sun is in Sagittarius. But the favourite time would seem to be Midsummer Eve or Midsummer Day. Both in France and Sweden special virtues are ascribed to mistletoe gathered at midsummer. The rule in Sweden is that 'mistletoe must be cut on the night of Midsummer Eve when sun and moon stand in the sign of their

potion prepared from mistletoe would fertilize barren cattle, and the Italians holding that a piece of mistletoe carried about by a woman would help her to conceive a child. Further, both peoples thought that if the plant were to exert its medical properties it must be gathered in a certain way and at a certain time. It might not be cut with iron, hence the Druids cut it with gold; and it might not touch the earth, hence the Druids caught it in a white cloth. In choosing the time for gathering the plant, both peoples were determined by observation of the moon; only they differed as to the particular day of the moon, the Italians preferring the first, and the Druids the sixth.

In respect of the healing virtues of mistletoe

might'. Again, in Wales it was believed that a sprig of mistletoe gathered on St John's Eve (Midsummer Eve), or at any time before the berries appeared, would induce dreams of omen, both good and bad, if it were placed under the pillow of the sleeper. Thus mistletoe is one of the many plants whose magical or medicinal virtues are believed to culminate with the culmination of the sun on the longest day of the year. Hence it seems reasonable to conjecture that in the eyes of the Druids, also, who revered the plant so highly, the sacred mistletoe may have acquired a double portion of its mystic qualities at the solstice in June, and that accordingly they may have regularly cut it with solemn ceremony on Midsummer Eve.

Be that as it may, certain it is that the mistletoe, the instrument of Balder's death, has been regularly gathered for the sake of its mystic qualities on Midsummer Eve in Scandinavia, Balder's home. The plant is found commonly growing on pear-trees, oaks, and other trees in thick damp woods throughout the more temperate parts of Sweden. Thus one of the two main incidents of Balder's myth is reproduced in the great midsummer festival of Scandinavia. But the other main incident of the myth, the burning of Balder's body on a pyre, has also its counterpart in the bonfires which still blaze, or blazed till lately, in Denmark, Norway, and Sweden on Midsummer Eve. It does not appear, indeed, that any effigy is burned in these bonfires; but the burning of an effigy is a feature which might easily drop out after its meaning was forgotten. And the name of Balder's balefires (*Balder's Bǎlar*), by which these midsummer fires were formerly known in Sweden, puts their connexion with Balder beyond the reach of doubt, and makes it probable that in former times either a living representative or an effigy of Balder was annually burned in them. Midsummer was the season sacred to Balder, and the Swedish poet Tegner, in placing the burning of

Balder at midsummer, may very well have followed an old tradition that the summer solstice was the time when the good god came to his untimely end.

Thus it has been shewn that the leading incidents of the Balder myth have their counterparts in those fire-festivals of our European peasantry which undoubtedly date from a time long prior to the introduction of Christianity. The Scottish pretence of throwing the victim chosen by lot into the Beltane fire, and the similar treatment of the man, the future Green Wolf, at the midsummer bonfire in Normandy, may naturally be interpreted as traces of an older custom of actually burning human beings on these occasions; and the green dress of the Green Wolf, coupled with the leafy envelope of the young fellow who trod out the midsummer fire at Moosheim, seems to hint that the persons who perished at these festivals did so in the character of tree-spirits or deities of vegetation. From all this we may reasonably infer that in the Balder myth on the one hand, and the fire-festivals and custom of gathering mistletoe on the other hand, we have, as it were, the two broken and dissevered halves of an original whole. In other words, we may assume with some degree of probability that the myth of Balder's death was not merely a myth, that is, a description of physical phenomena in imagery borrowed from human life, but that it was at the same time the story which people told to explain why they annually burned a human representative of the god and cut the mistletoe with solemn ceremony. If I am right, the story of Balder's tragic end formed, so to say, the text of the sacred drama which was acted year by year as a magical rite to cause the sun to shine, trees to grow, crops to thrive, and to guard man and beast from the baleful arts of fairies and trolls, of witches and warlocks. The tale belonged, in short, to that class of nature myths which are meant to be supplemented by ritual; here, as so often, myth stood to magic in the relation of theory to practice.

But if the victims – the human Balders – who died by fire, whether in spring or at midsummer, were put to death as living embodiments of tree-spirits or deities of vegetation, it would seem that Balder himself must have been a tree-spirit or deity of vegetation.

Now, considering the primitive character and remarkable similarity of the fire-festivals observed by all the branches of the Aryan race in Europe, we may infer that these festivals form part of the common stock of religious observances which the various peoples carried with them in their wanderings from their old home. But, if I am right, an essential feature of those primitive fire-festivals was the burning of a man who represented the tree-spirit. And in view of the place occupied by the oak in the religion of the Aryans, the presumption is that the tree so represented at the fire-festivals must originally have been the oak. The conclusion thus drawn for the European Aryans in general is confirmed in its special application to the Scandinavians by the relation in which amongst them the mistletoe appears to have stood to the burning of the victim in the midsummer fire. We have seen that among Scandinavians it has been customary to gather the mistletoe at midsummer. But so far as appears on the face of this custom, there is nothing to connect it with the midsummer fires in which human victims or effigies of them were burned. Even if the fire, as seems probable, was originally always made with oak-wood, why should it have been necessary to pull the mistletoe? The last link between the midsummer customs of gathering the mistletoe and lighting the bonfires is supplied by Balder's myth, which can hardly be disjoined from the customs in question. The myth suggests that a vital connexion may once have been believed to subsist between the mistletoe and the human representative of the oak who was burned in the fire. According to the myth, Balder could be killed by nothing in heaven or earth except the mistletoe; and so long as the mistletoe remained on the oak, he was not only immortal but invulnerable. Now, if we suppose that Balder was the oak, the origin of the myth becomes intelligible. The mistletoe was viewed as the seat of life of the oak, and so long as it was uninjured nothing could kill or even wound the oak. The conception of the mistletoe as the seat of life of the oak would naturally be suggested to primitive people by the observation that while the oak is deciduous, the mistletoe which grows on it is evergreen. In winter the sight of its fresh foliage among the bare branches must have been hailed by the worshippers of the tree as a sign that the divine life which had ceased to animate the branches yet survived in the mistletoe, as the heart of a sleeper still beats when his body is motionless. Hence when the god had to be killed – when the sacred tree had to be burnt – it was necessary to begin by breaking off the mistletoe. For so long as the mistletoe remained intact, the oak was invulnerable; all the blows of their knives and axes would glance harmless from its surface. But once tear from the oak its sacred heart – the mistletoe – and the tree nodded to its fall. And when in later times the spirit of the oak came to be represented by a living man, it was logically necessary to suppose that, like the tree he personated, he could neither be killed nor wounded so long as the mistletoe remained uninjured. The pulling of the mistletoe was thus at once the signal and the cause of his death.

But since the idea of a being whose life is thus, in a sense, outside himself, must be strange to many readers, and has, indeed, not yet been recognized in its full bearing on primitive superstition, it will be worth while to illustrate it by examples drawn both from story and custom. The result will be to shew that, in assuming this idea as the explanation of Balder's relation to the mistletoe, I assume a principle which is deeply engraved on the mind of primitive man.

8. The External Soul

The External Soul according to Folk-Tales

In a former part of this work we saw that, in the opinion of primitive people, the soul may temporarily absent itself from the body without causing death. Such temporary absences of the soul are often believed to involve considerable risk, since the wandering soul is liable to a variety of mishaps at the hands of enemies, and so forth. But there is another aspect to this power of disengaging the soul from the body. If only the safety of the soul can be ensured during its absence, there is no reason why the soul should not continue absent for an indefinite time; indeed a man may, on a pure calculation of personal safety, desire that his soul should never return to his body. So long as this object which he calls his life or soul remains unharmed, the man is well; if it is injured, he suffers; if it is destroyed, he dies. Or, to put it otherwise, when a man is ill or dies, the fact is explained by saying that the material object called his life or soul, whether it be in his body or out of it, has either sustained injury or been destroyed. But there may be circumstances in which, if the life or soul remains in the man, it stands a greater chance of sustaining injury than if it were stowed away in some safe and secret place. Accordingly, in such circumstances, primitive man takes his soul out of his body and deposits it for security in some snug spot, intending to replace it in his body when the danger is past. Or if he should discover some place of absolute security, he may be content to leave his soul there permanently. The advantage of this is that, so long as the soul remains unharmed in the place where he has deposited it, the man himself is immortal; nothing can kill his body, since his life is not in it.

Evidence of this primitive belief is furnished by a class of folk-tales of which the Norse story of 'the giant who had no heart in his body' is perhaps the best-known example. Stories of this kind are widely diffused over the world, and from their number and the variety of incident and of details in which the leading idea is embodied, we may infer that the conception of an external soul is one which has had a powerful hold on the minds of men at an early stage of history. For folk-tales are a faithful reflection of the world as it appeared to the primitive mind; and we may be sure that any idea which commonly occurs in them, however absurd it may seem to us, must once have been an ordinary article of belief. This assurance, so far as it concerns the supposed power of disengaging the soul from the body for a longer or shorter time, is amply corroborated by a comparison of the folk-tales in question with the actual beliefs and practices of savages.

The story of the external soul is told, in various forms, by all Aryan peoples from Hindoostan to the Hebrides. A very common form of it is this: A warlock, giant, or other fairyland being is invulnerable and immortal because he keeps his soul hidden far away in some secret place; but a fair princess, whom he holds enthralled in his enchanted castle, wiles his secret from him and reveals it to the hero, who seeks out the warlock's soul, heart, life, or death (as it is variously called), and, by destroying it, simultaneously kills the warlock. Thus a Hindoo story tells how a magician called Punchkin held a queen captive for twelve years, and would fain marry her, but she would not have him. At last the queen's son came to rescue her, and the two plotted together to kill Punchkin. So the queen spoke the magician fair, and pretended that she had at last made up her mind to marry him. 'And do tell me', she said, 'are you quite immortal? Can death never touch you? And are you too great an enchanter ever to feel human suffering?' 'It is true', he said, 'that I am not as others. Far, far away, hundreds of thousands of miles from this, there lies a desolate country covered with thick jungle. In the midst of the jungle grows a circle of palm trees, and in the centre of the circle stand six chattees full of water, piled one above another: below the sixth chattee is a small cage, which contains a little green parrot; – on the life of the parrot depends my life; – and if the parrot is killed I must die. It is, however,' he added, 'impossible that the parrot should sustain any injury, both on account of the inaccessibility of the country, and because, by my appointment, many thousand genii surround the palm trees, and kill all who approach the place.' But the queen's young son overcame all difficulties, and got possession of the parrot. He brought it to the door of the magician's palace, and began playing with it. Punchkin, the magician, saw him, and, coming out, tried to persuade the boy to give him the parrot. 'Give me my parrot!' cried Punchkin. Then the boy took hold of the parrot and tore off one of his wings; and as he did so the magician's right arm fell off. Punchkin then stretched out his left arm, crying, 'Give me my parrot!' The prince pulled off the parrot's second wing, and the magician's left arm tumbled off. 'Give me my parrot!' cried he, and fell on his knees. The prince pulled off the parrot's right leg, the magician's right leg fell off; the prince pulled off the parrot's left leg, down fell the magician's left. Nothing remained of him except the trunk and the head; but still he rolled his eyes, and cried, 'Give me my parrot!' 'Take your parrot, then,' cried the boy; and with that he wrung the bird's neck, and threw it at the magician;

and, as he did so, Punchkin's head twisted round, and, with a fearful groan, he died!

It can be shown that the notion of the external soul occurs commonly in the popular stories of peoples who do not belong to the Aryan stock. For instance it appears in the ancient Egyptian story of 'The Two Brothers'. This story was written down in the reign of Rameses II, about 1300 BC. It is therefore older than our present redaction of Homer, and far older than the Bible. The outline of the story, so far as it concerns us here, is as follows. Once upon a time there were two brethren; the name of the elder was Anpu and the name of the younger was Bata. Now Anpu had a house and a wife, and his younger brother dwelt with him as his servant. It was Anpu who made the garments, and every morning when it grew light he drove the kine afield. As he walked behind them they used to say to him, 'The grass is good in such and such a place', and he heard what they said and led them to the good pasture that they desired. So his kine grew very sleek and multiplied greatly. One day when the two brothers were at work in the field the elder brother said to the younger, 'Run and fetch seed from the village.' So the younger brother ran and said to the wife of his elder brother, 'Give me seed that I may run to the field, for my brother sent me saying, Tarry not.' She said, 'Go to the barn and take as much as thou wouldst.' He went and filled a jar full of wheat and barley, and came forth bearing it on his shoulders. When the woman saw him her heart went out to him, and she laid hold of him and said, 'Come, let us rest an hour together.' But he said, 'Thou art to me as a mother, and my brother is to me as a father.' So he would not hearken to her, but took the load on his back and went away to the field. In the evening, when the elder brother was returning from the field, his wife feared for what she had said. So she took soot and made herself as one who had been beaten. And when her husband came home, she said, 'When thy younger brother came to fetch seed, he said to me, Come, let us rest an hour together. But I would not, and he beat me.' Then the elder brother became like a panther of the south; he sharpened his knife and stood behind the door of the cow-house. And when the sun set and the younger brother came laden with all the herbs of the field, as was his wont every day, the cow that walked in front of the herd said to him, 'Behold, thine elder brother stands with a knife to kill thee. Flee before him.' When he heard what the cow said, he looked under the door of the cow-house and saw the feet of his elder brother standing behind the door, his knife in his hand. So he fled and his brother pursued him with the knife. But the younger brother cried for help to the Sun, and the Sun heard him and caused a great water to spring up between him and his elder brother, and the water was full of crocodiles. The two brothers stood, the one on the one side of the water and the other on the other, and the younger brother told the elder brother all that had befallen. So the elder brother repented him of what he had done and he lifted up his voice and wept. But he could not come at the farther bank by reason of the crocodiles. His younger brother called to him and said, 'Go home and tend the cattle thyself. For I will dwell no more in the place where thou art. I will go to the Valley of the Acacia. But this is what thou shalt do for me. Thou shalt come and care for me, if evil befalls me, for I will enchant my heart and place it on the top of the flower of the Acacia; and if they cut the Acacia and my heart falls to the ground, thou shalt come and seek it, and when thou hast found it thou shalt lay it in a vessel of fresh water. Then I shalt come to life again. But this is the sign that evil has befallen me: the pot of beer in thine hand shall bubble.' So he went away to the Valley of the Acacia, but his brother returned home with dust on his head and slew his wife and cast her to the dogs.

For many days afterwards the younger brother dwelt alone in the Valley of the Acacia. By day he hunted the beasts of the field, but at evening he came and laid him down under the Acacia, on the top of whose flower was his heart. And many days after that he built himself a house in the Valley of the Acacia. But the gods were grieved for him; and the Sun said to Khnumu, 'Make a wife for Bata, that he may not dwell alone.' So Khnumu made him a woman to dwell with him, who was perfect in her limbs more than any woman on earth, for all the gods were in her. So she dwelt with him. But one day a lock of her hair fell into the river and floated down to the land of Egypt, to the house of Pharaoh's washerwomen. The fragrance of the lock perfumed Pharaoh's raiment, and the washerwomen were blamed, for it was said, 'An odour of perfume in the garments of Pharaoh!' So the heart of Pharaoh's chief washerman was weary of the complaints that were made every day, and he went to the wharf, and there in the water he spied the lock of hair. He sent one down into the river to fetch it, and, because it smelt sweetly, he took it to Pharaoh. Then Pharaoh's magicians were sent for and they said, 'This lock of hair belongs to a daughter of the Sun, who has in her the essence of all the gods. Let messengers go forth to all foreign lands to seek her.' So the woman was brought from the Valley of the Acacia with chariots and archers and much people, and all the land of Egypt rejoiced at her coming, and Pharaoh loved her. But when they asked her of her husband, she said to Pharaoh, 'Let them cut down the Acacia and let them destroy it.' So men were sent with tools to cut down the Acacia. They came to it and cut the flower upon which was the heart of Bata; and he fell down dead in that evil hour. But the next day, when the earth grew light and the elder brother of Bata was entered into his house and had sat down, they brought him a pot of beer and it bubbled, and they gave him a jug of wine

The external soul

TOP. The Old Testament contains one of the many versions of the story of the external soul. Samson's strength and life resided in his hair – and that was his fatal weakness. Delilah cuts off Samson's hair. Grisaille painting by Mantegna, National Gallery, London
ABOVE. An Eskimo painter has expressed the idea of the external soul in her own words: 'My name is Pitseolak, the Eskimo word for sea pigeon. When I see pitseolaks over the sea, I say, "There go those lovely birds, that's me, flying!"' By Pitseolak, *Pictures Out of My Life*, 1970, from recorded interviews by Dorothy Eber, Montreal

and it grew turbid. Then he took his staff and his sandals and hied him to the Valley of the Acacia, and there he found his younger brother lying dead in his house. So he sought for the heart of his brother under the Acacia. For three years he sought in vain, but in the fourth year he found it in the berry of the Acacia. So he threw the heart into a cup of fresh water. And when it was night and the heart had sucked in much water, Bata shook in all his limbs and revived. Then he drank the cup of water in which his heart was, and his heart went into its place, and he lived as before.

A Tartar poem describes how the hero Kartaga grappled with the Swan-woman. Long they wrestled. Moons waxed and waned and still they wrestled; years came and went, and still the struggle went on. But the piebald horse and the black horse knew that the Swan-woman's soul was not in her. Under the black earth flow nine seas; where the seas meet and form one, the sea comes to the surface of the earth. At the mouth of the nine seas rises a rock of copper; it rises to the surface of the ground, it rises up between heaven and earth, this rock of copper. At the foot of the copper rock is a black chest, in the black chest is a golden casket, and in the golden casket is the soul of the Swan-woman. Seven little birds are the soul of the Swan-woman; if the birds are killed the Swan-woman will die straightway. So the horses ran to the foot of the copper rock, opened the black chest, and brought back the golden casket. Then the piebald horse turned himself into a bald-headed man, opened the golden casket, and cut off the heads of the seven birds. So the Swan-woman died.

The External Soul in Folk-Custom

The idea that the soul may be deposited for a longer or shorter time in some place of security outside the body is found in the popular tales of many races. It remains to shew that the idea is not a mere figment devised to adorn a tale, but is a real article of primitive faith, which has given rise to a corresponding set of customs.

When Mr James Macdonald was one day sitting in the house of a Hlubi chief, awaiting the appearance of that great man, who was busy decorating his person, a native pointed to a pair of magnificent ox-horns, and said, 'Ntame has his soul in these horns.' The horns were those of an animal which had been sacrificed, and they were held sacred. A magician had fastened them to the roof to protect the house and its inmates from the thunder-bolt. 'The idea', adds Mr Macdonald, 'is in no way foreign to South African thought. A man's soul there may dwell in the roof of his house, in a tree, by a spring of water, or on some mountain scaur.'

In folk-tales the life of a person is sometimes so bound up with the life of a plant that the withering of the plant will immediately follow or be followed by the death of the person. Similarly among the natives of the Pennefather River in Queensland, when a visitor has made himself very agreeable and taken his departure, an effigy of him about three or four feet long is cut on some soft tree such as the *Canarium australasicum*, so as to face in the direction taken by the popular stranger. Afterwards from observing the state of the tree the natives infer the corresponding state of their absent friend, whose illness or death are apparently supposed to be portended by the fall of the leaves or of the tree. In Uganda, when a new royal enclosure with its numerous houses was built for a new king, barkcloth trees used to be planted at the main entrance by priests of each principal deity and offerings were laid under each tree for its particular god. Thenceforth 'the trees were carefully guarded and tended, because it was believed that as they grew and flourished, so the king's life and power would increase'.

On a day when the cloud that settled on the later years of Sir Walter Scott lifted a little, and he heard that *Woodstock* had sold for over eight thousand pounds, he wrote in his journal: 'I have a curious fancy; I will go set two or three acorns, and judge by their success in growing whether I shall succeed in clearing my way or not.' On the old road from Hanover to Osnabrück, at the village of Oster-Kappeln, there used to stand an ancient oak, which put out its last green shoot in the year 1849. The tree was conjecturally supposed to be contemporary with the Guelphs; and in the year 1866, so fatal for the house of Hanover, on a calm summer afternoon, without any visible cause, the veteran suddenly fell with a crash and lay stretched across the highroad. The peasants regarded its fall as an ill omen for the reigning family, and when King George V heard of it he gave orders that the giant trunk should be set up again, and it was done with much trouble and at great expense, the stump being supported in position by iron chains clamped to the neighbouring trees. But the king's efforts to prop the falling fortunes of his house were vain; a few months after the fall of the oak Hanover formed part of the Prussian monarchy.

But in practice, as in folk-tales, it is not merely with inanimate objects and plants that a person is occasionally believed to be united by a bond of physical sympathy. The same bond, it is supposed, may exist between a man and an animal, so that the welfare of the one depends on the welfare of the other, and when the animal dies the man dies also. The analogy between the custom and the tales is all the closer because in both of them the power of thus removing the soul from the body and stowing it away in an animal is often a special privilege of wizards and witches. Thus the Yakuts of Siberia believe that every shaman or wizard keeps his soul, or one of his souls, incarnate in an animal which is carefully concealed from all the world. 'Nobody can find my external soul,' said one famous wizard, 'it lies hidden far away in the stony mountains of

Edzhigansk.' Only once a year, when the last snows melt and the earth turns black, do these external souls of wizards appear in the shape of animals among the dwellings of men. They wander everywhere, yet none but wizards can see them. The strong ones sweep roaring and noisily along, the weak steal about quietly and furtively. Often they fight, and then the wizard whose external soul is beaten, falls ill or dies. The weakest and most cowardly wizards are they whose souls are incarnate in the shape of dogs, for the dog gives his human double no peace, but gnaws his heart and tears his body. The most powerful wizards are they whose external souls have the shape of stallions, elks, black bears, eagles, or boars. Again, the Samoyeds of the Turukhinsk region hold that every shaman has a familiar spirit in the shape of a boar, which he leads about by a magic belt. On the death of the boar the shaman himself dies; and stories are told of battles between wizards, who send their spirits to fight before they encounter each other in person.

In Melanesia a native doctor was once attending to a sick man. Just then 'a large eagle-hawk came soaring past the house, and Kaplen, my hunter, was going to shoot it; but the doctor jumped up in evident alarm, and said, "Oh, don't shoot; that is my spirit" (*niog*, literally, my shadow); "if you shoot that, I will die." He then told the old man, "If you see a rat to-night, don't drive it away, 'tis my spirit (*niog*); or a snake which will come to-night, that also is my spirit."' It does not appear whether the doctor in this case, like the giant or warlock in the tales, kept his spirit permanently in the bird or in the animal, or whether he only transferred it temporarily to the creature for the purpose of enabling him the better to work the cure, perhaps by sending out his own soul in a bird or beast to find and bring back the lost soul of the patient. In either case he seems to have thought, like the giant or warlock in the stories, that the death of

the bird or the animal would simultaneously entail his own.

The theory of an external soul deposited in an animal appears to be very prevalent in West Africa, particularly in Nigeria, the Cameroons, and the Gaboon. In the latter part of the nineteenth century two English missionaries, established at San Salvador, the capital of the King of Congo, asked the natives repeatedly whether any of them had seen the strange, big, East African goat which Stanley had given to a chief at Stanley Pool in 1877. But their enquiries were fruitless; no native would admit that he had seen the goat. Some years afterwards the missionaries discovered why they could obtain no reply to their enquiry. All the people, it turned out, imagined that the missionaries believed the spirit of the King of Salvador to be contained in the goat, and that they wished to obtain possession of the animal in order to exercise an evil influence on his majesty. The belief from the standpoint of the Congo savages was natural enough, since in that region some chiefs regularly link their fate to that of an animal.

Among the Indians of Guatemala and Honduras the *nagual* or *naual* is 'that animate or inanimate object, generally an animal, which stands in a parallel relation to a particular man, so that the weal and woe of the man depend on the fate of the *nagual*'. According to an old writer, many Indians of Guatemala 'are deluded by the devil to believe that their life dependeth upon the life of such and such a beast (which they take unto them as their familiar spirit), and think that when that beast dieth they must die; when he is chased, their hearts pant; when he is faint, they are faint; nay, it happeneth that by the devil's delusion they appear in the shape of that beast (which commonly by their choice is a buck, or doe, a lion, or tiger, or dog, or eagle) and in that shape have been shot at and wounded'.

9. The Golden Bough

Thus the view that Balder's life was in the mistletoe is entirely in harmony with primitive modes of thought. It may indeed sound like a contradiction that, if his life was in the mistletoe, he should nevertheless have been killed by a blow from the plant. But when a person's life is conceived as embodied in a particular object, with the existence of which his own existence is inseparably bound up, and the destruction of which involves his own, the object in question may be regarded and spoken of indifferently as his life or his death, as happens in the fairy tales. Hence if a man's death is in an object, it is perfectly natural that he should be killed by a blow from it. In the fairy tales Koshchei the Deathless is killed by a blow from the egg or the stone in which his life or death is secreted and the Tartar hero is warned that he may be killed by the golden arrow or golden sword in which his soul has been stowed away.

The idea that the life of the oak was in the mistletoe was probably suggested by the observation that in winter the mistletoe growing on the oak remains green while the oak itself is leafless. But the position of the plant – growing not from the ground but from the trunk or branches of the tree – might confirm this idea. Primitive man might think that, like himself, the oak-spirit had sought to deposit his life in some safe place, and for this purpose had pitched on the mistletoe, which, being in a sense neither on earth nor in heaven, might be supposed to be fairly out of harm's way. In the first chapter we saw that primitive man seeks to preserve the life of his human divinities by keeping them poised between earth and heaven, as the place where they are least likely to be assailed by the dangers that encompass the life of man on earth. We can therefore understand why it has been a rule both of ancient and of modern folk-medicine that the mistletoe should not be allowed to touch the ground; were it to touch the ground, its healing virtue would be gone. This may be a survival of the old superstition that the plant in which the life of the sacred tree was concentrated should not be exposed to the risk incurred by contact with the earth. In an Indian legend, which offers a parallel to the Balder myth, Indra swore to the demon Namuci that he would slay him neither by day nor by night, neither with staff nor with bow, neither with the palm of the hand nor with the fist, neither with the wet nor with the dry. But he killed him in the morning twilight by sprinkling over him the foam of the sea. The foam of the sea is just such an object as a savage might choose to put his life in, because it occupies that sort of intermediate or nondescript position between earth and sky or sea and sky in which primitive man sees safety. It is therefore not surprising that the foam of the river should be the totem of a clan in India.

The view that the mistletoe was not merely the instrument of Balder's death, but that it contained his life, is countenanced by the analogy of a Scottish superstition. Tradition ran that the fate of the Hays of Errol, an estate in Perthshire, near the Firth of Tay, was bound up with the mistletoe that grew on a certain great oak. A member of the Hay family has recorded the old belief as follows: 'Among the low country families the badges are now almost generally forgotten; but it appears by an ancient MS and the tradition of a few old people in Perthshire, that the badge of the Hays was the mistletoe.

There was formerly in the neighbourhood of Errol, and not far from the Falcon stone, a vast oak of an unknown age, and upon which grew a profusion of the plant: many charms and legends were considered to be connected with the tree, and the duration of the family of Hay was said to be united with its existence. It was believed that a sprig of the mistletoe cut by a Hay on All-hallowmas eve, with a new dirk, and after surrounding the tree three times sunwise, and pronouncing a certain spell, was a sure charm against all glamour or witchery, and an infallible guard in the day of battle. A spray gathered in the same manner was placed in the cradle of infants, and thought to defend them from being changed for elf-bairns by the fairies. Finally, it was affirmed, that when the root of the oak had perished, "the grass should grow in the hearth of Errol, and a raven should sit in the falcon's nest". The two most unlucky deeds which could be done by one of the name of Hay was, to kill a white falcon, and to cut down a limb from the oak of Errol. When the old tree was destroyed I could never learn. The estate has been some time sold out of the family of Hay, and of course it is said that the fatal oak was cut down a short time before.'

The idea that the fate of a family, as distinct from the lives of its members, is bound up with a particular plant or tree, is no doubt comparatively modern. The older view may have been that the lives of all the Hays were in this particular mistletoe, just as in an Indian story the lives of all the ogres are in a lemon; to break a twig of the mistletoe would then have been to kill one of the Hays. Similarly in the island of Rum, whose bold mountains the voyager from Oban to Skye observes to seaward, it was thought that if one of the family of Lachlin shot a deer on the mountain of Finchra, he would die suddenly or contract a distemper which would soon prove fatal. Probably the life of the Lachlins was bound up with the deer on Finchra, as the

The external soul in plants
TOP. The oak tree at Penshurst Park planted at the birth of Sir Philip Sidney in 1554.

That taller tree which of a nut was set
At his great birth when all the Muses met.
    Ben Jonson

The *Sidney Oak* by Sir Edwin Landseer, Frederick Lee and Frederick Goodall, 1845. By permission of Viscount De L'Isle, VC KG, from his collection at Penshurst Place, Kent, England
ABOVE. Pair of euphorbias, planted at the birth of twins, by the Nguni, South Africa. Duggan-Cronin Gallery, Alexander McGregor Memorial Museum, Kimberley

life of the Hays was bound up with the mistletoe on Errol's oak.

It is not a new opinion that the Golden Bough was the mistletoe. True, Virgil does not identify but only compares it with mistletoe. But this may be only a poetical device to cast a mystic glamour over the humble plant. Or, more probably, his description was based on a popular superstition that at certain times the mistletoe blazed out into a supernatural golden glory. The poet tells how two doves, guiding Aeneas to the gloomy vale in whose depth grew the Golden Bough, alighted upon a tree, 'whence shone a flickering gleam of gold. As in the woods in winter cold the mistletoe – a plant not native to its tree – is green with fresh leaves and twines its yellow berries about the boles; such seemed upon the shady holm-oak the leafy gold, so rustled in the gentle breeze the golden leaf.' Here Virgil definitely describes the Golden Bough as growing on a holm-oak, and compares it with the mistletoe. The inference is almost inevitable that the Golden Bough was nothing but the mistletoe seen through the haze of poetry or of popular superstition.

Now grounds have been shewn for believing that the priest of the Arician grove – the King of the Wood – personified the tree on which grew the Golden Bough. Hence if that tree was the oak, the King of the Wood must have been a personification of the oak-spirit. It is, therefore, easy to understand why, before he could be slain, it was necessary to break the Golden Bough. As an oak-spirit, his life or death was in the mistletoe on the oak, and so long as the mistletoe remained intact, he, like Balder, could not die. To slay him, therefore, it was necessary to break the mistletoe, and probably, as in the case of Balder, to throw it at him. And to complete the parallel, it is only necessary to suppose that the King of the Wood was formerly burned, dead or alive, at the midsummer fire festival which, as we have seen, was annually celebrated in the Arician grove. The perpetual fire which burned in the grove, like the perpetual fire which burned in the temple of Vesta at Rome, was probably fed with the sacred oak-wood; and thus it would be in a great fire of oak that the King of the Wood formerly met his end. At a later time, his annual tenure of office was lengthened or shortened, as the case might be, by the rule which allowed him to live so long as he could prove his divine right by the strong hand. But he only escaped the fire to fall by the sword.

Thus it seems that at a remote age in the heart of Italy, beside the sweet Lake of Nemi, the same fiery tragedy was annually enacted which Italian merchants and soldiers were afterwards to witness among their rude kindred, the Celts of Gaul, and which, if the Roman eagles had ever swooped on Norway, might have been found repeated with little difference among the barbarous Aryans of the North. The rite was probably an essential feature in the ancient Aryan worship of the oak.

It only remains to ask, Why was the mistletoe called the Golden Bough? The whitish-yellow of the mistletoe berries is hardly enough to account for the name, for Virgil says that the bough was altogether golden, stem as well as leaves. Perhaps the name may be derived from the rich golden yellow which a bough of mistletoe assumes when it has been cut and kept for some months; the bright tint is not confined to the leaves, but spreads to the stalks as well, so that the whole branch appears to be indeed a Golden Bough. Breton peasants hang up great bunches of mistletoe in front of their cottages, and in the month of June these bunches are conspicuous for the bright golden tinge of their foliage. In some parts of Brittany, especially about Morbihan, branches of mistletoe are hung over the doors of stables and byres to protect the horses and cattle, probably against witchcraft.

The yellow colour of the withered bough may partly explain why the mistletoe has been sometimes supposed to possess the property of disclosing treasures in the earth; for on the principles of homoeopathic magic there is a natural affinity between a yellow bough and yellow gold. This suggestion is confirmed by the analogy of the marvellous properties popularly ascribed to the mythical fern-seed or fern-bloom. Fern-seed is popularly supposed to bloom like gold or fire on Midsummer Eve. Thus in Bohemia it is said that 'on St John's Day fern-seed blooms with golden blossoms that gleam like fire'. Now it is a property of this mythical fern-seed that whoever has it, or will ascend a mountain holding it in his hand on Midsummer Eve, will discover a vein of gold or will see the treasures of the earth shining with a bluish flame.

Now, like fern-seed, the mistletoe is gathered either at Midsummer or Christmas – that is, at the summer and winter solstices – and, like fern-seed, it is supposed to possess the power of revealing treasures in the earth. On Midsummer Eve people in Sweden make divining-rods of mistletoe, or of four different kinds of wood one of which must be mistletoe. The treasure-seeker places the rod on the ground after sun-down, and when it rests directly over treasure, the rod begins to move as if it were alive. Now, if the mistletoe discovers gold, it must be in its character of the Golden Bough; it is gathered at the solstices, and, like fern-seed, was probably thought to assume its golden aspect only at those stated times, especially midsummer, when fire was drawn from the oak to light up the sun. At Pulverbatch, in Shropshire, it was believed within living memory that the oak-tree blooms on Midsummer Eve and the blossom withers before daylight. A maiden who wishes to know her lot in marriage should spread a white cloth under the tree at night, and in the morning she will find a little dust, which is all that remains of the flower. She should place the pinch of dust under her pillow, and then her future husband will appear to her in her dreams. This fleeting bloom of the oak, if I am right, was probably the mistletoe in its character of the Golden Bough. The conjecture is confirmed by the observation that in Wales a real sprig of mistletoe gathered on Midsummer Eve is similarly placed under the pillow to induce prophetic dreams; and further the mode of catching the imaginary bloom of the oak in a white cloth is exactly that which was employed by the Druids to catch the real mistletoe when it dropped from the bough of the oak, severed by the golden sickle.

These considerations may partially explain why Virgil makes Aeneas carry a glorified bough of mistletoe with him on his descent into the gloomy subterranean world. The poet describes how at the very gates of hell there stretched a vast and gloomy wood, and how the hero, following the flight of two doves that lured him on, wandered into the depths of the immemorial forest till he saw afar off through the shadows of the trees the flickering light of the Golden Bough illuminating the matted boughs overhead. If the mistletoe, as a yellow withered bough in the sad autumn woods, was conceived to contain the seed of fire, what better companion could a forlorn wanderer in the nether shades take with him than a bough that would be a lamp to his feet as well as a rod and staff to his hands? Armed with it he might boldly confront the dreadful spectres that would cross his path on his adventurous journey. Hence when Aeneas, emerging from the forest, comes to the banks of Styx, winding slow with sluggish stream through the infernal marsh, and the surly ferryman refuses him passage in his boat, he has but to draw the Golden Bough from his bosom and hold it up, and straightway the blusterer quails at the sight and meekly receives the hero into his crazy bark, which sinks deep in the water under the unusual weight of the living man. Even in recent times, mistletoe has been deemed a protection against witches and trolls, and the ancients may well have credited it with the same magical virtue. And if the parasite can, as some of our peasants believe, open all locks, why should it not have served as an 'open Sesame' in the hands of Aeneas to unlock the gates of death?

Now, too, we can conjecture why Virbius at Nemi came to be confounded with the sun. If Virbius was, as I have tried to shew, a tree-spirit, he must have been the spirit of the oak on which grew the Golden Bough; for tradition represented him as the first of the Kings of the Wood. As an oak-spirit he must have been supposed periodically to rekindle the sun's fire, and might therefore easily be confounded with the sun itself. Similarly we can explain why Balder, an oak-spirit, was described as 'so fair of face and so shining that a light went forth from him', and why he should have been so often taken to be the sun. And in general we may say that in primitive society, when the only known way of making fire is by the friction of wood, the savage must necessarily conceive of fire as a property stored away, like sap or juice, in trees, from which he has laboriously to extract it. The Senal Indians of California 'profess to believe that the whole world was once a globe of fire, whence that element passed up into the trees, and now comes out whenever two pieces of wood are rubbed together'.

It is a plausible theory that the reverence which the ancient peoples of Europe paid to the oak, and the connexion which they traced between the tree and their sky-god, were derived from the much greater frequency with which the oak appears to be struck by lightning than any other tree of our European forests. This fact itself may well have attracted the notice of our rude forefathers, who dwelt in the vast forests which then covered a large part of Europe; and they might naturally account for it in their simple religious way by supposing that the great sky-god, whom they worshipped and whose

awful voice they heard in the roll of thunder, loved the oak above all the trees of the wood and often descended into it from the murky cloud in a flash of lightning, leaving a token of his presence or of his passage in the riven and blackened trunk and the blasted foliage. Such trees would thenceforth be encircled by a nimbus of glory as the visible seats of the thundering sky-god. Certain it is that, like some savages, both Greeks and Romans identified their great god of the sky and of the oak with the lightning flash which struck the ground; and they regularly enclosed such a stricken spot and treated it thereafter as sacred. It is not rash to suppose that the ancestors of the Celts and Germans in the forests of Central Europe paid a like respect for like reasons to a blasted oak.

My theory is that the god of the sky and the thunder was the great original deity of our Aryan ancestors, and his association with the oak was merely an inference based on the frequency with which the oak was seen to be struck by lightning. If the Aryans, as some think, roamed the wide steppes of Russia or Central Asia with their flocks and herds before they plunged into the gloom of the European forests, they may have worshipped the god of the blue or cloudy firmament and the flashing thunderbolt long before they thought of associating him with the blasted oaks in their new home.

Perhaps the theory has the further advantage of throwing light on the special sanctity ascribed to mistletoe which grows on an oak. The mere rarity of such a growth on an oak hardly suffices to explain the extent and the persistence of the superstition. A hint of its real origin is possibly furnished by the statement of Pliny that the Druids worshipped the plant because they believed it to have fallen from heaven and to be a token that the tree on which it grew was chosen by the god himself. Can they have thought that the mistletoe dropped on the oak in a flash of lightning? The conjecture is confirmed by the

The relativity of knowledge
TOP. Chemist's laboratory in 1747, John Johnson
Collection, Bodleian Library, Oxford
ABOVE. Department of Biochemistry, Dyson Perrins
Building, University of Oxford, Laboratory of
Chromatography. Photo: John Peacock, Oxford

name thunder-besom which is applied to mistletoe in the Swiss canton of Aargau, for the epithet
clearly implies a close connexion between the
parasite and the thunder; indeed 'thunder-
besom' is a popular name in Germany for any
bushy nest-like excrescence growing on a
branch, because such a parasitic growth is actually believed by the ignorant to be a product of
lightning. If there is any truth in this conjecture,
the real reason why the Druids worshipped a
mistletoe-bearing oak above all other trees of the
forest was a belief that every such oak had not
only been struck by lightning but bore among
its branches a visible emanation of the celestial

fire; so that in cutting the mistletoe with mystic
rites they were securing for themselves all the
magical properties of a thunderbolt. If that was
so, we must apparently conclude that the mistletoe was deemed an emanation of the lightning.

To conclude these enquiries we may say that if
Balder was indeed, as I have conjectured, a personification of a mistletoe-bearing oak, his death
by a blow of the mistletoe might be explained as
a death by a stroke of lightning. So long as the
mistletoe, in which the flame of the lightning
smouldered, was suffered to remain among the
boughs, so long no harm could befall the good
and kindly god of the oak, who kept his life
stowed away for safety between earth and
heaven in the mysterious parasite; but when
once that seat of his life, or of his death, was
torn from the branch and hurled at the trunk, the
tree fell – the god died – smitten by a thunderbolt.

And what we have said of Balder in the oak
forests of Scandinavia may perhaps, with all due
diffidence in a question so obscure and uncertain,
be applied to the priest of Diana, the King of the
Wood, at Aricia in the oak forests of Italy. He
may have personated in flesh and blood the great
Italian god of the sky, Jupiter, who had kindly
come down from heaven in the lightning flash
to dwell among men in the mistletoe – the
thunder-besom – the Golden Bough – growing
on the sacred oak beside the still waters of the
lake of Nemi. If that was so, we need not wonder
that the priest guarded with drawn sword the
mystic bough which contained the god's life and
his own. The goddess whom he served and married was herself, if I am right, no other than the
Queen of Heaven, the true wife of the sky-god.
For she, too, loved the solitude of the woods and
the lonely hills, and sailing overhead on clear
nights in the likeness of the silver moon she
looked down with pleasure on her own fair
image reflected on the calm, the burnished surface of the lake, Diana's Mirror.

10. Farewell to Nemi

We are at the end of our enquiry, but as often happens in the search after truth, if we have answered one question, we have raised many more; if we have followed one track home, we have had to pass by others that opened off it and led, or seemed to lead, to far other goals than the sacred grove at Nemi. Some of these paths we have followed a little way; others, if fortune should be kind, the writer and the reader may one day pursue together. For the present we have journeyed far enough together, and it is time to part. Yet before we do so, we may well ask ourselves whether there is not some more general conclusion, some lesson, if possible, of hope and encouragement, to be drawn from the melancholy record of human error and folly which has engaged our attention.

If then we consider, on the one hand, the essential similarity of man's chief wants everywhere and at all times, and on the other hand, the wide difference between the means he has adopted to satisfy them in different ages, we shall perhaps be disposed to conclude that the movement of the higher thought, so far as we can trace it, has on the whole been from magic through religion to science. In magic man depends on his own strength to meet the difficulties and dangers that beset him on every side. He believes in a certain established order of nature on which he can surely count, and which he can manipulate for his own ends. When he discovers his mistake, when he recognizes sadly that both the order of nature which he had assumed and the control which he had believed himself to exercise over it were purely imaginary, he ceases to rely on his own intelligence and his own unaided efforts, and throws himself humbly on the mercy of certain great invisible beings behind the veil of nature, to whom he now ascribes all those far-reaching powers which he once arrogated to himself. Thus in the acuter minds magic is gradually superseded by religion, which explains the succession of natural phenomena as regulated by the will, the passion, or the caprice of spiritual beings like man in kind, though vastly superior to him in power.

But as time goes on this explanation in its turn proves to be unsatisfactory. For it assumes that the succession of natural events is not determined by immutable laws, but is to some extent variable and irregular, and this assumption is not borne out by closer observation. On the contrary, the more we scrutinize that succession the more we are struck by the rigid uniformity, the punctual precision with which, wherever we can follow them, the operations of nature are carried on. Every great advance in knowledge has extended the sphere of order and correspondingly restricted the sphere of apparent disorder in the world, till now we are ready to anticipate that even in regions where chance and confusion appear still to reign, a fuller knowledge would everywhere reduce the seeming chaos to cosmos. Thus the keener minds, still pressing forward to a deeper solution of the mysteries of the universe, come to reject the religious theory of nature as inadequate, and to revert in a measure to the older standpoint of magic by postulating explicitly, what in magic had only been implicitly assumed, to wit, an inflexible regularity in the order of natural events, which, if carefully observed, enables us to foresee their course with certainty and to act accordingly. In short, religion, regarded as an explanation of nature, is displaced by science.

But while science has this much in common with magic that both rest on a faith in order as the underlying principle of all things, readers of this work will hardly need to be reminded that the order presupposed by magic differs widely from that which forms the basis of science. The difference flows naturally from the different modes in which the two orders have been reached. For whereas the order on which magic reckons is merely an extension, by false analogy, of the order in which ideas present themselves to our minds, the order laid down by science is derived from patient and exact observation of the phenomena themselves. The abundance, the solidity, and the splendour of the results already achieved by science are well fitted to inspire us with a cheerful confidence in the soundness of its method. Here at last, after groping about in the dark for countless ages, man has hit upon a clue to the labyrinth, a golden key that opens many locks in the treasury of nature. It is probably not too much to say that the hope of progress — moral and intellectual as well as material – in the future is bound up with the fortunes of science, and that every obstacle placed in the way of scientific discovery is a wrong to humanity.

Yet the history of thought should warn us against concluding that because the scientific theory of the world is the best that has yet been formulated, it is necessarily complete and final. We must remember that at bottom the general-izations of science or, in common parlance, the laws of nature are merely hypotheses devised to explain that ever-shifting phantasmagoria of thought which we dignify with the high-sounding names of the world and the universe. In the last analysis magic, religion, and science are nothing but theories of thought; and as science has supplanted its predecessors, so it may hereafter be itself superseded by some more per-fect hypothesis, perhaps by some totally dif-ferent way of looking at the phenomena – of registering the shadows on the screen – of which we in this generation can form no idea. The advance of knowledge is an infinite progression towards a goal that for ever recedes. We need not murmur at the endless pursuit:

Fatti non foste a viver come bruti
Ma per seguir virtute e conoscenza.

Great things will come of that pursuit, though we may not enjoy them. Brighter stars will rise on some voyager of the future – some great Ulysses of the realms of thought – than shine on us. The dreams of magic may one day be the waking realities of science. But a dark shadow lies athwart the far end of this fair prospect. For however vast the increase of knowledge and of power which the future may have in store for man, he can scarcely hope to stay the sweep of those great forces which seem to be making silently but relentlessly for the destruction of all this starry universe, in which our earth swims as a speck or mote. In the ages to come man may be able to predict, perhaps even to control, the wayward courses of the winds and clouds, but hardly will his puny hands have strength to speed afresh our slackening planet in its orbit or rekindle the dying fire of the sun. Yet the philo-sopher who trembles at the idea of such distant catastrophes may console himself by reflecting that these gloomy apprehensions, like the earth and the sun themselves, are only parts of that in-substantial world which thought has conjured up out of the void, and that the phantoms which the subtle enchantress has evoked to-day she may ban to-morrow. They too, like so much that to common eyes seems solid, may melt into air, into thin air.

Without dipping so far into the future, we may illustrate the course which thought has hitherto run by likening it to a web woven of three different threads – the black thread of magic, the red thread of religion, and the white thread of science, if under science we may include those simple truths, drawn from observation of nature, of which men in all ages have possessed a store. Could we then survey the web of thought from the beginning, we should probably perceive it to be at first a chequer of black and white, a patchwork of true and false notions, hardly tinged as yet by the red thread of religion. But carry your eye further along the fabric and you will remark that, while the black and white chequer still runs through it, there rests on the middle portion of the web, where religion has entered most deeply into its texture, a dark crimson stain, which shades off insensibly into a lighter tint as the white thread of science is woven more and more into the tissue. To a web thus chequered and stained, thus shot with threads of diverse hues, but gradually changing colour the farther it is unrolled, the state of modern thought, with all its divergent aims and conflicting tendencies, may be compared. Will the great movement which for centuries has been slowly altering the complexion of thought be continued in the near future? or will a reaction set in which may arrest progress and even undo much that has been done? To keep up our parable, what will be the colour of the web which the Fates are now weaving on the humming loom of time? will it be white or red? We cannot tell. A faint glimmering light illumines the backward portion of the web. Clouds and thick darkness hide the other end.

Our long voyage of discovery is over and our bark has drooped her weary sails in port at last. Once more we take the road to Nemi. It is evening, and as we climb the long slope of the Appian Way up to the Alban Hills, we look back and see the sky aflame with sunset, its golden glory resting like the aureole of a dying saint over Rome and touching with a crest of fire the dome of St Peter's. The sight once seen can never be forgotten, but we turn from it and pursue our way darkling along the mountain side, till we come to Nemi and look down on the lake in its deep hollow, now fast disappearing in the evening shadows. The place has changed but little since Diana received the homage of her worshippers in the sacred grove. The temple of the sylvan goddess, indeed, has vanished and the King of the Wood no longer stands sentinel over the Golden Bough. But Nemi's woods are still green, and as the sunset fades above them in the west, there comes to us, borne on the swell of the wind, the sound of the church bells of Rome ringing the Angelus. *Ave Maria!* Sweet and solemn they chime out from the distant city and die lingeringly away across the wide Campagnan marshes. *Le roi est mort, vive le roi! Ave Maria!*

Editorial Notes

In November 1889, the publisher, George Macmillan, received the following letter:

Trinity College, Cambridge, 8 November 89

Dear Sir,

I shall soon have completed a study in the history of primitive religion which I propose to offer to you for publication. The book is an explanation of the legend of the Golden Bough, as that legend is given by Servius in his commentary on Virgil. According to Servius the Golden Bough grew on a certain tree in the sacred grove of Diana at Aricia, and the priesthood of the grove was held by the man who succeeded in breaking off the Golden Bough and then slaying the priest in single combat. By an application of the comparative method I believe I can make it probable that the priest represented in his person the god of the grove – Virbius, and that his slaughter was regarded as the death of the god. This raises the question of the meaning of a widespread custom of killing men and animals regarded as divine. I have collected many examples of this custom and propose a new explanation of it. . . . This is a bare outline of the book which, whatever may be thought of its theories, will be found, I believe, to contain a large store of very curious customs, many of which will be new, even to professed anthropologists. The resemblance of many of the savage customs and ideas to the fundamental doctrines of Christianity is striking. But I make no reference to this parallelism, leaving my readers to draw their own conclusions, one way or the other.

The letter continued with the stipulation – unusual for an author whose typescript was not yet ready for submission, let alone accepted – that the book should have 'a frontispiece consisting of an engraving or mechanical reproduction of Turner's picture of the Golden Bough' and that 'a drawing of the mistletoe or Golden Bough should be stamped in gold on the cover', and was signed 'James G. Frazer'.

Macmillan's reader, John Morley, and George Macmillan himself were both enthusiastic, and the manuscript was at once accepted, marking the start of a long and happy working and personal relationship between Frazer and the Macmillan family.

The first edition appeared in two volumes in May 1890 and one cannot but be impressed by the extraordinary unity of intention displayed by its author over the next quarter of a century. Forty-six years later, when Frazer published his *Aftermath* to the twelve-volume edition, he was still assured that the underlying principles and conclusions of his earlier work remained unaltered. The work of the *Année Sociologique* in France and of the structural functionalists in England, had not led him to doubt his own interpretations nor to question his commitment to the comparative method.

One suspects that from early on, Frazer had it in mind to write a monumental work based on the comparative method, and that the first edition of *The Golden Bough* was intended as nothing more than a preliminary foray. Hence, when the first two-volume edition of 1890 was sold out, the second edition, published in 1900, comprised three volumes. In the preface to this second edition, Frazer implies that more volumes on the subject may be expected from his pen, and speaks of 'the plan I have traced out for myself'. The promise of more to come is explicitly renewed in his lectures on *The Early History of Kingship* (1905). The following year saw the publication of the first edition of *Adonis, Attis, Osiris* (1906) in one volume, followed by the publication of a revised edition in 1907. This was essentially a much enlarged version of three chapters from the first and second editions of *The Golden Bough*. The third and definitive edition was published in twelve volumes between 1911 and 1914.

To understand the history of *The Golden Bough* it is helpful to keep in mind Frazer's work both as an anthropologist and as a classical scholar. He initially read classics at Cambridge, and there is an intimate link between *The Golden Bough* and his contributions to classical scholarship. Of the latter the most important are his translation and commentary of Pausanias (1898), and his edition of Ovid's *Fasti* (1929). Ovid was one of the classical authors who recorded the custom of the priesthood of Nemi, which is the point of departure for *The Golden Bough*.

As Frazer repeatedly declared, *The Golden Bough* was not intended as a general treatise on primitive religion or superstition, but as a study of the rule of the priesthood at Nemi. It developed from this into a consideration of early kingship and, more generally, of the relationship between man and nature in primitive societies. But the original plan of *The Golden Bough*, as it appeared in its first edition, was never fundamentally changed through its two succeeding editions. The only significant addition to the subject matter was made in the second edition, where Frazer included a new chapter on the Saturnalia to follow up one on the killing of gods.

Frazer tended at times, as his very first letter to Macmillan indicates, to see his achievement as a mere catalogue of superstitious practices (a view held by many of his critics), into which future anthropologists could dip at leisure to find material for their own studies. It was partly this tendency that led him to continue adding more and more examples to the existing framework, even as late as 1936. But *The Golden Bough* is more than just a catalogue of superstitious customs. Among its other achievements, it is a very fine piece of literature. Frazer intended that it should be accessible to all who might be interested, not just to the initiated anthropologist and ethnologist, and this led him to take great pains over his style in the third edition.

In 1936, Frazer published the supplementary volume, entitled *Aftermath*, in which he presented further materials to clarify and amplify the main issues of the work. *Aftermath* is also an indirect reply to those who had criticized the theoretical and factual framework of *The Golden Bough*. Frazer included in this volume materials that emerged from the new style of intensive ethnography, and in the preface he stated his own position as follows:

> . . . as in all my other writings, I have sought to base my conclusions by strict induction on a broad and solid foundation of well-authenticated facts. In the present work, I have extended and strengthened the foundation, without remodelling the superstructure of theory, which on the whole I have seen no reason to change. But now, as always, I hold all my theories very lightly, and am ever ready to modify or abandon them in the light of new evidence. If my writings should survive the writer . . . they will live, if they live at all, as a picture or moving panorama of the vanished life of primitive man all over the world, from the tropics to the poles.

The Golden Bough, including *Aftermath*, making altogether thirteen volumes, has been reprinted five times. In 1922, Frazer, responding to widespread interest and at the request of his publishers, published a one-volume abridgment, which he had prepared himself. Until this publication *The Golden Bough*, though everywhere recognized as a work of the highest importance and stature, had not circulated widely. The abridgment was an immediate success, and its first and many subsequent impressions brought the work to a wide public all over the English-speaking world. Frazer's aim was to make the material of the full-length edition more widely available, but in the course of condensation much of the theoretical clarity and the stylistic elegance of the original were obscured. Useful as the abridgment is, it has led to those numerous ill-founded criticisms of *The Golden Bough* as being no more than a catalogue of superstitious practices.

The present rendering is also taken from the third edition, but includes the *Aftermath*, and preserves almost verbatim the wording of the original. Changes made for the sake of coherence very rarely extend to more than three or four words. The principles of selection are, however, very different from those of Frazer's own abridgment.

The thirteen-volume edition is some 1,300,000 words long, and most of it is devoted to illustrating the comparative method – in other words, to adducing examples from other cultures and periods for the various aspects of the rule of the priesthood of Nemi. Unlike Frazer's abridgment, the balance has been changed considerably in this book, and Frazer's theories, and the evidence he quotes in support of them, are reproduced in roughly equivalent proportions. As for the illustrations, wherever possible these reflect Frazer's comparative method by juxtaposing different pictures of similar customs from various periods and parts of the world. Themes and passages that could not be included in the text have at times found a place among the pictures, and in writing the captions I have drawn on the text of the complete work. Some pictures have been chosen by reference to Frazer's footnotes, to show visual images Frazer would himself have absorbed and used. There are no pictures in this book that do not arise directly from the full-length edition of *The Golden Bough*. The captions accordingly comment on the pictures in Frazerian terms, rather than taking an independent stance.

The abridgment and illustration have not been easy tasks because the work maintains throughout a large variety of themes. I have tried to do justice to this richness of content, while also guiding the reader's steps along the more important lines of Frazer's thought both in the text and in the prefaces to each of the seven parts. This has been a difficult undertaking, because many of Frazer's examples have multiple associations with different parts of his argument. Thus, to bring out one argument, it has often been necessary to sacrifice several others, and, in the interest of concision and clarity, to curtail some of the ramifications of those arguments that have been reproduced. Thus, very major cuts were made in the fields of ancient Greek and Roman religion, and almost everything regarding ancient Egypt has been deleted as being largely illustrative. *Adonis, Attis, Osiris*, Part IV of the third edition, has become *Adonis* in the present version, and chapters on related themes, as well as on the religion of ancient Italy, have been deleted. Apart from these major abridgments, and numerous lesser ones throughout the text (especially on the theme of fires and ancient calendars), the work has been systematically shortened in one of its ramifications: although Frazer's principal interest was with agricultural societies, he did extend his scheme to cover hunting and pastoral societies as well. Almost all references to these latter two have been deleted, since Frazer's argument can stand without them. Part V of the third edition, *Spirits of the Corn and of the Wild*, has accordingly become *Spirits of the Corn*. I hope that as a result Frazer's main themes, which concern the rule of the priesthood of Nemi and the functioning of the primitive mind, will emerge more clearly. However, it should be remembered that *The Golden Bough* is a difficult work, and no abridgment that ignores or seeks to slide over its difficulties can be faithful to Frazer's intentions. It would be too bold to hope that no errors of judgment have slipped into the text and pictures, but the present abridgment will have served its purpose if it leads even a few to an appreciation of the achievement of *The Golden Bough*.

SABINE MACCORMACK

Index

The index is designed primarily to give access to Frazer's main themes and material.

Figures in *italic* refer to black-and-white illustrations; those in **bold** to pages opposite the colour plates.